The Vultee
Vengeance in Battle

Peter C. Smith

Pen & Sword
AVIATION

First published in Great Britain in 2019 by
Pen & Sword Aviation
An imprint of
Pen & Sword Books Ltd
47 Church Street
Barnsley
South Yorkshire
S70 2AS

ISBN 9781526704566

Typeset in INDIA by Geniies IT & Services Private Limited

Printed and bound in the UK by TJ International, Padstow, Cornwall.

Pen & Sword Books Ltd incorporates the Imprints of Atlas, Archaeology,
Aviation, Discovery, Family History, Fiction, History, Maritime, Military, Military
Classics, Politics, Select, Transport, True Crime, Air World, Frontline Publishing,
Leo Cooper, Remember When, Seaforth Publishing, The Praetorian Press,
Wharncliffe Local History, Wharncliffe True Crime and White Owl.

For a complete list of Pen & Sword titles please contact
PEN & SWORD BOOKS LIMITED
47 Church Street, Barnsley, South Yorkshire, S70 2AS, England
E-mail: enquiries@pen-and-sword.co.uk
Website: www.pen-and-sword.co.uk

Contents

Foreword

In the American-built Vultee Vengeance dive-bomber, the RAF, along with the fledgling Indian Air Force, possessed the most accurate air-delivery aircraft of the Second World War. Its precision attacks were legendary and telling, its losses were minimal; hardly any Vultee Vengeances were lost to enemy anti-aircraft fire and absolutely none – zilch, zero – were lost to enemy fighter attack, despite all the direst predictions to the contrary. During the campaigns in the Arakan, the defence of Kohima and Imphal and supporting the Chindits, the weight of ordnance that the Vengeance was able to deposit on Japanese Army positions, troop assemblies and supply, fuel and munitions dumps was lethal to their cause. Whether it was the pinpoint destruction of road and rail bridges, enemy headquarters buildings and signals and wireless stations, this aircraft was the one the Allied ground troops called upon, praised and tried desperately to persuade the RAF to retain in front-line combat. But in vain.

The Japanese were fearless and ruthless in combat, attacking without thought of their own safety, and skilful in outflanking manoeuvres which kept the Allies' armies constantly out-thought. However, whenever the Japanese were forced onto the defensive, they proved equally, if not more so, skilful and adept at constructing deep bunkers that were hard to assault without incurring unacceptable casualties among the attackers. These bunkers were described as, capped with heavy log roofs, impervious to field or mountain artillery.[1] The soldiers of Nippon were also leading exponents of adapting natural features to form defensive positions that took full advantage of the jungle-covered hills, ravines, *chaungs* and mountains. Okinawa in the Pacific was a famous example of this capacity to construct such defence works, but it was all done earlier in Burma and the Arakan. The answer the Allies possessed was air power and all manner of aircraft were utilised

---

[1]   Grant, Ian Lyall, MC, *Burma: The Turning Point*, Leo Cooper, London, 2003.

to smash these positions, four-engine bombers altitude bombing in mass formations, medium level bombing at lower levels, both of which proved totally inaccurate against such targets. At the other extreme Allied fighters and fighter-bombers strafed with machine guns or dropped single bombs, few of which were precise enough and certainly lacked the ability to both hit and penetrate deeply enough to do the job properly. The Vengeance, by contrast, could deliver a combination of two heavy and two medium bombs per aircraft, in a steep dive, exactly where it was required and with six or twelve-aircraft attacks, were usually sufficient to make the difference.

Nor was there the risk, as with all other forms of air attack, of 'Blue-on-Blue'- incidents, of causing casualties from so-called 'friendly-fire' incidents, which so marred most Allied air support operations. The Chindits, operating far behind enemy lines, had to be totally convinced that the Vengeance was the aircraft to substitute for lack of heavy artillery, and they *were* so convinced, not so much by rhetoric as by results, Orde Wingate not being of the temperament to accept anything else. Nor did General Slim's men stint in their praise of the Vengeance, and they came to rely on her whenever things got really tough, as at Kohima and Imphal. It was the combination of accuracy coupled with penetration and smashing power that made the Vengeance (or VDB – Vengeance Dive Bomber – as it was commonly referred to in service) unique in British service.

Why was this so? The German Luftwaffe, with their much-feared Junkers Ju.87 *Stuka*, the Soviet Air Force with the speedy Petlyakov Pe-2 Peshka, the Imperial Japanese Navy with their carrier-borne Aichi D3A1/2 Val and the United States Navy with, initially, the Douglas SBD Dauntless and, later, the Curtiss SB2C Helldiver, had continually demonstrated the merits of dive-bombing. By contrast the British Air Ministry had resolutely set their collective faces against the concept in any shape, manner or form, and had fiercely opposed the purchase and use of the Vengeance. Facing imminent invasion in 1940, the Ministry of Aircraft Production, largely at the urgings of Lord Beaverbrook, who had Premier Churchill's ear, had by-passed the normal RAF procedures and ordered the type from American contractors, but the air marshals had steadfastly remained opposed and only very reluctantly put them into service. They continually downplayed all its many successes in combat, ignored its achievements in the field and, in effect, tried to rid themselves of this aircraft at every opportunity.[2] In this they finally succeeded, despite the pleadings of the men on the spot. And so, who today has even heard of this aircraft, other than from oft-repeated disparaging remarks from those who never flew them.[3] And yet, irony of ironies, it was the British who had *invented* dive-bombing, in 1917 with No. 84 Squadron on the Western Front.

The misrepresentation still abounds and continues. Although I have written before on the Vengeance, I felt that a fresh look was necessary and deserved. This time the widest possible take on the VDB is presented from a whole variety of sources – personal interviews and correspondence with survivors has been interspersed with both published and unpublished memoirs, personal diary extracts, interviews, squadron operational record books and similar official data and documents. We see through these varied extracts the aircrew being trained in a 'new' skill, coping not only with a new concept for which there was little precedent, and the minimal encouragement from 'on high', but with a brand-new aircraft, largely built by unskilled, newly-recruited labour in the USA. Engine problems and highly-unpredictable weather conditions added to a mix of complex problems. But gradually we see the six squadrons, filled with the whole range of nationalities in what was then the British Empire at its greatest extent, coming together in a coherent whole, honing their skills, learning

---

[2]   The RAF view was that the Vengeance was 'inferior in every way to the Fairey Battle'. This latter, a three-crewed, single-engine light bomber, had been almost wiped out in just two days of combat in May 1940 without achieving anything whatsoever.

[3]   See, quite apart from websites like 'Air of Authority' or similar assertions on the Wikipedia pages, from whence most modern 'researchers' seem to glean their information, self-styled 'authoritative' works like *Eagles in the Sky* (Mainstream Publishing, Edinburgh) in which Alan Carlaw, writing of the Burma Campaign, states that 'The Vengeance was not successful in this theatre of operation', a remark which Arthur Gill described as 'utter rubbish'. He informed Carlaw that 'During 41 years of flying, I flew nearly one hundred different types of aircraft, including Battles, Blenheims, Hampdens, Herefords, Hurri-bombers, Mosquitoes and after WW2 numerous types of jet bombers and fighters. Without exception, the Vengeance was the most accurate bomber I ever flew – before, during and since WW2.' Gill to Carlaw, dated 11 January 1994.

in combat and ultimately achieving enviable rates of success, despite all the odds stacked against them.

This then is the *real* Vengeance story, from the sharp end, told mainly in the words of the men themselves.

A brief word on place names. Since the end of the British Raj in India and Burma, there has been a wholesale renaming of cities, towns, villages and even the countries themselves. Thus, since the military takeover of Burma by the Sawmaung Regime in September 1988, and the resultant State Law and Order Restoration Council *diktat* of June 1989, the country is known as Myanmar while Rangoon is now Yangon, the Irrawaddy river is known as the Ayeyarwady, the Chindwin as the Chindwinn, the Chin Mountains and people are Zomi, Pegu is Bago, Arakan, where many of the Vengeance operations took place, is now Rakhine, Ramree Island is Yanbye Kyun and so on. Even the tiniest hamlets have, in many cases, been renamed. Even in the period covered by this volume, 1942-45, different spellings abounded to add yet more confusion.[4] Likewise, the Indian Empire has now become three independent states, India, Pakistan and Bangladesh, while Ceylon has become Sri Lanka and they, likewise, have changed the names of many of their place names: Akyab is Sittwe, Chittagong became Chotogram, Madras is Chennai, Calcutta is Kolkata, Bombay is now Mumbai, Bangalore is Bengaluru and Mysore is now Mysoru. I have attempted to append the alternative names to at least some of the major places in this book, but it is primarily an account of how things were in the Second World War and the permutations are too many and still too fluid to even attempt to list every village or collection of jungle bashas in a clearing. I ask the reader's tolerance in this respect.

Also, with regards RAF ranks a similar latitude is required. For the period described the progression was, very generally, for non-commissioned ranks, aircraftsman, leading aircraftsman (LAC), sergeant and flight sergeant with warrant officers being a special case; in the case of the Vengeance the rear-seat man was usually the wireless operator/air gunner (WO/AG), while for

---

[4]   Many Burmese people, especially those opposed to the military government, bitterly oppose these changes still today. For greater detail of how these name changes came about, the reader is recommended to turn to Donald M. Seekins' study, *Historical Dictionary of Burma (Myanmar)*, Rowan & Littlefield, Lanham, MD, 2017.

commissioned officers the path from cadet officer was usually pilot officer, flying officer, flight lieutenant, squadron leader, wing commander, group captain, air commodore, air vice marshal, air marshal and marshal of the Royal Air Force. Again, common sense will show that people mentioned in these pages will have moved up through these various ranks, and in wartime that could happen quite rapidly. I have endeavoured to show the ranks as they were at each point described, although promotions were often not notified until some considerable period had elapsed. The Commonwealth contribution to the Vengeance units was enormous and they were very mixed units regarding nationalities, races and religions, which, overall, reflected the diversity of the British Empire at that time. Thus Australians, Canadians, New Zealanders, Rhodesians, South Africans, as well as the many ethnic variations of the Indian sub-continent, are all reflected in the make-up of these squadrons, with even a few Americans bobbing up, being volunteers for the RAF or RCAF prior to their nation being propelled into the war on the Axis at the end of 1941. Again, I have done my best to reflect this diversity with the limited records available, such records being particularly scanty regarding non-commissioned personnel.

Acknowledgements

I would like to extend my heartfelt and sincere thanks to everyone who assisted me in tracking down the full story of the Vengeance aircraft in Burma. The list could be much longer, but many requested anonymity, while many, far too many, others have now passed on. Their achievements, however, largely ignored and even scorned by many historians of air warfare, deserve recording, as do they. So, thanks indeed to:

Jane Lisle, Arthur Gill's daughter; Nigel Gill, Arthur Gill's son, both of whom were wonderful in their support with his logbooks, photographs, documents and memoirs of 84 Squadron; John D. Topley, Squadron Leader Rodney Topley's son; Sara Mosher whose father, Burton, flew with 110 (H) Squadron and who has written her own book about their exploits; Adrian Gill, son of Squadron Leader John Gill, 110 Squadron; Jagan Pillarsetti, who runs the very informative and detailed *Bharat Rakshak* website on the history of the Indian Air Force, for his generous offer of help and assistance, and who is also writing his own book; Darren Hines for making available the logbook of Flight Sergeant Reginald Duncan, RCAF; Wally Blackwell; Edward Helliwell; and last, but not least, Hans Houterman – his knowledge of RAF officers is unrivalled and was of enormous help.

Pilots and navigators, designers and test pilots, mostly now passed on, whom I have interviewed or corresponded with down the years include: Reginald Duncan; Joseph O'Leary, one of only two RAF Vultee Vengeance pilots alive today, with a clear and concise memory and willingness to help; Hugh Bergel; Victor Bertagna; Ken Bowman; Eric M. Brown; Wayne Brown; Bob Browning; Jack Bryant; Dustin Carter; Dr Ira Chart; Theodore Coleman; D.R. Cuming; M. Jean Cuny; Peter Dallosso; J. Dickenson; Frank W. Davis; Colonel Gilbert Dou; F.R. Dyer; Jim Danahue; Air Commodore E.G. Fyfe; Ron Gabrielson; John E. Gerber; Squadron Leader Dennis Gibbs; Squadron Leader Arthur Murland Gill; Brian Hall; T.G. Handsforth, MT driver 84 Squadron; Louis Horman, Archives Technician, Reserarch

Team, Air Force Museum of New Zealand Walter E. Holt; Charles R. Irvine; Douglas Johnson; Squadron Leader Frederick Frank Lambert; Dr Peter Latcham; George A. Limbrick; 'Red' McInnes; Keith Meggs; Squadron Leader J. McMichael, Cyril McPherson; Douglas Morris; George Odgers; Edward D. Peden. Aubrey Pedler; E.L. Pidduck; Robert Piper; John Ramsden; Raymond George Ravenscroft; Stanley Raymond; Donald Ritchie; David Saunders; Hugh Seton; Christopher Shores; Richard L. Smith; Moye Stephens; L.R.M. Tibble; Ken Tonkin; T.G. Widdop; Stanley J. Worth. Finally, I would once again wish to thank my patient editor, Richard Doherty, for his diligence and for keeping me on track – tactfully but firmly so. To all these, and many others who have assisted my researches down the years, my grateful thanks, plus the acknowledgement that any errors herein are more likely to be mine than theirs.

Peter C. Smith, Riseley, Bedford, December 2018.

Chapter 1

Origins

Although the Royal Navy's Fleet Air Arm was an enthusiastic endorser of the dive-bombing concept, and sought to equip its carrier-borne squadrons with it, in the form of the Blackburn Skua it suffered severe handicaps. One was that, with limited funding, what monies there were had first to be spent on new warships to replace those scrapped under the terms of the notorious Washington Navy Treaty of 1922, which reduced the Royal Navy from its centuries-old position in order to placate soaring American ambitions to take her place post the Great War. The second restriction, again self-imposed by British politicians, was that the Air Ministry was given control over the Navy's aircraft programmes. Thus, the Skua, at the insistence of the Royal Air Force, was required to become a fighter aircraft, as well as a dive-bomber, two totally incompatible tasks.[1]

As for the RAF, their minds were firmly fixed on maintaining their independence and were intolerant of any air policy that smacked of the slightest subservience to either of the other two services. Paris (in the 1920s) or Berlin (in the 1930s) in flames and in ruins was the scenario on which the air ministers, buoyed up by the unproven theories of Lord Hugh Trenchard in the UK, General Giulio Douhet in Italy and Brigadier William Mitchell in the USA, and their sights were firmly and inflexibly set and remained so. Firmly convinced that air power alone could win the war and that armies and navies were now irrelevant, they scorned dive-bombing and paid only lip service to the concept.[2] Even when a first-class dive-bomber was produced in the late 1930s, the classic Hawker Henley, they used her, and not for the

---

[1] For the full story of how this came about see - Smith, Peter C., *Skua! The Royal Navy's Dive Bomber*. Pen & Sword, Barnsley, 2006.

[2] Douhet's view on tactical air support for the Army was that it was 'useless, superfluous and harmful', a view wholeheartedly adopted and advocated by most senior RAF officers, and whose ultimate exponent was Air Marshal Sir Arthur Harris. See Douhet, General Giulio, *The Command of the Air*, Air Force History and Museums Program, Washington DC, 1998.

last time, as a target tug. Trials and tests were conducted but their findings were shelved or rejected and, to fill the bill, the RAF's conception of army co-operation was the Westland Lysander spotter plane.

Consequently, when the Second World War arrived and the Luftwaffe's Junkers Ju.87 *Stuka*, used in combination with fast-moving tank columns, brought a new concept to warfare, the *Blitzkrieg* or Lightning War, close-support operations brought to perfection. This updated battle concept brought about the swift defeat of Poland and the equally rapid overrunning of the Low Countries and France, while the simultaneous eviction of the British Expeditionary Force (BEF) left the United Kingdom facing invasion with little in the way of any aircraft able to deal with an invading enemy in the same manner. Even when faced with this dire scenario the RAF could not, would not, face the truth. Typical was Air Marshal John Catesworth Slessor, who, with the expected invasion of England imminent, voiced the conviction that 'we don't want aircraft skidding around over Kent looking for enemy tanks, that is the job of the anti-tank gun'. From this stance they were never to budge.

Fortunately, the newly-appointed Minister of Aircraft Production, Lord Beaverbrook, did not share that blind faith that strategic bombing could win the war unaided. He set about finding a dive-bomber in a hurry and, being Canadian, naturally looked across the Atlantic at the vast and secure potential resources of American aircraft manufacturers, far from any risk of German retribution. In this desperate search he was aided by good fortune. The Vultee Corporation, based at Downey, California, had appointed Richard Palmer as vice president and his was one of many firms visited by a French Army Air Force Officer Purchasing Team during the period 1938-40. To their requests for a dive-bomber the company's Field Division had begun development of the V-72, a low-wing, all-steel, monoplane. When France crashed down in total defeat the British were able to take over this concept and tailor it to their own needs. The need was for speed, but such were the numbers required that another company, Northrop, was seconded to begin a second production line and the two firms produced the Vengeance, whose specification the British changed almost weekly, together. This led to delays and, instead of the spring of 1941, it was almost eighteen months later that the first models began to be shipped to the British.

When the Vengeance was first forced upon and, albeit reluctantly, tardily accepted by the RAF, the priority was to equip squadrons in areas where they might be the least involved in hard combat action. South Africa was to have one squadron, India, including both the Indian Air Force itself and RAF squadrons operating in that theatre, (which, it must be remembered and stressed, at the original time of planning was not yet a war zone) was to receive sufficient numbers to be able to equip six squadrons; the Royal Canadian Air Force was to have two squadrons, while the Royal Australian Air Force to have no less than nine squadrons so equipped. In the event, although the Indian and RAF units received their due quota, but much later than promised, the RAAF only received enough for four squadrons and neither the RCAF nor the SAAF were able to form any Vengeance squadrons of their own.

As for the Burma Campaign itself there are many fine studies to be had, both with regard to the land and the air side of things, but for those puzzled by the constant 'stops-and-starts' imposed by the weather conditions, principally the monsoon season, a brief explanation is perhaps required. At the risk of over-simplification, the region's meteorological boundaries consist of three phases, a 'hot and dry' season, roughly lasting from March to May; a 'wet and rainy' season, approximately from late May to October, and a 'cool and dry' season, from November through to February. Military operations were thus limited during that time when the rain did not so much fall as pound down, turning dirt forward airstrips into morasses, while for the required 'inch-perfect' dive-bombing, thick clouds were a constant impediment to accuracy, as will be seen, and continued to be a constant frustration. The Japanese, numerically superior on the ground, but drastically inferior in the air, would welcome such conditions while the six active Vultee Vengeance squadrons, chafing at the bit, would curse them.

In addition to climate restrictions, the British were continually hampered by the Allied Supreme Command's policy of 'Germany First', which was to lead to the repeated cancelling of plans for grand offensives to be made, as the priority for men, materials, aircraft, landing craft and supplies, was never South-East Asia but always the Mediterranean and then Europe. Those charged with the defence of Britain's Empire in South-East Asia had already seen the results of Premier Winston Spencer Churchill's policies of arming the Soviet Union (the world's leading armaments manufacturer, and co-rapist of their original Polish ally) ahead of their own people, sending aircraft, tanks and munitions to Marshal Josef Stalin and neglecting

Singapore, Malaya and Burma in 1941. This policy continued, and the Allies were time and again forced to abandon anything other than the most limited offensives until 1945.

Nonetheless, once the new aircraft were put to the test, they proved able to reverse all the dire predictions and became valuable assets in aiding the land forces both contain and then take the offensive against the hitherto 'invincible' Japanese Army. The early marks of the Vultee Vengeance had many difficulties with their power-plants and mechanics, but these were eventually overcome. Among the many ironies was that, just when the Vengeance had been refined to perfection, with the Mark IV, the Air Ministry had its way and these machines, which would have been in their element in the first six months of 1945, were relegated instead to target-towing. The Vengeance, and her crews, deserved better.

Chapter 2

No. 7 IAF Squadron

Motto: *Shatrunjay -Vanquish the Enemy*

The squadron was first formed on 1 December 1942 at Vizagapatam on the Bay of Bengal following the decision of the Indian Government (The Raj) to form two self-sufficient, fully mobile, light bomber squadrons under India Order No. 707. The Commanding Officer designate was Squadron Leader Hemango Choudhuri (or Chaudhuri), a Volunteer Reserve officer. Cambridge-educated 'Hem', son of a Calcutta barrister and with two brothers in the Indian Army, was a volunteer reserve pilot who flew privately.[1] He was to prove himself an outstanding and inspirational leader, though not flawless. Air Chief Marshal Pratap Chandra Lal described him in his memoirs in this way. 'He was well-read, played games to keep fit, drank heavily but, as he said, could hold his drink. He was cheerful, witty, and at times extremely boisterous. He was more western than Indian, a Brown *sahib*. His flying was competent and a little over-confident.'[2]

The squadron itself was formed largely with personnel from the Indian Air Force Volunteer Reserve Flights of No. 104 General Reconnaissance Squadron IAF, the Indian Flight of No. 353 Squadron RAF, No. 3 Coastal Defence Flight and No. 6 Coastal Defence Flight.[3] This had Lieutenant K.K. Mukherji, an Indian Royal Navy officer attached as the Sea/Air Liaison

---

[1]   He originally worked for the Railways Division of the British-founded Andrew Young Company of Calcutta (now known as Kolkata), West Bengal, whose widespread interests included jute, cotton, coal, tea, engineering, electrical, power, chemicals, insurance, railways, shipping, paper and printing. He returned there post-war.

[2]   Lal, Air Chief Marshal Pratap Chandra, *My Years with the IAF*, Lancer Publications LL.c., Atlanta, Ga., 1986. Choudhuri himself resumed his pre-war career when hostilities ceased. He made his final dive while soloing from his beloved Barrackpore Flying Club at Calcutta, 'One fine day he went up and was flying over the river. He swooped down in a dive from which he failed to pull out, plunging straight into the water.'

[3]   AHQ Formation Order 268, dated 18 November 1942.

Officer.[4] Initially existing obsolete Hawker Audax and Westland Wapiti biplanes belonging to the latter two flights were their only establishment machines as the Vultee Vengeance shipments were still not ready.

Problems with the aircraft themselves, as delivered, were compounded by the difficulty in finding sufficient Indian personnel, not just pilots and navigators, but the mechanics and ground crew, motor transport and maintenance teams, to set up and run this very different aircraft with its very different mission specification. The Vultee Vengeance was a very different beast indeed to the docile and placid biplanes like the venerable Audax and the like, with which the Indian teams had been used to dealing with over the previous decade. Everything had to be learnt from scratch.

These problems were never fully overcome by the Indian Vengeance units, especially 8 Squadron, and eventually it was only by drafting in two different tranches of RAF and Commonwealth pilots and aircrew to make up the numbers, that this latter unit got into action ahead of her companion.

The aircrew underwent their W/T Course at Bombay (now known as Mumbai) and their operational training at the No. 152 Operational Training Unit (OTU) from 22 October 1942, and were based at Peshawar in north-west India, close to the Afghan border. Before that, however, all personnel had to undergo a refresher W/T (Wireless Telegraph) course at Andheri at Salsette Island in southern Bombay (now Mumbai). These conversion courses were completed by 5 March 1943 whereupon the squadron shifted over to Phaphamau, the small and now defunct Indian Pilot Training Establishment airfield south Allahabad, Uttar Pradesh (then known as the United Provinces).[5] They were part of No. 227 Group, but it was not until 20 April 1943 that the first pair of Vengeance aircraft was delivered, and these were joined by three more (EZ826, EZ 837 and EZ 867) on 7 May. This was followed by an order to move to Bairagarh near Bhopal, Madhya Pradesh, for their ATU[6] course. En route the Vultees were commandeered by the local commander of the RAF Pilot Training Establishment (PTE) at Bamrauli

---

[4]   This officer, sometimes referred to as Mukerjee, later transferred to the Royal Indian Navy where he served aboard the minesweeping sloop *Rohilkhand* (ex-*Padstow*) at the liberation of Singapore before attaining the rank of captain in the Indian navy post-war.

[5]   Long defunct and not to be confused with the present-day satellite airfield, which is on a different site.

[6]   ATU – Advanced Training Unit.

to conduct a flypast over the field to celebrate the recent Allied victory in Tunisia. Once established at Bairagarh, flight and gunnery training then followed for all the nineteen pilots at the Kohat[7] bombing range.

On 10 July, 7 Squadron, whose *raison d'être* was operational mobility in every sense of the word, received the first batch of twelve NC (E).[8] Inducted tradesmen from the RAF Chaklala airfield near Rawalpindi, Punjab, and their initial batch of twelve 3-cwt[9] trucks arrived from No. 8 Civil Repair Organisation at Lahore on the 11th.

Like other units, No. 7 had found familiarisation with the new Vultee a testing time in more ways than one, not least because of the unreliability of the rear cockpit-mounted machine guns, which took a lot of time to fix and which necessitated the tail gunners to conduct their training back in the stately old Audax! Other problems were encountered, not least the Wright Cyclone radial engines, which required endless maintenance to make them fit for operations. Some idea of the scale of the problem can be gleaned by listing some of accidents that took place with the Vengeance with No. 152 Operational Training Unit (OTU) at Peshawar. The squadrons found the Vengeance a handful.[10]

Date	Serial	Pilot	Crew	Location	Damage
15 February 1943	AN844	P/O Ernest John Butler, RAFVR.	Cpl Philips	Close to Jamrud	Failed to pull out of a dive – a/c destroyed, crew killed. Mk. I 154 OTU
25 March 1943	AN865	–	–	Peshawar	Cat A structural failure

---

7   Now part of northern Pakistan.

8   Non-Combatant (Enrolled) – as serving non-combatants they were subject to Air Force discipline but not granted Military Service Pay (MSP). Because of this they often regarded themselves as a cheap way of unfairly maintaining the IAF unit's ground crew numbers – it was not until 2014 that they finally achieved a more equal status.

9   1 cwt = 50.8023kg.

10   See AIR 29/703, IIM/FP348/12 & 1A, *152 Operational Training Unit – Peshawar, India* November 1943 to March 1944.

Date	Serial	Pilot	Crew	Location	Damage
15 April 1943	AN902	–	–	Peshawar	Nose-over-salvaged
16 April 1943	AN977	Sqn Ldr Niranjan Prasad	–	Peshawar	Belly landing
24 April 1943	AP125	P/O Mustafa Kamal	P/O Mohammad Jamiluddin Khan	6 miles from out Peshawar	Dive brakes on. Crew injured.
24 April 1943	AP111	–	–	Crashed Peshawar	Brakes seized up – salvaged crew unhurt.
28 April 1943	EZ800	–	–	Belly landing Peshawar	Hydraulic failure
29 April 1943	AN997	P/O H.B. Waterson	P/O Mohan Karam Chand (8 Squadron)	Crashed near Bombing Range	Destroyed – crew killed
7 May 1943	AP104	P/O Churukara George Immanuel Philips	–	Landed off runway	Undercarriage collapsed
29 May 1943	AN913	P/O Kulwant Singh Sandhu	Sgt Rustomji	Crashed on Bombing Range	Destroyed – crew killed.
5 June 1943	AN865	Sgt W.A. Garbutt	–	Landed wheels up technical problem	
9 June 1943	AN865	Sqn Ldr Leonard Frank Penny	–	Landed port undercarriage unlocked	Uninjured
19 June 1943	EZ813	Sgt W.A. Garbutt	–	Engine failure landed one mile from Peshawar	Uninjured
30 June 1943	AP112	Sgt Peter Frederick Robinson	F/O Kenneth Burton Mosher, RCAF	Disorientated –Landed Afghanistan	Crew returned to unit – aircraft abandoned
17 July 1943	EZ884	Sgt Joseph N. Parrish	–	Engine failure – ditched in Klall river	Uninjured – aircraft salvaged

Date	Serial	Pilot	Crew	Location	Damage
24 August 1943	AN865	Sgt N.P. Neuman	–	Starboard undercarriage failed –Ground looped Peshawar	Uninjured
16 September 1943	AN802	Sgt Churchley	–	Belly landing Peshawar	First solo on type
22 September 1943	AN715	Sgt Warren	–	Undercarriage collapse Peshawar	Damaged
2 October 1943	AN902	Sgt Charles Guy Morris, RAFVR	Sgt Leonard Walkington, RAFVR	Crashed on bombing range	Destroyed and both crew (82 Squadron) killed.
8 November 1943	AN715	P/O Ronald Francis Norman	–	Undercarriage failure – belly landed Peshawar	
11 November 1943	AN953	P/O J. Andrews	–	Fuel leak into cockpit blinded pilot –crashed Peshawar	Pilot seriously injured
4 December 1943	AVV691	Sgt Hume	–	Crashed on landing due obstruction Peshawar	Uninjured
28 January 1944	ES878	Sgt F. Brown	Sgt Harris	Crashed on Bombing Range	Both crew killed.
17 February 1944	AN629(AN 649)	F/O Victor John Hillman, RCAF	WO Thomas Barlow	Crashed 16 miles SW of Chakwal at Marakabar in turbulence after flying into clouds.	Both crew killed
8 August 1944		P/O Bhawanishankar Kagal Dayanand	–	Failed to recover from dive.	Pilot killed

Like many incidents a certain amount of post-war embellishment has taken place, with myth replacing fact and being repeated. Owen Thetford's oft-quoted statement, in combat operations, 'the Vengeance always operated with a fighter escort' is one such tale.[11] In truth, as we shall see, they hardly ever had a close escort although sometimes what was termed 'fighter cover over the target area' was promised. But rarely was close escort provided. While at Peshawar the legend is that a pair of RAF officers were sent out to show the Indian pilots how to dive bomb. One of these officers, described, at least according to Maukund Murthy, by Joe Ezeliel as 'a hot-shot pilot' who was 'called in to explain to the Natives that the Vengeance was perfectly safe to pull out of a dive, no matter what'. He allegedly was 'a Squadron Leader who apparently thought little of the Indian pilots'. This officer 'called all the Indian pilots into a group and harangued them, and questioned their courage and technical capabilities, equally. He then walked out to the nearest Vengeance, started her up, taxied her out, took off, climbed to 10,000ft[12], deployed his dive brakes and – well, just dived.'

The United States Navy was a great exponent of dive bombing, and they made it pay all through the war. As the RAF had continually rejected this method of attack between the wars, and since, selected pilots had been sent to Pensacola Naval Air Station in Florida to learn the ropes. The Americans utilised a telescopic sight to line up the target, but this had the disadvantages of 'fogging up' as the aircraft descended through different layers. Royal Navy dive-bomber pilots who flew the Blackburn Skua also used this method but, as Joseph O'Leary recalled to me, 'I have heard about this idea. Don't know how it worked. Would not touch it with a barge-pole. I **** decide when to pull out! Two RAF types, who had done a dive-bombing course with the US Navy, came to give us the "gen". They had telescopic sights. "Show us," we said to Expert A, gave him a VV, he fitted his sight, had a go – and speared in! Expert B, discredited, went away! The yellow line on top of the forward fuselage was all we needed.' As for the ring-and-ball sight which Fleet Air Arm pilots used to turn a diving Skua around its axis to stay on target against a fast-moving ship, O'Leary stated, 'A ship can't move all that

---

fast! More of a problem was 'weathercocking' in the dive. Aileron turns to bring target on line were easy.'[13]

Air Commodore Lal, as he had then become, was at that time newly reinstated at Peshawar with the job of overall instructor for Vengeance training with 152 OTU and he described this incident in his memoirs in this way.

> At that time none of us knew anything about dive-bombing. We had to develop our own ways of attack. An RAF officer, who had been to America and visited the factory where these aircraft were designed, took one up for a demonstration. He went into a dive and never recovered from it. He went straight into the ground; the aircraft blew up and he was killed. This was rather a spectacular way to demonstrate the bombing. Anyway, we went on to develop our own techniques and in fact trained some RAF Squadrons and then No. 7 Squadron.[14]

The unfortunate pilot was not a squadron leader at all but, in fact, a pilot officer, 24-year-old Ernest John Butler, RAFVR (124152) who, while demonstrating the technique in Vengeance AN844 of 154 OTU, made a fatal terminal dive into the bombing range on Monday 15 February 1943.

According to the same source at the subsequent inquiry into the disaster it came to light that a probable cause of the accident was that the aircraft's centre of gravity (CG) without anyone in the rear cockpit, or any compensating ballast, was too far forward. This led to an irrecoverable terminal dive which even her nose-up trim could not reverse. This sounds reasonable, except for the fact that Butler had a rear-seat man with him, Corporal Phillips. So perhaps there was another factor here. It would certainly seem so for, some weeks later later, on 29 April, Pilot Officer H.B. Waterson with Pilot Officer Mohan Karam in Vengeance AN 997, met the same fate. And, on 28 January 1944, Sergeant F. Brown and Sergeant Harris, flying ES 878, also dived to their deaths on the range. As can be seen in the 152 Accident Listing, this

---

[13] Joseph O'Leary to the Author, 15 October 2016.

[14] Lal, Air Chief Marshal Pratap Chandra – *My Years with the IAF*, Lancer Publications LLC., Atlanta, Ga., 1986.

theory about single-seating sorties upsetting the aircraft's centre of gravity
(CG) did not prevent single pilot flights taking place from June to December
1943 without any fatalities.[15]

It was not just the dangers of the dive-bombing technique itself
that brought a steady toll of casualties at Peshawar down the years. The
uncertainties of the Indian sub-continent's volatile weather added to the
tally of loss. Jumping forward, one typical example of such losses due to
the vagaries of the weather was that which took place on 17 February 1944.
A flight of three Canadian-piloted Vultees, led by Flying Officer Milton
War Sills, RCAF, with Pilot Officer John Grant Gunderson, RCAF as
No. 2 and Flying Officer Victor John Hillman RCAF, as No. 3, took off
from Peshawar at 1305 to carry out a cross-country circular navigation
training flight following a route which took them over Attoch, Khisman,
RAF Chaklala (Chakwal), Attoch and back to base. The base's duty
Meteorological Officer on that day, Warrant Officer L.J. Powdrill, cleared
the flight as the forecast was for good weather, but with 10/10th cloud
cover from a base of 6,000 feet.

Initially, all proceeded to plan with clearing skies along each leg as far as
Khushab. Conditions then began to deteriorate again on the next leg and
clouds, at first thin but increasingly dense, were encountered. So thick did
the cover become that Sills, quite correctly, ordered the unit to return. As he
did so the flight was suddenly violently buffeted by strong air currents. In the
course of this, Sills' radio broadcast was not received by his two companions.
Gunderson, however, was able to see his leader make the turn and complied,
even though by this time their blind-flying instruments had malfunctioned.
Fortunately, both Vengeance survived this ordeal and broke free of the clouds

15 Perhaps one should not pay too much heed about the memory of a then 8-year-old about
his father's talk being recalled many decades later. Ezekiel was credited with crashing a
Vengeance, 'without wings' on a small clump of trees amazingly without death or serious
injury to either occupant. He was also said to have described the Vultee as a bad copy of the
German Stuka – Junkers 77 [sic] dive-bomber: 'the Yanks put together an untested plane
and dumped it under Roosevelt's lend-lease and the British Government dumped it on us,
natives, who were being [pre]sumptuous enough to want our own 'native' Air Force.' See:
http://chodsrinivas.blogpot.co.uk/2014/04/the-plane-my-dad-crasheddads-airforce.html
Tuesday 8th April 2014.

and each made an independent decision to head to Khushab[16] to land. No word or sight came of Hillman's aircraft unfortunately. The two Vultees eventually sighted each other and re-united, deciding to land instead at RAF Sargodna, Punjab, which both reached safely, landing at 1450 but Hillman's aircraft had disappeared.

The following day a local reported a crashed aircraft burning near Marakpur, some sixteen miles south-west of Chakwal. The report was scorned but when an investigation party arrived at the scene of the accident they found the Vengeance, AN 629, had gone in at an angle of 45 degrees, had indeed suffered a fire and that were no survivors. The aircraft's junction box was recovered from the wreckage with signs of electrical fire damage. The hypothesis was that, in the storm, a lightning strike had knocked out this box, with the result that all electrical services, and that of course included the electrical petrol pumps, would have been rendered inoperative and the engine had then completely cut out through fuel starvation. The choices for the crew were stark, either to bale out, which in the conditions prevailing would have been suicidal, or attempt an emergency landing and that Hillman had opted for the latter.

A Board of Enquiry was held, and their conclusions as recorded in a report dated 3 March,[17] was that 'It is thought that the pilot was attempting to execute a forced landing, but owing to the bad weather and violent air currents the aircraft went out of control and low cloud base prevented control being completely regained before the aircraft struck the ground'.

To counter criticisms of Powdrill for okaying the flight and not anticipating the risks, Flight Lieutenant Khan Bahadur Haj Golmastkhan, No. 152 OTU's Commanding Officer, recorded that he 'thoroughly' agreed with the decision to fly the route. He stated that while in his view pupils had to be properly warned against attempts to fly though what he termed 'heap' cloud, and that this was always impressed upon them during lectures and at pre-flight briefings,

> I consider it essential, however, for pupils to be competent to fly through scattered cloud. I am of the opinion that an OTU would be

---

[16]   Nowadays the site of Pakistan's Nuclear Research facility.
[17]   AIR 27/703 op. cit.

failing to discharge its training obligations if crews, capable of flying only in fair weather, were passed on to operational squadrons. It is felt that it must be accepted as inevitable that, by virtue of its advance nature, flying training at an OTU must be carried out in conditions more hazardous than those justifiable at units engaged in more elementary flying training.

This was fair comment, and more losses were indeed taken by the Vengeance from the unforgiving elements controlled by Mother Nature than were ever inflicted by the Japanese enemy.

On arrival at Campbellpur the squadron had come under control of the RAF No. 233 (Composite) Group commanded by Air Commodore Henry John Francis Hunter CBE RAF, a stern disciplinarian. After their long period of transition and training the squadron's first blooding took place almost a year to the day since formation, after they were had shifted base to Mirashah. They were assigned targets in Northern Wazaristan against insurgents who had ambushed a peaceful convoy. At 1530 two Vengeance aircraft, AN 678 piloted by Squadron Leader Karori Lal Bhatia (later a VC holder) with Flying Officer Victor Srihari as navigator, and AN 664, flown by Flight Lieutenant Pratap Chandra Lal, (later to become Air Chief Marshal Lal DFC) with Flying Officer Kartik Chandra Sarkar as his rear-seat man, were despatched after a preliminary reconnaissance flight by Lal in a Hawker Audax biplane. Lal was the Flying and Navigational Instructor and in charge of the conversion to the Vengeance by both No. 7 and No. 8 Squadrons, but he managed to get assigned an operational role as a 'private' pilot.[18] He managed 'with great difficulty' to persuade his superiors that he should go on operations. 'I did not join the Air Force simply to become an Instructor.' He transferred to 7 Squadron while they were at Campbellpur,[19] east of the Kabul River from Peshawar. As usual, all such counter-insurgency operations were carefully monitored due to the political sensitivity of the area and a political agent was on hand at the base to oversee the mission when the aircraft took off. Their targets were caves hiding insurgents along

---

[18]   This was a 'warm-up' for Lal, who, in October 1943, finally managed to get himself out of instructing and into combat flying.

[19]   Now known as Attoch.

the Tochi River (also known as the Gambilla River) at Tsepal Phasi, in the North-West Frontier Province. Bhatia made the first strike in AN672 and was followed down by Lal, whose camera-equipped Vultee photographed the bomb strikes which confirmed direct hits were made with the 500lb general purpose (GP) IV10 bombs.

On 12 December a record squadron long-range flight was chalked up by A Flight, led by Flight Lieutenant Eric Wilmot Pinto, which covered the one thousand miles between the base and Nagpur in a single day. It was not until 21 December that a second strike was made on the tribesmen, again directed against the same cave refuge targets. This time four Vengeances were despatched, led by Flying Officer Karori Bhatia with Sergeant Ohri in AN664, Flying Officer Mandhar Sakhare and Sergeant Jagad in AN795, Flying Officer Keki Gocal and Flying Officer Arthur Chacko in AN758 and with the Squadron CO, Squadron Leader Hem Choudhuri, flying as No 4 in the formation in AN748 with Flying Officer Victor Srihari to film the results. However, the camera failed through electrical faults although hits were visually observed.

Further anti-insurgency sorties were flown from the primitive airfield at Miranshah Fort, Waziristan, and they suffered the indignity of night sniper fire from the local Wazir and Mahsud tribesmen in return.[20]

Intense training involved dives from 12,000 feet at the optimum 80–degree angle and the dropping of 8lb[21] practice bombs whose stannic chloride charge emitted white smoke to aid the various control teams in plotting accuracy of aim on the target, a fifteen-yard diameter white circle.[22] Joseph O'Leary elaborated this basic to me in more depth by stating that 12,000 feet was the optimal altitude to start a dive: '10,000 feet is the minimum (anything less is a bit of a rush, and, as every rifleman knows, the longer the barrel, the more accurate the weapon.' As for the pull-out altitude, he had written 'five seconds too late and you're dead' but he told me later,

---

[20] The British Army had been trying to hold down these fierce, resilient and resolute fighters for decades under the Raj, and the RAF had taken over in the 1930s. Neither had much success and when the Pakistan military took over the chore after 1947 neither did they. Today it all continues, and CIA drone strikes have replaced aircraft, to little avail!

[21] 1 lb = 0.453592 kg.

[22] Yeats-Brown MC, Major Francis Charles Clayton, *Martial India*, Eyre & Spottiswood, London,1945. A former cavalry officer Yeats-Brown was the author of the well-known *Lives of the Bengal Lancer* and spent time with 152 OTU researching.

I recalculated – it's 2.5 seconds. We pulled out when the altimeter passed 3,500, as the instrument lagged, that was roughly a true 3,000. If you pulled till 'grey out' (all pilots did – wouldn't you?) you should be level at 1,000, more or less. The Vultee Vengeance behaved nicely, no judder – just 'mushed' – but that was taken into account in the calculation. So that 1,000 is your margin. The Vultee Vengeance is vertical at terminal velocity (300mph approximately) when you pull. That's 400 feet per second… . If you did 'black-out', neither you nor anyone else would know any more about it (this was, in fact, the 'standard' VV accident).

As to how the pilot coped with the physical effects of the dive, O'Leary noted the 'open' mouth, or 'chew gum' or 'keep swallowing' advice (to clear ears) was used. "Did the Vultee Vengeance pull out smoothly? 'Yes, it did.'[23]

In the New Year of 1944, at the behest of No. 223 Group, the squadron prepared to move to undertake more intense training in close-support missions, working closely with army units in preparation for combat operations in Burma. On 19 February two formations of Vengeances took off for Gwalior in central India. The leading group of nine aircraft under Squadron Leader Choudhuri fared the worst. This section of the squadron (which had had by this time received the nickname 'Battleaxes') was subjected to a sobering ordeal for massive dust storms were encountered en route which reduced visibility to a minimum. Three aircraft were lost all told, that flown by Flying Officer Ajit Singh with Sergeant Sohrab Rostamji Desai and another piloted by Flying Officer Mangal Gururaj Stitaram Rao with Sergeant Muhammad Ali Khan Darling and also lost in this machine was Aircraftsman 1st Class Wadekar, a technician who had not wanted to take the train and had somehow hitched a ride.

More fortunate were the third crew, the experienced Flying Officer Pilot Officer Keki Gocal and his rear-seat man, Sergeant S.K. Ghosh, who managed to get down in one piece and survived. Lal, leading the following second batch of eight Vengeance, recalled that:

---

23   Joseph O'Leary to the Author,13 October 2016.

We ran into very bad weather before we were over Lahore, about mid way between Campbellpur [now Attoch] in the Punjab and Delhi, where we were due to refuel before the next leg to Gwalior. I saw one of the crashes and landed at Lahore to ask the RAF there to see if there were any survivors. Only two persons survived, five persons were killed. My flight came through intact.[24]

For the survivors who reached Gwalior on the 20th and the replacement crews and aircraft which arrived later, training was then undertaken over the next month before the first combat tour got underway in earnest.

Lal recorded that the squadron 'was inducted into Burma mainly to work for, and with, General Wingate's soldiers, the Chindits, to fight the Japanese.' Major General Orde Charles Wingate DSO** was a brave but very unorthodox soldier. His idea was to train up a force of jungle fighters, able to travel light but be able to outfight the enemy in those special habitats and conditions, and then deploy them deep behind enemy lines where they would strike unexpectedly and cause havoc to their supplies and bases before fading back into the green maze again. They would be flown in by the RAF; they would be re-supplied and then evacuated by air before the enemy could corner them. He had 77 Indian Brigade, which had served in the first Chindit expedition in 1943, to which 14, 16 and 111 Brigades were ultimately added, along with both Nepalese Gurkha elements and native Kachins.[25]

While they were in combat the Chindits' only heavy artillery, apart from 25-pounders, would likewise be laid on from the air and, because accuracy was a pre-essential, only the dive-bomber was considered the most suitable close support weapon.[26] Wingate himself, from previous experience, was

---

[24] Lal, Air Chief Marshal Pratap Chandra, *My Years with the IAF*, Lancer Publications LLC., Atlanta, Ga., 1986. Lal claims the CO of 221 Group was Hunter, but it fact this position was held by Air Commodore (later Air Vice Marshal) Stanley Flamank Vincent DFC, – while Hunter was AOC of 223 Group.

[25] Special Force executed the second expedition in 1944, Operation THURSDAY, and deployed six brigades, three of them from 70th Division (the former 6th Division). Most re-supply was by USAAF Skytrains; US light aircraft were also used to evacuate casualties.

[26] One of the greatest of all Second World War close air support myths is the halting of the German Panzer attack at Mortain, France, (Operation LÜTTICH) in August 1944. Rocket-firing RAF Hawker Typhoon aircraft and American Republic P-47 Thunderbolt fighters with bombs, claimed to have destroyed over 200 German tanks. Careful analysis later proved beyond

highly sceptical about both the accuracy and the efficiency of RAF bombing aircraft, but, after some detailed discussion which we will examine later, he came around to the idea that the Vultees were capable of providing heavy blows, with speed and precision, should his force run into any enemy he could not either deal with or evade.

With a formation of six to twelve Vengeances operating some thirty miles behind the front line each aircraft toting two 500lb bombs and two 250lb wing bombs, almost four tons of lethal payloads could be implanted accurately into any enemy position 'in about 30 seconds'. Joseph O'Leary points out that such a weight of ordnance was 'more than a battery of 25-pounders could put down in a morning, even supposing they could bring up so many rounds'. Repeat the dosage with another Vultee squadron and even the formidable defensive positions that the Japanese specialised in might be neutralised.

It also gives a better understanding from the men on the spot at the time to some post-war pundits' comments. One of the most ridiculous statements ever made about the Vengeance was that by J. Rickard who wrote on 9 November 2009, 'The Vengeance was not a very effective dive-bomber…'. And again 'The Vengeance was not a particularly successful aircraft ….'

While the big bombers like the four-engined Consolidated B-24 Liberators of the USAAF could 'pattern bomb' with immunity from a great height, their enormous payloads rarely hit anything worthwhile, while the twin-engined North American Mitchell B-25 medium bombers proved equally erratic; the Vengeance on the other hand placed its bombs exactly on artillery positions, bunkers and the like, as the artillery forward observation officers repeatedly appreciated.[27] Also, as O'Leary pointed out, 'the concentration of the bombing meant that, even if every Jap were not killed in the strike, the

---

any doubt that airborne rockets knocked out just *seven* tanks and bombs a mere *two*! It was calculated that a Typhoon pilot firing eight rockets had, at best, a 4 per cent chance of hitting a tank. Still the myth is perpetuated *ad nauseam* while the accuracy of the Vengeance was legendary, but is ignored or dismissed. See Gooderson, Dr Ian, *Air Power at the Battlefront: Allied Close Air Support in Europe 1943-45*, Routledge, Abingdon, Oxon, 2013.

[26A] Rickard, J. *No. 8 Squadron (IAF): Second World War,* http://historyofwar.org/air/units/IAF/8-wwII.html.

[27] Careful post-war analysis by the USAAF bears this out, the respective accuracy rates for these aircraft were – Liberator 50 per cent, Mitchell 60 per cent and Vengeance 100 per cent.

noise and blast would stun him long enough for our forward troops, who would be close nearby, to rush the position and finish him off with grenade, rifle and bayonet before he came to his senses.' Certainly, no heavy bomber could risk being utilised in conditions where the two opposing sides were nearly invisible and eyeball-to-eyeball in the jungle as in Burma. Close Air Support (CAS) so scorned by the upper hierarchy of the RAF, came into its own in this type of warfare.

On the Army side of things many conventional British generals, including the redoubtable Lieutenant General William Joseph Slim, were far from convinced by Wingate's strategy, many considered such units a waste time and manpower, but eventually it went right up to the top via the Supreme Allied Commander (SAC) South-East Asia, Admiral Lord Louis Mountbatten to Premier Winston Churchill himself and go–ahead was given. Both 7 Squadron IAF and No. 84 Squadron RAF were therefore assigned to this task and detailed training began.

The squadron then moved to Gwalior which was the main base for the Chindits' jungle warfare training as it had similar jungle terrain to the Chindits' areas of operation, and began training to work alongside them and the other Vengeance squadrons allocated to the same task. Here for the next two months both forces used the Madhya Pradesh forests to work up reliable communications between the men on the ground and the dive-bombers whose job was to take out pinpoint targets of opportunity under the forest canopy. This entailed Air Control Groups on the ground able to communicate swiftly with the men in the air. With a tropical equatorial climate, including high temperatures (100+ degrees), high humidity, malarial conditions along the Betwa (Vetravati) River, which substituted for the Chindwin, and the monsoon season (March to September) looming, it was far from the ideal place or time to fight pitched- battles, but events decided otherwise.

The positioning of the enemy when close to friendly forces has always been, and remains, a tricky problem. Specialised aircraft required specialised aircrew trained to use them of, course, but also the very closest liaison with the ground troops. Early methods were for the army to lay down white smoke markers (known to the Vengeance pilots as *fluff*) with mortars but of course the Japanese were far from stupid and on the appearance of the Vengeances would lay down their white smoke markers on Allied positions. Changing the smoke colours from day-to-day was one way around this but required even more close connection with the ground troops to ensure the correct smoke colour and patterns were known by everyone prior to each mission.

On 12 March fifteen of the squadron's Vultees flew into the Uderbund airstrip some twelve kilometres (about 7.5 miles) from Kumbhirgram, Assam, near the Barail Hills of north-east India, close to the principal RAF base at Silchar, Assam[28] under Warrant Officer Bhaskaran. By the 21st the transfer was complete, and they readied themselves for their first proper combat missions. However, on the 24th General Wingate died in a plane crash. Lal related that:

> His forces, some of them scattered around northern Burma, seemed not too badly affected through the loss of their leader. However, when we started to support them with our Vengeances we found that they had been dropped at points which were beyond our range. We could not fly there and back with the fuel that we carried in our aircraft.

Disappointment was muted because around this time the massive Japanese thrust toward Imphal and Kohima began to develop, and all available airborne firepower had to be switched to these targets. At these decisive battles the following Vengeance squadrons participated: No. 7 IAF and Nos. 82, 84 and 110 RAF.

Combat missions now began and a total of forty-eight targets on this first tour of duty included enemy vital crossings and supply bases along the Chindwin River, Myothit, in the Magway district of central Burma, the Japanese Army positions near Imphal, enemy convoys on the Tiddim Road, which was the main supply route up to Imphal for the Japanese 33rd Division under Lieutenant General Motoso Yanagida who had been driving back 17th Division under Major General David Tenant 'Punch' Cowan, again; against enemy positions at Maungdaw in Rakhine State, in south-east Burma, just across the Indian border to which it was joined by twin tunnels and which had fallen to the British offensive on 8 January 1944, and the far tougher nut of Razabil. At this latter place the Japanese army had dug in deeply and created a formidable fortress with interlocking fire and bunkers

---

[28]   The present-day Silchar Airport near Agaktala.

in their usual manner. Direct assaults by infantry, tanks and artillery, with the occasional totally futile heavy bomber altitude attacks, proved costly and fruitless and initially failed. Renewed operations to take this strong position by infiltration was initiated in March[29] rather than head-on called for precision support which was in part provided by No. 7 Squadron.

On 28 March 1944 six Vengeances, under the command of Squadron Leader Choudhuri, made an attack on Kenji on the Chindwin.[30] The targeting was, in the main, accurately conducted, but casualties were taken. No. 7 Squadron, as part of 224 Group, 167 Wing, has allegedly been subjected to some less-than-flattering criticisms recently by the likes of the son of Flying Officer Joe Ezekiel (1709) (but who also wrote in stark contradiction, that the Vengeance was 'the ideal weapon of war against the targets in the mountains and thick jungles.') and the like, so it behoves us to once more examine some of their missions in details to find out the real facts. We will here reproduce some examples in depth from the squadron's sortie reports.[31]

On 29 March the squadron was operating from Uderbund airstrip and one section was assigned to dive bomb Japanese positions in the village of Nawngpu-awng. Maps and photographs were studied at the pre-mission briefing and six Vengeance Mk IIs were allocated to this mission. They were armed with 500lb instantaneously-used bombs and six 500lb bombs with a .025 min delayed-action fuse for penetration. The strike was led by Flight Lieutenant Pratap Lal and was composed as follows:

Aircraft	Pilot	Aircrew
J	Flt Lt Pratap Chandra Lal	Flt Lt Mandhar Sarkare
Q	F/O Sudindra Ibraham	Sgt Jagad
X	F/O Vellore Radhakrishnan	Sgt Dilbagh Singh
O	F/O Karori Bhatia	F/O Umesh Sunder Tonse
F	F/O Jagdish Kochhar	F/O Vernon Shib Chunder Bonarjee
L	F/O Nusly Duggan	Sgt Ohri

This formation followed a route that took them over Imphal airfield and then on across the Chindwin River south of its confluence with the Uyu

---

29   WO 203/1173 – HS/ALFSEA 247/8 & WO 203/1175 – HS/ALSEA 131/9.
30   AIR 27/110/27.
31   AIR/27/111.

River and taking final departure after identifying Homalin. They followed the Uyu River east and found alto cumulus cloud with a 10,000-foot base over the target with a visibility of fifteen miles, easily identifying their target and made their dives from east to west. There was no reaction from the enemy and five of the six aircraft made accurate deliveries with bursts in among the buildings in the road loop west of the *chaung* (waterway or small stream) in the centre of the village. Buildings collapsed and obscured the target with clouds of dust and white smoke. The sixth aircraft overshot to the north and one bomb dropped harmlessly in the river but the second of the salvo burst in a village on the opposite bank of the river starting a fire.

The 30th saw a strike by five Vengeance-IIs under the command of Choudhuri against enemy troop concentrations in Thayaung village (map reference SF 3410). Composition of the force was as follows:

Aircraft	Pilot	Aircrew
M	Sqn Ldr Choudhuri	F/O Murat Singh
K	F/O Mandhar Maharudrappa Sakhare	F/O S.K. Ghosh
J	P/O Palokat Mathews	F/O Vernon Bonarjee
P	F/O John Karori Lal Bhatia	F/O Victor Srihari
L	F/O Nusly Duggan	Sgt Ohri

Each Vengeance was carrying a pair of 500lb GP LD 37D bombs. The five aircrew were briefed by the senior Air Liaison Officer (ALO) using ¼-inch and 1-inch[32] maps and photographs. They took off at 1100 and took a route that took them over the Imphal valley south of that town, reaching the Chindwin River between the island in the river just north-west of the target and the loop in the river further up. The Vultees then followed the line of the river, crossing it slightly south of Thayaung and making their attack from south-east to north-west. At exactly midday the dives went in from a height of 9,000 feet down to 2,000 feet. The bombs from four of the planes were observed to detonate across the centre of the village while the two bombs from the fifth machine exploded in the eastern outskirts and several buildings were seen to disintegrate before dust and smoke obscured the target. Duggan's aircraft was the last plane down and attempted to take photographs. The section returned to Uderbund at 1256.

---

[32]   1 in = 2.54 cm.

The second part of this strike consisted of a further five Vengeances who were tasked to strike the village of Sanda (map reference 3214). This section, led by Flying Officer Chadagam Satyanarayana consisted of-

Aircraft	Pilot	Aircrew
N	F/O Chadagam Satyanarayana	F/O Cecil Henry Naire
D	F/O Edulji Hormusji Dadhabboy	F/O Jamset Bapuji Dordi
C	F/O Codanda Mudappa Cariappa	F/O Pananadan Chernruvari Ramakrishna
E	F/O Dorad Engineer	F/O Kalpalli Menon
H	F/O Dinshaw Burjorjee	Sgt Tonse

The aircraft carried a mixed bomb load, all toting one 500lb GP NITI, (Nose Instantaneous, Tail Instantaneous) while three also carried one 500lb GP (General Purpose) with time delay (TD) .025 and the other pair each had an LD 37D. They followed much the same route as the other section but crossed the Imphal valley to south of the town to the alternative target and followed the river until reaching the target zone, which with a ten-mile visibility below the cumulus cloud layer, they recognised by a distinctive 'winding *chaung*' noted in the briefing photographs. The dives were also made at midday in the direction north-east to south-west. The attack was made from an altitude of 9,500 feet down to 3,900 feet and all the bombs fell in the centre of the village, scoring direct hits on many of the buildings before the smoke and dust obscured them. Once more no enemy activity was observed, and the section returned to base at 1256.

Enemy troop concentrations at Maungdaw (SF 5599) were the targets of dive-bombing strikes on 31 March. Squadron Leader Choudhuri led a full twelve-plane sortie from Kumbhirgram at 1104. The force was made up of the following aircraft and crew.

Aircraft	Pilot	Aircrew
D	Sqn Ldr Hemango Choudhuri	F/O Murat Singh
F	F/O Muhammad Khan	Flt Sgt S.K. Ghose
B	F/O Keki Nadirshah Gocal	n/a
H	F/O Mohit Mohan Ghose	F/O Sadanand Sadashiv Nadkarni
C	F/O Miza Rahman	F/O Ghansyam Pandurang Pagnis
E	F/O Joseph 'Joe' Jacob Ezeikel	F/O Ripa Daman Sahni
O	Flt Lt Pratap Lal	Flt Lt Ketik Chandra Sarkar

Aircraft	Pilot	Aircrew
K	F/O Sudindra Kumar Ibrahim	Sgt Jagad
P	F/O Satinderlal Rikhye	F/O G.B. Singh
N	F/O Kochnar	F/O Vernon Bonarjee
M	P/O Dinshaw Burjorjee	F/O Tonse
J	P/O Palokat Mathews	Sgt Dilbagh Singh

Following the briefing with maps and photographs of the target from the Senior Air Liaison Officer, the squadron lifted off at 1104 and proceeded to the Chindwin river following a course slightly north of Kangla airstrip and crossed the river over its bend west of Homalin before turning north and following it until they identified their target in 25⁰ 5'N, 95⁰ 2' E by the pear-shaped sandbank in a river bend to the north-east. The enemy had hidden themselves but, with a ten-mile visibility, the Vengeances had no difficulty in target selection. 'Hem' Choudhuri's section (six machines) made their attacks from east to west, while Flight Lieutenant Lal took five aircraft in an approach from north-east to south-west to confuse enemy gunners. Five of the attacking aircraft scored direct hits around the centre of the target where two roads met, while five others struck an area between the river and a parallel road, hitting with a mixed range of ordnance; the eleventh aircraft overshot, and her bombs landed in the river itself. The final Vengeance could not release either of her bombs due to an electrical fault. All aircraft returned to base by 1300.

April Fools' Day 1944 proved no joke and no let-up in operations. Two strikes were launched from Uderbund at 1000 and 1003, their respective targets and compositions being as follows:

Aircraft	Pilot	Aircrew
G	F/O Karori Bhatia	F/O Victor Srihari
N	F/O J.S. Kochnar	F/O Vernon Bonarjee
P	F/O Nusly Duggan	Sgt Ohri
K	F/O Mandhar Sakhare	F/O R. Ghosh
J	P/O Palokat Mathews	Sgt Dilbagh Singh

Only five aircraft were despatched, the sixth, 'M', with Pilot Officer Umesh Burjorjee as pilot and Flying Officer Tonse as navigator, had been detailed off but were unable to take part due to electrical faults that developed prior to take-off. Bomb loads were the usual mixed batch with five 500lb GP NITI, four 500lb GPTD .025 and one 500lb GPLD 37D being carried.

Following the usual briefing this group lifted off at 1000 and followed the usual route to the target, which was the village of Kawya, with an alternative target of Thaungdut village, flying to Imphal and crossing the Chindwin 'over the notch in the river north of the bend above the point the Uyu river flows into the Chindwin'. No GPU references in those days – you flew via visual points of reference. The formation turned north and passed over the target, but it was obscured by low cloud (10/10th cumuli-nimbus) with a base at about 1,500 feet with two-mile visibility and heavy rain. This rendered dive-bombing out of the question, so the aircraft turned back and, flying up the eastern side of the river, headed toward the secondary target.

The Vultees re-crossed the Chindwin north of the bend above Thaungdut and identified the target by the U-bend of the river from the briefing photographs. Here they found better weather with cloud cover 6/10th cumulus with a 6,000-foot base and six-mile visibility. As usual no enemy activity was observed, and the attack went in from the south-east to the north-west with the dives commencing at 1828.8m (6,000 feet) and bomb release at 1,500 feet. Before the usual smoke and dust obscured the target, it was seen that direct hits were made on at least two buildings. The Vengeances returned to base at 1226.

The second section lifted off from Uderbund at 1003 with the aim of hitting concentrations of Japanese troops located at Sittaung, Paunghyin Township, in Mawiaik District on the right-hand side of the Chindwin. The section comprised the following personnel-

Aircraft	Pilot	Aircrew
H	F/O M.M. Ghose	F/O Sadanand Nadkarni
F	F/O Muhammad Khan	Flt Sgt S.K. Ghose
B	F/O Edulji Dadhabboy	F/O Jamset Bapuji Dordi
C	F/O Miza Abdul Rahman	F/O Ghansyam Pagnis
	F/O Dorad Engineer	F/O Kalpalli Menon
E	F/O Joseph Ezekiel	F/O Ripu Daman Sahni

While only fifteen miles from base the formation encountered the same 10/10th thick cumulus clouds as their predecessors. These blanketed the hilltops and presented a blank wall up to 16,000 feet. They attempted to find a break but after fifteen minutes flying they found nothing but the same unbroken barrier. The operation was aborted by Flying Officer Ghose, but the formation became dispersed as they turned back in the murk. Ghose himself (at 1104), along with Khan (1117) and Dorad 'Dolly' Engineer (1141) finally made it back to base okay, but Miza Rahman had to put down at the Tulihal air strip. Joe Ezekiel was reported missing but eventually he was also reported to have safely managed to land at Tulihal.

Flying Officer Edulji Hormusji Dadabhoy, piloting Vengeance AN797 and his rear-seat man, Jamshet Bapuji Dordi, were not so lucky. They became hopelessly lost in the overcast and ran out of fuel. Both men baled out of the aircraft which itself crashed in a valley to the west of Imphal. Dordi fortunately landed safely and he somehow made his way back to Allied territory over the course of the next two days and rejoined at base at 1700 on the 3rd, but Dadabhoy was lost and was presumed dead; his body was never found. It was a bitter reminder that, in this unwelcoming part of the world, Mother Nature was often more dangerous than the Japanese foe.[33]

The war meanwhile ground remorselessly on. On 2 April, despite the unpromising weather, another mission was scheduled, the principal target this time being Yegan (map Reference SF 6164) with an alternative of Segyaung, at Phaungbyin in Sagaing south-east of Imphal (SF 2900). Twelve aircraft were allocated to this strike, as follows.

Aircraft	Pilot	Aircrew
D	Sqn Ldr Hemango Choudhuri	F/O Murat Singh
H	F/O J.S. Kochhar	F/O Vernon Bonarjee
G	F/O Muhammad Latif Khan	Flt Sgt S.K. Ghose
C	F/O Miza Rahman	F/O Ghansyam Pagnis
N	F/O Chadagam Satyanarayana	F/O Cecil Naire
O	Flt Lt Pratap Lal	Flt Lt Kartik Sarkar
Q	F/O Sudindra Kumar Ibrahim	Sgt Jagad
P	F/O Satinderlal Rikhye	F/O Gurbachan Singh
K	F/O Mandhar Sakhare	F/O Rathindra Ghose
J	P/O Dinshaw Burjorjee	F/O Umesh Tonse
M	F/O Vellore Radhakrishnan	Sgt Dilbagh Singh
E	F/O Dorad Engineer	F/O Kalpalli Menon

[33] Nothing daunted from this ordeal, Dordi went on to serve with No 12 Squadron earning a Mention in Despatches (MiD) and had a distinguished career in the Indian Air Force, retiring in September 1967 as an air commodore.

Take-off was at 1225 but Flying Officer Dorad Maneckhan Engineer's aircraft crashed during take-off and so only eleven Vengeances were despatched. However, once more while only about thirty miles out from Uderbund, the section encountered impassable weather. 'Massing of towering cumulus covering hill tops and rising to above 15,000ft [4572m] with layers of alto-stratus at 12-13,000ft. [3657.6 -2962m]' Visibility varied between one and ten miles. Choudhuri decided to turn back rather than risk losing more aircrew on a mission that such conditions would have rendered impossible anyway and the eleven Vultees were back on the ground at 1330.

Another twelve-plane strike was readied for 3 April with the aim of hitting concentrations of Japanese troops sited in Myothit village in the Magway District, which was a slightly longer-range mission than normal. The route to be taken after the usual briefing with ¼-inch and 1-inch scale maps and fresh photographs was slightly to the north of Wangjing. The composition of the force, which was despatched from Uderbund at 0845, was thus:

Aircraft	Pilot	Aircrew
A	Sqn Ldr Hemango Choudhuri	F/O Murat Singh
C	F/O Miza Rahman	F/O Ghansyam Pagnis
G	F/O Muhammad Latif Khan	Flt Sgt S.K. Ghose
D	F/O Mohit Ghose	F/O Sadanand Nadakarni
H	F/O Joseph Ezekiel	F/O Ripu Sahni
F	F/O Chadagam Satyanarayana	F/O Cecil Naire
J	Flt Lt Pratap Chandra Lal	Flt Lt Mandhar Sakhare
K	F/O Nusly Duggan	Sgt Ohri
N	F/O Satinderlal Rikhye	F/O Gurbachan Singh
O	F/O Karori Bhatia	F/O Victor Srihari
P	F/O Ibraham	Sgt Jagad
M	F/O Vellore Radhakrishnan	F/O Vernon Bonarjee

Once the formation had reached the area they easily picked up the Yu River with its distinctive bends and with a fifteen-mile visibility over the target zone they could see the road to Tamu quite clearly. Myothit was also identified by the leader who had a photo of the village with him while the U-bend in the river and the prominent pagoda at the eastern end of the village were further recognition features. At 0933, the twelve Vultees tipped over at an altitude of 8,000 feet and made their attack dives down to a 'bombs-off' height of 2,500 feet, crossing from east to west. There was some light AA fire from a 40mm type gun located some third of a mile from the track and Flying Officer Muhammad Latif Khan's aircraft, the third machine off the stack, suffered minimal damage from shrapnel. Despite this all aircraft delivered equal numbers of 500lb GP NITI and GPTD .025-inch. All but one Vultee's bomb-loads detonated along the track leading to the pagoda from the main highway and some buildings were demolished by direct hits. One aircraft undershot slightly but the attack was considered 'very successful'. All aircraft returned to base at 1030.

That same afternoon two additional six-plane sorties were made. Flight Lieutenant Pratap Chandra Lal led the first against Kawya and they took off from base at 1445. This section consisted of:

Aircraft	Pilot	Aircrew
O	Flt Lt Pratap Lal	Flt Lt Kartik Sarkar
N	F/O Vellore Radhakrishnan	F/O Shanil Kumar Mukkherji
P	F/O Satinderlal Rikhye	F/O Gurbachan Singh
K	F/O Mandhar Sakhare	F/O Rathindra Ghosh
J	P/O Palokat Mathews	Sgt Dilbagh Singh
M	P/O Dinshaw Burjorjee	F/O Umesh Tonse

The unit flew over Imphal where they found thick cloud cover blocking their planned outward route. They therefore diverted and struck the Chindwin River at the U-bend opposite Thaungdut, turning north upriver and passing its junction with the Uyu River before crossing the right-angled bend. The target was identified by the prominent stream as featured on the briefing photograph. There was no enemy opposition when at 1550 the Vengeances flew their mission from north-east to south-west, carrying out their dive attacks from 7,500 feet down to 3,000 feet. The usual mixed bomb loads were deposited, and most of the bombs landed amongst the huts in the village centre. One aircraft undershot, and her bombs burst in trees slightly to the east of the village. Flying Officer Radhakrishnan's machine was equipped with a 5-inch focal lens camera to record the attack. All the aircraft were safely back at base by 1650.

The second formation had as its leader Flying Officer Mohit Mohan Ghose and they were allocated reported Japanese concentrations in the village of Maungkan, which is located on the east bank of the Chindwin River, at Homalin Township in the Hakamtl District, north of Kawya and south of Tason. They followed the first strike off from Uderbund at 1550.

Aircraft	Pilot	Aircrew
D	F/O Mohit Ghose	F/O Sadanand Nadkarni
C	F/O Miza Rahman	F/O Ghansyam Pagnis
H	F/O Joseph Ezekial	F/O Cecil Naire
F	F/O Chadagam Satyanarayana	F/O Wairs
A	F/O Keki Gocal	F/O Vernon Bonarjee
E	F/O Codanda Cariappa	F/O Panangadan Ramakrishnan

The formation crossed the Chindwin at the bend above Homalin and followed the river up to the pear-shaped sand bend in the riverbank before diving in at 1704 from 10,000 feet to a bomb-release height of 3,000 feet. While it was ascertained that bombs of all the aircraft detonated in the northern section of the village, once again the actual target was obscured by dust and smoke and could not be fully assessed, but fires were seen burning in the village as they took their departure. All aircraft landed safely at 1805.

It was expected that more serious opposition might be encountered for 7 Squadron's next mission. The Japanese had captured the airstrip at Tamu (94° 5'N, 24° 10' E) earlier and now it was seen that they were utilising it, not only for their aircraft, but as a staging base in their advance. Concentrations of troops and much motor transport had been photographed and it was decided to try and knock them about. Although the dive-bombers were, as per usual, not given an escort as such, they were told that the Supermarine Spitfires of No. 615 Squadron would provide what was termed 'general cover' in the area.[34] The squadron was on this occasion led by Flight Lieutenant Pratap Lal and organised thus:

Aircraft	Pilot	Aircrew
J	Flt Lt Pratap Lal	Flt Lt Kartik Sarkar
Q	F/O Sudindra Kumar Ibrahim	Sgt Jagad
K	F/O Vellore Radhakrishnan	F/O Shanil Kumar Mukkherji
O	F/O Karori Bhatia	F/O Victor Srihari
F	F/O Nusly Duggan	Sgt Ohri
M	F/O Jagdish Kochhar	F/O Vernon Bonarjee

---

[34]   This, the 'County of Surrey' Squadron, was commanded by Squadron Leader David William McCormack DSC*, RAAF, and was based at Silchar West airfield in Assam with Supermarine Spitfire Vcs. McCormack was later killed when eight Spitfires crashed on encountering a severe monsoon storm on 10 August 1944.

Aircraft	Pilot	Aircrew
D	F/O Mohit Ghose	F/O Sadanand Nadakarni
C	F/O Miza Rahman	F/O Ghansyam Pagnis
H	F/O Joseph Ezekiel	F/O Ripu Daman Sahai
E	F/O Chadagam Satyanarayana	F/O Wairs
G	F/O Dorad Engineer	P/O Kalpalli Menon
A	F/O Codanda Cariappa	F/O Panangadan Ramakrishnan

The group took off at 1350 on 4 April and set a course that took them to Palel. However, Flying Officer Karori Lal Bhatia's aircraft developed electrical failure and was forced to turn back, landing back at base at 1403. The remaining eleven machines then followed the line of the road to Tamu, which they identified by its distinct layout as shown on the briefing photographs. The attack went in at 1441 on a line from south-east to north-west and making their dives from 9,000 feet down to 3,000 feet before release. All the bombs fell in the target area, among the felled trees, but, as always, the damage could not be assessed due to dust and smoke from the explosions, although Flying Officer Kocher's aircraft took photographs on the way in with a 5-inch focal lens camera. Just a lone single radial-engined enemy fighter was observed in a blast pen to the west of the airstrip itself. A newly-constructed emergency strip lain across a paddy field[35] north-east of the main runway was also noted. The group returned to Uderbund at 1540.

Next day, 5 April, two smaller sorties were mounted. The first section consisted of six Vengeance IIs under the command of Squadron Leader Choudhuri, organised as follows.

Aircraft	Pilot	Aircrew
B	Sqn Ldr Hemango Choudhuri	F/O Murat Singh
D	F/O Kesargod Bhat	Sgt Allah Bakhashi
E	F/O Chadagam Satyanarayana	F/O Cecil Naire
H	F/O Keki Gocal	F/O Vernon Bonarjee
C	F/O Codanda Cariappa	F/O Panangadan Ramakrishna
G	F/O Muhammad Latif Khan	Flt Sgt S.K. Ghose

This group was tasked with striking reported Japanese troop concentrations at Thitt Seikkon, which housed a station on the rail link from the south up

---

[35]   *Padi* (Rice) which became the Anglo-Saxon 'Paddy' down the years.

which the enemy were moving their troops and supplies. Take-off commenced at 0917 but almost immediately the Vengeance of Flying Officer Muhammad Latif Khan suffered a catastrophic electrical failure and was forced to abort. The remaining five aircraft continued, taking a route between Sapam and Wangjing, two fair-weather airstrips being utilised by the RAF, and then crossed the Chindwin River south of the U-bend at Thaungdut where they turned north and followed the river to the target. A distinctive sandbank in the middle of the river made identification simple and there was no reaction from the Japanese.

The weather conditions at this juncture were 5/10th cumulus clouds with a base of 10,000 feet and visibility was ten to twelve miles. More seriously they encountered a strong crosswind, and this caused problems. Dives were commenced at 1015, tracking from the north-east to the south-west, the aircraft peeling off at 8,500 feet and releasing at 2,500 feet. Bombs delivered were five 500lb GPNITI, three 500lb GPTD .025 and two 500lb GPLD 37D. Three Vultees placed their ordnance along the eastern edge of the village due to the strong winds, while the other two undershot and these burst on the sandbank in the river slightly to the north-west. Not altogether a successful outcome and it is doubtful if any Japanese were much troubled by it.

The second group, also six aircraft strong, was led by Flying Officer Karori Bhatia and was composed of the following:

Aircraft	Pilot	Aircrew
O	F/O Karori Bhatia	F/O Victor Srihari
Q	F/O Nusly Duggan	Sgt Ohri
L	F/O Satinderlal Rikhye	F/O Gurbachan Singh
J	F/O Palokat Mathews	Sgt Dilbagh Singh
F	P/O Dinshaw Burjorjee	P/O Umesh Tonse
K	F/O Mandhar Sakhare	F/O Rathindra Ghosh

Again, one aircraft, K piloted by Flying Officer Mandhar Sakhare with Flying Officer Rathindra Ghosh as rear-seat man, had to abort the mission prior to take-off due to electrical problems.

The remaining five machines of this section left from Uderbund at 0930. Their allocated target was Letpantha village and their route took them over Imphal airfield and then over the Chindwin at its elbow bend at Tilawng near Homalin, before turning upriver until the new shorter loop of the river west of their target was identified. The dives were commenced from 9,000 feet down to a 2,000-feet release height in a south-east to north-west run and the usual mixed bomb load was deposited, three aircraft hitting the centre of the settlement and the other two in the south-western segment. All five aircraft were safely back at base by 1125.

We move forward to 8 April and a full squadron strike was mounted against Japanese troops at Pakpin near Homalin. The full composition of the force was:

Aircraft	Pilot	Aircrew
A	Sqn Ldr Hemango Choudhuri	F/O Murat Singh
G	F/O Muhammad Latif Khan	Flt Sgt S.K. Ghosh
E	F/O Kesargod Bhat	Sgt Allah Bakhashi
B	F/O Mohit Ghoshe	F/O Sadanand Nadakarni
C	F/O Miza Rahman	F/O Ghansyam Pagnis
H	F/O Joseph Ezekiel	F/O Jamshet Dordi
F	Flight Lieutenant Pratap Lal	F/O Vernon Bonarjee
Q	F/O Sudindra Kumar Ibrahim	Sgt Jagad
N	F/O Vellore Radhakrishnan	F/O Shanil Kumar Mukkherji
O	F/O Karori Bhatia	F/O Victor Srihari
K	F/O Mandhar Sakhare	F/O Rathindra Ghosh
M	F/O Jagdish Kochhar	Sgt Dilbagh Singh

The squadron lifted off from Uderbund at 1310 and steered a course directly over Imphal airstrip before crossing the Chindwin just south of Homalin before following the Uyu River toward the apex of the 'W' shaped by the river. The *chaung* which joined the Uyu just to the north of this point made targeting easy as this could be checked from photographs carried by both Choudhuri and Lal. By this time the Japanese had gone to cover on the approach of the formation, but visibility was excellent with just 4/10th cumulus with a 9,000-foot base and a ten-mile view. The attack run was made on a course from the north-east to the south-west and dives commenced at 8,000 feet down to bomb release at 3,000 feet. The bomb bursts from ten of the Vultees were observed in the north-eastern part of the village amongst the huts, many of which were demolished, along the main road itself while one aircraft was off-target and its bombs landed in the fields slightly to the east. As they flew off the formation witnessed a huge fire and dark brown columns of smoke rising to some 6,000 feet in the direction of Nampesna (map Ref 97580). The squadron returned unmolested back at base at 1525.

Another dual strike was organised by No. 7 Squadron on 9 April. The two six-plane sections were led by Flight Lieutenant Satinder Lal and Flying Officer Chadagam Satyanarayana respectively.

The first section was sent against enemy troop concentrations reported at Thanan, Sagaing, a village north of Tamu some twelve miles north-west of Thaungdut on the Japanese supply road up from Tonhie, and was composed thus:

Aircraft	Pilot	Aircrew
N	Flt Lt Pratap Lal	F/O Vernon Bonarjee
P	P/O Satinderlal Rikhye	F/O Gurbachan Singh
Q	F/O Sudindra Kumar Ibrahim	Sgt Jagad
M	F/O Mandhar Sakhare	F/O Rathindra Ghosh
O	P/O Dinshaw Burjorjee	F/O Umesh Tonse
L	P/O Palokat Mathews	Sgt Dilbagh Singh

After the usual briefing the section lifted off from Uderbund at 0955 and flew over the enormous all-weather airfield at Tulihal.[36] It was built of interlocking PSP[37] en route to the target area. They identified the distinctive Sunpawngnga *chaung* that led north-west from there to the Namya and Taban *chaungs* to the point on the Chindwin where it bends east to the target, which was 'very clearly visible'. There was 2/10th cumulus clouds at 3,000 feet with good visibility at up to fifteen miles. The target area was already found to be burnt and damaged from earlier visitations from other Allied units but the Vultees concentrated on a small area at the junction of several tracks which seemed to be a choke-point for Japanese supply convoys.

At 1055 they commenced their attack run from south-east to north-west, diving in from an altitude of 9,500 feet, with bomb release at 3,000 feet. Five of the aircraft pinpointed their ordnance exactly on the junction of the tracks; the sixth targeted a brownish rectangular patch 200 yards to the

---

[36] Constructed, it is said, maybe apocryphally by Americans using one set of dimensions to the plans of the British using another, so that it ended up by being four times the necessary size!

[37] Pierced Steel Planking metal, and covered in *Bithess* sheeting.

south-west from which smoke was seen, assumed to be camouflage netting covering stores and supplies. On their way back out from this attack Sergeant Dilbagh Singh in Vengeance P reported sighting a party of between forty to fifty enemy soldiers near Lonopi village, Ukhrul on the Burmese-India border. It was a worrying indication of how far the enemy was pressing further into Allied territory. The squadron returned to base at 1145.

The second group comprised the following:

Aircraft	Pilot	Aircrew
A	F/O Chadagam Satyanarayana	F/O Cecil Naire
E	F/O Kesargod Bhat	Sgt Allah Bakhashi
H	F/O Codanda Cariappa	F/O Panangadan Ramakrishnan
G	F/O Muhammad Latif Khan	Flt Sgt S.K. Ghose
C	F/O Dorad Engineer	P/O Kalpalli Menon
B	F/O Keki Gocal	F/O Jamshet Dordi

They had as their assigned objective Japanese troop concentrations in Nawnguawng village. They took the normal route over Imphal. East of this point Flying Officer Codanda Mudappa Cariappa's aircraft lost contact with the rest of the formation due to heavy clouds. The rest of the unit crossed the Chindwin south of the confluence with the Uyu River, then proceeded to the 'W' bends as before and identified the target from photographs carried by Chadagam Satyanarayana. Dives were made from an altitude of 9,000 feet down to 3,000 feet in an east to west attack. Two aircraft were seen to burst between the *chaung* and the village centre and the road running parallel to it, while the other three Vengeances hit and demolished huts west of the *chaung* along the road leading south-west from the river bank. The five-aircraft returned safely to base at 1240 where they found that Cariappa had landed safely at midday with full bomb load intact.

Maungkan village was attacked again on the 10th by a six-plane strike led by Squadron Leader Choudhuri. The formation consisted of the following:

Aircraft	Pilot	Aircrew
A	Sqn Ldr Hemango Choudhuri	F/O Murat Singh
G	F/O Dorad Engineer	P/O Kalpalli Menon
D	F/O Codanda Cariappa	F/O Panangadan Ramakrishnan
H	F/O Mohit Goshe	F/O Sadanand Nadakarni

Aircraft	Pilot	Aircrew
C	F/O Miza Rahman	F/O Ghansyam Pagnis
B	F/O Joseph Ezekiel	F/O Jamshet Dordi

This was another 'milk run' along the well-worn route over Imphal strip and across the Chindwin to the north of Kawya, making reference to the island in the sweep of the river here and turning north up the river to the village, itself identified by the chaung to south-west and the pear-shaped sandbank pointing toward it, all verified by photographs carried by the leader. Weather over the target was good, 2/10th scattered cumulus with a base at 10,000 feet and fifteen-mile visibility. The attack went in at 1130 from north-east to south west with dives being initiated from 8,000 feet altitude down to 'bombs-off' at 3,000 feet. The bombs comprised six 500lb CPN Rod T.1, four 500lb GPTD .025, one 500lb GPLD 37A and one 500lb GLD 37B. Five of the Vultees placed their bombs between the forks on the roads in the north-eastern part of the village, while those of the sixth aircraft demolished huts along the road at the south-western tip. 'Bombing considered effective', ran the report, and all aircraft returned safely to Uderbund at 1225.

A more satisfying target was selected for No. 7 Squadron's attention on 11 April. This was a Japanese ammunition and storage dump located at Pinpoint SF 2623. The site covered an area parallel to and adjacent to the Chindwin River and was of approximately 200 by 800 yards in extent, running north-east to south-west. During the briefing the usual maps and photographs were studied, and, in addition, a large-scale chalk drawing of the target was on display. Choudhuri himself led this important sortie in two six-plane boxes and whose composition was as follows:

Aircraft	Pilot	Aircrew
A	Sqn Ldr Hemango Choudhuri	F/O Murat Singh
D	F/O Kesargod Bhat	Sgt Allah Bakhashi
E	F/O Muhammad Latif Khan	Flt Sgt S.K. Ghose
H	F/O Mohit Ghose	F/O Sadanand Nadkarni
C	F/O Miza Rahman	F/O Ghansyam Pagnis
B	F/O Joseph Ezekiel	F/O Jamshet Dordi
M	Flt Lt Pratap Lal	F/O Vernon Bonarjee
K	F/O Mandhar Sakhare	F/O Rathindra Ghosh
Q	P/O Dinshaw Burjorjee	F/O Umesh Tonse

Aircraft	Pilot	Aircrew
O	F/O Karori Bhatia	F/O Victor Srihari
P	F/O Satinderlal Rikhye	F/O Gurbachan Singh
L	F/O Jagdish Kochhar	F/O Shanil Kumar Mukkherji

It was an early start and the whole formation took departure from Uderbund at 0610 flying over the all-weather airfield at Palel, itself under increasing threat from the advancing Japanese ground troops, before crossing the Chindwin below the familiar U-bend in the river at Thaungdut. They turned north and found gloriously clear weather over the target area, a cloudless sky for once, with a slight haze reducing visibility to six to eight miles. The identifying points were therefore clearly made out – the shape of the sandbank in the river itself, the *chaung* meeting the river to the north and well-worn trails, all made sighting easy. There was no enemy opposition but as they approached the Vultee crews could see that the target area was already covered with dust and smoke from a previous visitation.

The attack duly went in at 0708, tracking from north-east to south-west, with dives being made from 9,000 feet down to 3,000 feet. Both Choudhuri and Lal carried 5-inch focal lens cameras which were duly employed during the dives and the bomb loads, twelve 500lb GPN Rod TI, three 500lb GPTD .025, two 500lb GPID 37A and two 500lb GPLD 37D weapons, were duly delivered onto the enemy. The Squadron Leader's section made concentrated bursts inside the north-eastern part of the target area and Lal's section hit slightly to the south-west with the angle of tracks. This was considered a very successful strike. As they left the area 'bluish' smoke seen rising from the north-east section of the target. The squadron returned to base without incident at 0755.

Another very important long-range mission was undertaken on 12 April, this being an attack on the advanced divisional headquarters at Mulam (RC 386) near Churachandpur in Manipur, a village located some 73 kilometres (45 miles) north of Imphal. For this attack a full squadron strike was organised as composed thus:

Aircraft	Pilot	Aircrew
O	F/O Karori Bhatia	F/O Victor Srihari
Q	F/O Sudindra Kumar Ibrahim	Sgt Jagad
N	F/O Jagdish Kochhar	F/O Shanil Kumar Mukkherji

Aircraft	Pilot	Aircrew
K	F/O Mandhar Sakhare	F/O Rathindra Ghosh
P	F/O Satinderlal Rikhye	P/O Gurbachan Singh
L	P/O Dinshaw Burjorjee	F/O Umesh Tonse
A	F/O Chadagam Satyanarayana	F/O Cecil Naire
C	F/O Dorad Engineer	F/O Kalpalli Menon
H	F/O Codanda Cariappa	F/O Panangadan Ramakrishnan
K	F/O Muhammed Latif Khan	Flt Sgt S.K. Ghosh
D	F/O Kesargod Bhat	Sgt Allah Bakhashi
B	F/O Keki Gocal	F/O Vernon Bonarjee

The team was fully briefed by a senior ALO before departure and they took off from Uderbund at 1645, and flew straight to the southern end of the Imphal Valley and continued until they arrived at the Tiddam Road near to the village of Taranga Obi, identified by a track meeting the road from the west and a road crossing the stream a little to the south. Here the squadron followed the Tiddam Road until a prominent bend east of Mulaw with a loop to the south enabled them to pinpoint their position with photographs carried by Karori Bhatia. The weather here was 2/10th cumulus cloud with a base at 10,000 feet, but thick haze obscured the target reducing visibility to two-three miles only.

There was no enemy opposition as, at 1728, the two boxes turned to make their bombing run from south-west to north-east going into their attack dives from an altitude of 10,500 feet with a release height of 6,000 feet. Pilot Officer Vernon Bonarjee's aircraft only dropped a single bomb as he failed to select the 500lbGPN Rod TI carried on the starboard crutch. Concentrating on the target Flying Officer Karori Bhatia failed to select either of his bombs. Of the remaining aircraft nine dropped directly in the village and detonations from them were seen on target before being obscured by the haze and dust. Two other Vultees slightly overshot and dropped their ordnance to the north-east of the village. All aircraft had safely returned to base by 1810.

The enemy was pressing ever closer to the Imphal and Kohima and, on 13 April, 7 Squadron was given a precision target close to the front, this being a Japanese position described as 'at ring-contour of hill top at BK 434758'. The squadron leader led this twelve-Vultee attack which left base in two sections, the first at 0912 and the second at 0927. The following units took part:

Aircraft	Pilot	Aircrew
N	Sqn Ldr Hemango Choudhuri	F/O Marat Singh
O	F/O Muhammad Khan	Flt Sgt S.K. Ghosh
H	F/O Mohit Ghose	Flt Lt Ramaswami Sitaram
C	F/O Miza Rahman	F/O Ghansyam Pagnis
B	F/O Joseph Ezekiel	F/O Jamshet Dordi
M	Flt Lt Pratap Lal	F/O Vernon Bonarjee
Q	F/O Sudindra Kumar Ibrahim	Sgt Jagad
P	P/O Satinderlal Rikhye	F/O Gurbachan Singh
G	F/O Karori Bhatia	F/O Victor Srihari
K	F/O Mandhar Sakhare	F/O Rathindra Ghosh
L	F/O Jagdish Kochhar	F/O Shanil Kumar Mukkherji
E	F/O Kesargod Bhat	Sgt Allah Bakhashi

The squadron flew straight to now-threatened Imphal, crossing the airfield and turning to port straight to the target. Identification was crucial as friend and foe were now very close to each other. The loop tracks enclosing the area and Kangla airstrip due south gave excellent points of reference while the precise position of the enemy position, overlooking Allied defences, was unmistakeable, being at the apex of a 'V' formed by the spurs of the hill itself. The British artillery on the ground also fired smoke rounds into the target to further aid identification.

The Vengeances attacked at 1004 from south to north so that any overshoots would still land in hostile territory and harm any defenders. Eleven 500lb GPTI and eleven GPTD bombs were released in dives down from 11,000 feet to 6,000 feet and all these bomb bursts were concentrated on the target itself. However, the bombs of Pilot Officer Satinderlal Rikhye's aircraft 'hung-up' on him during the dive and only became free during the pull-up, dropping away and bursting to the north-west in map reference BK 015780. This was the only hitch and the aircraft returned to base in two sections at 0945 and 1045 respectively.

There was no let-up at this crucial period and a second full-squadron mission was launched that same afternoon. The target was Japanese troop concentrations at Ekban-Ekwan and high ground in the hills to the east at map reference BK 325844 overlooking Imphal. The enemy had cut the road between Imphal and Kohima at Kangatongbi (24° 59'N, 93° 54' E), just north of the former and were pressing hard. Squadron Leader Choudhuri and Flight Lieutenant Pratap Lal once again led the two boxes into action thus:

Aircraft	Pilot	Aircrew
A	Sqn Ldr Choudhuri	F/O Murat Singh
E	F/O Muhammad Khan	Flt Sgt S.K. Ghosh
O	F/O Kesargod Bhat	Sgt Allah Bakhashi
M	F/O Mohit Ghose	Flt Lt Ramaswami Sitaram
C	F/O Miza Rahman	F/O Ghansyam Pagnis
B	F/O Joseph Ezekiel	F/O Jamshet Dordi
N	Flt Lt Pratap Lal	F/O Vernon Bonarjee
Q	F/O Sudindra Kumar Ibrahim	Sgt Jagad
K	F/O Mandhar Sakhare	F/O Rathindra Ghosh
P	P/O Satinderlal Rikhye	F/O Gurbachan Singh
N	P/O Dinshaw Burjorjee	F/O Umesh Tonse
L	P/O Palokat Mathews	Sgt Dilbagh Singh

The normal route was taken to overfly Imphal airstrip with a turn to port to follow the Manipur Road to the target. The bend in the road north of Kangatongbi provided a marker as did the bend in the *chaung* to the north-east. The precise aiming point was identified as the spur on the hill to the north of the bend and from photographs carried by Choudhuri. The attack was made at 1440 on a line from north-east to south-west, with dives commencing at 9,000 feet and pull-out at 4,000 feet. Eleven of the aircraft bombed with great accuracy and many huts suffered direct hits. Flying Officer Muhammad Khan overshot in the dive towards the bomb line and, quite correctly, did not release; he took his bombs back to base with him and landed safely with the others at 1535.

The following day 7 Squadron returned to the same target by the same route, leaving Uderbund at 0630. This time the configuration of the strike was this:

Aircraft	Pilot	Aircrew
Q	F/O Karori Bhatia	F/O Victor Srihari
N	F/O Dinshaw Burjorjee	F/O Umesh Tonse
P	F/O Palokat Mathews	Sgt Dilbagh Singh
K	F/O Mandhar Sakhare	F/O Rathindra Ghosh
M	P/O Vellore Radhakrishnan	F/O Shanil Kumar Mukkherji
L	F/O Jagdish Kochhar	F/O Vernon Bonarjee
C	P/O Rathindra Gosh	Flt Lt Ramaswami Sitaram
D	F/O Kesargod Bhat	Sgt Allah Bakhashi
G	F/O Joseph Ezekiel	F/O Jamshet Dordi
A	F/O Chadagam Satyanarayana	F/O Cecil Naire

Aircraft	Pilot	Aircrew
E	F/O Dorad Engineer	P/O Kalpalli Menon
B	F/O Codanda Cariappa	F/O Panangadan Ramakrishnan

Again, they found a clear, cloudless sky with ten-mile visibility. Despite this a bad error was made. Perhaps it was the intensity of the previous non-stop operations, maybe tiredness or just plain human error but on this occasion after turning left up the Kohima Road to the bend north of Kangatongbi, Flying Officer Karori Bhatia made a wrong call, mistaking the village at map reference RK 285283 for the target and attacking it, He made his dive-bombing attack in a run from the north-west to south-east. Disnhaw Burjorjee, Vellore Radhakrishnan and Jagdish Kochar followed him down and bombed before the mistake was realised and a warning was broadcast. Their bombs burst in the southern part of this village and damaged several huts.

The rest of the squadron circled the area and made sure that they had clearly identified both the bend in the road and that in the river west of the target and they also saw the bomb craters and demolished huts from their previous day's attack. Then, and only then, the rest of the unit carried out their own attacks on a line from north-west to south-west and dived from 10,000 feet down to 5,000 feet to hit the village (map reference RK 28843) at 0702 with seven 500lb GPTI and seven 500lb GPTD .025 bombs. Flying Officer Codanda Cariappa was part of this attack but failed to fully press home the firing button and had to bring his bombs back to Uderbund. The aircraft landed back at base at 0750.

Squadron Leader Choudhuri led the next full-squadron strike which was mounted on 15 April. Their target was again Japanese troop positions in a designated triangular area formed by map references RK 426733, RK 446783 and RK 449800. At the briefing by a senior ALO, using maps and an enlarged chalk drawing, the identification features were stressed as being a junction of tracks which formed an inverted 'V' while a bend in the track to the west and a marked bend in the *chaung* running along it gave further markers. The formation consisted of the following:

Aircraft	Pilot	Aircrew
A	Sqn Ldr Hemango Choudhuri	F/O Murat Singh
D	F/O Kesargod Bhat	Sgt Allah Bakhashi

Aircraft	Pilot	Aircrew
G	F/O Muhammad Khan	Flt Sgt S.K. Ghose
H	F/O Mohit Ghose	Flt Lt Ramaswami Sitaram
C	F/O Miza Rahman	F/O Ghansyarn Pagnis
B	F/O Chadagam Satyanarayana	F/O Cecil Naire
N	Flt Lt Pratap Lal	F/O Vernon Bonarjee
Q	F/O Sudindra Kumar Ibrahim	Sgt Jagad
M	Pilot Officer Palokat Mathews	Sgt Dilbagh Singh
K	F/O Karori Bhatia	F/O G. Surihani
P	F/O Satinderlal Rikhye	F/O Gurbachan Singh
L	F/O Jagdish Kochhar	F/O Shanil Kumar Mukkherji

After lifting off from Uderbund at 0920 the formation's first point of passage was the airstrip of Tulibal[38] before turning west and, leaving beleaguered Imphal off their port side, proceeded to the target area. The weather was good, the sky was cloudless, and visibility was ten miles, thus all the marker points discussed were easily made out. The only activity seen on the ground was white mortar smoke at 1001 at map reference RK 4978, laid it was assumed by the Japanese ground troops. The attack went in four minutes later, the Vultees tracking across from south to north, and making their dives down from 11,800 feet to a release altitude of 5,000 feet. Bombs deposited to the discomfiture of the enemy were twelve 500lb GPNITI, six 500lb GPTIN Rod and six 500lb GPTD. Ten aircraft salvoes were observed to burst on the eastern slopes of the hill spur near a small east-pointing ridge, while two other salvoes burst exactly on the hill top itself. This accuracy atoned for the failure of the previous day. The squadron returned to base at 1000.

The Japanese Air Force was not a large factor in the campaign, but it was far from totally ineffective. An attack was made on the base dropping many 5lb anti-personnel bombs and eight of the ground team were killed, with many more injured.[39]

Nawngpu-awng was the target for 16 April. Located on the east bank of the Chindwin at Homalin Township in the Hikamti District of Sagaing, it

---

[38] Nowadays an Indian Army base.

[39] Those who died in the raid were Corporal Allah Bakhsh, Leading Aircraftsman Mukunda Raul, Aircraftsmen 2nd Class Altaf Husain, Guru Ashirbam, Lal Sarkar, Saldanha and Guru Ashirbam and enrolled follower Muhammad Amin Khan.

was a staging post for enemy reinforcements and supply convoys coming up to the front. The prospect for a strike was not good as the weather over Uderbund was closing in; nonetheless, such was the seriousness of the situation that an attempt was made, and a six-plane sortie led by Flight Lieutenant Pratap Lal took off at 0902. This comprised:

Aircraft	Pilot	Aircrew
M	Flt Lt Pratap Lal	F/O Vernon Bonarjee
N	P/O Dinshaw Burjorjee	F/O Umesh Tonse
P	P/O Palokat Mathews	Sgt Dilbagh Singh
K	F/O Mandhar Sakhare	F/O Rathindra Ghosh
Q	F/O Sudindra Ibrahim	Sgt Jagad
L	F/O Satindelal Rikhye	P/O Gurbachan Singh

Each aircraft carried one 500lb GPTI and one 500lb GPTD bomb. The unit flew over Imphal and over the Chindwin River at the U-bend south of Homalin itself, turning to port up the line of the Uyu River until they reached the target, south of the distinctive 'W' bend. There was 6/10th cloud cover with stratus at 12,000 feet with a ten-mile visibility range. At 1013, while Lal reported sighting 'some suspicious looking bombers' south-west of the target, but this did not deter the attack There was no reaction from the Japanese either in the air or on the ground, and, at 1016, the attack went in smoothly from north-east to south-west, with the dive commencing at 9,500 feet down to a release height of 3,000 feet. All twelve bombs detonated in the western part of the village, but results were, as always, obscured by dust and debris.

While returning, word was received that Uderbund had become totally 'weathered-out' and the unit was ordered to land at nearby Kumbhirgram which had fared better with the elements, and which they did at 1141. Things had improved by the mid-afternoon and the six Vengeances left that airstrip at 1510 for the short hop over to base, where they landed ten minutes later.

On 17 April 7 Squadron mounted two full strikes. The first was led by 'Hem' Choudhuri and the target was enemy forces concentrated at Kalewa. Although the dive-bombers were promised cover over the target by McCormack's Spitfires of No. 615 Squadron, they, as usual, were unescorted to and from the area. The unit was constructed thus:

Aircraft	Pilot	Aircrew
A	Sqn Ldr Hemango Choudhuri	F/O Murat Singh
C	F/O Chadagam Satyanarayana	F/O Cecil Naire
H	F/O Keki Gocal	Flt Sgt K.C. Bull
G	F/O Mohit Ghoshe	F/O Jamshet Dordi
E	F/O Codanda Cariappa	F/O Vellore Radhakrishnan
B	F/O Dorad Engineer	F/O Kalpalli Menon
F	F/O Karori Bhatia	F/O Victor Srihari
N	F/O Dinshaw Burjorjee	F/O Umesh Tonse
J	P/O Palokat Mathews	Sgt Dilbagh Singh
M	F/O Mandhar Sakhare	F/O Rathindra Ghosh
Q	F/O Sudindra Ibrahim	Sgt Jagad
L	F/O Jagdish Kochhar	F/O Vernon Bonarjee

Departure from Uderbund was taken at midday after the usual briefing and a straight course was followed direct to the target. Unfortunately, Sakhare in Vengeance M found that his oil-filler cap had been left open and had to return early, landing back at base at 1235. The remaining eleven aircraft pressed on to carry out the mission. The Myittha runs eastward and joins the Chindwin at the 'S' bend just below the town and this made for easy identification as did the Labin *chaung* on the eastern bank which also met the Chindwin in the knuckle of the bend, as well as two smaller *chaungs* to the west. The Vultees attacked in a line from south-east to north-west from an initial height of 9,500 feet to a pull-out altitude of 4,500 feet.

For once the enemy showed some mettle with numerous light AA batteries situated mainly on the east bank opening fire with red flashes from 1256 onward in a vain attempt to deter any further damage to the already badly knocked about target. It was assumed the Japanese had something to defend here. The enemy barrage burst with white smoke at between 5,000 and 6,000 feet. Seven specific AA positions were noted and reported back to 168 Wing for future reference. Choudhuri in Vengeance A led down G and H and most of these AA guns fell silent. The rest of the force followed them down to make their drops and the batteries opened again as Karori Bhatia in 'F' began his dive but the bursts were well above them at 9,000 feet and the explosions emitted black instead of white smoke.

The dive-bombers were untroubled by the defensive fire and delivered ten 500lb GPTI bombs, ten 500lb bombs with .025min fusing, one 500lb GPTIN Red and one 500lb GPLD with 72-hour delayed action fuse into the target area at 1300. Seven struck directly into the village, flattening huts with several direct hits, two others targeted the new ferry jetties. They squadron landed back at base at 1410.

The second mission that day was a full strike against the locality of Fort White,[40] which lies on the eastern side of the Letha range between Kale and Tiddim, being some eighty miles from the latter.

The targeting concentrated on enemy troop formations and a large ammunition/storage dump some ten to eleven miles east of the second stockade. Because of its location and the distance to be flown over enemy air space fighter cover, in the form of a Spitfire sortie, was promised over the target. This twelve-plane mission was entrusted to the safe hands of Flight Lieutenant Pratap Lal and his team was as below:

Aircraft	Pilot	Aircrew
M	Flt Lt Pratap Lal	F/O Vernon Bonarjee
Q	F/O Sudindra Ibrahim	Sgt Jagad
J	P/O Palokat Mathews	Sgt Dilbagh Singh
K	F/O Mandhar Sakhare	F/O Rathindra Ghosh
P	F/O Satinderlal Rikhye	F/O Gurbachan Singh
L	F/O Jagdish Kochar	F/O Shanil Kumar Mukkherji
A	F/O Mohit Ghose	Flt Lt Ramaswami Sitaram
G	F/O Muhammed Khan	Flt Sgt S.K. Ghose
H	F/O Keki Gocal	F/O Panangadan Ramakrishnan
C	F/O Miza Rahman	F/O Ghansyam Pagnis
E	F/O Joseph Ezekiel	F/O Jamshet Dordi
B	F/O Dorad Engineer	F/O Kalpalli Menon

The route followed by No. 7 Squadron on this mission led directly to Tiddim itself and then, passing to the right of Kennedy Peak, they headed directly for Fort White along the road. A track leading to the road from the south-east immediately east of Fort White itself gave a recognition point as did the junction of two chaungs to the north of the western end and the tip of the valley to the east when checked with maps carried by Lal. The weather here

---

[40] This was originally a stockade constructed by the British Army in 1889 during their campaign to annex the Chin Hills. It was named in honour of Field Marshal Sir George White VC. It served as a base for the Chin-Lushal Expedition. It was occupied by the Japanese in 1942 and not finally re-taken until 10 November 1944. The area is nowadays known locally as Tangmual.

was overcast with 'very dense' haze which reduced visibility down to a mere 200–500 yards.

At 1715 the Vultees tipped over from 10,000 feet and made their dives down to 5,000 feet in a west to east line of attack. While in the dive 'a circular spot with white lines showing' was observed north of the road at the eastern end of the target range, which was thought to have probably been a camouflaged area. Bombs from five aircraft detonated in the area between the road and the stream to the north, while the other seven bomb loads were concentrated to the southern area. The raid was considered successful and the whole force returned to Uderbund at 1815.

Continued reports of enemy troop at Masein, Kalewa Township, Kale District on the east bank of the Chindwin River, occupied the attentions of 7 Squadron on 19 April. Accordingly, a full strike was organised, led by Squadron Leader Hemango Choudhuri and organised thus:

Aircraft	Pilot	Aircrew
A	Sqn Ldr Hemango Choudhuri	F/O Murat Singh
G	F/O Muhammad Khan	Flt Sgt S.K. Ghose
F	F/O Chadagam Satyanarayana	F/O Cecil Naire
D	F/O Mohit Ghose	F/O Kalpalli Menon
C	F/O Miza Rahman	F/O Ghansyam Pagnis
B	F/O Joseph Ezekiel	F/O Jamshet Dordi
J	Flt Lt Pratap Lal	F/O Vernon Bonarjee
P	F/O Satinderlal Rikhye	F/O Gurbachan Singh
N	P/O Dinshaw Burjorjee	F/O Umesh Tonse
O	F/O Karori Bhatia	F/O Victor Srihari
K	F/O Jagdish Kochhar	F/O Shanil Kumar Mukkherji
L	P/O Nusly Duggan	Sgt Jagad

Take-off from base was at 1302 and Spitfire cover over the target was promised. It was a straight flight out to the target area, arriving at the river just south of the Paluzawa *chaung* north of Masein. Pointers used for identification were the distinctive tributaries of that stream and here they turned south keeping the Chindwin itself to port while photographs of the target were carried by the squadron leader to further assist. There was 7/10th cloud cover with a 12,000-foot base and a slight haze restricted visibility to between two to three miles. The attack was made from south to north with the dives commencing at 9,500 feet and pull-out 4,500 feet, with the usual

50-50 per cent of mixed ordnance. Eleven aircraft saw their bombs explode in the village itself covering an area between the 'V' of the intersecting roads and the area to the west of the junction. Some bombs burst amongst the hutments along the road at the apex of the 'V'. One aircraft overshot, and its bombs detonated on the east bank of the *chaung* to the west of the target near its junction with the river.

Although the usual dense dust and debris obscured the target afterwards the subsequent report stated that the attack was 'considered very effective'. All aircraft were back at Uderbund at 1510.

The following day, 20 April, 7 Squadron was tasked with an attack on the Tiddim Road at a bend east of Mualkawi, with the object of denying its use to the enemy. This highway was the main Japanese supply route and along this metalled and torturously winding road from south of Bishenpur came the resources that were maintaining the tough, fanatical troops of Lieutenant General Motoso Yanagida's 33rd Infantry Division which Slim later described as having 'the reputation of being the toughest Division in Burma'.[41] As they strove to annihilate Major General David Tennant 'Punch' Cowan's 17th Indian Division in Operation U-GO. Slim also described the fighting along this vital artery as some of the heaviest in the entire Imphal-Kohima battle, with Churachandpur (Lamka) on the west bank of the Tutiha (Khuga) river, some forty kilometres from Kohima, being the lynchpin of the continued Japanese thrusts northward for it was here that convoys of lorries arrived and transferred their cargoes to mule trains sustaining the forward troops in the jungle-clad hills. Since the offensive had commenced the Japanese had forced their way to within ten kilometres of Imphal

For this attack, Squadron Leader Choudhuri organised the strike thus:

Aircraft	Pilot	Aircrew
A	Sqn Ldr Hemango Choudhuri	F/O Murat Singh
G	F/O Muhammad Khan	Flt Sgt S K Ghosh
D	F/O Kesargod Bhat	Sgt Allah Bakhashi
C	F/O Mohit Ghose	Flt Lt Ramaswami Sitaram
F	Flying Office Ramchandra Ghisad	Sgt Prabhu
B	F/O Nur Khan	Sgt Harrington

---

[41] Slim, Field Marshal 1st Viscount William, *Defeat into Victory*, Cassel, London, 1956.

Aircraft	Pilot	Aircrew
J	Flt Lt Pratap Lal	F/O Vernon Bonarjee
O	F/O Sudindra Ibrahim	Sgt Jagad
P	F/O Gubachan Singh	Sgt Wijyendran
Q	F/O Mandhar Sakhare	F/O Rathindra Ghosh
N	F/O Solomon Purushotam	Sgt Chatterjee
L	P/O Palokat Mathews	Sgt Dilbagh Singh

Take off from Uderbund was at 0910 and the loop of the road itself, south of Mulam village, forty-five miles[42] south of Imphal, was picked up without difficulty. They followed the road keeping it off their left wingtips passing the bridge over the Manipur River where the Vultees turned to the left and made their approach using photographs carried in the leader's aircraft and the sight of Kualkawi village to the west. There was dust on the road itself north-east of a bend as the dive-bombers attacked at 1005 from an altitude of 11,900 feet down to a 6,000-feet release and pull-out. Five of their bombs detonated on the road itself, two at the bend and three on the road south of the bend. Two others burst on the hillside above the road to the north-east. The first box followed in two minutes later. The area was left covered in dust clouds. The formation returned to base at 1055.

Operations continued 21 April with another full squadron mission to strike at the Tiddim Road. Cutting this route was vital and a continuous task, and this day 7 Squadron was tasked with blocking the road at the strip bend at map reference RO 981642 by causing landslides from the steep-sided jungle-clad slopes. A difficult task which, due to the narrow valley and constricted approach, only dive-bombers had any hope of achieving. Led by the Choudhuri the twelve-plane formation was despatched thus:

Aircraft	Pilot	Aircrew
A	Sqn Ldr Hemango Choudhuri	F/O Murat Singh
G	F/O Muhammad Khan	Flt Sgt S.K. Ghosh
D	F/O Kesargod Bhat	Sgt Allah Bakhashi
E	F/O Chadagam Satyanarayana	F/O Cecil Naire
F	F/O Dorad Engineer	P/O Kalpalli Menon
B	P/O Keki Gocal	F/O Panangadan Ramakrishnan
O	F/O Karori Bhatia	F/O Victor Srihari

[42]   1 mile = 1.60934km.

Aircraft	Pilot	Aircrew
P	F/O Gurbachan Singh	Sgt E A Wijayendran
R	P/O Dinshaw Burjorjee	F/O Umesh Tonse
J	F/O Mandhar Sakhare	F/O Rathindra Ghosh
M	F/O Narayan Shamu Prasad	Sgt S. Vaidyanath
L	F/O Nusly Duggan	F/O Vernon Bonarjee

The force took off at 1116 and followed the most direct route to the target, but unfortunately Flying Officer Engineer's aircraft developed engine trouble early on and was forced to return to base, landing safely at 1135. The remaining eleven Vultees crossed the Tuivai River and upon reaching the Tiddim road south of the target zone, turned to port and identified the acute bends in the road picked out with the aid of the half-inch map and photographs carried by the leader. There was 8/10th cumulus cloud with a base of 10,000 feet here with visibility from two to three miles. There was no movement on the road at this time and, at 1207, the squadron made a line-astern approach from south-east to north-west, peeling off at an altitude of 9,500 feet and releasing at, 5,500 feet. Half the ordnance comprised 500lb MCTD bombs with a time-delay of eleven seconds, to these were added five 500lb GPLD bombs – three with 12-hour delay and two with 6-hour delay fuses, and six 500lb MCLD bombs one with 6-hour delay and five with 12-hour delay fuses.

It was clearly observed that nine of the instantaneously-fused bombs exploded on the road itself and both Khan and Chadagam Satyanarayana independently confirmed that these caused the required landslide which blocked the road. Two bombs overshot and burst on the slopes below the road. This was later confirmed by study of photographs taken by Keki Gocal and Nusly Duggan, the last men in. At the end of this very successful bombing the eleven Vengeances returned to Uderbund at 1245.

The following day was a frustrating one. An ARMOP strike was launched against Moirang where Japanese troop concentrations were reported. This time the group included several newer faces and was arranged as follows:

Aircraft	Pilot	Aircrew
A	Sqn Ldr Hemango Choudhuri	F/O Murat Singh
E	F/O Codanda Cariappa	Sgt S. Ball
D	F/O Kesargod Bhat	Sgt Allah Bakhashi
G	F/O Mohit Ghose	F/O Kalpalli Menon
H	F/O Joseph Ezekiel	F/O Jamshet Dordi

Aircraft	Pilot	Aircrew
F	F/O Keki Gocal	F/O Ghansyam Pagnis
O	Flight Lieutenant Pratap Lal	F/O Vernon Bonarjee
J	F/O Nusly Duggan	Sgt Dilbagh Singh
Q	P/O Ajit Singh	Sgt Harbans Singh
K	F/O Gurbachan Singh	Sgt E.A. Wijayendran
P	F/O Satinderlal Rikhye	F/O Gurbachan Singh
M	F/O Solomon Purushotam	Sgt Chatterjee

Conditions were far from promising but despite louring conditions the twelve Vengeance IIs lifted off and headed out. The weather further deteriorated *en route* and they found the area covered in a thick haze rising to 12,000 feet. There was cumulus cloud with its base at 9,500 feet and visibility was recorded as 'Nil. Looking towards sun 500 yards, or less when looking away'. This gloom made target identification impossible and left them no choice but to return home with their bombs and await a better opportunity. Most of the squadron made it back through the murk and landed back at base at 1508 but Flight Lieutenant Pratap Lal and Flying Officer Purushotam lost contact in the poor visibility and did not land until 1525.

They returned to Tiddim Road again on 23 April. They were instructed to hit the highway at map reference RP0734 east of Mualkawi, north of Tunzang in Chin Province. The composition of the force was as below:

Aircraft	Pilot	Aircrew
A	Sqn Ldr Hemango Choudhuri	F/O Murat Singh
H	F/O Chadagam Satyanarayana	F/O Cecil Naire
E	F/O Malik Nur Khan	Sgt Harrington
C	F/O Mohit Ghose	Flt Lt Ramaswami Sitaram
G	F/O Dorad Engineer	F/O Kalpalli Menon
F	F/O Masom Ali Vazir	Sgt S. Ball
O	F/O Karori Bhatia	F/O Victor Srirari
P	F/O Sudindra Ibrahim	Sgt Jagad
L	F/O Narayan Prasad	Sgt E.A. Wijayandran
R	F/O Mandhar Sakhare	F/O Rathindra Ghosh
J	P/O Palokat Mathews	Sgt Dilbagh Singh
M	F/O Jagdish Kochhar	F/O Sham Kumar

After the usual briefing the force left base at 1105 and set a straight course for the target, reaching the Tiddim Road just south of the target zone.

They found good weather, with 2/10th cumulus cloud and visibility from six to eight miles. They picked out the road bridge over the Manipur River and turned left to follow the line of the road northward, its bends being picked off from the map and photographs carried by the leader. The target was already covered with dust clouds and, at 1207, 'Hem' led in the attack from east to west, with the attack dives being initiated from 11,000 feet down to a release height of 6,000 feet. Various 500lb bombs with differing delays ranging from eleven seconds to six hours were dropped but Flying Officer Vazir's aircraft suffered hydraulic failure and he could not release, having no choice but to take his bombs back home with him. One aircraft overshot with her bombs bursting on the slopes below the road but the other ten made concentrated hits on the road itself with excellent results.

While pulling out of his dive Squadron Leader Choudhuri caught sight of a convoy of five to ten enemy 3-ton supply trucks heading north-east between mile stones 114 and 116 toward Imphal. He took the fleeting opportunity to pay these some attention and made a strafing run with his front wing guns along this column, expending 280 rounds of .300-inch and 120 rounds of .303-inch ammunition on them. With some satisfaction he noted at least one was hit and swerved, smashing into a tree. There was not time for more and the squadron headed back to Uderbund where they arrived at 1255.

The true measure of the dive-bombers' success in this, and similar road-cut missions, lay not in their own observations, nor from camera shots but from the enemy himself. When Lieutenant General Renya Mutaguchi, commanding the Japanese Fifteenth Army, signalled on 18 April (prematurely as it happened) his praise and appreciation for the capture of Kohima and its vital ridge, the commander of the besieging Japanese 31st Division, Lieutenant General Kotoku Sato, signalled straight back to him, 'We do not require praise for doing our duty, we require supplies!'[43]

A longer-range mission deep into enemy territory was mounted by 7 Squadron on 24 April. The target assigned to them was a large Japanese camp, ammunition and supply base, just west of the town of Pyingaing

---

[43] Sato and Mutaguchi were old foes. The former had already publically expressed the opinion that the latter was an imbecile and that the *U-Go* plan was doomed to failure before it even began. 'We shall probably all starve to death,' he had gloomily (and prophetically) predicted to his subordinates at the onset of the battle.

Myauk (23^0 15' N, 94^0 83E – nowadays also known as Pyingaing). It is located well south of Imphal, between Ye-U in the east and Kale in the west. For this mission (and for the first and only time) the Vultees were allocated their own escort of Spitfires as it was expected that this vital dump would be strongly protected from the air as well as the ground. A full squadron sortie left Uderbund at 0710 and comprised the under listed:

Aircraft	Pilot	Aircrew
A	Sqn Ldr Hemango Choudhuri	F/O Murat Singh
B	F/O Kesargod Bhat	Flt Sgt S.K. Ghosh
G	F/O Keki Gocal	Sgt Baijnath
F	F/O Mohit Ghose	F/O Sadanand Nadakarni
C	F/O Miza Rahman	F/O Ghansyam Pagnis
E	F/O Nur Khan	Sgt Harrington
O	Flight Lieutenant Pratap Lal	F/O Vernon Bonarjee
P	F/O Purshotam Dhaven	Sgt Jamshet Cama
J	F/O Dinshaw Burjorjee	F/O Umesh Tonse
K	F/O Gurbachan Singh	Sgt E.A. Wijayandran
Q	F/O Ajit Singh	Sgt Harbans Singh
H	F/O Joseph Ezekiel	F/O Jamshet Dordi

The squadron initially flew to the Imphal area, picking up the Spitfires from the Palal satellite airstrip at 0800 and then heading straight for the target area. Unfortunately, Vengeance Q, the mount of Flying Officer Ajit Singh, developed severe hydraulic problems and was forced to turn back, landing safely at base at 0840.

The remaining force of eleven Vultees crossed the Chindwin between Ode and Kindaut, vectoring on the distinctive bend to their left and the river island to their right. From there their next staging point was the Maukkadaw *chaung* NNE of the enemy camp, with a smaller *chaung* running immediately east of the target area and the road south easy to identify from maps and photos carried by the leader.

There was no interference from the Japanese air force, nor from the defending ground forces and the weather had 2/10th cumulus cloud cover with one-mile visibility, compounded by a thick haze extending up to above 10,000 feet. At 0837 the attack run was made from south to north over the camp, with the dives commencing from 9,000 feet down to bomb release at 4,000 feet. A mixed array of ordnance was deposited upon the Japanese supply base consisting of ten 500lb MCTD bombs with eleven-second time delay fusing, eight 500lb MCTI, two 500lb MCLD with six-hour fusing and one with twelve-hour time delay and a single 500lb GPLD with the same fusing. One aircraft undershot the target, her bombs detonating on the road alongside the dump, but the other ten made 'concentrated' hits within the target area. The resulting dust and already hazy conditions made target assessment impossible beyond that. The squadron returned to base without any complications at 0950.

A return to the Fort White area occupied 7 Squadron the following day, 25 April. This section was led by Flight Lieutenant Pratap Lal with the following:

Aircraft	Pilot	Aircrew
N	Flt Lt Pratap Lal	F/O Vernon Bonarjee
Q	F/O Sudindra Ibrahim	Sgt Jagad
P	F/O Satinderlal Rikhye	F/O Gurbachan Singh
O	F/O Karori Bhatia	F/O Victor Srihari
K	F/O Mandhar Sakhare	F/O Rathindra Gosh
M	F/O Nusly Duggan	Sgt E.A. Wijayandran

This group took departure from base at 0920 and flew directly toward the Tiddim Road, crossing it at Khuaivum then turning to follow it up using Fort White and Tiddim itself as reference points en route. Just south-east of the old stockade the road made a slight bend, and this helped pinpoint the target itself. There was no enemy reaction, the weather encountered had 9/10th cloud cover with a base at 12,000 feet and a visibility of two to three miles. At 1030 the Vultees led in to conduct shallow dives down from 11,500 feet to 9,000 feet and all bombs were seen to explode within the designated target area. It was a routine mission of the type they had conducted many times before and it was a shock when it became clear that Vengeance M did not rejoin the formation after the attack. Flying Officer Duggan's mount was last seen over Tiddim at 9,000 feet after pulling out. The rest of the force returned to Uderbund at 1120 and Duggan and Wijayandran were posted as 'missing'.[44]

---

[44] It later transpired that Duggan's Vengeance, AN 678, had met very thick weather with nil visibility and became hopelessly lost. They eventually ran out of fuel and made a crash-landing way off course at the Shillong, a 4,000-foot hill station in Assam. Both crew members survived this ordeal and Duggan later was posted to 1 Squadron at Kohima and then to 15 Squadron. He finally retired from the IAF in April 1956.

The other half of the squadron led by 'Hem' was that day tasked with a mission in the same area; this time the target was Fort White village itself. The sub-section was led by Choudhuri himself and consisted of:

Aircraft	Pilot	Aircrew
A	Sqn Ldr Hemango Choudhuri	F/O Murat Singh
D	F/O Muhammed Khan	Flt Sgt S.K. Ghosh
G	F/O Keki Gocal	Sgt Baijnath
C	F/O Mohit Ghose	F/O Sadanand Nadakarni
F	F/O Codanda Cariappa*	Flt Sgt S. Ball
H	F/O Dorad Engineer	F/O Kalpalli Menon

*The 7 Squadron Report for this date shows Flying Officer Keki Gocal as pilot of both G and F, but this is here corrected.

The weather prospects were far from good but, nonetheless, the unit took off from base at 0920. When only twenty-five miles from Uderbund the formation ran into what was described as 'bad haze and clouds'. The official description was 10/10th clouds at 3,500 feet, with a maximum visibility of one to two miles. 'Hem' recorded that they 'attempted to get through to south of course' but meeting similar conditions that way he aborted the sortie. This was apparently the same conditions that Duggan had encountered on his return trip. The Vultees landed back at base at 1005.

On the 26th a mission was readied with enemy troop concentrations at Ukhrul as the target. This village lay some twenty-five miles north of Imphal and had been captured by the Japanese 56th Infantry Regiment, part of Major General Shuichi Miyazaki northern attacking force, on 21 March during the Battle of Sangshak. The weather was again poor but due to the seriousness of the situation it was felt that an attempt had to be made to aid their hard-pressed colleagues on the ground. A full squadron strike therefore took off from Uderbund at 0850 and headed east into the overcast.

Aircraft	Pilot	Aircrew
A	Sqn Ldr Hemango Choudhuri	F/O Murat Singh
G	F/O Muhammad Khan	Flt Sgt S.K. Ghosh
D	F/O Kesargod Bhat	F/O Kalpalli Menon

Aircraft	Pilot	Aircrew
F	F/O Mohit Ghose	F/O Sadanand Nadakarni
C	F/O Miza Rahman	F/O Ghansyam Pagnis
H	F/O Joseph Ezekiel	F/O Jamshet Dordi
O	Flt Lt Pratap Lal	F/O Vernon Bonarjee
Q	F/O Purshotam Dhaven	Sgt Jamset Cama
N	P/O Dinshaw Burjorjee	F/O Umesh Tonse
K	F/O Gurbachan Singh	Sgt Chatterjee
L	F/O Jagdish Kochar	F/O Shani Kumar Mukkherji
B	P/O Ajit Singh	Sgt Harbans Singh

At 0920, while en route to the target the formation met the Vengeance of 110 Squadron returning westward ten minutes prior to their scheduled time. The formation leader from the British unit broke away closed with 'Hem' and signalled visually for 7 Squadron to turn back, it was presumed because the target area was 'weathered out'. Choudhuri there turned the unit back for home but when they were close to their base they were told to keep clear as there was an 'Air Raid Red' warning of an imminent Japanese attack. Accordingly, 'Hem' took the formation to the 'scramble rendezvous'.[45] When the all-clear was given the force returned and landed safely with bombs intact at 1105.

That same afternoon Flight Lieutenant Pratap Lal led a full squadron strike against an ARMOP (Army Originated Operation) at Kohima. The British XXXIII Corps would assign a pinpoint target on the G2 Mosaic for them to hit.[46] It was to be a two-squadron strike totalling four six-plane

---

[45] This was a safe area away from the field as laid down by 168 Wing in their Operational Instructions No. 4.

[46] XXXIII Indian Corps, under General Montagu George North Stopford, was in overall control of Kohima area, but the main British supply base, and enormous ammunition dump some eleven miles long by one mile wide, lay at Dimapur, and was sparsely defended and terribly vulnerable. Here also was located 202 Line of Communications Group under Major General Robert Philip Lancaster Ranking. As the campaign had developed the commander of the Japanese 31st Division, General Kotoku Sato, had wanted to seize Dimapur, and it was well within his power to do so. Had that happened it would have been a catastrophe for the British and an enormous boon to the Japanese attackers. However, his superior, General Renya Mutaguchi, overruled Sato and the chance was lost. Even so the road connecting Dimapur to the hard-pressed defenders of Kohima, under Colonel Hugh Richards, had been cut off by a Japanese roadblock at Zubza.

boxes mounted in conjunction with 110 Squadron once more. Lal's force consisted of:

Aircraft	Pilot	Aircrew
N	Flt Lt Pratap Lal	F/O Vernon Bonarjee
L	F/O Jagdish Kochar	F/O Shanil Kumar Mukkherji
K	F/O Mandhar Sakhare	F/O Rathindra Ghosh
O	F/O Karori Bhatia	F/O Victor Srihari
Q	F/O Satinderlal Rikhye	F/O Gurbachan Singh
J	P/O Narayan Prasad	Sgt Harbans Singh
F	F/O Mohit Ghose	F/O Sadanand Nadakarni
D	F/O Nur Khan	Sgt Harrington
G	F/O Ramchandra Ghisad	Sgt Prabhu
A	F/O Chadagam Satyanarayana	F/O Cecil Naire
G	F/O Keki Gocal	Sgt S. Ball
H	F/O Dorad Engineer	F/O Kalpalli Menon

The formation proceeded to within twelve miles south-east of Kohima, following 110 Squadron closely. The target area when reached had 9/10th cumulus cloud cover rising from a base of 12,500 feet to up beyond 15,000 feet and a rainstorm was developing fast. They watched as the leading box of 110 Squadron entered the cloud and vanished from sight. The second 110 Squadron box, realising the situation made accurate targeting almost impossible, turned back at 1358 and Lal turned 7 Squadron back with them. They landed back at Uderbund, with *full* bombloads intact, at 1435. It was an extremely frustrating time for all concerned but over the jungle-clad hills the weather was inevitably always a deciding factor.

What was described as 'an unmade village', located at map reference RK 3289, was the target for 7 Squadron on 27 April. An ARMOP request was for strikes against Japanese troop concentrations here and a two-box attack was duly mounted with twelve Vultees, their departure from base at 1248. The attack was made up thus:

Aircraft	Pilot	Aircrew
A	Sqn Ldr Hemango Choudhuri	F/O Murat Singh
B	F/O Muhammed Khan	Flt Sgt S.K. Ghose
D	F/O Kesargod Bhat	Sgt Allah Bakhashi
F	F/O Mohit Ghose	F/O Sadanand Nadakarni

Aircraft	Pilot	Aircrew
G	F/O Joseph Ezekiel	F/O Jamshet Dordi
E	F/O Keki Gocal	Sgt S. Ball
O	F/O Karori Bhatia	F/O Victor Srihari
L	F/O Jagdish Kochhar	F/O Shanil Kumar Mukkherji
H	F/O Solomon Purushotam	Sgt Chatterjee
K	F/O Mandhar Sakhare	F/O Gurbachan Singh
Q	F/O Sudindra Ibrahim	Sgt Jagad
J	F/O Narayan Prasad	Sgt Harbans Singh

The route taken was over the Imphal airstrip before turning left and retaining the Imphal-Kohima road on that side until the bend in the road to the north-east after Kanglatongbi village was well as the slight zig-zag in the road farther north, adjacent to the target itself. The map reference was located in the middle and just west of this part of the road, with the track leading to north from Safarmaina,[47] below Eye, very clear. Thick cloud (10/10th cumulus) with a base at 9,000 feet obscured the damage from previous strikes and, as usual, there was no sign of the enemy who had gone to ground. The attack went in at 1332 with dives commencing at 8,500 feet down to 5,500 feet. The whole force returned to base at 1415.

The final strikes of April were mounted on the 28th. The target was Sangshak village (map reference RK 7887) where Japanese troop concentrations remained. A full-strength strike was mounted with the following aircrew.

Aircraft	Pilot	Aircrew
C	Sqn Ldr Hemango Choudhuri	F/O Murat Singh
B	F/O Ramchandra Ghisad	Sgt Prabhu
D	F/O Ravubha Godel	Sgt Baijnath
F	F/O Mohit Ghose	F/O Sadanand Nadakarni
E	F/O Malik Nur Khan	Sgt Harrington
H	F/O Dorad Engineer	F/O Kalpalli Menon
O	Flt Lt Pratap Lal	F/O Vernon Bonarjee
Q	F/O Purshotam Dhaven	Sgt Jamset Cama
N	F/O Dinshaw Burjorjee	F/O Umesh Tonse
K	F/O G.S. Singh	F/O Shanil Kumar Mukkherji
L	F/O Satinderlal Rikhye	F/O Gurbachan B Singh
J	P/O Ajit Singh	Sgt Dilbagh Singh

---

[47] In the days of the Raj a large base for Indian Army sappers and miners.

After briefing with half-inch maps, enlarged chalk drawings and photographs of the target the formation took to the air from Uderbund at 0600 for the fifty-minute flight which took them over Imphal and they kept the road to from there to Ukhrul over on the port side to Sansak. They duly identified the village by the track leading south-west from the road, but found the area covered with smoke from burnt and blasted hutments at that end of the settlement. Although there had been no mention of any fighter cover at the briefing earlier, both Spitfires and Hurricanes were sighted over the target area at 10,000 feet. There was no enemy opposition from either air or ground, however, and the squadron led in the assault from north-east to south-west diving in from 9,800 feet to bomb release at 6,000 feet. Ten Vultees duly delivered their ordnance into the relatively untouched eastern part of the village, with one machine undershooting and another overshooting. The explosions added considerably to the dust clouds which masked the target. The unit returned to base at 0750.

In the same afternoon Flight Lieutenant Pratap Lal led another mission, returning to the Tiddim Road to deny its use to the enemy. The pinpoint selected was a bend south of Maulkawi. Again, lowering cloud made the chances of success difficult but at 1405 the formation lifted off from Uderbund and formed up in two six-plane boxes thus:

Aircraft	Pilot	Aircrew
J	Flt Lt Pratap Lal	F/O Vernon Bonarjee
N	F/O Purshotam Dhaven	Sgt Jamset Cama
P	F/O Satinderlal Rikhye	F/O Gubachan B. Singh
O	F/O Karori Bhatia	F/O Victor Srihari
M	P/O Ajit Singh	Sgt Harbans Singh
L	F/O Nusly Duggan	Sgt Dilbagh Singh
A	F/O Mohit Ghose	Flt Lt Ramaswami Sitaram
D	F/O Kesargod Bhat	Sgt Allah Bakhashi
G	F/O Chadagam Satyanarayana	F/O Cecil Naire
C	F/O Miza Rahman	F/O Ghansyam Pagnis
F	F/O Ramchandra Ghisad	Sgt Prabhu
B	F/O Malik Nur Khan	Sgt Harrington

The formation set course to the Tiddim Road at the point that it emerged from the southern tip of the Imphal Valley. While still some way west of this aiming point they encountered very bad weather, 10/10th bluish-grey altostratus cloud at 13,000 feet with 4/10th towering cumulus covering the hilltops beyond 13,000 feet and a thick smoky haze rising to 12,000 feet. Visibility was one to two miles at best. Although an attempt was made to get through without success, these conditions made the mission impossible to complete with any hope of success and they reluctantly returned to base. In the turn the formation lost touch with Vengeance D piloted by Flying Officer Bhat, who found himself in the lead and alone. He landed back at Uderbund at 1525, while the rest of the force got down safely twenty-five minutes later.

These operations by 7 Squadron have been taken in their fullest detail from the official ORBs quite deliberately to show the relentless, non-stop pace of the Vengeance contribution to the Imphal-Kohima battles. Several other Vengeance squadrons also took part in these battles and their contribution will also be described, mainly from pilots' logbooks and memoirs, but many military and air historians have: 1) totally ignored the fact that the Vengeance was engaged in these operations, listing all other squadrons and aircraft types but deliberately omitting the dive-bombers; 2) made out that the dive-bombers' contribution was negligible; and 3) stated outrightly, or hinted, that the contribution of the Indian squadrons was not on a par with its RAF counterparts. Even those who have staunchly insisted that 7 and 8 Squadrons more than pulled their weight have accused them of exaggerating their results, or as one correspondent put it 'gilding the lily' a trifle. By reproducing the war diary of one of these units *no* further doubt ought now to remain.

Fairer assessments of the Vengeance have been made: for example, Air Vice Marshal Arun Kumar Tiwary went on record that 'its flying was impressive as the unit undertook a multitude of missions'.[48] It was also claimed that Warrant Officer Bhaskaran maintained 100 per cent serviceability from February to May 1944, although considering the primitiveness of the strips they operated from, and the weather, this is a more arguable statement.

In fact, resumption of operations by 7 Squadron in May was delayed by the onset of the *chota* (in English 'little') monsoon which, as we have seen, had been steadily closing down operations or making them very difficult for over a week. Although not as prolonged as a full monsoon, this rainy period is just as intense while it lasts and usually consists of about seven to ten days

---

[48]   Tiwary, Air Marshal Arun Kumar, *Indian Air Force in Wars*, Lancer LLC, Delhi, 2012.

of rain and high winds which breaks the winter spell of fine weather in the Arakan each year. The improvised runways were, in the main, merely levelled clay strips over the old *padi* fields, and the non-stop downpour quickly rendered them totally unserviceable. The squadron's CO recorded in the Operational Record Book (AIR27/110) that on 1 and 2 May, 'Although not so 'chota' the strip is covered all over with six inches deep water ...'. This rendered it 'A veritable swamp. It is difficult to imagine that it will ever be serviceable for flying. Already there is a heated discussion going on among some NCOs as to whether it would be better for the Squadron enlist for an aircraft-carrier[49] or to or to ask for a conversion course on to submarines. The opinion is divided.' This deluge eased, and the strip appeared to be drying out from the glutinous mess it had become, so, rather optimistically, on the 4th Squadron Leader Choudhuri attempted a taxiing test during the afternoon. 'It was a real test between the Wright Cyclone engine and the tenacity of the soft ground. The latter won.' During the 5th the ground continued to dry out and operations were resumed on 6 May from the all-weather concrete strip against two targets 'to everyone's delight'.

The CO led the first mission of the day with twelve aircraft to provide support for the army in the Kuwai area. The strike itself was recorded as being 'very successful' and the ground troops at the front confirmed this: 'Reports today's bombing are extremely successful. Well done.' The second attack of the day was mounted against Kumbi village itself. However, shortly after take-off, Flight Lieutenant Eric Wilmot Pinto of the second box and Flight Lieutenant Gubachan Singh of the first box had to return to base with engine problems. The rest of the formation continued the mission but then Flight Lieutenant Pratap Lal's aircraft developed both engine and R/T troubles. Lal had to turn back, and the rest followed him home, so the mission was aborted.

The 7th saw No. 7 Squadron launch an eleven-plane attack against Ponnagayun led by Squadron Leader Pratap Lal. Although described as a 'biggish' target the bombs were well distributed and the whole area target

---

[49] The Vengeance was originally brought in to attack any repeat raid by Japanese carriers like the Nagumo Force. However, it was becoming apparent that the main fleet had its hands full in the Pacific but that Japanese submarines continued to be a threat. The two warship types called for very different response in bombing techniques and patrolling.

area was covered. That evening the squadron was visited by the Air Officer Commanding (AOC) India Command, Air Vice Marshal Meredith Thomas CSI CBE DFC AFC RAF, a First World War ace; he met all the officers that evening and commended them on their work to date.

The following day, 8 May, No. 7 Squadron undertook what was listed as a 'semi-strategical' mission at Kalewa near Mutaik Chandos. The Kalewa township area, located at the confluence of the Chindwin and Myittha rivers in the Kale district of north-west Burma, was the main Japanese line of communication and was studded with supply dumps and transit camps and included a School of Jungle Training. The bombing was carried out accurately and many enemy *bashas* (Assamese word for a dwelling made of natural materials) were left demolished or in flames. The CO wrote, 'If the jungle warfare school had any fire-fighting instructors they must have been delighted at being provided with something for exhibiting their prowess.'

A second attack was sent out that same evening against the same area and was led by Flight Lieutenant Pinto. Unfortunately, operations were marred fight from the off by a bad accident when Flying Officer Muhammad Latif Khan's aircraft developed engine trouble right from the off, and this resulted in a fatal crash-landing as he tried to return to the runway. The Vengeance skidded to a halt and within a short time caught fire. Both 500lb bombs detonated in a large explosion which destroyed the machine. During the brief period between the crash and the explosion a feat of great heroism was witnessed when Squadron Leader Davis, the Engineering officer of HQ 168 Wing, who happened to be at the base, unhesitatingly ran in and managed to extract the rear-seat man, Flight Sergeant S.K. Ghoshe, from the aircraft. Others attempted to release the pilot, but Khan was found to be already dead and entangled in his harness and his body had to be hastily abandoned to the flames. This was Ghoshe's third crash and survival but, nothing daunted, it was recorded that he was soon sitting up in hospital and asking when he could undertake his next mission!

The rest of the squadron headed toward the target area but soon encountered very bad weather conditions en route. Indeed, so bad did it get with thick cloud and rain that Flight Lieutenant Pinto quickly saw that to continue was hopeless and turned the squadron back. Choudhuri wrote that 'It was a consolation to see them on *terra firma*. Other squadrons who were also on this mission did not share his vision and were scattered all over the sky in distress.'

The squadron returned to battle on 9 May with Choudhuri heading up a pinpoint strike at the behest of the army. Their target was a hill slope at map reference RE353838. The bombs were delivered exactly as requested, it being noted that 'The accuracy .... earned genuine compliments from the local ALOs (Air Liaison Officers)'. The second strike was directed once more at the 'semi-strategic' targets in the Kalewa area around map square 008675. They reported fairly good bombing results and after the attack the unit landed back at base at 1425 hours and found that an urgent request had been received from the ALO at the front. After a hasty re-arming, the aircraft were back in the air at 1445 to strike at Toupoeri and they duly delivered what was termed 'A very successful strike ...'.

This was offset by the fact that on that same day Vengeances AN 976 and FB 976 of the squadron collided three-and-a-half miles SSE of Dohazari, crashing with the loss of Flying Officer Muhammad Latif Khan as recorded above.

On 11 May 7 Squadron was placed at the disposal of the Air Surveillance & Control (ASC) for the day and hopes ran high that this would see much action. Unfortunately, only one call was made on their services – enemy positions at Potsangbam (known to the British soldiers as 'Pots and Pans'). Their bombing was, in the main, good, but marred by just a single salvo which crossed the bomb-line which was set more than 200 yards north of the target itself. Fortunately, there were no casualties amongst the Allied troops in that vicinity. The following day, while still allocated to ASC for targets, the squadron was again sent out against the same target, lifting off at 0658 with a second strike mounted against Toupoeri at 1512. These strikes were acknowledged by the army in a signal which read 'Ground forces report your bombing as excellent. Good show'.

The 13th saw the battle at Potsangbam in full swing.[50] The Japanese positions at Upokpi were 7 Squadron's next target and were subject to 'really concentrated' bombing in the squadron's only attack of the day. The following day Squadron Leader Choudhuri led the Vengeances back to Kalewa once more to leave yet more *bashas* aflame at map reference 975876, while on the 15th the army requested an attack on Moriang, which was successfully delivered.

---

[50]   Grant, Brian Lyall, *Burma: The Turning Point*, Pen & Sword, Barnsley, 2003.

The ASC allocated another target on 16 May but due to appalling weather the attack was made with some difficulty through driving rain over the enemy positions. Dive-bombing was out of the question, but bombs were delivered in shallow dives and the results were described in the ORB as 'excellent in view of the conditions'. Meanwhile, back at the field, orders were received from AHQ for Squadron Leader Choudhuri to be posted away from the squadron. His replacement was named as Squadron Leader Aizad Baksh Awan.

On 17 May dive-bombing was resumed and was concentrated exclusively on the northern part of Moriang village, stronghold of the last Japanese defenders. Accuracy was crucial and excellent results achieved so that the army was able to capture the whole village shortly afterward. The following day Japanese supply dumps and troop concentrations were struck while on the 19th the Vengeance attacks were once more allocated by the ASC, the first of which was at pinpoint RK 2934, but which was hampered by bad weather and heavy cloud over the target. The afternoon strike went in against Toupokpi village and against resulted in it being occupied by Allied troops that same day. On the 20th enemy concentrations at pinpoint 113872 were dive-bombed.

Squadron Leader Awan duly arrived at the base on 21 May but the following day he put in an application to HQ regarding the proposed change, and, with this postponement, he did not assume command after all at this time but took over on 6 June. Thus, Choudhuri continued to lead the Vengeances during their last period of intense activity with the squadron when operations resumed on 23 May with an attack on Japanese troop concentrations (Group 'F') but once more the weather over the target was extremely bad making both accurate navigation and bombing tricky. Two attacks followed on the 24th, the first led by Flight Lieutenant Pinto against enemy bunkers, which made accurate shooting and the second, under Squadron Leader Choudhuri, targeted Japanese troops and machine-gun positions.

During the 25th there was heavy and continuous rain all morning, the sky was overcast with 10/10th cloud. The target was the vitally strategic Manipur river bridge and two aircraft, piloted by Flight Lieutenant Pratap Chandra Lal and Flying Officer Dinshaw Maneck Burjorjee, flew reconnaissance missions and sent back reports that dive-bombing was possible. Accordingly, a seven-plane strike was mounted, led by Flight Lieutenant Pinto, and duly delivered their attacks. The bridge itself was hard to approach, being hemmed in all around by high hills while the weather, although better than at base, was far from ideal. Nonetheless, Flying Officer Palokat John Mathews (2887) scored a direct hit on the eastern end of the bridge, a strike that was later confirmed by both further reconnaissance and by Group. The entry in the ORB noted that 'The damaging of this very strategic bridge reflected very creditably on the squadron'.

Squadron Leader Choudhuri led the next morning's attack against another ASC-assigned objective, the village of Irengram, in company with 110 Squadron. *En route* both squadrons received a recall signal over the R/T because of bad weather over the target. The story was much the same on the 27th and 28th of the month; the former was notable for continuous rain, the winds blowing the airmen's *bashas* flat and the rain penetrating everything. Clearly no flying was possible or practical, the ORB noting that 'Seems as if the *burra* (big) monsoon has broken'. On the 28th also no flying was possible until the evening and, although an attempt was made then, with aircraft taxiing out on the runway in readiness, wiser counsels prevailed, and the mission was aborted before any took off.

The main monsoon was clearly upon them, but last attempts were made on the 30th. Squadron Leader Choudhuri led an attack on both sides of a track at pinpoint RK365885, where the bomb line was 'very close indeed' to friendly troops. However, excellent bombing was made. An attempt to block the Imphal road at Milestone 93 by creating a landslide was led by Flight Lieutenant Pratap Lal. 'Mission accomplished' was the subsequent report. Sadly, there was one last loss for the squadron that day also.

The casualty owed nothing to Japanese action. Flying Officer Dorab Maneckshaw Engineer had become separated from his companions and lost. He eventually sighted a formation of USAAF North American B-25 Mitchell twin-engined bombers near Henzada, apparently heading home, and tried to join up with them. The Americans seemingly were unable to distinguish between a Vengeance and a Japanese Nakajima Ki-43 Oscar, although there was little resemblance, and opened fire, killing Flight Sergeant K.C. Ball with a shot through the head.[51]

---

[51] In addition, there had been two non-fatal accidents away from the front. On 25 April Flying Officer Nusly Jamshedji Duggan, flying Vengeance AN678, crashed near Shillong, in north-east India but both he and his crewman, Flight Sergeant Wijeyedran, survived. In an accident

No. 7 Squadron's record for these final months' operations was certainly not second-rate. They had flown a total of 252 sorties totalling 621 operational hours. They had only had nine non-flying days, due entirely to the weather, and had averaged sixteen sorties per day, many of them mounted at the very last moment at critical junctures in the land fighting. Accuracy had been maintained despite the worsening conditions. Lal recalled that 'The dive bombing contributed not a little to the victory of the Allied troops in various battles in the area'. He added, sagaciously, 'The credit goes not only to the pilots who tend to enjoy the limelight; their success depended greatly on the percentage of serviceability, the quality of maintenance of the aircraft which is the responsibility of the ground crew.'[52]

Choudhuri noted that conditions had been far from ideal, 'what with weather, indecision regarding change of Command and the impending move of the squadron'. He added, 'It is to be hoped that things will be sorted out in the next few days.'

Early in June the squadron was removed from the front and flew to Ranchi. Command devolved to Squadron Leader Aizad Baksh Awan, (a Cranwell graduate), who commanded from 6 June to 20 July. He was relieved the next day by Squadron Leader Pratap Chandra Lal and led the squadron for the next three months before they moved to Kohat near Peshawar in November, at which base they were to convert to Hawker Hurricane fighter-bombers before re-deploying to Imphal.

From the wealth of information gained by a study of 7 Squadron's combat data one interesting point to arise is the total unreliability of many of the 'facts' published on the Vultee Vengeance hitherto. Although it was certainly laid down in the training manuals that attacks were made from an optimum target height of 12,000 feet, and this is solemnly trotted out in most accounts, it is a hard fact of actual combat that the Vultees attacked from varying heights and hardly ever thus. What dictated their approach were weather conditions – especially the cloud base – location or size of

---

on 8 May, Flying Officer Mohammed Ibrahim Khan, formerly of No. 7 Squadron, piloting Vengeance AN834, suffered engine failure while with the Indian Air Training Command (IATC) at Peshawar.

[52]   Lal, Air Chief Marshal Pratap Chandra – *My Years with the IAF*, Lancer Publications LL.c, Atlanta, Ga., 1986.

the target itself, the bomb-load to be distributed, and the nature of the surrounding terrain. Thus, if we just examine just a selection from one month-long period of 7 Squadron's operations it can be seen that it makes a total nonsense of 'accepted' procedure.

Date (1944)	Target	Height Dive Started	Height of Pull-Out
30 March	Thayaung	9,000ft	2,000ft
30 March	Sanda	9,500ft	3,900ft
1 April	Kawya	6,000ft	1,500ft
3 April	Myothit	8,000ft	3,500ft
3 April	Kawya	7,500ft	3,000ft
3 April	Maungkan	10,000ft	3,000ft
4 April	Tamu	9,000ft	3,000ft
5 April	Thitt Seikkon	8,500ft	2,500ft
5 April	Letpantha	9,000ft	2,000ft
8 April	Pakpin	8,000ft	3,000ft
9 April	Thanan	9,500ft	3,000ft
9 April	Nawnguawng	9,000ft	3,000ft
10 April	Maungkan	8,000ft	3,000ft
11 April	SF2623	9,000ft	3,000ft
12 April	Mulam	10,500ft	6,000ft
13 April	BK 434758	11,000ft	6,000ft
13 April	Ekban-Ekwan	9,000ft	4,000ft
14 April	Ekban-Ekwan	10,000ft	5,000ft
15 April	RK42673/44678/449800	11,800ft	5,000ft
16 April	Nawngpu-awng	9,500ft	3,000ft
17 April	Kalewa	9,500ft	4,500ft
17 April	Fort White	10,000ft	5,000ft
19 April	Masein	9,500ft	4,500ft
20 April	Tiddim Road	11,900ft	6,000ft
21 April	Tiddim Road	9,500ft	5,500ft
23 April	Tiddim Road	11,000ft	6,000ft
24 April	Pyingaing	9,000ft	4,000ft
25 April	Fort White	11,500ft	9,000ft
27 April	RK3289	8,500ft	15,500ft
28 April	Sansak	9,800ft	6,000ft

The optimum tip-over height of 12,000 feet was *never* utilised in practice, while pull-outs varied from 9,000 feet to a mere 1,500 feet.

Chapter 3

No. 8 IAF Squadron

Surakshya Va Akraman
Offence in Defence

Although officially raised at Kajamalai, RAF Trichinopoly (now called Tiruchirapalli) in Southern India in December 1942, the assembly of the first cadre of pilots and navigators did not actually take place until two or three months later. On formation the Commanding Officer of No. 8 Squadron from 1 March 1943 was Squadron Leader Niranjan Prasad, a former army major who had volunteered to fly for the air force. He had first seen service with 1 Squadron IAF in Burma. According to one source, Squadron Leader Thelkethil Joseph Thomas, who was an Indian other rank wireless and electrical mechanic (WEM) on the squadron at that time, Prasad ran the new squadron like an army unit with strict discipline, and on one occasion threatened to 'break' the NCOs if they did not clamp down on their men and put them on charges.[1]

However, another (British) observer had quite the contrary view; in his opinion Prasad took a more academic 'fatherly' approach, writing 'We had an Indian C.O. He struck me as a very reserved, scholarly, intellectual type, far better suited as a Staff officer than in the rough-and-tumble of Squadron life.'.

One young pilot officer (Churukara Philips) later noted that he introduced into the fresh young organisation that was the embryo 8 Squadron elements of tradition, instituting their own squadron mess with silverware, trophies and the like, and instilled a respect for the proper and correct officer behaviour in the youngsters and that he was well-loved by his men.[2]

---

[1] *Memories of 8 Squadron IAF* – Squadron Leader Thelkethil Joseph Thomas (Rtd) (185097) – http://www.lchr.org/a/54/4atjt6.html.

[1A] *Danny42C pprune* forum, January 2012, with permission of the author.

[2] In my earlier history of this aircraft, *Vengeance! The Vultee Vengeance Dive Bomber*, Airlife Publishing, Shrewsbury, 1982, I have been criticised for being 'muddled' as to the morale in the squadron, but the variation in veterans' memories is quite stark in their contrasts in this, and other matters.

The initial batch of pilots comprised Pilot Officers Abdul Naeem Aziz, Jotindar Singh Dhillon, Baldev Singh Dogra, Mohammad Jamiluddin Khan, Bal Bhagwan Marathay, Mohan Krishnarao Nerurkhar, Churukara George Immanuel Philip, Kulwant Singh Sandhu and Sharan Singh Sawhney. There was also on this 13th Training Course at Peshawar a leavening of much more experienced aircrew, including Flying Officers Purnendu Chakrabarty and Homi Burjorji Dorabji. Others at 152 OTU included Flying Officer Ibrahim Khan, Pilot Officers Sarosh Jehangir Dastur, Shanil Kumar Mukkherji (who went to 7 Squadron), Vallikkat Kottayl Karunakar (who only served until January with 8 Squadron and then returned to 152 OTU), Pilot Officer Muhammad Sadiq and Pilot Officer Kodendear Chengappan Madappa, and 8 Squadron was later complemented by Flight Sergeant S. Saindass and Sergeants V. Cabinetmaker, George Verghese (who was later a commissioned Flying Officer), B.H. Ghyara, G.P. Biswas and R. Pillai.

This group was assembled at Peshawar from various units and, since their recent qualification had been flying a variety of second-rate aircraft types like the Westland Lysander, the Hawker Audax and the Westland Wapiti on coast defence patrols, the Vultee was to be a whole new experience for these fledglings. Their training was carried in conjunction with No. 82 Squadron RAF, and the two squadrons had friendly rivalry and often acted in combined operational matters, in much the same was as did No. 7 Squadron IAF and No. 110 Squadron RAF, both being part of 224 Group in the Second Arakan Campaign.

Prasad had, as his immediate subordinates, Flight Lieutenants Hari Chandra Dewan and Kanwar Haveli Shah Chopra. The latter was described as 'the exact opposite of Squadron Leader Prasad'. A moustachioed, cheerful extrovert, he was the life and soul of the party and very popular with everyone. The commander of B Flight was recorded by this source to have later been Flight Lieutenant 'Bill' Boyd Berry RAF, 'an excellent Flight leader and well liked. His crews were a mixture of British and all the Dominions, all of them from one or other of the four original ex-Blenheim squadrons.'

While still based at Peshawar and working up, the squadron was put on show in front of the Governor of the North-West Frontier Province, Sir George Cunningham OBE, to commemorate the Tenth Anniversary of the founding of the Indian Air Force.

[2A] *Danny42C* pprune forum, January 2012 with permission of the author.

To equip the proposed new Vengeance squadrons for the IAF the Coastal Fights had been disbanded and the Indian other ranks (IORs), including Wireless and Electrical Mechanics (WEM), were sent to the sole aircraft depot in India at that period (late 1942) which was based at Drigh Road, Karachi. Here they were accommodated in tented camps and this ground crew underwent familiarisation training on the Vultee, a number of which were being taken out of their shipping crates and being put together in the assembly hangars. Little was known about the Vengeance at this time, other than it was an American-built, all-metal dive-bomber. As the RAF had firmly set its face against dive-bombers and dive-bombing for two decades, the workings and techniques of this machine had to be learned almost 'off the cuff' from what few manuals and documents were available. So, while the pilots and other flight crew had to learn the techniques from scratch, the ground crew gradually got to know the plus and minus points of the Vengeance over a period of three months.

All kinds of problems were encountered, and some remarkable tales were subsequently told about the problems encountered. Flight Lieutenant Jock Poyner, RAFVR, recalled that he served with No. 168 Wing on the ground team on the Burmese border at RAF Madhiganj in 1942-43 assembling the Vengeance. He stated that the aircraft were unpacked and assembled to plan 'but not a single one could take off. The engine fired but they could only manage to trundle along the runway'. He recalled that the problem was so bad that American engineers were brought in 'but they, too, could not solve the problem'. Many years later he met a former signals officer from Madhiganj in 1943 and, while reminiscing, brought the subject up. He was told that the reason the engines failed was because Nazi sympathisers at the American factory had sabotaged them. 'They were clever because the engines had passed the manufacturer's tests and because they were not found out until near the end of the war.' That such unsubstantiated gossip could still find credence years after the war just added to the Vengeance's misrepresentation.

In fact, away back in 1980, Walter C. Holt, a lead electrical man on the Hawthorne Vengeance production line, had told me that he found himself being watched by a British inspector while he soldered electrical plugs for the aircraft. The inspector seized the paste and took it away for analysis. It later transpired that this was because fifteen Vengeances which had come from the line had arrived in Australia with inoperative plugs. Others, presumably, had gone to India, and had shown the same fault. 'Sabotage was suspected.' In fact, tests revealed nothing of the kind. What was discovered from further investigation was that during the long sea voyages to both destinations, with the aircraft stowed on the decks of the transports, their crates being only covered with canvas, the salt air had penetrated and produced wire corrosion which resulted in some of these failures.

The problems with the Wright Cyclone engine with frequent seize-ups occupied the minds of all concerned right through the war as related, but most had more prosaic causes. Some engines only lasted about seven or eight hours of flying time, according to 'Red' McInnes a pilot with 110 Squadron.

E.L. Pidduck, on 84 Squadron's ground team, told me that the electrically-driven fuel pumps were prone to failures, according to two Vultee reps on site, Spencer J. Leech and Mr Anderson, of the neoprene washers, and 'lacking the best equipment to de-fuel tanks meant changing them while still full *in situ*'; all the piston rings had to be changed due to rust (mechanics described them as having the appearance of Swiss cheese) and other problems, which meant 'all 18-cylinders to be changed on makeshift stands, no hangars, no shade, just press on to get them in the air again...'.[3]

The Vultee's Cyclone engine did not get a totally bad press, however. One RAF mechanic, John Jackson, recalled that 'One aircraft we worked on was called a Vultee Vengeance, which was a dive-bomber. We were the only squadron in the Royal Air Force with dive-bombers (sic).' He also recalled that the RAF 'did not have many aircraft with radial engines, unlike the Americans, who did not have many inline engines. I can't think why we preferred inline engines, as they are more susceptible to damage. I've know an American engine come in with one cylinder hanging off, but still running on seven cylinders. A bullet had gone through one cylinder and locked the piston. This broke the con-rod and that broke the cylinder off.'

The Vengeance was urgently required but there remained a dearth of pilots. Following an IAF Unit Commanders' Conference at Delhi AHQ, the decision was made that, in view of the lack of enough qualified Indian aircrew, Commonwealth pilots, navigators and wireless operators/air gunners would be drafted in from existing dive-bomber units. Thus, on 25 November 1943, many British, Australian, Canadian, two South Africans

---

3   Smith, Peter C., *Vengeance!* 1982, op. cit.

and a New Zealander all entered 8 Squadron's ranks in batches to join the Pathans, Sikhs and other diverse Indian religions in a totally polyglot organisation with English as the common tongue.

Squadron Leader Thelkethil Joseph Thomas (Rtd) (185097) was one of the IAFVR team from the Cochin Coastal Flight that formed the nucleus of No. 8 Squadron IAF when it was formed at Kajamalai, a few miles from Trichinopoly railway junction. On 23 June the squadron transferred to Phaphamau, Allahabad, the proud possessor of a concrete all-weather runway among the paddy-fields and canals of the region. The aircrew were sent to Bhopal on 12 August for further training courses and then, in October, the squadron re-located once more, this time to a USAAF bomber base with a much longer concrete runway and more solid accommodation, located at Charra, Jharkhand State, north-west of Calcutta, close to Purulia and Ranchi. Here was located the bulk of 70th Division under Major General George William Symes, charged with defending the Orissa coast from any Japanese invasion and as the only reserve force for the frontier armies. Thomas later recalled that the specialist equipment that came with the Vultee included 'an engine-driven generator, electrical fuel pumps, swivelling landing lights etc. To add to the troubles of electricians, the battery on the aircraft was a low capacity one.'

A period of intensified training then ensued with a programme that was accelerated by the need for the dive-bombers to get combat fit. Dive-bombing practice was increased, along with more cross-country navigation, air-to-air gunnery with drogue firing, and the absorption of the tactical doctrine for the squadron's impending army co-operation role. Prasad himself recalled about the Vengeance: 'In a near vertical dive, the Vengeance could do a complete aileron turn to drop the bombs smack onto the target. The aircraft had no major vices and was easy to fly.' On the downside Prasad stated that it was 'grossly underpowered and the climb rate was consequently slow' and also that cockpit visibility was poor while taxiing, but that, overall, 'the Vengeance carried out the dive bombing task very well and was successful whenever employed …'.[4]

[3A] *Memories of 8 Squadron IAF*, Squadron Leader Thelkethil Joseph Thomas (Rtd) (185097) – htttp://www.lchr.org/a/54/4atjt6.html

[4] See Pushpindar Singh, *History of the Indian Air Force, Volume 1*, Society for Aerospace Studies, New Delhi, 2007, and Singh, Pushpindar- *Aircraft of the Indian Air Forces 1933-1973*, B. Chowdn, New Delhi, 1974.

On 26 November, as related, the first tranche of Commonwealth pilots and navigators officially transferred into the squadron from various other Vengeance outfits and joined the squadron at Charra from Phaphamau airfield,[5] Flight Lieutenants Boyd 'Bill' Berry, (later a flight commander) and Robert Dempster, Flying Officers George Davies, William Charles Hughes, Carswell Harold Niven (an Australian serving in the RAFVR), Joseph Dennis O'Leary and H.P. 'Dusty' Curtis, another Aussie; Pilot Officers Donald 'Doc' Osborne (a South African), Warrant Officers Patrick Lloyd Brinkley (RAAF) and Arthur James 'Paddy' Lamb, (RAFVR) and Sergeants Roy Alfred Fotheringham (RAAF) and Lloyd all being pilots. Navigators joining were Flying Officer J. Andrews, Reginald Robert Cookson, RAAF, and Frank Woodmansey, RAFVR, Flight Sergeant Keith 'Stew' Stewart-Mobsby and Sergeants Jones and Mankinson and Wireless Operator/Air Gunners Flight Sergeant Charles R. Irvine and Sergeants Wall and B.A.E. Winter.

One of those British pilots, Joseph O'Leary, later commented that the Indians *in situ* 'were all good chaps but most had come straight from the OTU in Peshawar. How much bombing practice they had had there, I don't know, but it can have been nothing like the four months' intensive work we'd been able to put in on the Darnodar range early in the year.' He also stated that 'The Indian ground crews were very inexperienced, and needed close supervision by RAF NCOs and airmen trawled, like us, from the squadrons. This Indian nucleus had had their aircraft for some weeks before we arrived, but they had done little with them. Certainly, they had done no bombing. Much more to the point, they hadn't swung any compasses, or belted-up a single round of ammunition for their guns.'[6]

Both these tasks were essentials, and both were extremely time-consuming. The added complication in this American-built aircraft was that the machine guns were of two different types and calibres. The four wing-mounted forward-firing machine guns on the Vultee were .300 Colts with 500rpg in span-wise-mounted boxes fired via an optical sight. Originally also, the rear defence was a twin Colt .300 on a Bell hydraulic pivot with 500rpg. When the first Vengeances arrived in India they went to 301 MU

---

[5]   A satellite airstrip north across the River Ganges from RAF Allahabad.

[6]   O'Leary, op. cit.

at Drigh Road, Karachi[7] and they made several alterations on the spot. One of these had been to replace the rear-seat Colts with the British Browning .303 on a flexible mounting and this was described as 'not a difficult conversion'. Why was this done? Well, reasons vary according to source: one common rumour was that it was because there were ample ammunition stocks for the Brownings whereas the Colts were restricted in availability.[8] Another suggestion has been that the Colts were found to be unreliable and Brownings were substituted as more dependable. However, many armament experts regarded the Colt as the more efficient weapon of the two, so this may *not* be the reason. It was, perhaps, a combination of the two; at all events AHQ India sanctioned the change and ordered that all further deliveries of the Vengeance were to be adapted in the same manner.

This decision to re-arm the Vengeance Is, IAs and other early marks may have made for a more satisfactory defence, or facilitated more attainable ammunition supplies, but it meant a real headache for the ground teams who had to load the Vultees with two different types of ammunition. The rounds were, of course, not compatible, the .300 being a slightly longer round than the .303 although one pilot recorded that inexperienced Indian ground crew loaded the wrong rounds into the belt and *forced* it through an aligning apparatus on at least one occasion![9] There was also the question of the appropriate mix of ammunition selected, ball, incendiary or tracer, and this too was a question for the individual squadrons, but the recipe, whatever ratio of each type, had to be hand-prepared and loaded into the spring clips. The wing-mounted Colts, used for strafing in low-level operations, were retained and, on several occasions, were most certainly used effectively by the Vengeance (including No. 7 IAF) in action against

---

[7] Drigh Road airfield dated from 1918 and was formerly No. 1 (India) Depot for the RAF before it became the home of 301 MU and almost every military aircraft that arrived in the sub-continent passed through its hands for assembling, checking and testing before being flown out to the various squadrons.

[8] The original Browning design dated from 1919 and the British version became the standard RAF bombers' defence weapon of the Second World War. It had a rate of fire of 1,150rpm and a range of 1,500 yards. It was belted with 250 rounds per belt.

[9] In the United States, those Vengeances taken over by the United States Army Air Forces (USAAF) already had their machine guns upgraded to .50 calibre weapons, and this was ultimately also done to those later supplied to the RAF, but this came too late to affect the issue in the Burmese operations.

Japanese motor transport, *bashas* and suspected troop concentrations. They tended to overheat with prolonged use though and the mounting boxes were liable to judder themselves out of alignment so that many pilots refused to use them. There was never any question of air-to-air duelling with enemy fighter aircraft of course.

As for relations between two flights one British pilot defined it as 'a state of mutual voluntary *apartheid*, eyeing each other warily ...'.[10] Even among the Indians there was a mixture of various religions and sects and these included different diets and other cultural complications. Add in the rich mix of Australians, British, Canadians, New Zealanders and South Africans to this already complex polyglot and it should be of little surprise that there were ethnic tensions, without the clashing of the Raj and the undercurrent of independence. Basically, the Indians wanted the British out only slightly less than they wanted the Japanese (including Chandra Bose's rag-tag 'Indian National Army' (INA) and suchlike) to take over.

Feelings were not helped by so many different messing arrangements and such and were all parts of the facts of life that separated the groups. Considering the complex make-up of the No. 8's personnel, it is not surprising that there were tensions between them; what should be applauded is the fact that the squadron operated so successfully at all. There was certainly no sort of Utopian harmonious agreement among the factions, save for the most important, which was the defeat of the Japanese. This pulling together for the common objective is surely is to be lauded rather than the current twenty-first-century practice of retrospectively concentrating on any little things that divided them.

The squadron's continual movement did not help them all shake down. The squadron moved to Phaphamau, Allahabad, then on to Charra, near Ranchi, spent a week at Chairnga, and then moved into Double Moorings for several months. From here it conducted limited offensive operations supporting the British offensive in Arakan by XV Corps under Lieutenant General Sir Philip Christison with the ultimate objective of seizing the island of Akyab (now Sittwe), a low-lying tract at the confluence of the Kaladan, Mayu and Lay Mro rivers at the southern tip of the Mayu Peninsula. This had been occupied by the Japanese since 1942 and contained a vital deep-water supply port for their armies and an all-weather airfield. No. 8

---

[10] pprune op. cit., by permission of the author.

Squadron operated initially against targets on Akyab Island itself and then further inland to support the army's advance.

The squadron had, as noted, moved at extremely short notice via Calcutta to Chittagong where they were based at Double Moorings, a *kutcha*[11] strip This move took place between 2 and 11 December and, by the 12th, the Vengeances were flying combat missions within a few days of their arrival. Initially the squadron only had A Flight under Flight Lieutenant Hari Chand Dewan and B Flight under Lieutenant Kanwar Haveli Shah Chopra.[12] There was no C Flight at this stage as there remained insufficient pilots and aircrew to form one. `

Squadron Leader Niranjan Prasad was determined to lead the first Indian dive-bomber squadron into action and got his wish on 15 December 1943. Philip concisely described the procedure this way – 'The Army gives you the target, and our job was to neutralise that post. Usually these were Gun Position or something like that, which the Army wanted out of the way, and the dive-bombers were called.' As the six Vengeances taxied out and took to the air it was recorded that 'Most of the Officers are present on the runway to watch the first operational take off'.[13] As well as Prasad, Flying Officers Purnendu Chakrabarty and Churukara Philip and three pilots from the Commonwealth induction, Flight Lieutenant Bill Berry, Warrant Officer W.M. Osborne and Flying Officer H.P. Curtis, took part in the mission.

Their task was put succinctly in the sortie report: 'Destroy Stores and kill Japs in Apaukwa PM 996243.' The unit was organised thus:

Pilot	Aircrew
Sqn Ldr Niranjan Prasad	Flt Lt Jagjit Singh
F/O Purnendu Chakrabarty	Sgt M.J. Khan
F/O Churukara Philip	Flt Sgt G. Verghese
Flt Lt William Berry	Sgt B.A.E. Winter
WO W.M. Osborne	Sgt Arthur Field
F/O H.P. Curtis	F/O J. Andrews

---

[11] An Indian word meaning crude, imperfect or temporary; most who worked from that field would say it qualified for all these definitions.

[12] Both Chopra and Dewan had flown missions from the UK, flying Vickers Wellington and the larger Vickers Warwick bombers with the RAF before being transferred back to India. Chopra was later moved, ostensibly for 'medical' reasons, and replaced by a British flight commander.

[13] AIR 27/111.

The two 'Vics' took off from Double Moorings at 1440 with the weather described as generally fine and with 3/10th cloud at 12,000 feet. The target itself was identified by the bend in the River Kaladan with the town on its southern bank and a roadway. No movement was obvious, but the town showed obvious signs of previous damage as the Vengeances tipped over at 1535 and commenced their steep diving attacks from 9,000 feet. They registered diving speeds of 200mph and released at an altitude of 2,000 feet. Ten GPNITD bombs were dropped and their bursts were observed at several points within the town with others along the waterfront where the *chaung* ran into it and still more in the centre of the target. Vengeance AN 763 had her bombs hang up on her and returned safely to base with them. All the aircraft landed at 1645. During their withdrawal they reported two large fires burning close to Nphony Leik PM 5836 and another at Aiethonyaw PM 4021. They were thought to be villages alight or maybe bush fires.

A notable milestone for 8 Squadron was the bombing of the Japanese Army HQ in Kangyibyin village (PM 48817) on Christmas Eve. This made a change from the normal Army Support, Close (ASC) missions which dominated the Vultees' combat life. Squadron Leader Niranjana Prasad led this raid also with three Indian teams and three Commonwealth teams, all flying Mark II Vengeances as below:

Pilot	Aircrew
Sqn Ldr Niranjana Prasad	Flt Lt Jagjit Singh
F/O Purnendu Chuckerburty*	F/O Tapeswar Basu
F/O Homi Dorabji	F/O Saroshi Dastur
F/O H.P. Curtis	F/O Officer J. Andrews
F/O Joseph O'Leary	F/O Frank Woodmansey
WO Arthur Lamb	Sgt James.

*Chuckerburty, after his combat period was over, returned to Peshawar and was sadly killed in a flying accident there on 21 January 1945

The two[14] flights left Double Moorings at 0910 and found the weather over the target excellent, with no cloud and no wind, ideal for dive bombing.

---

[14] On twelve-plane attacks it was generally the case that one flight was formed from the Commonwealth pilots and the other consisted of the Indian pilots and aircrew; but often smaller, six-plane, missions were composed of a more diverse mix of crews, three from each of the flights.

The village was located south of the main Nyaungyaung to Buthidaung west-to-east road. They observed no movement from the enemy and attacked. All the bombs fell inside the target area, some in the middle of the village, and some just to the north-east of the centre. Six bombs overshot some 100 yards north-west and four others fell 500 yards to the south, but sixteen heavy bursts were observed in the middle and north-east of the village which sent up large clouds of dust and debris. All six Vengeances returned safely to base at 1100.

Unfortunately, on 28 December, the squadron suffered a further loss when Flying Officer Frank Woodmansey, with Sergeant Rogers in the rear seat, crashed into the sea while returning to base after a practice dive-bombing during the afternoon. It was later confirmed the Vengeance (EZ 895 or EZ 898) went into the sea killing both men. Woodmansey's body was never recovered.

A typical pair of missions for 8 Squadron took place on 10 January and we can analyse them as we did for those of 7 Squadron. The first was launched from Double Moorings at 0925, with Squadron Leader Niranjan Prasad at the head of eleven Vultees, nine Mark IIs and two Mark IAs, thus:

Pilot	Aircrew
Sqn Ldr Niranjan Prasad	Flt Lt Jagjit Singh
F/O Purnendu Chakerbutty	F/O Tapeswar Basu
F/O Abdul Aziz	Flt Sgt B.H. Ghyara
Flt Lt Kanwar Chopra	F/O Philip Chandran
F/O Churukara Philip	Flt Sgt George Verghes
F/O Charan Sharma	F/O Muhammad Sadiq
Flt Lt William Berry	F/O John Brinkley
F/O Carswell Niven	Flt Sgt Irvine
WO Arthur Lamb	Sgt Jones
F/O Ranendu Sen	F/O Sharadchandra Bombawalla
F/O Jotindar Singh Dhillon	F/O Alfred Jagjiven

Their instructions were to bomb Japanese troop positions in a restricted area of 100 yards around Pinpoint PM 444447 where two *chaungs* joined to be identified from the map and photos studied at the briefing. Additionally, the Army were to lay on further parameters in the form of a smoke barrage which would indicate the 'bomb line' and 8 Squadron was to concentrate its attack south of this line. Philip recalled that these bomb lines were often as close as twenty-five yards to friendly forces, so exact was the placing of the ordnance by the dive-bombers. Although the practised procedure at this time was to tip over from 12,000 feet, dive at 80 degrees and release at 4,000 feet, retracting the dive brakes and escaping at high speed, the weather conditions usually made this impossible. Even when the cloud base was down to 5,000 feet such was the urgency that the Ground Liaison Officers (GLO) would call them in anyway and they would comply. In such instances, full dive-bombing being impossible, the attacks would be made with a shallower approach, the environs allowing of course, nipping in between the forest-clad hills, releasing at 2,500 feet and levelling out at 800 feet before making a treetop getaway.

On this occasion the weather proved good over the target. This was duly complied with, the attack going in at 1025 in a steep dive from 11,000 feet down to 1,500 feet at a speed of 310mph. Altogether they dropped eight 500lb GPNITD and twenty-eight 250lb GPNI bombs on the enemy. There was no sign of any movement from below, nor any air opposition, and it was recorded that 'All bombs fell in concentration South of Smoke', with the explosions causing 'clouds of dust and smoke covering the whole target'. Mission accomplished the force returned to base at 1125.

The second strike took off at 1430 that afternoon under the charge once more of Prasad, against the same troop concentration. This time the squadron deployed thus:

Pilot	Aircrew
Sqn Ldr Niranjan Prasad	Flt Lt Jagjit Singh
F/O William Hughes	F/O J. Andrews
F/O Abdul Aziz	Flt Sgt B.H. Ghyara
Flt Lt Kanwar Chopra	F/O Philp Chandran
F/O Charan Sharma	F/O Muhammad Sadiq
F/O Churukara Philip	Flt Sgt George Verghes
Flt Lt William Berry	F/O John Brinkley, RAAF
P/O Saradindu Das Gupta	Flt Sgt G.P. Biswas
P/O Joseph O'Leary	Flt Sgt Keith Stewart-Mobsby
Flt Lt Robert Dempster	Sgt Mankinson
F/O Ranendu Sen	F/O Sharadchandra Bombawala
F/O Carswell Niven	Flt Sgt Irvine

There were again ten Mark II Vengeances and two Mark IAs in the mix and the ordnance toted was similar to the first raid. Lift-off was at 1430 and the attack went in at 1525, with steep dives being made from 11,000 feet down to 2,000 feet This time they were met by tracer and small-arms fire as they withdrew at low altitude. Again, the target was covered with smoke and dust. All the planes returned to Double Moorings undamaged at 1620. Such missions evoked many signals of thanks from the front-line Army units which were chalked up on boards for the returning flyers to see. On occasion, when a particular important target had been destroyed, their 'bosses', the 3rd Tactical Air Force, under Air Marshal Sir John Baldwin, which controlled events, also sent congratulatory signals.[15]

The runways used by 8 Squadron varied from what might be termed the sublime to the most basic of basics and this affected the performance of the Vengeance of course. The take-off run of the Vultee, like every other bomber aircraft, was affected not only by this factor but by the type of ordnance embarked for each mission, the type of bomb, distance to the target which dictated fuel load and so on. This was perfectly normal, but only the Vengeance has ever been criticised for it. I put the question to Dennis O'Leary, who was as generous in his response as he was in other matters.

> Cannot be precise here, but from recollection (we never measured the Take-Off run), I would first say that 1: I always carried the same bomb load on all my trips, 2 x 500lb GP internally and two x 250lb GP on the wing racks. But after I left 110 at Khumbirgram on 17 November 1943 there was a hang-up accident there when an incendiary fell off on landing. 2: In the Arakan we almost always operated from a *kutcha* (a levelled paddy field) strip in dry weather (these all turned to mud in the monsoons). At Khumbirgram we were on concrete. My first three ops (May 1943) were flown from Chittagong (tarmac). At Cannanore, rolled crushed *laterite*. It didn't seem to make much difference, except that the dust on the *kutchas* was a nuisance.
>
> In Arakan, we always moved up (or back!) to keep about fifty miles behind the land battle. This kept the turnaround time to a minimum; but anything less would not allow time to assemble a

---

[15]   8 Squadron reported to 3 TAF, 224 Group and 167 Wing.

'box' and climb to bombing height of 12,000 feet before reaching the target. In hilly Assam, we were based at Khumbirgram, the targets were more spread out, mostly roads, stores and fuel dumps, riverside villages used by the Japanese as staging posts to hide store by day for river transport by night, that sort of thing. There was little visible Japanese troop- activity until the last great land battles at Imphal and Kohima, where the fighting was so hand-to-hand that we dare not bomb for fear of 'blue-on-blue' incidents. Some of the targets were 200 miles away, about the limit of our radius of action.

I would say that the trips were around 3,000 feet, and I know I had 3,000 at Cannanore. It was enough, although I've said that 'Acceleration was poor, there were always complaints about the long take-off run.' I can't recall an instance of a Vultee Vengeance not getting off in the distance we had. Winds were light during the dry season, at Cannanore all take-offs were out to sea, all landings from the sea irrespective of wind.

So, how long was the take-off run on a bombed-up Vengeance? I'd guess 2,500 feet. Sorry, that's the best I can do.[16,17]

Another day's operation can be examined as another 'typical' day for 8 Squadron at this period, taking at random events that occurred on 17 January. There were a twelve-plane strike and two six-plane sorties mounted that day. The first was under Squadron Leader Niranjan Prasad and was made up thus:

Pilot	Aircrew
Sqn Ldr Niranjan Prasad	Flt Lt Jagjit Singh
Sgt E.P. Hall	F/O Reginald Cookson
F/O Abdul Aziz	Flt Sgt Mohammad Ashraf Sheikh
Flt Lt Kanwar Dewan	Flt Lt Kulwant Singh Sandhu
F/O William Hughes	F/O J. Andrews
F/O Charan Sharma	F/O Muhammad Sadiq

---

16 Dennis O'Leary to the author, Friday, 30 December 2016.

17 One of the spurious reasons that General Douglas MacArthur's Command put forward to replace the Australian Vengeance squadrons in New Guinea around this time was that they took too long to take off from their forward airstrips. This was hotly disputed by the RAAF on the spot, but USAAF General Kenney's view prevailed without any further discussion.

Pilot	Aircrew
Flt Lt William Berry	Sgt B.A.E. Winter
F/O Carswell Niven	Flt Sgt Irvine
F/O Jotindar Dhillon	F/O Alfred Jagjivan
WO W.M. Osborne	Flt Sgt Arthur Field
P/O Joseph O'Leary	Flt Sgt Keith Stewart-Mobsby
WO Sams	Sgt David Edward Victor Dove, RAAF

Their target allocation was Japanese positions on hill features between Letwedet and Htindaw on the main Maungdaw to Buthidaung Road The area was to be the target of the next planned Chindit assault led by the 1st Battalion Queen's Royal Surrey Regiment. The Vultees were briefed to strike at Pinpoints 457449 and 459448 two hills (which the British named 'Cain' and 'Abel') that straddled the road. For this mission AHQ must have expected some Japanese aerial opposition because 8 Squadron were allocated a rare close escort, this being five Hawker Hurricanes from 6 Squadron, IAF. It was known that, farther north, the Japanese had built two airstrips at Idaw to protect the important road to Myitkina, and just to the north-east was the strategic rail junction of Naba. What was *not* known then was that the Japanese were planning an offensive of their own. Japanese aircraft were rarely seen, however, and the Vengeances were under strict orders not to engage in unnecessary heroics should they appear, but the fighter escorts, themselves rare, were even more rarely ever required in practice.

Joseph O'Leary commented that 'the Hurricane was so inferior to the Oscar in almost all respects apart from its ability to absorb punishment, that our escort would have its work cut defending itself, never mind us.' The Hurricanes in any case 'appeared only randomly, and we could never see any particular reason for it, perhaps when they had nothing more important to do.'[18] Of course, it was possible that AHQ had intelligence on Japanese intentions on certain occasions, or if a mission took the Vengeance closer to enemy airfields.[19]

It has also been alleged that the RAF had no radar defences in the region, but this is not true. The RAF had established the HQ of No. 221 Group,

---

[18] O'Leary, pprune, op. cit., with the author's permission.

[19] These Hurricane IICs were from 5 Squadron RAF, Squadron Leader Guy Joseph Charles Hogan, DFC AFC, initially based at Imphal itself. The Hurricane had recently replaced the Curtiss Mohawk IV in this squadron.

under Air Vice Marshal Stanley Flamank Vincent, DFC AFC, at the main airstrip at Imphal itself. This was one of just two all-weather strips, the other being Palel, while satellite 'fair-weather' strips were located at Kangal, Sapam, Tulihal and Wanjing. Other radar sets were located at Moirang, Kangla and near Dimapur. To provide early warning, radar posts and observer sites had been established out from the Imphal plain toward the Chindwin River valley. These AMES (Air Ministry Experimental Stations), coding for mobile short-range radar units, were located at Kangala, Tiddim and Wabagai but the lynch-pin radar was based at a site close to Tamu, in the Kabaw Valley. This set was the only one which could locate enemy aircraft east of the mountains shielding Imphal and provided a 100-mile warning. This set had a direct land-link back to Imphal itself, vital because the hills interrupted much of the radio and radar signals.[20] When the Japanese had advanced, the 20th Division, under Major General Douglas Gracey, defending this area was pulled back to the 4,334-foot high Shenam Saddle position overlooking the 2,926-foot Imphal plain, but not before the AMES radar set had been destroyed by enemy shellfire. The RAF therefore lost this vital radar outpost.

Hit-and-run raids by Japanese aircraft were now became a distinct possibility. Japanese air raids by up to a maximum of thirty fighters at a time and a dozen medium bombers, now took place against Imphal (where they killed twenty men from AHQ), Palel and Tulihal. They also intercepted the defenceless Douglas C-47 Skytrains (Dakotas) transport planes flying in supplies to the beleaguered garrison and on 25 April, destroyed five of them along with their crews. The Japanese 5th Air Division, was commanded by Lieutenant General Tazoe (Teizo) Noboro, with his headquarters at Maymyo (Pyin Oo Lwin). He had opposed the whole idea of Operation U-GO (Operation C) warning it would be wasteful.[21] The land commander,

---

[20]   383 AMES had been formed at Imphal in 1943; 15059 AMES had been formed in March 1944, but was pulled back to Amarda Road in April. AIR 29/178 - IIM/FE531/1 and 1A. *383 Air Ministry Experimental Station (AMES). Formed at Imphal (India) in February 1943* & AIR 29/193 IIM/FE15059/1, *15059 Air Ministry Experimental Station (AMES). Formed at Imphal (India) in March 1944. Based at Amarda Road (India) in April 1944 and Baigachi (India) in June 1945.* 1944 Apr- 1945 Dec. National Archives, Kew, London.

[21]   In this Tazoe was prophetic for his whole command had been reduced from 370 aircraft at the start of the campaign to a mere 161 aircraft by June 1944, and these were opposed by Allied air power totalling over 1,500 aircraft.

Lieutenant General Renya Mutaguchi, had already declared that air support was not necessary for his infantry divisions and deemed it irrelevant for warfare among the jungle-clad hills on the India-Burmese border which did not bode well for Nipponese air co-operation. The Japanese had fine aircraft, often better than the British, including the Nakajima Ki-44 *Shoki* ('Tojo') fighter and the Nakajima Ki-49 *Donryu* (Storm Dragon or 'Helen') twin-engined bomber of the 62 *Sentai*, 3rd *Chutai*, usually remembered as the Sally, but this was the Mitsubishi Ki-21.[22]

As for the Vengeances' own defence against enemy interceptors, the 'official' line was for the Vengeance boxes to stay in tight formation to offer mutually protecting fire from the rear gunners. O'Leary considered the Vengeance's *real* best protection was its camouflage when acting as a mock attacking fighter, 'if I took my eye off the 'box', it had simply disappeared.' In the event there were never any interceptions by Japanese fighters. He mused many years later, that 'our Vengeance operations must rank among the safest ones in all the war. Nearly all our people flew all their sorties over a two-year period without a scratch. The Jap fighters never tried to intercept us, and their AA fire was largely ineffective. Very few of our losses could be put down to them with any certainty. Almost all were due to flying accidents, as ever the result of carelessness, stupidity, weather or sheer bad luck.'[23]

Regarding Japanese anti-aircraft defence O'Leary stated to me that, in the attacks on Akyab Island, where he flew his first three sorties with No. 110 Squadron in 1943, 'There they had "heavies", which could reach us at 10-12,000 feet as we came in, and down low plenty of Bofors-type 40mm for us after pull-out. Apart from that, we often collected small-arms hits from the ground as we were coming back low level – obviously from troops taking casual "pot-shots". As far as I am concerned little damage ever resulted (although I believe there were one or two cases of a VV exploding in mid-dive, presumably from a direct hit).' He was equally prosaic about his combat missions: 'it was as exciting as taking a bus into town. Different targets every day, but same procedure.'[24]

---

[22] Japanese Studies in World War II, Monograph No. 59 (1), *Burma Operations Record, Phase III, 1944-1945*, Prepared for Military History Section, HQ, Army Forces Far East.

[23] O'Leary, op. cit., by permission of the author.

[24] Joseph O'Leary to the Author 2 October 2016.

For this 17 January mission the squadron had two Mark IA and ten Mark II Vengeances, and all were airborne from Double Moorings at 0925 and proceeded to the target in two six-plane boxes. For this mission they did have a nominal close escort of five Hawker Hurricane fighters. The weather was fine along the route remained good at 1025 when they arrived over the actual enemy hill positions. There was no enemy reaction whatsoever and the attack dives commenced at 1030, the Vultees making a south-east to north-west run and diving in from 11,000 feet down to a pull-out height of 3,000 feet.

In total eighteen bombs burst in the centre of the target while four others undershot and fell on the northern feature of the hill, while two more bombs fell in the paddy fields at the eastern edge. The hill was left covered in dust and white smoke. As they withdrew enemy road traffic was observed on the road and sprayed with machine-gun fire. The squadron returned to Double Moorings at 1125. After the de-briefing it was decided to attack the same target again in two sections.

The first of these sections out was five Vengeances, four Mark IIs and one Mark IA, which made up a strike under Flight Lieutenant Kanwar Chopra. These aircraft left the Double Moorings base at 1515 with these aircrew:

Pilot	Aircrew
Flt Lt Kanwar Chopra	F/O Philip Chandran
F/O Surjit Singh` Jaspal	Sgt Sadiq Ahemed
F/O Charan Sharma	F/O Muhammud Sadiq
Flt Lt Kanwar Dewan	Flt Lt Ranbir Singh Sandu
F/O William Hughes	F/O J. Andrews

They found the weather over the target area 'generally good but hazy' and were able to attack as planned at 1615 on a line from north-east to south-west in steep dives from 11,000 feet to 3,000 feet and deposited their 500lb GPTI bombs with three-, nine- and twelve-hour delay fuses into the enemy positions[25] The Japanese were adroit in camouflage and deception, dug themselves into deep bunkers and were rarely caught out in the open during

---

[25]   The standard RAF GP (General Purpose) bombs with Time Instantaneous (TI) fuses were fitted with quarter-second tail (TI) fuses and tenth-of-a-second nose (NI) fuses with various Time Delays (TD) or Long Delay (LD) fusing as with the Type 37D. Extended rod (T1) fuses were sometimes used when exposed troop concentrations were the target, but this was rare in Burma.

the hours of daylight. Major General Douglas David Gracey, acknowledged this fact, stating, 'The capture of a Japanese position is not ended until the last Jap in it (generally several feet underground) is killed. Even in the most desperate circumstance, 99 per cent of them prefer death or suicide to capture. The fight is more total than in Europe, The Jap can be compared to the most fanatical Nazi youth and must be dealt with accordingly.'[26]

Blocking or impeding the Japanese army supplies was ultimately to starve more of them to death than direct bombing. The enemy troops were told that more than ample supplies would be provided when Allied bases were overrun, thus giving them the added spur of hunger to their already indoctrinated commitment to the attack at any cost and inbuilt superiority. It must be remembered that the Japanese commanders were callous and indifferent of large losses provided they attained their final objectives and the Japanese soldier was that taught self-sacrifice was noble and surrender or defeat was shameful. After the mass slaughter of the First World War the Allied commanders (or most of them) tended to be rather more circumspect with their men's lives. Thus, when hitting enemy targets with mixed instantaneous and varying time-delay ordnance, the Allied troops on the ground had to be aware of exactly what was involved or else they might prematurely move into highly dangerous areas.

Chopra reported that all these fell in the centre of the target, save two which hit slightly north of the feature. There was no opposition and all aircraft had returned to base by 1715.

Next up was Flight Lieutenant Boyd 'Bill' Berry who led a six-plane sortie from Double Moorings at 1535:

Pilot	Aircrew
Flt Lt William Berry	Sgt B.A.E. Winter
F/O Carswell Niven	Flt Sgt Irvine
F/O Jotindar Dhillon	F/O Alfred Jagjivan
P/O Joseph O'Leary	Flt Sgt Keith Stewart-Mobsby
WO W.M. Osborne	Flt Sgt Arthur Field
WO Arthur Lamb	Sgt David Dove RAAF

[26] See also Mead, Richard, *Churchill's Lions: A biographical guide to the key British generals of World War II*, Spellmount, Stroud, 2007.

This was virtually a repeat run with the attack runs again being made from north-east to south-west but this time, to avoid near misses, the dive-bombing was conducted at 1635 from an initial height of 8,000 feet down to just 2,000 feet. Bill Berry reported all twelve bombs fell right in centre of target which was considered duly 'softened up'. The section all safely landed back at base at 1725. On 19 March a Commonwealth contingent, fresh from the OTU, arrived at Manbur, a satellite airstrip to Cox's Bazar, and these included Pilot Officers John Grant Gunderson, Flying Officers Austin Ormond Buck, Hazen Edward Dougherty, Everett Embert Ettinger, William Ernest Jay MacBain, Hugh W. Seton and Milton Ward Sills, Warrant Officers George Logan Allan, James Burns Conlon, RAAF, and Frederick Anthony Kennedy, (RAAF), Flight Sergeants Burrows and John David Steele, (RCAF) and an engineer, Sergeant John Bell, who augmented 8 Squadron's personnel yet further.

It has been alleged that No. 8 Squadron never mounted twelve-aircraft strikes but, as we have already seen, this is not the case and the arrival of this fresh intake increased the number of such missions. We will examine in detail three further such missions as examples of this work rate. On 23 March a five-Vengeance attack was mounted from Manbur by No. 8 Squadron with four Mk II and two Mk IA aircraft. Their task was to bomb enemy positions at Point 162, after initially making a dummy attack on Point 1301 at 1215. This initial strike was made up of the following aircraft and aircrew:

Pilot	Aircrew
F/O H.P. Curtis RAAF	F/O John Brinkley RAAF
WO Arthur Lamb	Flt Sgt Barker
F/O Jotindar Dhillon	F/O Alfred Jagjivan
Sgt Lloyd	Flt Sgt Jones
Sgt Roy Fotheringham RAAF	Flt Sgt David Dove, RAAF

Take-off was at 1130 and they had a close escort of six Hawker Hurricane fighters. One of the IAs had to turn back within twenty minutes due to electrical failures. The mission was duly carried out without loss, the aircraft retuning at 1250. Examination of the twenty camera exposures revealed 'excellent' results. But this was but a warm-up to the main event.

Squadron Leader Niranjana Prasad led a mixed-crews, eleven-aircraft attack with eight Mark II and three Mark IAs from the Manbur base.

Their mission was to attack and soften up Japanese troops dug in on the hill feature at Point 16, an enemy stronghold which dominated their lines of communication to Maungdaw and which had repeatedly thwarted the Army's various attempts at storming it. The composition of this force was as below:

Pilot	Aircrew
Sqn Ldr Niranjan Prasad	Flt Lt Jagjit Singh
F/O Churukara Philip	Flt Sgt George Verghese
F/O Abdul Aziz	Flt Sgt Mohammad Ashraf Sheikh
F/O Purnendu Chakerbutty	F/O Tapeswar Basu
F/O Ghansham Tahilramani	Sgt Shanker Rao
Sgt Wall RAF	F/O Reginald Cookson RAAF
F/O H.P. Curtis RAAF	F/O John Brinkley
Flt Lt Carswell Niven	WO Irvine RAF
WO Arthur Lamb	Flt Sgt Barker
F/O Jotindar Dhillon	F/O Alfred Jagjivan
Sgt Lloyd RAF	Flt Sgt Jones RAF

Take-off was at 1600 and it took only half-an-hour to reach the target, which was identified on the east of Letwedet and on the hill feature south of the pronounced loop of the Letwedet *chaung*. The weather over the enemy position was clear on arrival but no enemy movement could be seen. The whole two-box formation attacked at 1630, the six Mk II Vengeances depositing sixteen 500lb GPTI bombs and the three Mk IAs dropping six 500lb GPTI in steep dives down from 8,000 feet to a release height of 2,000 feet. It was logged that all the bombs burst 'in close concentration on target' and, as so often before, a cloud of dust resulted which so covered the enemy position that nothing could be seen, although the camera aircraft made thirty exposures for later analysis. There was no defensive fire but on the return to base a Mk II Vengeance, P flown by Flying Officer Chakerbutty and Flying Officer Basu, was forced to make a crash-landing at Lyons (map reference 0811) the undercarriage collapsing and the aircraft skidding in a paddy field at the end of the runway. Chakerbutty observed thick blue smoke, and then oil pour out which rapidly covered the aircraft. Fortunately, both aircrew got out and away safely without any injuries.

It was in March that Niranjana Prasad himself left the squadron. This caused much resentment among the Indian aircrew, apparently because after Prasad departed his place was taken by Squadron Leader Ira Allison Sutherland (NZ402909) who commanded 8 Squadron from 27 March 1944 to 8 December 1944. He was born on 11 April 1913 and was awarded the DFC and MiD before he was killed flying de Havilland Mosquitoes with No. 82 Squadron in India on 28 June 1945.[27] The humid atmosphere compromised the adhesives that bonded the plywood machine and the fabricated main spar failed. The particular aircraft that killed Sutherland had already been declared unfit for operations and should never have been authorised.] He was described as 'a tough New Zealander with a hard reputation as a martinet'. It is also rumoured, in another memoir, which one of the squadron flight commanders[28] just could not 'get on' with Sutherland and was apparently impertinent to him once too often, with the result that he had him shipped out.

The next big mission, with two 'boxes' totalling twelve Vengeance, a mix of Mk IA and IIs once more, was carried out on 10 April. Led by Flight Lieutenant Bill Berry, the composition of the strike was thus:

Pilot	Aircrew
Flt Lt William Berry	Flt Sgt B.A.E. Winter
F/O William Hughes	F/O J. Andrews
F/O Milton Sills	F/O James Burns Conlon RAAF
WO W.M. Osborne	WO Arthur Field
Flt Lt Carswell Niven	WO Irvine
F/O Churukara Philip	Flt Sgt George Verghese
F/O H.P. Curtis	F/O John Brinkley
Sgt Lloyd	Flt Sgt Jones
F/O William McBain	P/O Frederick Kennedy
F/O Jotindar Dhillon	F/O J. Andrews
Sgt Roy Fotheringham, RAAF	Flt Sgt David Dove RAAF
F/O Austin Buck	Sgt Browline

---

[27] This particular aircraft, like many 'Mossies', suffered from aircraft skin delaminating; the glue that held the 'Wooden Wonder' came apart in the tropics and killed several good former Vengeance pilots before the problem was solved. This adhesive, known as Casein Glue, was based on milk protein, and it was blended with water, hydrate time and sodium hydroxide. After the Mosquitoes' accidents in Burma and India this adhesive was replaced by a formaldehyde-based glue.

[27A] (*Danny42C* pprune forum, January 2012, by permission of the author).

[28] Only identified as the squadron adjutant, a Bengali flying officer.

Their target was Imbauk village, Banmauk Township in the Sagaing Region. (24^0 36' N, 95^0 58' E) in north-central Burma on the road from Rangoon. The Japanese had been pressing the 25th Indian Division here since 5 April and fierce fighting had seen the front changing hands almost daily with hand-to-hand combat and heavy losses on both sides. The formation took off from Mumbar at 1055 and made their attack in clear weather at 1137, after first confirming their target to the north-west of Dangyaung. The Vengeance commenced their 'steep dives' from an altitude of 9,000 feet with release height at 1,500 feet to achieve maximum accuracy, so close were the two sides.

The first box concentrated on the north feature, with scattered bombing, two bombs landing in the centre of this position, two more slightly to the east and nine bombs covered an area from the centre of north feature to the centre of the south feature. Another hit was made on the extreme north-east pimple of the south feature, while two more bombs overshot into a paddy field east of the feature. The second box's bombing was 'very well concentrated'. Fourteen bombs burst on the south feature covering it from north to south. Total ordnance delivered on the Japanese positions was sixteen 500lb and six 250lb GPTI, while the Mk IAs dropped eight 500lb GPTI.

This dive-bombing attack was backed up by heavy artillery fire which enabled the 8th/19th Hyderabad Regiment to recapture the vital 'Bird' position the following night, although, ultimately, it could not be held.

Another 'two-box' sortie was conducted on 26 April. It was led by Squadron Leader Ira Sutherland and was made up of the following aircrew:

Aircraft	Pilot	Aircrew
S	Sqn Ldr Ira Sutherland	Flt Sgt B.A.E. Winter
P	F/O William McBain	P/O Frederick Kennedy
K	F/O Hazen Dougherty	WO George Allan
B	Flt Lt Carswell Niven	WO Irvine
D	F/O Everett Ettinger	Flt Sgt John Steele RCAF
F	Sgt Roy Fotheringham, RAAF	F/O Reginald Cookson
J	F/O H.P. Curtis	F/O John Brinkley
E	F/O Jotindar Dhillon	Flt Sgt G.P. Biswas
A	F/O William Hughes	F/O J. Andrews
O	F/O Hari Dewan	Flt Lt Kalwant Sandhu
T	F/O Austin Buck	Sgt Burrows
M	F/O John Gunderson	Sgt John Bell

Their targets were specific, Japanese infantry dug-in on pimples 502483, 503484 and 505483. These were strongpoints located to the south of Pinpoint 121, on the west bank of the Kalapanzin River, to the north-east of Sin-chbyin village. The Japanese diversionary operation, HA-GO, was carried out along the coastal area by their 55th Division, under Lieutenant General Tadashi Hanaya. He planned to cut through to Bawli Bazar and thus destroy the 7th Indian Division in the eastern area of the Mayu Mountains, clamping them between twin northern and southern pincher movements. The scheme was that 55th Division was to move against Nganyaung, and smash 5th Division at Maungdaw, west of the Mayu mountains. The Japanese termed this whole ambitious plane the 'Northern Arakan Operation' to distinguish it from their even more deadly attacks on the Allied supply bases at Imphal and Kohima.

Once underway this serious threat required urgent attention and this attack was part of the Allied response. The ten Vengeance IIs and two Vengeance IAs lifted off from Mumbar at 1500. The weather was clear over the area and the attack commenced at 1546, with tip-over at 10,000 feet and bombs-off height at 1,500 feet. Twenty 500lb GPTD 025 and eighteen 250lb GPTI bombs were dropped by the Mk IIs and four 500lb GPTD 025 and two 250lb GPTI bombs were dropped by the Mk IAs. The plan was for four aircraft to cover each pimple and the bombs were stick dropped in steep dives resulting in very concentrated bombing, 'all bombs seen burst on target except one bomb in paddy south-west of target'.

The forty exposures taken during the attack with the 5-inch focal length camera showed excellent results. This was confirmed later by the Army themselves who sent a signal, 'bombing excellent – many corpses found'.

Losses from enemy action remained rare, but the units continued to take intermittent casualties. On 16 May 1944 Flying Officer Hazen Edward 'Doc' Dougherty, RCAF, flying Vengeance AN618, with rear-seat man Sergeant J.M. Khan, was No. 5 in a box formation of six Vengeances according to the subsequent CO's report. Their target was enemy lines of communication in the Arakan Hills. The Allied troops on the ground some 2–3,000 yards from the target reported that Dougherty was doing aileron turns during the latter part of the dive, 'practically a spin', and that he did not commence his recovery until at a very low altitude. The bombs had been released and were observed to have struck the target. Flying Officer Ghurukara Philip (later a group captain) the pilot of No. 6 aircraft astern of 'Doc' in the attack, noticed nothing special other that the low recovery altitude, and reported the aircraft was almost level again when the starboard wing hit the side of the hill in enemy-held territory. 'Such was the nature of the terrain that he catapulted across the valley, turning on his back and crashed on the other side. There was no fire.' It was all over in seconds. The army observers also stated that there was no sign of fire. One of the unit's Vengeances circled the position, given as 20^0 50' N, 92^0 27E near the village of Baguna, for a time and later the army sent out patrols, but they failed to locate the wreck and both crewmen were listed as MIA. The rear-seat man of No. 4 aircraft ahead of Dougherty observed something trailing from his aircraft as it went in and expressed the opinion that the machine had struck a cable stretched across the valley and might also have been hit by small-arms fire. Sutherland wrote to Doc's father that there was little hope that his son had survived and also that the fact that the army sent patrols into hostile territory in an effort to locate the aircrew thus risking other lives to find them 'gives you an idea of how much the bombing carried out by your son and companions is appreciated by our troops'. Philip was more pragmatic, recalling later that Dougherty and he had been playing cards before the operation and that the Canadian still owed him money!

There were near-misses also. Saskatoon-born Flight Lieutenant Everett 'Eb' Ettinger recalled one such incident in an interview with a RCAF press officer. During a take-off one tyre burst and this damaged the hydraulic system of his Vengeance, AN 837, meaning his flaps, wheels and bomb release equipment were all rendered useless. It was a hopeless dilemma and there was no option but to attain a safe altitude, put the Vengeance into a gentle bank and allow the WAG to bale out, which was done safely. Everett then flew his machine out toward the coast, baling out over land and hoping the Vengeance would end her days in the drink. Unfortunately, while he was descending by parachute to the ground, Ettinger was appalled to see his pilotless aircraft, with rudder apparently jammed, begin circling and ultimately heading straight toward him. As he later recalled it narrowly missed him, not once, but twice, before crashing to earth. 'I was glad to see the end of that aeroplane', he recalled.[29]

Joseph O'Leary gave another instance. Over the target his wing-man in the back 'Vic', Flying Officer George Davies, was hit by light flak while in his attack dive. The enemy AA pierced the aircraft's hydraulic system which immediately began spewing out the fluid. He was able to retract his dive brakes at the end of the dive and then the system went out totally leaving him with the bomb doors still open and one undercarriage leg left dangling down. It was standard practice for the front 'Vic' to get themselves home as planned leaving the cripple to follow. O'Leary and Australian Warrant Officer Arthur James 'Paddy' Lamb closed Davies' machine and slowed to his reduced speed so that their rear-gunners could offer him some limited protection should a Japanese fighter put in an appearance, tempted by such easy prey. Two of the escorting Hurricanes also dropped back and took up positions one mile behind them, sweeping to maintain formation.[30]

The flight, though slow, was without incident and Double Moorings was reached safely, and O'Leary and Lamb duly landed. Davies was left to puzzle out what to do next. He tried shaking the second undercarriage leg down (although how he would have locked it is unclear) but without success and in the end, they bowed to the inevitable. Heading out over the coast they duly parachuted to safety and were rescued, while their trusty mount that had got them home, took her final plunge into the Bay of Bengal.

On 24 February O'Leary himself, flying Vengeance IA EZ993 was lucky to escape from a crash landing in Arakan with a full fuel and bomb load when his engine failed at low level. He attempted a crash-landing at Mambur airstrip, a satellite field in Arakan Survive, but could not quite reach it. The Vultee ploughed through the jungle for half-a-mile, shredding the wings off en route. These contained the main fuel tanks of course, which was helpful

---

[29] Ettinger had been assigned to 8 Squadron IAF in December 1943, but instead joined 110 Squadron that same month. Unfortunately, Ettinger only postponed his demise; he was shot down and killed in a Spitfire with No. 273 Squadron while attacking targets on the Taungop-Prome road on 20 April 1945.

[30] O'Leary noted that these Hurricanes had a much lower performance in every way to an *Oscar* that they would never have been much use in any dog fight. The *Oscar* was the codename allocated to the Nakajima Ki-43 Army Type 1 *Hayabusa* (Peregrine Falcon), a single-seater that destroyed more Allied aircraft than any other type during the war, but they never got a Vengeance.

to the aircrew's survival; the pilot was still sitting on the 20-gal capacity 'trap' which, as O'Leary himself recorded, was 'quite sufficient to barbecue both crew members'.[31] Survive he did, but it resulted in hospitalisation and a period of recuperation leave which meant that although he did rejoin the squadron again, it was not in time to take part in any further combat missions. He was destined to become a Vengeance instructor but even that was overtaken by events.

Ira Sutherland, not a soft man by all accounts, wrote that 'The aircrew are really an International group. It is an IAF Squadron and besides Indians – who in themselves are divided into Sikhs, Punjabis, Bengalis and other sects – there are a lot of Canadians … Englishmen, Scots, Australians and myself, a lone New Zealander – really a mixed bag! 'Doc' mixed in and got on extremely well with everyone; he was generally liked.' Dougherty was, in fact, one of several (fourteen) Canadian pilots flying with the squadron who were transferred into No. 8 Squadron on 29 February 1944 prior to the offensive. There were insufficient trained Indian pilots to maintain operations, so many Commonwealth flyers were assigned, including Australian Flight Lieutenant Carswell Harold Niven, RAFVR, who was later killed flying FB956 and initially interred at Quetta.

However, in contrast to the above rosy picture of harmony, Squadron Leader Thelkethil Joseph Thomas, at that time on the ground staff with 8 Squadron as a member of the Indian Air Force Volunteer Reserve (IAFVR), is on record as stating that the 'atmosphere in the Squadron was not all that good. There was intense anti-British feeling. The period was 1943-44. The turmoil in Indian politics kept this hatred alive'.[32]

---

[31] This feature's potential for mayhem had been commented on long before, as far back as 30 November 1941 in fact. Moye Stephens, test pilot at the Northrop Plant, at Mines Field, Los Angeles, had written. 'Another item which was questioned was the incorporation of a small, intermediary, fuel trap tank in the fore part of the cockpit. It serves as the focal point for fuel lines from the various wing tanks. Its outlet led directly to the carburettor. At the start of my take-offs, the outlet connection developed a leak which drenched a canvas-covered dynamotor directly beneath the tank. Cutting the combination ignition and electrical system master switch (another debatable feature) was the only means of shutting down the dynamotor. It was fortunate the failure hadn't chosen to delay its appearance for a few seconds further into the flight.'

[32] Thomas, Squadron Leader Thelkethil Joseph, *Memories of No. 8 Squadron, IAF*. Veterans Project – Interviews, Profiles and Memoirs, Wing Commander Joseph Thomas. Updated 21 March 2015.

As the monsoon weather worsened from May onward, the small airstrips suffered and became almost untenable. Part of the squadron had to operate from adjacent runways with even fewer facilities and even when sorties were possible they were sometimes aborted or had to be conducted at low level. A few new and improved Vultees began arriving from the Karachi Depot toward the end and were combat tested but time was running out.

Among the final combat missions in July were those flown on the 6th and 7th. On the 6th a force comprising five Mark III and one Mk II Vengeances was led by Flight Lieutenant Carswell Niven to bomb the village of Ntiwi, Rakhine State. They took off from Cox's Bazar at 1529, as follows:

Pilot	Aircrew
Flt Lt Carswell Niven	WO George Allan
F/O Everett Ettinger	Flt Sgt John Steele RCAF
F/O Austin Buck	Flt Sgt Burrows
F/O William Hughes	F/O J. Andrews
F/O Churukara Philip	Flt Sgt George Verghese
F/O Milton Sills	WO James Conlon RAAF

The village lay on the Mayu River which empties into the Bay of Bengal above Sittwe and needed softening up as part of the Allied campaign to take Maugdaw. The weather proved good with 4/10th cumulus cloud cover at 9,000 feet but the village itself appeared deserted. Nonetheless, they knew very well that the enemy was adept at camouflage and concealment and so decided to continue with the attack. At 1600 they made 'steep dives' in from 7,500 feet down to 1,500 feet in runs from north to south.

The Mk II Vengeance dropped two 500lb GPNITIR and two 250lb NITI bombs while the other five dropped ten 500lb NITIT and ten 260lb NITI bombs, all of which were observed to explode evenly dispersed in the village. After the dive-bombing, all six-aircraft returned and conducted two low-level strafing runs, one from from east to west and then another from west to east. The unit returned to base at 1645.

Next day, and again under the command of Flight Lieutenant Niven, another six Mk III Vengeances took off from Cox's Bazar at 1450 with instructions to bomb a reported 400-strong Japanese force located in the village of Satpaung (PG 7728).

Composition of the force was as follows:

Pilot	Aircrew
Flt Lt Carswell Niven	WO George Allan
F/O William McBain	P/O Frederick Kennedy RAAF
F/O Everett Ettinger	Flt Sgt John Steele RCAF
F/O William Hughes	F/O J. Andrews
Sgt Lloyd	Sgt Jones
F/O Milton Sills	WO James Conlon RAAF

As can be seen at this latter stage 8 Squadron IAF was flying combat missions with no Indian pilots at all; the majority were Australians or Canadians: Allan, James Conlon, RAAF, Frederick Anthony Kennedy, RAAF, William Ernest McBain, Milton Ward Sills, RCAF, and John David Steele, RCAF; Carswell Niven was an Australian serving with the RAF, and J. Andrews, William Hughes, Jones and Lloyd were also RAF.

Satpaung in Chin State was a village on the east bank of the Kaladan River, south-west of Dalentine and some 200 miles south of Imphal. The Vultees arrived over the village at 1530 and found the weather clear, with 3/10th to 4/10th cloud. Target selection was for each section of three aircraft to hit one of the two groups of *bashas* and dives commenced at 9,000 feet down to a 3,000 feet release altitude. Twelve GPNITI bombs and twelve 250lb NITI bombs were dropped 'in a steep dive'. It was reported that one stick scored a direct hit on three huts, another burst slightly east of the target and the remainder burst on target in close concentration. As they withdrew they noted five or six new *bashas* on a bend in the river noting them as potential new targets. All the aircraft landed back at base at 1600.

Soon after this the squadron was withdrawn from the front having clocked up an impressive 1,420 combat sorties. The squadron was moved all the way back to Samungli, Quetta, Baluchistan, close to the Afghan border.

They were scheduled to be initially re-equipped as a Hawker Hurricane IIC unit and later became a Supermarine Spitfire squadron. Ironically, they spent most of their time dive-bombing in this iconic fighter plane. 'The spirit of the Vengeance lives on' was one final remark in their wartime ORB.

Their withdrawal from the front did not prevent further losses. One 8 Squadron RAF pilot, Flight Lieutenant Caswell Harold Niven, RAFVR, an Australian, and his Wireless Operator/Air Gunner (WOP/AG) Eric

Douglas Willcock, were killed when their Vengeance, FB956, crashed while landing at Samungli Care and Maintenance Base near Quetta, Balochistan, on 6 August.[33]

One of the last Vengeance fatalities was Flying Officer William Ernest Jay 'Boon' McBain of Winnipeg, who was killed, along with his passenger, AC1 M T Haque, on 14 August 1944 piloting FB952 on a routine local test flight after a minor inspection. According to his CO, Ira Sutherland, McBain had taken off from Quetta climbed in circles to *circa* 12,000 feet, 'about 1828m 6,000ft to 7,000 feet above ground level'. The aircraft then began a test dive and, although various eyewitness reports were described as 'conflicting' the consensus was that this dive was at a 'very steep angle.' 'The pilot must have left it late before beginning his pull out but when he did pull out he did so so violently that the aircraft assumed an almost horizontal position.' Even so, this failed to check the downward momentum and the Vengeance 'squashed' into the ground some 5,000 feet above sea level. As Sutherland wrote to McBain's mother: 'It is very sad to think that 'Boon' came through some months of operations against the Japs – during which he acquitted himself very creditably … and then be killed in an accident during a training flight.' Bitter irony indeed.

Also poignant was the fact that, as they were being withdrawn, the Vengeance I, IAs and IIs were being replaced by the far superior Vengeance IV. The latter was described to me by Britain's foremost test pilot, Captain Eric 'Winkle' Brown, thus: 'True dive-bombers like the Ju.87, the Dauntless and the Vengeance were, of course, always superior in that role to fighters adapted for dive-bombing as a secondary role.' He also told me that 'the Vengeance IV eradicated all the original faults, until it was probably the nearest in efficiency to the Ju.87.'[34] This potential was all wasted for the IAF, like its British and Australian counterparts, mainly employed them for target-towing.

It might have been very different. It was an incredible fact, but a fact nonetheless, that, as related earlier, the Mosquito killed Squadron Leader

---

[33]   AIR 28/821 IIM/FV707/1 & 1A. *21 Care & Maintenance Party, later RAF Station Samungli (CMP India), Dec 1943 – April 1945.*

[34]   Brown, Captain Eric, to the Author. See also his analysis in *Wings of the Weird and Wonderful. Vol. 2*, Airlife Publishing, Shrewsbury, 1985.

Ira Sutherland, Wing Commander Haley Charles Stumm DFC, Squadron Leader Charles Joseph Merryfield MBE, RAAF, and indeed, for a time, so many other Commonwealth pilots, that serious consideration was given to converting back to the Vengeance! Joseph O'Leary, at that date working with No. 1580 (Calibration) Flight on the Vengeance at Cholaveram, confirmed this to the author, stating that, at the end of October, 'I was sent down to Yelahanka to convert Mosquito pilots onto Vengeance (the glue panic was at its height, and it was feared the 'Mossie' would never be fit for the tropics).'[35] This policy was finally reversed again on the very day he arrived at Yelahanka, leaving him 'high and dry', but he later returned to the Vengeance III as a flight lieutenant with No. 1340 (Special Duties) Flight at Cannanore (Kannur), Kerala State, where he relieved an old acquaintance from 110 (H) Squadron days, Flight Lieutenant V.B. 'Red' McInnis.[36] This unit had formerly had a special duty as they experimented with spraying mustard gas and phosgene gas for the trials of the Chemical Defence Research Establishment for the purposes of evaluating methods of protecting our troops should the Japanese, in extremis, ever use them against us. These trials were continued even after VJ day until their full completion.

Dennis O'Leary described the set-up thus:

> I was established with a Harvard and three Vengeance Mk. IIIs. One of these, FB 986, was a veteran from one of the old Squadrons and still bore its faded letter 'M' for 'Mother' (in the old phonetics); it was my favourite as it never seemed to give any trouble. Of course, there was no question of dive-bombing on this job. Accuracy was not needed when putting gas down. All we had to do was get the stuff into quite large fields at Porkal or Kumbla (about 40 miles north up the coast where the CDRE had laid out ranges for their trials.
>
> No conventional bomb types were used. Internally we carried loads of 2 x 6-packs of 65lb tins mustard gas (square sectioned,

---

[35]   Presumably this was for those Mosquito pilots fresh out from the UK who had not had any previous experience of dive-bombing.

[36]   Flight Lieutenant V. Bud (Bohdan) 'Red' McInnis, (J 17891) from Barrie, Ontario, was a Cadet Pilot at No. 8 Service Flying Training School at Lakeburn and was awarded his wings on 27 February 1942. He served at 152 OTU and with 110 (H) Squadron before joining 1340 Flight.

very like the ubiquitous 4-gallon fuel can), and 'Chedlets' – smaller segmented things (named after the well-known packets of processed cheese, the shape of which they closely resembled).

Besides these, there were 500lb mustard gas clusters, and a 4lb bomb. An entry in my log book shows batches of 42 being dropped from 4,000ft. This was most unusual, and I cannot recall why (all other gas ordnance was dropped low-level). There was no need for any of these items to be of ballistic shape, and there were no fuses. We just dropped them, and they burst open on impact.

The cans sometimes leaked from the soldered lids and seams, and made most unpleasant cargo. The 'post-box' slot on the Vengeance cockpit floor carried up fumes from the bomb bay, so we always flew with canopies fully open, not that that was any hardship in the heat. I cannot remember any hang-ups, for the release mechanism was very simple, but even so we were always glad to get the gas canisters out of the bays. Looking back, I'm amazed at how casually we worked with this dangerous stuff … I never saw a mask worn (and we certainly didn't have any). Of course, my armourers only had to load the containers into the bays, and fit spray tanks to the wing racks.

These wing racks were a different proposition. It would be dangerous to carry the thin-skinned tins out in the airflow (and think of the drag they would cause), so spray tanks were fitted to the bomb racks. From memory, these were cylinders about 15 inches in diameter and four to five-foot long. They would hold about ten gallons. There was a spigot at the back of (and projecting below) the tanks, and a filling point in the nose. There was 'tap' arrangement: this would be very hard to design, as the original release circuit was just a simple on-off.

The solution was ingenious. There was this small circular opening at the front of the tank, and a similar one in the tail pipe. The tanks were filled with liquid gas (this was an unpleasant job), and Bakelite discs fitted into the apertures to seal them. Each disc carried a tiny explosive charge and detonator, wired up to the cockpit switch. You pressed the button, both disks exploded, the ram effect from air pressure drove all the contents out of the rear nozzle, and the rush of air 'scoured' all the gas out of the tank. That way, it would be less of a danger to my ground crew after landing, and ready for refilling by the CDRE's armourers. As with the tins, the spraying was of course done low-level.

At the end of these trials, once cleaned out, the tanks were adapted for more peaceful uses as anti-malarial sprays. McInnis was in charge between September 1944 and the spring of 1945, but when O'Leary took over the unit was experimenting with using these same containers to control mosquitoes and these trials continued until March 1946 when he was 'demobbed'.[37]

---

[37]   Dennis O'Leary to the Author 27 September 2016, 6 December 2016 and 10 May 2017.

Chapter 4

No. 45 (R) Squadron RAF

Per Ardua Surgo
(Through Difficulties, Arise.)

F ormerly a Bristol Blenheim squadron No. 45 was commanded
from 1 November 1942 by Argentinian-born Squadron Leader
Anthony Traill, RAFVR. The squadron had been operating in the
Mediterranean area in the Western Desert, Iraq and Palestine, but in March
1942 left for India, without its Blenheims. New aircraft did not arrive until
August 1942 when the squadron received Vultee Vengeance dive-bombers,
initially Mark I and II and finally Mark IIIs, which it would keep for the next
two years. With these aircraft, in July 1942, the squadron began anti-submarine patrols, operating from Cholavarum, close to Madras, and this duty
continued until 5 March 1943. During the period October to November
1942, the squadron was placed under the temporary command of Flight
Lieutenant Norman William Bayly, RAAF, while Squadron Leader Traill
was leading the detachment at Karachi (2 July to 28 October 1942), Traill
resuming command from November right through to January 1944.

In May 1943 the squadron moved to Salbani, West Bengal, nearer to
the Burmese border. From there the squadron began bombing operations
against the Japanese in Burma, performing this duty from June 1943 to July
1944. At this time the Squadron had no fewer than twenty-six Australians
on its strength including ex-12 Squadron Vengeance veterans.

The first Vengeance IA deliveries were made to the squadron in December
1942 at their base at Cholavarum. Between March and May the squadron
returned to Asanol and in May moved to Digri. There followed six months
of training. Once re-equipped with the Vengeance II things improved.

Just what was involved in re-equipping and re-training a twin-engine,
Bristol Blenheim medium-bomber-equipped squadron and preparing it for
a totally different and more efficient method of inflicting maximum damage

to the enemy can be illustrated by the trials and tribulations encountered by 45 Squadron between January and June 1943.[1]

On 30 December 1942 a section of pilots from No. 45 Squadron flew to Karachi to take delivery of five Vengeance aircraft which were ultimately destined for 84 Squadron, 45 being responsible for their initial maintenance with two to be retained on temporary loan for their own training. The detachment left for Karachi full of hope curiosity and optimistic for the future. On arrival at Drigh Road the following day those hopes were immediately dashed. They found that these aircraft were deficient in flying instruments and tool kits and Australian Flying Officer Andrew Furmage outright refused to take them on charge to the squadron. There ensued 'a serious disagreement with the Chief Technical Officer and the Station Commander ... about this state of affairs'. In the end the Vengeance were all fully kitted up as required and flown over to Karachi airport itself to join four others waiting at the Reception Centre to be taken on charge. However, on 4 January 1943 the squadron's ground crews checking out these machines reported that 'the assembly work on the aircraft was very much below standard'. On 5 January the compasses of all nine aircraft were swung and local flying was conducted on four of them, the remaining four being similarly treated the following day. After twenty-five hours flying by each of these aircraft they were to be grounded and automatically withdrawn from No. 45 Squadron's charge. On the 9th four of these Vengeances were ferried over to 319 MU for storage. Of the others two completed the allotted air time on the 11th and were grounded for a major inspection, and new piston rings had to be fitted to their engine cylinders. It was a far from auspicious start introduction to their new mount.

Meanwhile Flight Sergeant Douglas Ernest French, an experienced observer, joined from 82 Squadron and became Squadron Leader Traill's faithful companion. Wing Commander John Hugh McMichael, as the Officer Commanding Vengeance training in the squadron, flew out to Karachi on the 13th to form the Vengeance Development Flight and was joined next day by the pilots Flying Officers Andrew Hastie Furmage and Maloney, Pilot Officer George William Hartnell, RAAF, and Warrant Officer Gilbert Challans Hockley, with their respective

---

[1]   This section is largely based on the Operational Record Book of 45 Squadron, AIR 27/457.1.

rear-seat men, Flying Officer Arthur John Laney, a navigator, and Flight Sergeants Robert Montrose 'Bob' Barclay, RAAF, Thomas Lord and Reginald Wilson. By the end of January, the squadron had managed a total of forty-five hours flying time in the Vengeance. On 2 February 45 Squadron was transferred from 225 Group to 221 Group, with plans to relocate at Panagarh near Asansol. There were large numbers of Australians on strength and eight of these, Sergeant Pilots H.P. Curtis, Colin Thomas Fryar, Arthur Huon, Hugh MacClennan, Hugh Foster Shattock, Sergeant Navigator Cedric Edward Birkbeck and Wireless Operator/Air Gunner Cyril Barclay, were all promoted to flight sergeants, RAAF, on the 6th. Meanwhile, Flying Officer Karl Ernest Christensen, another pilot, had joined the squadron. Other promotions were Flying Officer Geoffrey Greer Furmage, RAAF, to flight lieutenant on the 11th and Sergeants Allan Henry Halley, RAAF, and A.H. Lebas, RCAF, to pilot officers RCAF on the 15th while two days later Flight Sergeant Douglas French, RAFVR, became a pilot officer.

Transfers now began. Three Vengeances under Warrant Officer Gilbert Challans Hockley flew to Asanol via Vizagapatam and Cuttack on the 20th and were followed by two more under Flight Sergeant Hedley Charles Jewell on the 25th and another flown by Pilot Officer A.H. Lebas next day. Total flying time on the Vengeance was seventy hours that month. When the advance parties arrived at Asanol on 1 March they found more neglect, the base was 'untidy and neglected'. Everything was left dirty and broken and the facilities had not apparently even been looked at since the last occupants had pulled out some months before. This was put to rights as best they could within a week and 168 Wing transferred their HQ from Madhaiganj to nearby RAF Camp Kundulia. That same day Squadron Leader Anthony Traill, RAFVR, with Squadron Leader Dennis Gibbs, the CO of 82 Squadron, as his passenger, also flew to Asanol, leaving Pilot Officer Keel in temporary command of 45 Squadron until the transfer had been completed. This was done on the 6th when Flying Officer Poul Ulrik Keel, RAFVR, with Flying Officer George George and Flight Sergeant J. Hadley, and Sergeant Arthur Field, RAAF, flew the last two aircraft across.

Two days later a party comprising Flight Lieutenant Herbert Wilson, Flying Officers Kelly, (the squadron doctor), Pilot Officer George Hartnell, with Vultee Technical Representative Mr Jones[2] and the main party left Cholavarum for Asanol while Flying Officer Donald Edwards and Sergeant Worrall were despatched to 312 MU at Cochin to get whatever Vengeance spares they could rustle up. The return of a Japanese Navy task force to the Indian Ocean, even if doubtful at this time, was always something the dive-bombers had to reckon on as a possible target, and on 8 March Pilot Officer D. French was sent to the GR School at Aridheri, Bombay, for a warship recognition course; others from the various Vengeance squadrons also attended at this time.

No. 45 Squadron logged the first of what was to prove several minor accidents with their new aircraft on 11 March, an aircraft swing on take-off and her pilot was unable to correct the swing. The Vultee ended up in a ditch alongside the runway, damaging the starboard main plane and oleo leg, but both aircrew were unharmed. There were also further promotions, on the return of Squadron Leader Traill from leave: Flying Officer Poul Ulrik Keel, RAFVR, became a flight lieutenant and OC A Flight. More Australian flight sergeant navigators became warrant officers RAAF, Lenin Charlton, Ernest James Hallett, Denys Arthur Golder and R. Southern. On the 18th Edwards and Worrall returned with all the spare parts they had been sent for and were full of praise for the help and co-operation they had received from 312 MU in the process.

Better news was received the next day, a signal from AHQ Bengal informing the squadron that they were to collect sixteen of the fully modified Vengeance IAs from Karachi in three batches of four aircraft at a time and that these would replace existing aircraft which were to be sent to 320 MU. Accordingly, Flight Lieutenants Andrew Furmage and Vernon James Hedley, Hedley Charles Jewell, Flight Sergeant Brown and Sergeant F. Terry were sent off to Karachi for the first transfer. Another pilot, Pilot Officer Maurice Gordon Fountain, MIERE, joined the squadron the same day. On the 25th Flight Sergeant H. Curtis with Flight Sergeant John Brinkley as his rear-seat men was also despatched and Warrant Officer W. Donald 'Doc' Osborne, Flight Sergeant Arthur Neville Huon and J. Hadley and Flying Officer S. Matthews, RNZAF, all pilots followed, with Sergeant A. Field, Flight Sergeant Cedric Edward Birbeck, H. Garfath and Flight Sergeant G.F. Williams.

---

[2]   The other attached Vultee Technical Representative was Mr Spencer J. Leech.

Three of the new Vengeances arrived back at base on the 29th, crewed by Halley/Hallett, Jewell/Terry and Howat/Stone with next day three more crewed by Furmage/Barclay, Neil/Brown and Curtis/Brinkley and being joined on 2 April by two more, with Warrant Officer W.M. Osborne and Flight Sergeant Arthur Field, RAAF, and Sergeant S.C. Matthews with Flight Sergeant G.F. Williams. These welcome additions were rather offset by another accident on the 8th: one aircraft, attempting to land in a strong cross-wind, saw he was drifting too much and opened up to go around for another try. On his second approach he overshot and continued his landing into labourers and equipment which were employed extending the runway. The Vengeance ended up on her nose but with nothing more serious than a buckled airscrew. Next day, on conclusion of bombing practice on the range, another Vengeance, flying low to communicate with the range party on the ground, flew into a tree and damaged the port main plane. A further pair of IAs was flown over to the squadron from Karachi by ANC pilots on the 12th while the 13th saw the arrival of the first Vengeance II, flown in by Warrant Officer Gilbert Hockley and Flight Sergeant Thomas Albert Lord.

With regard to personnel matter Flight Lieutenant Herbert Harman Wilson became the new adjutant on the 14th and Pilot Officer Donald Stuart Edwards was promoted to flying officer on the 12th, with Flight Sergeants Curtis, Colin Fryar, Hunt, Hugh Neil and Foster Philips Shattock all becoming warrant officers on the 9th. Five more new aircraft were required to bring the squadron up to its full strength of sixteen machines, but further problems were encountered when Pilot Officers Allan Halley and Lebas, Warrant Officers Arthur Huon, Foster Shattock and Sergeant J. Howat were despatched to 320 MU to fetch them, but they were refused as that unit stated that the Vengeances supplied for 110 Squadron earlier were a 45 Squadron allotment! More problems arose when the bombing range at Nadiha on the River Damodar, which had been used in March, was put out of bounds and not to be used at all. It had been extended and this work was completed, but, as the work had not been officially approved, AHQ Delhi banned its use. It was pointed out that three Vengeance squadrons, 45, 82 and 110, were all using the one single range at Silampur and there was considerable congestion which led to delays in completing training programmes.

Another accident added to their woes, Flying Officer Poul Ulrik Keel and Flying Officer George George were returning from a formation exercise and made a normal approach and touch-down. As the aircraft's wheels touched the runway the starboard main wheel immediately started spinning horizontally outside of the oleo-leg. The pilot instantly corrected a violent tendency to ground-loop and the aircraft finally came to rest some full yards off the runway, having racked up on its nose then back to three points. On inspection it was found that the bracket which keeps the main wheel in a fore-and-aft position had sheered through completely, thus leaving the wheel to spin. It was not that this could have caused a serious accident, but, due to the pilot's 'steady and immediate action' there were no injuries.

On top of all this the INA (Indian National Army) added their petty two pennies' worth and on the 26th ten of these subversives were arrested for attempting to steal aircraft fuel and sabotage the aircraft on the base. But the build-up continued despite it all, and another new Vengeance arrived on the 28th, flown again by an ARC pilot, and the squadron clocked-up 150 hours Vengeance flying time during April, On 5 May Pilot Officer A.H. Lebas, RCAF, and Warrant Officer Foster Shattock flew in two more Vengeance IIs from Karachi. Further Australian promotions were Warrant Officer J. Vernon, a navigator, and Flight Sergeant John Brinkley to pilot officers in the RAAF, Pilot Officer George Hartnell to flying officer, Warrant Officer Arthur Huon (pilot) and Ernest Hallett (navigator) and Flight Sergeant Clark all to pilot officers RAAF. On the 15th two more Aussies became flying officers, RAAF, Curtis and Poul Keel. On the 17th four Vengeances of A Flight left for Dighri and two days later four from B Flight arrived from Asanol. Air-to-air firing practice was conducted at the Ramnagar Bombing Range from the 22nd and, two days later, Pilot Officers Robert Barclay and Arthur Lamb with eight sergeants left for Karachi to ferry more Mark IIs back to base. Flying Officer Robert Alfred Turton, RNZAF, a navigator, was another addition to the team.[3]

The tempo was increasing now and Squadron Leader Traill led six Vengeances to Alipore to conduct fighter affiliation exercises with five of No. 615 Squadron's Hurricanes on the 27th and with Nos. 17 and 607 Hurricanes the following day. Some 151 Vengeance flying hours were

---

[3]   Sadly, he was transferred to a Mosquito squadron and, eleven days later, on 2 November 1943, he was killed when his aircraft broke up in mid-air just south of Kyaungyi Village. His memorial is at the Taukkyan War Cemetery, Rangoon.

racked up that month. It was noted that 'Ten selected aircrews' were being brought up to operational standard as quickly as possible, ready for combat. This was delayed by modifications to the wing guns, but these were almost completed. These ten aircrew were almost ready by 2 June and at this time full operational bomb-loads were being carried. Further fighter affiliation took place with 17 Squadron on the 8th and next day 45 Squadron was told by 221 AHQ that it 'is to be on the top line' ready to take over combat from 82 Squadron at Chittagong shortly. On the 10th/11th Squadron Leader Traill and Flying Officer Edwards flew to Chittagong to arrange for the operational detachment to move forward and on the 16th the modifications to the .300 machine-gun mountings were completed and fitted to all the Vengeance aircraft 'standing by' for operations. Trials of these mountings took place the following day and it was noted that there was now 'very little tendency' for the guns to move in their new mountings.

The twenty-first formation flying practice was conducted by six Vengeances and finalised by dives down toward the base runway itself. 'From the ground the dives appeared to be excellent, achieving angles between 80^0 and 90^0.' A signal from AHQ 221 advised that eight Vengeances should be detached to Chittagong on 26 June and on the 24th of the month Flying Officer Christiansen with Flight Sergeant Robert Douglas Hilditch, as his WOp/AG left for Chittagong as the advance party, being followed by Pilot Officer Arthur Huon, Flying Officer Cyril Birbeck, Neil and Pilot Officer Brown and Flying Officer Donald Edwards with the maintenance party. Back at base the ground crews worked late into the night to ensure all the aircraft were ready.

On the 27th the first seven of 45 Squadron's Vengeance IIs left for battle, 'the first operation since the raid on Mingalawon on 21st March 1942'. It had been a long haul but now 45 was ready. The composition of the force for the flight to Chittagong was as listed below:

Aircraft	Pilot	Aircrew
AN 618	Sqn Ldr Anthony Traill	P/O Douglas French
EZ 844	P/O R. Curtis	P/O John Brinkley
EZ 843	P/O Allan Halley RAAF	P/O E. Hallet (Navigator)
EZ 848	WO Gilbert Hockley	Flt Sgt A. Field
AN 621	WO W.M. Osborne	Flt Sgt Thomas Lord
AN 626	Flt Sgt Hedley Jewell	Sgt F. Terry

Aircraft	Pilot	Aircrew
EZ 847	Flt Sgt S. C. Matthews	P/O G.F. Williams
EZ 850	F/O Karl Ernest Christensen	Flt Sgt Robert Hilditch

The detachment took a course from Dighri via Kulna to Chittagong, arriving safely. The following day, 27 June, the first of 45 Squadron's Vengeance combat operations took place. They were given an escort of ten Hawker Hurricane IICs from 261 Squadron, commanded by Squadron Leader Cyril Frank Counter DFC, RAFVR, for this mission. Their target was Akyab town and they took off at 1330, taking a route from Cox's Bazar via Oyster Island. They found the weather difficult, 'very bad monsoon conditions over land', but on reaching Akyab island itself they found it clear of cloud. The actual strike forces was made up as follows:

Aircraft	Pilot	Aircrew
AN 618	Sqn Ldr Anthony Traill	P/O Douglas French
EZ 647	Flt Sgt Hedley Jewell	Sgt F. Terry
EZ 648	WO W.M. Osborne	Flt Sgt Arthur Field RAAF
EZ 650	F/O Karl Ernest Christensen	Flt Sgt Robert Hilditch
EZ 644	F/O R. Curtis	F/O John Brinkley
AN 621	WO Gilbert Hockley	Flt Sgt Thomas Lord
AN 626	P/O Allan Halley (Spare)	P/O Ernest Hallett

At 1430 the Vengeances peeled off from 9,000 feet and made their dives from south to north down to bomb release height of 2,000 feet, making a low-level escape. They were met by a small amount of heavy-calibre flak. All the aircraft bombed although Traill's initial bomb detonations obscured the aiming point and the following aircraft had to bomb into the smoke rising from the target. All aircraft had landed back safe and sound at 1545.

The result was summarised in a signal from AHQ Delhi, dated 29 June: 'Am very glad to see that 45 Squadron have come back into force against Japanese. First operation appears very successful. Good Luck and good hunting.'

A second operation followed the next day with the target being designated as *kutchas*[4] buildings at the north ends of two lakes south of Myohaung on the main road south. The sortie was composed of the following aircrew:

---

[4]   *kutcha* = large huts built of mud bricks.

Aircraft	Pilot	Aircrew
AN 618	Sqn Ldr Anthony Traill	P/O Douglas French RAFVR.
EZ 847	Flt Sgt Hedley Jewell	Sgt F. Terry
EZ 843	P/O Allan Halley	P/O Ernest Hallett
EZ 850	F/O Karl Ernest Christensen	Flt Sgt Robert Hilditch
EZ 848	WO W.M. Osborne	Flt Sgt Arthur Field
AN 621	WO Gilbert Hockley	Flt Sgt Thomas Lord
EZ 844	P/O R. Curtis (Spare)	P/O John Brinkley

Twelve Hawker Hurricane IICs from 261 Squadron were made available as fighter escort but, as usual, no aerial opposition was met. They took off at 0845 and followed an outward route from Cox's Bazar via the Naf peninsula to Myohaung down the main Teknaf highway. This close to the monsoon season the weather was bad, with 10/10th cover from ground level up to 8,000 feet all the way down. There was a gap in this morass which extended a few miles up the Kaladan river. The attack went in as planned and ten 500lb GP, NETD (Nose-extended, time delayed) bombs with .025-second delay were dropped, all of which fell in the target area and two demolishing buildings at the northern tip of western lake. The Vengeance climbed back up to 10,000 feet to avoid the cloud cover for their return journey, all arriving back at base at 1050.

A third attack was mounted on 29 June, the target again being Myohaung where concentrations of enemy troops were observed at a building to the south of the settlement. *Kutcha* buildings close to the previous attack zone of the 27th were the assigned targets on this occasion. The formation was thus:

Aircraft	Pilot	Aircrew
AN 618	Sqn Ldr Anthony Traill	P/O Douglas French RAFVR
EZ 848	Flt Sgt Hedley Jewell	Sgt F. Terry
AN 621	WO Gilbert Hockley	Flt Sgt Thomas Lord
EZ 848	WO W.M. Osborne	Flt Sgt A. Field
EZ 844	P/O R. Curtis	P/O John Brinkley
AN 626	P/O Allan Halley	P/O Ernest Hallett
EZ 843	P/O Hugh Martin Neil	P/O F. Brown

Departure was taken at 0710 and once more 261 Squadron provided a ten-Hurricane escort and the Vengeances operated in two four-plane boxes.

This time, however, the weather beat them, the weather over the Naf peninsula remained bad and the whole sortie had to be aborted with the bomb loads of sixteen 500lb GP NITD .025, having to be brought back to base. The aircraft, nonetheless, became separated and while Anthony Traill landed at 0840 and Gilbert Charles Hockley and Hugh Martin Neil at 0855, the others straggled in over the next quarter of an hour, but all landed safely.

On 30 June they were assigned the same target again with eight Vengeances being deployed as below:

Aircraft	Pilot	Aircrew
AN 618	Sqn Ldr Anthony Traill	P/O Douglas French RAFVR
EZ 847	Flt Sgt Hedley Jewell	Sgt F. Terry
AN 621	WO Gilbert Hockley	Flt Sgt Thomas Lord
EZ 845	WO W.M. Osborne	Flt Sgt A. Field
EZ 848	P/O Hugh Neil	P/O F. Brown
EZ 850	F/O Karl Ernest Christensen	Flt Sgt Robert Hilditch
EZ 844	P/O R. Curtis	P/O John Brinkley
AN 626	P/O Allan Halley	P/O Ernest Hallett

All eight Vengeances took off at 0700, again in two four-plane boxes, protected by seven Hurricanes from No. 67 Squadron. This time they attempted an alternate route but again found 10/10th cloud cover with a base from 3,000 to 4,000 feet. They found a gap over the Kaladan river some ten miles north of their objective but were able to dive-bomb from 4,000 feet down to a release height of 1,500 feet. This time 'Very successful results' were recorded. The first box concentrated their attentions on buildings at the north tip of the west lake, while the second quartet hit two 100-foot buildings on the west bank of the eastern lake. They were met by accurate small-arms fire, one Vengeance having her elevator holed and aerial cut, but the buildings 'were seen to disintegrate after direct hits and the two larger ones were damaged by near-misses'. One aircraft suffered a bomb hang-up. Once more, having completed the attack, they had to climb above the murk in order to steer a course for home, all getting down safely between 0900 and 0915. The verdict was that, for operational purposes, two four-plane boxes was more efficient than one six-plane box.

Daily sorties continued, but the weather was almost always poor, and some missions had to be aborted because of it. The 1st of July saw eight

Vengeances, with an escort of ten 261 Squadron Hurricanes, taking off at 0740 to dive-bomb Japanese storage buildings in the northern end of Akyab Tow. Fourteen bomb bursts were observed on various buildings in the target area and the aircraft were back at base by 0940. A second sortie was sent away at 1150, with six dive-bombers with a nine-Hurricane escort. One bomb 'hung up' on Vengeance 'E' during her dive, but all the rest were planted into *busti* huts at Mawnubyin and Khadnbaik on Akyab Island and all planes were safely home by 1400. On the 2nd a raid by eight Vengeance with eight Hurricanes of 67 Squadron as escorts, left at 0720. Their target was the Narigan Bridge on Akyab Island, but this was 'weathered out' and the force returned without making any attack at 0940. It was a similar story on 7 July, when six Vengeances with eight 67 Squadron Hurricanes attempted to dive-bomb more huts at Thaungdara, with buildings at Buthidaung being the secondary target. Although the main target was picked out through a gap in the clouds, no attack was delivered and, likewise, the alternative target was by-passed due to poor visibility. A second attempt was made at 1605 the same day, with seven Vengeances escorted by nine Hurricanes; this time they were able to complete the dive-bombing of Thaungdara with all bombs falling in the target area and starting a fire. All aircraft returned at 1800.

On 8 July 261 Squadron Hurricanes again escorted 45 Squadron Vengeances who dive-bombed enemy storage facilities at Buthidaung with all the bombs falling amidst the buildings and one large storage facility receiving a direct hit. Their escorts lost one Hurricane in the Buthidaung area, but all Vengeances returned safely to Chittagong at 1245. A further eight Vultees were sent off to attack Thrungdara once more, with eight escorting Hurricanes from 261 Squadron. Fourteen bombs were observed to burst in the village, with direct hits being made on buildings starting first with grey smoke, and all aircraft returned safely at 1655. The following day at 0545 six 45 Squadron Vengeances returned once more to Maungdaw, covered by seven of 67 Squadron's Hurricanes, and delivered ten 500lb GP bombs into the target area, once more scoring several direct hits. A different target occupied the attentions of two of 45 Squadron's aircraft late that day, when, along with four of 67 Squadron's Hurricanes, they were sent to destroy a PRU Spitfire that had crashed on the beach at Alethangyaung. They hoped to destroy its cameras and other top-secret equipment before the enemy could strip them out and examine them. The raid was made but neither Vengeance scored a direct hit on the crash-landed Spit, so a second attempt was made with two more dive-bombers, crewed respectively by Squadron Leader Traill/Pilot Officer French and Flight Sergeant Hedley Jewell/ Sergeant F. Terry, taking off at 1600 that day. They were armed with four 250lb bombs with NITD Rods and four 250lb bombs with eleven-second time-delay. Seven bombs fell within twenty yards of the target, which was surrounded by Japanese troops, while one delayed-action bomb was observed to go right through the Spitfire's fuselage before exploding and this was deemed to have caused enough damage to ensure the secret equipment was unsalvageable. A rough body count estimated at least 120 Japanese were killed in these two attacks. This success was attained even though the weather was 10/10 at 700 feet, with rain and visibility in the rain down to 1,000 yards. All aircraft were back at base by 1800.

The 10th of July saw eight Vengeances with six Hurricanes from 261 Squadron taking off from Chittagong at 0705 to attack and hopefully breach the *Bund* (embankment) of the Royal Lake at Akyab, used by the Japanese to offload war supplies. As such, it was well defended by flak. The secondary target was again Buthidaung. They took route 170 degrees over the Mayu peninsula and thence to the target, but EZ 841 (Pilot Officer Arthur Huon and Pilot Officer Cedric Birkbeck) was forced to return to base within five minutes due to engine trouble. The remaining seven Vengeances dive-bombed from 8,000 feet down to 2,000 feet at 0820, dropping fourteen 500lb GP NITD .025 bombs. Unfortunately, no direct hits were scored, and the *bund* remained intact. The Japanese heavy AA bursts were inaccurate for both height and direction and caused no problems, while the 20mm light flak, including red tracer, was heavy from the northern end of the north-to-south runway of Akyab airfield in the vicinity; a Bofors-type 40mm located in a clump of trees at Kaungdaga placed accurate bursts with ten-fifteen yards of the boxes.

The detachment's final sortie during the Akyab Offensive took place on 11 July. The composition of this strike was thus:

Aircraft	Pilot	Aircrew
AN 618	Sqn Ldr Anthony Traill	P/O Douglas French
EZ 847	Warrant Officer W.M. Osborne	Flt Sgt A .Field
EZ 865	Flt Sgt S. Matthews	P/O G.F. Williams

Aircraft	Pilot	Aircrew
EZ 851	F/O George Hartnell, RAAF	Flt Lt Arthur John Laney
AN 626	P/O R. Curtis	P/O John Brinkley
EZ 849	Sgt J. Howat	F/O George George

Once more 67 Squadron provided six Hurricanes as escorts, and once again they were not required. Take-off was at 0815 and they took the most direct route to their target which was a large Japanese storage building at Minbya, with Buthidaung as the secondary target. They encountered a layer of cloud over the river at 0930 which meant that they could not visually pinpoint the storage building itself, but they made dives from 8,000 feet through thin cloud and deposited eight 500lb GP NITD 025 bombs into the direct target zone. Those that dropped were unable to observe specific results while Flight Sergeant Matthews could not find an aiming point and took his bombs back to base. In addition, Pilot Officer Curtis was forced to re-land at Chittagong in AN 626 after ten minutes with engine problems but took off again, determined to make the mission, and arrived over the target alone at 0945, diving down from 3,000 feet and scoring direct hits on three red-roofed buildings. He was also able to note extensive damage to other buildings done from both this day's and previous days' bombings. The weather was 9/10th cumulus cover from a base of 4,000 feet up to 7,000 feet. All aircraft had returned safely to Chittagong by 1045.

The monsoon had now set in and, on 14 July, 45 Squadron's detachments was withdrawn, making the flight back to base between 1125 and 1325.

In the interim, back at Chittagong, under the temporary command of Flight Lieutenant Norman William Bayly, RAAF, with Navigator Flying Officer George George as acting flight commander of both A and B Flights,[5] the rest of the squadron was continuing to train and refit, when the weather permitted for on several days the rain was so heavy and continuous that operations were severely curtailed. It did not matter initially because on 6 July it was reported that one of 82 Squadron's Vengeance aircraft had been found to have a weakness in the construction of her boost tab, with the result that Flight Lieutenant Davis, the Engineering Officer of 168

---

5   The arrival on 8 July of Flight Lieutenant John Hunter Stevenson, RAAF, from 82 Squadron, eased the situation as he became one flight commander.

Wing, grounded all the Vultees until they had been modified to overcome the weakness. By the 8th the modification was completed and the aircraft air-tested satisfactorily. The next day a conference was held with Wing Commander Robert Findlay Boyd, the CO of 168 Wing, with Squadron Leader Lionel George Marten (Admin) and Squadron Leader Daniel Cecil Richmond Rouse Jenkins RAFVR (Senior Medical Officer) 168 Wing, along with Flight Lieutenants Norman William Bayly and Rodney Charles Topley, acting COs of 45 and 110 Squadrons, on adjusting working hours to aid in maximising conditions for the ground staff's health. On the days when bombing practice was practical at the Silampur Range, inevitably dive-bombing had to be replaced by low-level bombing until the weather improved.

One experiment that 45 Squadron did initiate at this period was the testing of SCI canisters.[6] These cylinders were fitted with aluminium front and rear fairings to give streamlining and minimise drag and had a long discharge pipe with a Bakelite plug. Smoke-laying was a problem but as long ago as the 1920s a more sinister role was contemplated, spraying poison gas on enemy troops, and experiments with harmless emissions had taken place pre-war. Orders for 500 of these devices had been placed in 1938 and they were tested in August of that year. Eventually ten times that number were produced. They had an overall length of 7-feet 9-inches, excluding the discharge pipe, and were ultimately live tested in the Gold Cost (now Ghana) by 110 Squadron, as related later. (See Jefford, Wing Commander Clive Graham 'Jeff' – *The SCI* – article in RAF Historical Society *Journal* No. 45, 2009: Witney, Oxford. The Windrush Group).

On 28 July Flight Sergeant Hedley Jewell, with Major A.R. James of the South African Air Force as his aircrew, commenced experiments with the SCI. It was noted that 'It is proposed to carry out experiments with the aid of SCI experts to determine whether or not these canisters can be dropped from a Vengeance aircraft in a ninety-degree dive.' The following day Squadron Leader Anthony Traill and Group Captain James Barclay Black DFC, the CO of 168 Wing, conducted further tests. It was found that the canister could be safely deployed from a Vengeance in a 45-degree dive.

---

6   SCI = Installation, Smoke Curtain, which was a 250lb, fully-lagged, mild-steel cylinder mounted on the universal bomb carrier (UBC) beneath the wings.

The months of August and September were largely 'washed out' by the weather; even training was continually disrupted by the low cloud and endless rain. Some squadron activity was conducted of course, and another detachment was made, this time to Ranchi to undertake training in Army Co-operation from 16 August. The 45 Squadron pilots sent included Flying Officers Ronald Parker, Douglas Ernest French, George William Hartnell, Arthur Neville Huon, James Reginald Vernon, RAAF, and G.F. Williams; Pilot Officers Cedric Edward Birbeck, RAAF, John Brinkley, A.H. Lebas, RCAF, Jack Nankervis, RAAF, Warrant Officer W.M. Osborne; Flight Sergeant Arthur Field, R.H. Edwards, Hedley Jewell, S.C. Matthews, William McBain; and J. Hadley and Allen G. Terry. Squadron Leader Anthony Traill flew Group Captain James Black, from 221 Group, over to visit them on the 20th, leaving Flight Lieutenant John Hunter Stevenson in temporary command. They commenced the training with Army Captain Charles Evans Darlington as their liaison officer. This officer had been the district commissioner for the Hukawng area before the war, and knew the territory intimately. He was to have imparted his local knowledge to the Vengeance crews, which would have invaluable, but unfortunately Air HQ ordered the curtailment of this work on the 23rd.

Instead, on 30 August the Command Tactics Officer, Wing Commander Stephen Claude Alfred Stephen Clause Alfred Leathers, and Wing Commander Patrick Edward Meagher, Air I of 221 Group for a conference in Calcutta to discuss Vengeance tactics with the OC 168 Wing and the commanding officers and flight commanders of both 45 and 110 Squadrons and also of 5 (Hurricane) Squadron. As a result, a programme of Tactical Trials was decided upon, to be commenced immediately. Target Indication experiments were initiated with three Vengeances flying with Army officers as aircrew for their own air experience and target identification from various heights to show them the problems from the air. There were also practice bombings (mainly low-level due to the weather) in conjunction with the 4th/1st Gurkha Rifles against tanks, Bren-gun carriers, Bofors guns and motor transport targets.

From 1 September also Vultees from Digri tried out various formation flights; eleven Vengeances in two boxes of four and one of three, were attacked twice by the usual trigger-happy Americans that day, once by a Lockheed P-38 Lightning fighter and then again, while they were circling to land, the three aircraft box was shot at by a Consolidated B-24 Liberator.[7] As result of such experiments it was decided to adopt the six-plane box rather than the four. But the atrocious conditions curtailed many experiments. From the 16th there were many lectures on chemical warfare delivered by Captain Gorfinkel of the South African Air Force and trials were conducted with three Vengeances in this, and by four Vengeances dive-bombing while four others simulated chemical attacks. But during these two months there was very little flying recorded.

On the final day of September, it was announced that a detachment was to be sent to Ranchi and an advance partly under Pilot Officer Allen Halley was despatched thither. On 1 October eight Vengeance Is flew over to Ranchi, as listed herewith:

Aircraft	Pilot	Aircrew
EZ 898	Flt Lt John Stevenson	Flt Sgt Sidney Siddle
EZ 847	F/O Ronald Curtis	F/O John Brinkley
EZ 835	P/O Arthur Lamb	Flt Sgt J. Paterson
EZ 828	P/O Gilbert Hockley	F/O Ernest Hallett RAAF
EZ 843	Flt Sgt S.C. Matthews	F/O Flying Officer G.F. Williams
EZ 851	F/O Hugh Neil	F/O James Vernon RAAF
EZ 865	Sgt J. Howat	Sgt Charles Romans
EZ 848	WO W.M. Osborne	Flt Sgt Arthur Field

The detachment's Main Party, under Flying Officer John Ernest Arnold, arrived on 2 October and next day three of these carried out a low-level 'shoot-up', with both front and rear guns, of the Army Battle Craft School, along with a *vic* from 84 Squadron. Further exercises followed: the 4th saw an exact replica of a Japanese pillbox, of the type used in the Arakan, dive-bombed by three aircraft from 11,000 feet down to 5,000 feet (ASL), the target height being 2,000 feet (ASL). Six 500lb GP Mk IV NITI bombs were dropped but there were zero direct hits; the closest they came was forty yards distant and, not unexpectedly, the pillbox was undamaged. There was obviously much more to do. There was a live bombs exercise flown against a hill feature in co-operation with the Army, but again results

---

[7]   Consolidated had absorbed Vultee by this time, but being built by the same company did not prevent such 'blue-on-blue' mishaps.

were unimpressive; all the bombs struck the hill but none the brow, which was the intended aiming point. Another exercise was conducted on the 6th with four aircraft but one had to land early after the attack due to a petrol leak. It was not a good introduction.

Meanwhile, between October 1943 and February 1944, the main squadron was re- located to Kumbhirgram. Squadron Leader Anthony Traill flew to the detachment at Ranchi and then went on a brief period of leave, his place being taken by Flying Officer George Hartnell during this time, while Pilot Officer Philip Crossley DFC joined the squadron from Amarda Road. Group Captain James Barclay Black DFC, the Commanding Officer of 168 Wing, made his first flight in a Vengeance on the 6th and three crews conducted dive-bombing practice but on this day Sergeant Charles Howard Romans and Flight Sergeant James Hay Tough Howat were both unfortunately killed in a flying accident. The 8th of the month saw a signal from 221 Group Headquarters, advising 82 Squadron that they must be prepared to move to Kumbhirgram at short notice and that the Ranchi detachment be recalled 'forthwith'. The only serviceable aircraft of the three at Ranchi re-joined on the 9th, leaving the other pair to be put back in service and catch up as soon as they could; Flight Lieutenant John Stevenson assumed temporary command of the squadron. On the 11th seven Vengeances, along with a Dakota transport plane, flew to Kumbhirgram.

The first of the new Mark II Vengeances were ready for delivery and were flown in to Digri on the 14th, with another following the day after and four more flying straight to Kumbhirgram itself. At that airfield an advance party of six Vengeances were on stand-by ready for combat operations from the 14th but their first call did not come until two days later when, led by Flight Lieutenant John Stevenson, they took off at 1047 to hit stores and an enemy headquarters at Kalemyo. Despite cloud cover the attack was duly delivered at 1140 with dives from 12,000 feet down to 3,500 feet and ten 500lb GP NITI bombs were dropped, at least seven of which were seen to detonate in the target area. Vengeance EZ 900, crewed by Pilot Officer Hedley Jewell and Sergeant Allen G. Terry, failed to release at the time, but was instead delivered into an alternative target from a height of 5,000 feet at Hpannyeik. The formation returned to base at 1236.

Meanwhile Squadron Leader Anthony Traill, his leave interrupted, had arrived back in the squadron.

On the 17th the detachment again was briefed and ready to attack Japanese store dumps and possible troop concentrations at Mawlaik (Pinpoint RP 9423) from 0800 this day but bad weather first delayed and then caused the operation to be called off. But it was back on for the 18th and the six Vultee dive-bombers, again led by Flight Lieutenant John Stevenson, left Kumbhirgram at 0855 to complete the mission. They left base at 0855 and made their attack at 0942, diving from 11,000 feet down to 4,000 feet and dropping twelve 500lb GPNITI bombs, of which at least nine fell in the target zone, causing fires and leaving it covered in a pall of smoke. They landed back at 1032.

Meanwhile Squadron Leader Traill flew to Imphal and, from 1041, held a consultation with Group Captain Herbert Seaton Broughall MC DFC, a Canadian-born RAF officer, from 170 Wing and conducted a pathfinding exercise with Curtiss Mohawk fighters of No. 155 Squadron. Traill recorded: 'The Mohawk pilots after many operations covering the area, know the location of many targets which are likely to be given to No. 45 Squadron and many of these targets are invisible from the air.'[8]

It was decided to combat-trial this method as soon as possible and assess its merits or otherwise as soon as conditions allowed. Meanwhile, on 20 October, Squadron Leader Traill led six Vengeances from Kumbhirgram and bombed Myo-Hia, (Pinpoint RU 505647). One Vengeance, EZ 900 with Flying Officers Ronald Curtis and John Brinkley as aircrew, was forced to return at 1211 with due to a leaky filler cap. Two Mohawks acted as target markers, but their smoke could not be picked out by the dive-bombers, partly due to cloud. They nonetheless visually identified it for themselves and all ten bombs fell in and around the assigned area, while strafing was also done. There was no opposition. Meanwhile the main party was arriving from Digri and unloading supplies and equipment.

On 22 October Squadron Leader Anthony Traill led six Vengeances from base at 0958, but once more one aircraft, EZ 851 with Flying Officers Hugh Neil and F.F. Brown as crew, had to turn back early at 1011 with undercarriage problems. The remaining five machines proceeded and duly carried out the dive-bombing attack on Japanese troops and supplies at Kalewa (Pinpoint RU 8268). They met some anti-aircraft fire but were untroubled by it and

---

8   AIR 27/457/5.

the target and buildings along the Kalewa to Kalaymyo Road were also machine-gunned.

On the 24th Flight Lieutenant John Stevenson took six Vengeances to conduct an army close support mission and strike at enemy troops on the Vowmalumual Summit (Pinpoint RU 313705). The force contained both Mk IA and the new Mark II Vengeance and was disposed thus:

Aircraft	Type	Pilot	Aircrew
EZ 898	Mk II	Flt Lt John Stevenson	Flt Sgt Sidney Siddle
EZ 851	Mk II	F/O H.M. Bell RCAF	F/O F.F. Brown
EZ 850	Mk II	F/O Ronald Curtis	F/O John Brinkley
AN 617	Mk IA	P/O Gilbert Hockley	F/O Thomas Lord
AN 625	Mk IA	P/O Arthur Lamb	P/O Robert Hilditch RAAF
AN 711	Mk IA	Flt Sgt J. Marshall	Flt Sgt J. Paterson

Unfortunately, due to very bad weather conditions and the close proximity of the Allied forces, target identification was crucial but proved impossible to be certain and so, at 1515, they instead attacked the alternative target of Pyinthazeik, hitting with ten 500lb bombs. The departing planes left behind a column of blue smoke that was visible for five miles.

On the 25th Squadron Leader Anthony Traill led six Vengeances, with two of 155 Squadron's Mohawks as pathfinders, from base and conducted a precision attack on the enemy positions at Pinpoint RU 346685. This experiment had unforeseen and adverse results. While 45 Squadron's attack was adjudged 'very successful' in bombing the indicated target, 110 Squadron, which was co-operating in the trial, mistook ground fire for target indication smoke from the Mohawks and delivered their bomb loads into an area where hand-to-hand fighting was in progress, with resultant casualties on both sides.

At 1518 another six-plane box, under the command of Flying Officer George Hartnell, left to strike Japanese positions and stores at Webula (Pinpoint RU 3845) but this area was 'weathered out' so once more an alternative target was hit, this being enemy positions at Ngapa (Pinpoint RU 5440), which they bombed at 1535. Accurate bombing was observed from the five Vengeances which attacked, and they left the village under a pall of smoke visible from twenty-five miles away. Vengeance AN 711, with Flight Sergeants J. Marshal and J. Paterson as her crew, did not attack due to bombs 'hanging up'.

On the 26th Squadron Leader Anthony Traill and Flight Lieutenant Rodney Charles Topley DFC, the acting commanding officer of 110 Squadron, flew to Imphal to attend analysis of the previous day's misfortune at the HQ of 150 Wing, under which 45 Squadron was operating at the time. The result of these deliberations was that the decision was made to discontinue, with immediate effect, the use of 155 Squadron's Mohawks at pathfinders. In Traill's absence Flight Lieutenant John Stevenson led six Vengeances off at 1432 and, at 1535, struck at troops and stores at Webula which had been the objective of the previous day's mission. Direct hits on one building were seen but AN 625, crewed by Pilot Officers Arthur Lamb and Robert Douglas Hilditch RAAF, were unable to bomb because the bomb-release button had 'fallen off' during the outward track, so she brought her cargo home with her, but in a defused condition.

The 28th saw a six-plane strike launched at 0830 but their target, No. 2 Stockade, was obscured by thick cloud and they returned to base with their bombs at 1010. The following morning Flight Lieutenant Stevenson took nine Vengeances from Kumbhirgram at 0940 to attack a Japanese company of troops and a headquarters building near to Hata (RU 3514) the actual point of attack being 4702 (RU 3212).

This force was made up of the following:

Aircraft	Type	Pilot	Aircrew
EZ 898	IA	Flt Lt John Stevenson	Flt Sgt Sidney Siddle
EZ 851	IA	P/O Hugh Neil	F/O F.F. Brown
EZ 850	IA	F/O Ronald Curtis	WO John Brinkley
EZ 848	IA	WO W.M. Osborne	Flt Sgt Arthur Field
EZ 900	IA	F/O Hedley Jewell	Sgt F. Terry
EZ 865	IA	Flt Sgt S.C. Matthews	WO G.F. Williams
AN 731	II	Flt Sgt J. Hadley	F/O James Vernon
AN 656	II	P/O Allen Halley RAAF	P/O Ernest Hallett
AN 711	II	Flt Sgt J. Marshall	Flt Sgt J. Paterson

Yet again the weather intervened to the advantage of the enemy and blanket cloud cover prevented this attack from being delivered. In lieu the force had to select the 'Last Resort' target of Kokko (RU 624194) and this was dive-bombed at 1055. In compensation it was recorded that 'Excellent bombing' was achieved and validated. 'Buildings were seen to be hit and demolished.' Many fires were started and one particularly large fire in the centre of the north-western end of the village had the initial appearance of one huge sheet of flame of more than 100-feet high. This turned into a column of brownish-yellow smoke which rose to more than 1,000-feet high and was still visible at fifty miles distant. All the aircraft returned intact to base at 1141.

The final missions for October were carried out by two formations of Vengeances, led respectively by Flying Officer George Hartnell and Squadron Leader Anthony Traill, who both left at 0640.

Hartnell's group was to report on the possibility of making strikes on a reported company of Japanese troops at Point 4702 (Pinpoint RU 3812) near Hata (RU 5514). In the event cloud cover again ruled out locating this objective and instead they made a series of individual bombings of Tintha between 0755 and 0804. Most bombs were seen bursting in the centre and at the corners of the village, and while one aircraft machine-gunned this target others strafed villages and *bashas* to the north on their way out.

Squadron Leader Anthony Traill's box was assigned No. 2 Stockade as its target along with assessing the possibility of dive-bombing Point 5151 (RU 3378) one mile north-north-east of Pimpi Village (Pinpoint RU 3277). The dive-bombing of the stockade was accomplished at 0745 with ten 500lb GT Mk IV NITI bombs being dropped among *bashas* and buildings in the location. One aircraft, EZ 849, had to turn back early with engine problems. The other location was not sighted properly although a few pilots thought they *might* have spotted the latter position. It was concluded that this location would prove a very difficult objective to hit.

November continued in much the same vein with the weather thwarting 45 Squadron's attempts to aid their Army colleagues on many occasions but, whenever the seemingly endless cloud lifted sufficiently, attacks were continued, albeit with difficulty. Thus, there were no sorties on the 1st, 3rd, 4th and 7th of the month while on the 2nd two attacks were made, Flight Lieutenant John Stevenson leading B Flight against No. 2 Stockade and nearby concealed dumps at 1347. This attack was delivered at 1505 and two camera-equipped aircraft recorded its accuracy. Next Flying Officer George Hartnell took A Flight to bomb No. 3 Stockade, departing at 1414. Vengeance EZ 711 with Flight Sergeants J. Marshall and J. Paterson, was forced to turn back with technical problems. Thick cloud ruled this site out and so the 'Last Resort' target of Yesagyo (Yaesagyo) became their focus. The leading *vic* dived from 12,000 feet to release at 4,000 feet. However, the second *vic* of this group bombed Contha Village (Pinpoint RP 5803), west of the Myittha river, by mistake. On return Flying Officer George Hartnell's EZ 731 had problems with her undercarriage and only landed at 1643 after several early attempts had failed.

The 4th saw Squadron Leader Anthony Traill return to No. 3 Stockade for another six-plane assault at 1440. For once the weather proved excellent but, conversely, by the time they reached the area the lowering sun cast a shadow that left the target zone as a dark patch. Nonetheless, the location was known to the aircrews and the attack was delivered in steep dives from 11,000 feet down to 3,500 feet at 1544 with twelve 500lb bombs, including some time-delay of five and eight hours, being placed in and around the stockade and along the road to the east.

The 6th had an attack on Le-U (Pinpoint SF 4422), led by Flight Lieutenant John Stevenson, leaving Kumbhirgam at 1302 and making their dives at 1404. This area was reported to contain both Japanese troops and supplies and, while two salvoes overshot, the main weight of ordnance was duly positioned in the immediate vicinity of the target area. Next five Vengeances dive-bombed Kawya (Pinpoint SF 5389) on the 8th. Composition of this force was:

Aircraft	Mark	Pilot	Aircrew
EZ 986	IA	F/O George Hartnell	F/O Robert Barclay RAAF
EZ 850	IA	P/O Arthur Lamb	P/O Robert Hilditch RAAF
EZ 849	IA	Flt Sgt S. O'Connor	Sgt M. Macrae
EZ 841	IA	P/O A.H. Lebas RCAF	F/O James Vernon RAAF
EZ851	IA	Sgt J. Banham	Sgt R. Sumner
AN 731	II	P/O Allen Halley RAAF	F/O Ernest Hallett RAAF

The aircraft left base at 1000 but Pilot Officer Arthur Lamb had to turn back after twenty-five minutes flight time due to petrol pump trouble. The remaining five Vengeances attacked at 1053, dropping ten 500lb GP Mk. IV NITI bombs both in the middle of and in the immediate vicinity of the village. Enemy reaction was non-existent, and all planes were back down safely at 1145.

The 9th saw all available Vengeances from both 45 and 110 Squadrons scrambled away due to the imminence of an enemy air raid on the base, but it failed to materialise. The AOC of 221 Group, Air Commodore Herbert

Rowley, along with Group Captain James Black DFC, visited No. 168 Wing and both squadrons on the 10th but the following day, after the earlier false alarm, Kumbhirgram was attacked by enemy aircraft. Warning of an incoming raid was received at 0850 and the air raid warning sounded at 0908 and again at 0912. They sighted eighteen Japanese Kawasaki twin-engine Ki-48-IIb bombers, escorted by six Nakajima Ki-43-I fighters[9], at an estimated height of 18,500 feet. The raid was unopposed in the air, but the heavy AA guns claimed one possible. All save one of 45's Vengeance got airborne and this latter was damaged by bomb splinters in the attack which concentrated on the dispersal area at the south-eastern end of the runway, several 100kg high-explosive and more than fifty small high-explosive bombs being dropped. The squadron suffered no casualties but there were losses among 110's ground crews and four of their aircraft were damaged in this raid. They took this unwelcome attention as a confirmation that they were hurting the enemy as attacks of this nature were few and far between.

A strike was sent out at 0910 that day, with Squadron Leader Anthony Traill leading six Vengeances in an attempt to destroy a pontoon bridge at Hpaungzeik. They made their dives at 1010 with one direct hit on the south-western end of the bridge and many very near misses reported. The damage was confirmed by the subsequent examination of photographs taken at the time. Another mission was launched at 1309 with the aim of destroying storage dumps near Pindaya (Pinpoint SA 8333). The five-plane strike was composed thus:

Aircraft	Mark	Pilot	Aircrew
EZ 898	IA	Flt Lt John Stevenson	Sgt Sidney Siddle
EZ 850	IA	P/O Arthur Lamb	P/O Robert Hilditch RAAF

[9]   The Imperial Japanese Army Air Force designation for the Ki-48-IIb was the *Sokei*, to which the Allies gave the code-name 'Lily'. She was fast but, like so many Japanese aircraft, lacked defensive protection and armour as a result. The Ki-43-I, the *Hayabusa* or Peregrine Falcon, was a single-engine fighter, with a performance much superior to the British Hawker Hurricane which, although better armed, was pedestrian by comparison and outclassed in manoeuvrability. The Allies codenamed her as 'Oscar', and she destroyed more Allied aircraft than any other interceptor in the South-East Asia area of operations. Superficially at least, she resembled the Navy's Mitsubishi Zero-Sen fighter, and was frequently reported as such by Allied pilots.

Aircraft	Mark	Pilot	Aircrew
EZ 851	IA	Flt Sgt W.V. Tolar	Sgt Joseph Fenwick RAAF
EZ 841	IA	Sgt J. Banham	Sgt R. Sumner
AN 617	II	F/O Gilbert Hockley	WO Thomas Lord

They attacked at 1411, with mixed results. While three sets of 500lb bombs burst with equally-spaced detonations covering the target area, two others fell outside it, one falling short and the other overshooting. There was no opposition and the team were landing back at their airfield by 1509.

That same day there occurred what Squadron Leader Anthony Traill termed 'an extraordinary incident involving one of the few known parachute descents from Vengeance aircraft'.[10] At 1600 Flight Sergeant S.C. Matthews had taken Vengeance EZ 865 up on a test flight to check out new wireless equipment. In the rear seat was Sergeant McCandlish, one of 45 Squadron's wireless personnel. To see how the set reacted to manoeuvres, Matthews waggled his wings a little and then made a few shallow dives. He spoke to McCandlish over the intercom asking him 'All right?', but the latter misheard this as 'Bale out'. Getting no response, Matthews repeated the question and put his thumb up and this McCandlish took as a firm confirmation he should get out pronto, which he duly did at 1620, much to the astonishment of the pilot! The aircraft was at an altitude of 1,500 feet at the time and the descent was made with dignity and without any injury.

Two strikes were delivered on 12th November, the first with six aircraft, led by Flight Lieutenant John Stevenson against an enemy hutted camp (Pinpoint RU 5642) a mile north-east of Ngapa, and this strike was repeated by a further five VDBs under Flying Officer George Hartnell at 1051. These strikes were delivered at 1128 and 1200 respectively and were mainly accurately placed.

An even more intense day of operations was seen on the 13th, with 45 and 110 Squadrons delivering three attacks apiece. No. 45 Squadron's first contribution was led by Squadron Leader Anthony Traill and they lifted off from Kumbhirgam at 1123 and made a successful attack on Webula (Pinpoint RU 3945) at 1225. Some red-roofed buildings were struck and some *bashas* also demolished. At 1500 Flying Officer George Hartnell took

---

[10]   AIR 27/457/6.

six more Vengeances to dive-bomb No. 2 Stockade yet again, with what were reported to be 'Good results'. Enemy reaction was minimal, but the final mission had a more dramatic outcome.

At 1514 Flight Lieutenant John Stevenson, of B Flight, with his regular WO/AG, Flight Sergeant Sidney Siddle, RAFVR, in EZ 898 took a force of seven Vengeances, four 45 Squadron machines and three from 110 Squadron, to bomb Kalemyo. This attack was duly successfully delivered at 1600, but when the dives were completed, and the formation re-assembled Stevenson's aircraft was missing. After debriefing the story emerged in some detail. Stevenson's machine was seen to successfully recover from the dive but trailing a vapour trail astern. He proceeded on a north-easterly course at an altitude of 3,000 feet and managed to gain another 1,000 feet in the process. Flight Sergeant S. Matthews, piloting EZ 856, and Flight Sergeant W.V. Tolar, flying EZ851, attempted to form up on either side of Stevenson, but he waved them away to keep clear of him. At this time the engine was 'coughing and spluttering' and still leaving a trail of oil or petrol behind it as it flew up the Meyinzaya Valley, heading north on its eastern edge.

As his two companions obeyed his orders and broke away, Stevenson's aircraft began to lose height with the smoke trail blackening and thickening astern. At 1605 Flight Sergeant Matthews, by this time some 1,500 feet above EZ 898, witnessed one of the crew bale out. Flight Sergeant W.V. Tolar was convinced that it was the WO/AG who had baled out at Point RU 5292. Almost immediately after this Stevenson's aircraft went straight down without any sign of the second crew member having left the machine. The aircraft at this point appeared to have resumed a straight and level course with the pilot showing signs of having been wounded or affected by the fumes. EZ 986 crashed at around Pinpoint RU 5298, exploding on impact and bursting into flames.

It was assumed that Stevenson had been killed in the crash, but the reports indicated that Siddle had been seen to bale out. Stevenson, a popular and very able officer, was mourned but, on the 21st of the month, a phone call was received at Kumbhirgam from 170 Wing, which announced that Stevenson 'had walked into an advanced Army post at Point RP 1413, north of Tiddim'. He was transferred to Imphal and re-joined 45 Squadron two days later. Stevenson was thus able to correct the false impressions that had abounded since his premature 'demise' had been announced.

It appears that when their aircraft had been hit Sergeant Siddle prepared to bale and he turned his seat and stood up in readiness. This had been observed by other aircrews close by, but immediately afterwards, according to Stevenson, Siddle settled back down in the aircraft again. Stevenson was temporarily able to regain some control of his Vengeance and continue his course but EZ 898 was now losing height rapidly and soon it was clear nothing more could be done, so Stevenson baled out but Siddle failed to do so.[11]

During most of the 14th the squadron was on stand-by as usual from 0700. This readiness was briefly interrupted at 1132 when a warning of the approach of a group of enemy aircraft was received and the Vengeances were scrambled away. This warning, like so many others, proved a to be a false alarm but, on returning to base, Sergeant J. Banham in Vengeance EZ 851 landed 'wheels up' at 1328, blocking the runway for two hours. Both the pilot and his gunner were unharmed, but their mount suffered Category 2 damage. Once the wreck had been cleared the squadron resumed stand-by but it was not until 1517 that the call came and Squadron leader Anthony Traill led five Vengeances away with the task of bombing reported enemy movements along the track between Nos. 2 and 3 Stockades. Conditions were poor, but the attack was put in at 1610 nonetheless, along a line of east to west. Bomb bursts were seen close to both track and stockade, although observations of the results proved difficult.

At 0810 on the following day the six available aircrews were in the middle of being briefed in readiness for another attack on No. 3 Stockade at Natang, with the pontoon bridge at Hpaungzeik as the secondary target. The squadron was aware that Fort White, regarded as the keystone of the British defence in IV Corps area, had fallen to an enemy attack during the night, and 17th Indian Division had been driven out. But it was not until the briefing session was almost over that this objective was substituted as the main target for the unit's main strike. The rapidly-deteriorating situation on the ground brought about this response and, at 0957, Flying Officer George Hartnell led the six Vengeances toward that disputed locale. Regrettably cloud cover made this attack impossible to carry out and the secondary

---

[11] The author can attest that Flight Sergeant Sidney Siddle's name and rank is as inscribed on the Singapore Memorial.

target, No. 3 Stockade, was similarly hampered, so the 'Last Resort' target, a pontoon bridge at Pinpoint RU 5971, was dive-bombed instead, again with difficulty due to local weather conditions. They approached at an altitude of 11,500 feet from the south-west and Flying Officer Hartnell, in EZ 865, immediately went into an 85-degree dive on a northern heading at 1114, releasing his bombs at 2,500 feet. Fight Sergeant W. Tolar, piloting AN 625, followed him straight down, but the other quartet circled the target and then attacked in sequence from 10,000 feet at minute later. No direct hits were scored, however, and the bridge appeared intact as they left the scene.

Nor could the disputed position be attacked the next day but, at 0914 on the 17th, the only six serviceable Vengeances took off from Kumbhirgram at 0914 led by the acting commander of B Flight, Pilot Officer Gilbert Hockley. Twenty-four minutes into the outward leg one aircraft, EZ 848 piloted by Flight Sergeant J. Hadley, had to turn back to base with technical problems, but the remaining five aircraft carried on and completed the attack on Fort White (Pinpoint RU 2371) at 1027. The group made an eastern approach at 12,500 feet and, heading west, made shallow dives with release at 8,500 feet. Such an approach could not guarantee their usual accuracy, but bombs were seen to detonate at the eastern end of the Fort causing a small fire.

On the 18th the squadron was on standby all day although no operations were ordered but enemy troop concentrations at Yasagyo (Pinpoint RP 5803) were targeted for an ARMOP the following day with Squadron Leader Anthony Traill leading six Vengeances from base at 0930, disposed thus:

Aircraft	Pilot	Aircrew
EZ 886	Sqn Ldr Anthony Traill	F/O Douglas French RAFVR
EZ 841	P/O A.H. Lebas RCAF	F/O James Vernon RAAF
EZ 865	Flt Sgt J. Marshall	Flt Sgt J. Paterson
EZ 837	P/O L. Halley	F/O Ernest Hallett RAAF
EZ 879	Flt Sgt J. Hadley	Sgt A Gobbie
EZ 850	Flt Sgt W. Tolar	Sgt Joseph Fenwick RAAF

They approached the area from the north-west at an altitude of 11,500 feet and, as they entered the dive, made a turn to the north-east at 1020. Release height for their weaponry was 3,000 feet and twelve 500lb GP NITI bombs were dropped. It was reported that all bombs appeared to fall within the target area. The force returned intact at 1109. It was on the 19th also that 45 Squadron lost three pilots, Flying Officers Ronald Parker Curtis and Patrick Loyd Brinkley along with Warrant Officer W.M. Osborne and a WO/AG, Flight Sergeant Arthur Field, all of whom were posted away to No. 8 Squadron Indian Air Force on this day.

The 20th November saw an attack mounted against Thukali[12], the No. 2 Stockade area of Nansaungpu, but it was once more 'weathered out'. On the 21st six Vengeances made a successful attack on Mawlaik and another good strike was made on Japanese bunkers and positions at Pinpoint RU 228738 on the 22nd, but an attack on Fort White (Thangmual) on the 23rd was not a good one. Flying Officer George Hartnell led six aircraft from base at 0946 but one had to return early with engine problems, one other was unable to identify the target with certainty so, quite correctly, brought his bombs home. The remaining quartet carried out shallow dives due to conditions, but this resulted in 'disappointing' results as most bombs delivered in this fashion resulted in overshoots.

The 24th saw both 45 and 110 Squadrons standing by all day ready to make an attack on Point 8198, (Pinpoint RU 228738), at Milestone 22, which was a key position overlooking Fort White and its environs and approaches and which, now in enemy hands, had been turned into formidable fortress which the Japanese named *Kimozan* (Golden Peak). The plan was for each of the Vengeance squadrons to contribute a six-plane box and the whole force would rendezvous with Curtiss Mohawks over Imphal, their task being to strafe the area on completion of the Vengeances' dive-bombing, but, in the event, bad cloud over the area caused this operation to be aborted. It was hoped to make the attack the next day. The Senior Intelligence Officer from AHQ Bengal, Wing Commander Richardson, visited the base and provided both squadrons with the latest information on the confused ground situation in their intended target zone. The fluidity of the situation was emphasised when, next morning, advice was received that 'on no account was the previous day's target to be attacked'. Instead the target was changed to an area 400–500 yards on either side of the vital supply route of the Falam Track immediately to the south and south-east of Fort White. The plan was for Pilot Officer Gilbert Hockley to lead a force of twelve Vengeances, six from each of the two squadrons, to this bombing zone but, yet again, weather

---

[12] Now Tulsuk.

conditions were so bad than no attack could be delivered, and all aircraft returned with the bomb loads intact.

Indeed, no further combat missions proved possible for the rest of the month, save for one abortive mission mounted on the 29th, with enemy troop concentrations in the Fort White area as the main objective, which was once more totally blanked in thick cloud. Thus 45 Squadron's total combat sorties for November were restricted to just 133. But being constantly on stand-by restricted maintenance and serviceability was lower than usual for this reason.

On 1 December Australian Flying Officer George Hartnell led B Flight with nine Vengeances on a sortie which left base at 1002 and made a successful attack on Milestone 52 at position RU 2374. For these 'road cuts' precision was essential with time-delay fuses to the 500lb GP bombs to keep the enemy supply lines shut. The practice of flying missions on alternate days, with 110 Squadron taking over in turn and turn about, was followed at this time. Thus 45 was stood down from operations on 2 December but ready 'on-call' for any emergency request from the army. Next day Squadron Leader Traill led six aircraft on a strike which took off at 1415. Although one aircraft had to return with engine trouble the remaining five made a good attack on Milestone 52, position RU 2374. The 5th saw Traill leading a strike by twelve aircraft against a Japanese camp and dumps between Kaungkasi (SL 5184) and Letpangwe (SL 5382). The squadron was on stand-by from 0620 on the 7th 'at maximum effort at full readiness' but was not called upon. It was the same the following day, but this did not prevent accidents during three non-operational flights. Flight Sergeant J. Marshall took Vengeance 'Q' (AN 711) up for a local test but quickly became aware of a flow of petrol from his engine. He immediately landed back down and taxied to the Flight office prior to switching off, but, as the engine came to a halt, it backfired, and the flames enveloped the entire machine which was destroyed save for parts of the tail unit. Fortunately Marshal and his rear-seat man were able to escape unscathed.

The next combat mission took place on the 9th, with take-off at 0755 with Traill leading twelve Vengeances to make a heavy strike on the area of Milestone 52, located about a mile north of Fort White. Meanwhile, congratulatory reports came in from Army sources describing their earlier dive-bombings of the 1st and 3rd, the results of which were given as 'excellent'. Briefing for six crews in readiness for another planned attack with a take-off time of 0900 was made, but the operation was cancelled due to the cloud cover over the target zone. On the 12th twelve Vengeances were airborne at 0845 with a mission to take out a Japanese bunker at position MS 52, but again cloud cover rendered this attack impossible. Around this time warning was received of another incoming raid and the aircraft were aerially dispersed as a precaution. At 1500 Traill led twelve aircraft away and, despite similar awful cloud conditions, they made a successful attack on the position

The 14th saw a briefing for twelve crew at 0715 when they were instructed to harass Japanese artillery positions in a land battle already in progress. The Vengeances were despatched in two sections of six aircraft apiece with a two-hour time gap between them, with Traill leading the first attack; Hurricane fighter protection was provided on this occasion for both sorties. On the approach of the Vengeances, Japanese guns, which had been heavily engaging Allied positions, suddenly ceased firing and the dive attacks were delivered against limited ground opposition. The second attack was deemed a limited success only as two aircraft had to return with their bombs due to hang-ups. Later in the day 45 Squadron was visited by the top brass with the Commander-in-Chief, Air Chief Marshal Sir Richard Edmund Charles Peirse KCB DSO AFC, along with Air Marshal Sir John Eustice Arthur Baldwin KBE CB DSC, Air Officer Commanding AHQ, Bengal, delivering a pep talk to the crews.

Between the 16th and 21st 45 was on stand-by but was only called upon once, on the 18th, when Pilot Officer Gilbert Hockley, the acting commander of B Flight, led eleven Vengeances off at 1445 and made a successful attack on enemy stores and supply dumps at Pyinthazeik (RU 5866). Not until 22 December was another combat mission carried out and that day Squadron Leader Traill led a force of nine Vengeances, along with a further three from 110 Squadron, to attack enemy targets at Kalemyo.

On Christmas Eve the Vengeances delivered Santa's gifts to the Japanese when at 0844 Flying Officer G.W. Hartnell, commanding A Flight, led a force of nine 45 Squadron Vengeances, along with three more from 110 Squadron, to attack enemy bunkers at MS 52 (map ref RU 2374). A feature of this strike was that the exact target locations were indicated to the dive-bomber crews by shell bursts from Allied artillery forces in the vicinity, a great advance. On the 26th the target of the day was a Japanese army camp at Kontha (RU 5703), with Squadron Leader Traill again leading a force of twelve Vengeances which took at 1000. However, cloud cover made observations difficult, but it was not considered a good attack and lacked the usual concentration. Additionally, five bombs 'hung-up' and were jettisoned while three more were brought back to base. One aircraft was holed by small-arms fire. They returned to Kontha on 28 December with Pilot Officer Gilbert Hockley leading a formation of six Vultees against enemy troop concentrations there. One aircraft had to abort but the other five made successful attacks. At 1413 Flying Officer George Hartnell, RAAF, led a second strike with six Vengeances against a Japanese army HQ and supply dumps at Paluzawa (RU 85099).

The year did not end well for 45 Squadron. On the 30th bad weather delayed the departure of a twelve-aircraft strike led by Squadron Leader Traill against enemy troops and ration concentrations on the Kalemyo to Fort White road between positions MS10 and 11. However, due to a misunderstanding, most bombs were delivered further along between MS 10 and 11 in a mass overshoot. On analysis it was discovered that Traill had slightly overshot the target with a point of aim at the eastern extremity of the target zone, whereas their points of aim should have been distributed over a distance of a mile to the west. It emerged that the formation assumed that the lead had bombed a point at the western end of the target and that they therefore bombed almost on him and even further to the east.

The next day all the crews who had taken part in the previous day's abortive attack were assembled and Traill tore them off a colossal strip using photographic evidence. In the words of the report, their error 'was very forcibly brought home' to them by the CO. Traill stressed, 'in no small measure, the vital necessity especially when operating as Army Support (when frequently the bomb line is in the immediate vicinity of the target) of every pilot identifying the target and never bombing on someone else's bombs'. Fortunately, on this occasion, the target and the bomb line were many miles apart.

Between 2 and 9 January 1944 both 45 and 110 Squadrons conducted further joint missions together. The squadron resumed sole operations on the 10th, but a twelve-strong attack against Japanese troop concentrations at Mawku (RP 9234) had to be aborted east of the Kale and Kabaw valleys due to bad weather.

On 17 January Squadron Leader Traill led a twelve-plane attack against an enemy-occupied strongpoint at Kyaukchaw on the Yu river at Pinpoint RU 9162. This formation was composed thus:

Aircraft	Pilot	Aircrew
EZ 986	Sqn Ldr Anthony Traill	F/O Douglas French
AN 821	Flt Sgt J. Marshall	Flt Sgt R. Sumner
AN 796	Flt Sgt S.C. Matthews	F/O G.F. Williams
AN 779	F/O Arthur Lamb RAFVR	P/O Robert Hilditch RAAF
AN 879	Sgt D. Carter	F/O Eric Leonard 'Sandy' Sandifer
AN 819	P/O Arthur John Laney	P/O Stanley Potts
AN 818	F/O Arthur Huon	F/O Cedric Birbeck
AN 656	F/O A.H. Lebas	P/O James Vernon RAAF
EZ 848	Flt Sgt J. Badley	Sgt A. Gobbie
EZ 837	WO J .Levey	Sgt H. Garfath
EZ 879	Flt Sgt S. O'Connor	F/O Jack Nankevis DFC RAAF
AN 710	Sgt J. Scanes	P/O Leonard Arthur Mears

The strike departed at 1433 and found the weather over the target area good, with 3/10th cloud. They made their attack at 1535 from a height of 14,000 feet down to bomb release at 3,000 feet. They planted two dozen 500lb GPTI bombs and an equal number of 250lb GPTI bombs at 1535 and photographs confirmed their hits.

The following day was a frustrating one. Twelve Vengeances took off at 1300 for a massive combined strike with 110 Squadron on Wuntho Railway Station (SM 3359). One 45 Squadron machine had to land at Palel airstrip at 1332 due to technical problems, the remainder circled for a further forty minutes waiting for 110 Squadron to form up on them, but this was not achieved and so Squadron Leader Anthony Traill led his unit out at 1340. By the time they reached the Chindwin river bad weather lay ahead and this factor, coupled with an estimated insufficiency of fuel remaining, was enough for the commanding officer to abort the mission. Meanwhile Vengeance AN 819 (Flight Sergeant W. Tolar and Sergeant Joseph Fenwick RAAF) had also developed technical problems and had landed back at base at 1437. The remaining ten aircraft got down safely at 1511 with their complete bomb loads.

Better fortune was to be had on the 19th when Flight Lieutenant George Hartnell led a twelve-Vengeance sortie from base at 1216 made up of these aircraft and aircrew:

Aircraft	Pilot	Aircrew
EZ 847	Flt Lt George Hartnell RAAF	F/O Robert Barclay
AN 827	WO J. Levey	Sgt H. Garfath
EZ 879	Flt Sgt S. O'Connor	P/O Keith Bottrill
AN 896	P/O H. Jewel	F/O Jack Nankervis
AN 772	Sgt J. Scanes	F/O Leonard Mears
AN 656	P/O A.H. Lebas	F/O James Vernon
AN 818	F/O Arthur Huon	F/O Cedric Birkbeck RAAF
AN 796	F/O Arthur Lamb	P/O Robert Hilditch
AN 821	Flt Sgt S. Matthews	F/O G. Williams
AN 679	F/O Hugh Neil	P/O F. Brown
EZ 865	Sgt V. Emson	Sgt Arthur McKee RAAF
AN 710	Sgt D. Carter	F/O Eric Sandifer

They arrived over Mawku at 1324 and made a good attack. In total they dropped twelve 500lb GPTI, twelve 500lb GPLD, fourteen 250lb GPTD and twenty 250lb GPLD bombs on this rail junction.

After a day without operations, the 21st saw another full strike with twelve Vengeances planned under the command of Squadron Leader Traill. The force comprised:

Aircraft	Pilot	Aircrew
EZ 896	Sqn Ldr Anthony Traill	F/O Douglas French
EZ 879	P/O Charles Jewell	F/O Jack Nankervis
AN 772	Flt Sgt S. Matthews	F/O G.F. Williams
AN 679	F/O Hugh Neil	P/O F. Brown
AN 731	P/O Arthur Laney	P/O Stanley Potts
AN 865	P/O V. Emson	Sgt Arthur McKee RAAF
EZ 847	Flt Lt George Hartnell	F/O Robert Barclay
AN 837	WO J. Levey	Sgt H. Garfath
AN 656	Flt Sgt S. O'Connor	P/O Keith Bottrill
AN 818	F/O Arthur Huon	F/O Cedric Birkbeck
EZ 848	Flt Sgt J. Hadley	Sgt A. Gobbie
AN 710	Sgt D. Carter	F/O Eric Sandifer

Take-off was at 1420, but Emson and McKee's aircraft failed to leave the runway due to technical faults, so only eleven aircraft left for the strike. Their objective was a Japanese encampment at Pinlebu (pinpoint SL 8680) which they hit at 1529. Such Japanese troop concentrations were rarely located but when they were then the Vengeance dropped 500lb GP and LD bombs, some fitted with 4.5-inch extension rods to the nose fuses to spread the blast wider above the ground.[13] Targets for conventional ordnance also included *bashas*, bunkers and other defence works.

So, 45 Squadron delivered a very mixed bombload into the Japanese centre this day, including nineteen 500lb GPTI with extension rods, three 500lb GPLD, sixteen 250lb GPTI and six 250lb with the rods. Meanwhile, Vengeance AN 656 was forced to make a refuelling stop at Palel but was airborne again by 1650 and the rest of the force had already landed back at base by 1649. This same target was revisited next day with much the same force. The attack was delivered at 1327 and all dropped successfully except EZ 848 (Flying Officers A.H. Lebas and James Vernon) which had one starboard wing bomb which refused to release and was later successfully jettisoned on the enemy at Wayongon on the journey home.

By contrast the next strike, made on 27 January, proved another bad day for 45 Squadron. Although eleven aircraft were allocated for this mission against Japanese troops and stores at Mawlaik (pinpoint RP 9223), one Vengeance, AN 772 (Flight Sergeant S. Matthews and Flying Officer G.F. Williams), failed to take off due to technical problems. Of the ten that did leave at 1403, three turned back due to weather conditions, one of them being forced to jettison its bombs. Seven aircraft were left to attack, but accuracy was poor due to the extreme weather conditions; aircraft L (Vengeance EZ879) became lost and crashed near Nowgaung (Nowgong), Assam. Pilot Officer Hedley Charles Jewell, RAFVR, the pilot, was killed,[14] but Pilot Officer Keith Bottrill, the navigator, baled out safely.

---

[13] These had been invented by German Junkers Ju. 87 Stuka pilots during the Greek and Crete campaigns of 1941 and were known as *Dinortstabe* after the commander of *Stukagruppen.2*. For eyewitness detail of how they originated and were initially deployed and developed see Smith, Peter C., *The Junkers Ju.87 Stuka*, p.182, Crecy, Manchester, 2011. They were soon copied by the Allied air forces.

[14] Jewel was posthumously promoted to flying officer on 20 March.

Nor was this the end of their woes. On the same day Squadron Leader Traill flew AN656 to Delhi for instructions concerning conversion of the unit to Mosquitoes. *En route* the aircraft crashed near Ghagra river, Traill and Flying Officer Douglas Ernest French, RAFVR, were both killed. Command of the squadron had temporarily devolved upon Squadron Leader Donald Stuart Edwards, between January and February.

Although one source states that 'During March 45 Squadron alone was to undertake 987 sorties',[15] in truth the squadron's Summary of Events[16] records a very different story. On 1 February it recorded that the squadron continued its preparations for the imminent move. The squadron, along with 110 Squadron, was now scheduled to re-equip with Mosquitoes, and they were replaced at Kumbhirgram by 7 IAF and 82 RAF Squadrons as the critical situation at Kohima and Imphal developed.

On 2 February ten Vengeances, led by Flight Lieutenant George Hartnell, took off for 322 MU, Cawnpore via Alipore. On arrival there on 3 February these ten aircraft were handed over for disposal and meanwhile the balance of Vengeances had also left Kumbhirgram for Cawnpore the same day, led by Flight Sergeant J. Marshall. The main party of 45 Squadron, under the command of Squadron Leader Donald Edwards, left Kumbhirgram for Yelahanka on 4 February, leaving behind a rear party to clean up, including Flying Officers Arthur Lamb and Keith Bottrill, on temporary attachment to 138 Wing. The new CO, Wing Commander Haley Charles Stumm DFC, arrived by air from HQ 3rd Tactical Air Force (3TAF) on the 10th but, far from flying combat missions in the Vengeance, it was recorded on the 17th of that month that the only aircraft 45 Squadron possessed were 'a few Bisleys'.[17] These were later joined by a solitary Avro Anson.

It was also recorded that the first Mosquito Mk VI, LR250, arrived at Yelahanka on 1 March (not 29 February) and that 'Great interest was shown'. The second Mosquito, HP867, did not arrive until 5 March.

On arrival at Yelahanka No. 45 Squadron commenced conversion to the de Havilland Mosquito VI. Far from being 'potent fighter bombers',

---

[15] Shores, Christopher, *The Air War in Burma: The Allied Air Forces Fight Back – 1942-45*, p. 171, Grub Street, London, 2005.

[16] AIR 27/457.12.

[17] The Bristol Bisley ground-attack variant, also known as the Blenheim V.

a series of fatal crashes followed, including one on 13 May 1944 when Wing Commander Stumm himself was killed, flying Mosquito HP939, when the tail broke off. This further delayed their adoption until problems with the glue holding it together were solved and so the Mosquito did not actual get into any combat action until 28 September 1944.

Chapter 5

No. 82 (United Provinces) Squadron RAF

Super Omnia Ubique
(Over All Things Everywhere)

After serving in North Africa and Malta, 82 Squadron, a medium-bomber outfit, became based at Karachi, Sindh, from 24 May 1942. On 12 June it moved to Quetta, Baluchistan, but only remained there until 6 July when it again shifted base to Cholavarum in the Madras Presidency (now Tamil Nadu) to form a Vultee Vengeance dive-bomber unit. Their first aircraft in their new role were Mark I and Mark 1a Vengeances which arrived in August. In November Squadron Leader Dennis Raleigh Gibbs took over from Wing Commander John Hugh McMichael. Commencing 17 November, they conducted limited coastal and anti-submarine patrols but, when it became clear that the Japanese were not going to repeat their carrier attacks on India and Ceylon, it was decided to move the dive bombers to the Burma Front. On 26 February an advance party was sent to Madhaiganj airfield, West Bengal, (23°38'N, 87°21'E), to the north-west of Calcutta,[1] where a new base was under construction. On 5 March 1943 a detachment was also sent to Karachi. The move to Madhaiganj took place on 12 April, but eleven days later became based at the more suitable airfield at Asansol where concrete runways were built. Here the squadron received replacement machines, Vengeance IIs.

On 26 October 1942 Flying Officer Edward Loughrey 'Ted' Reis RAAF and his British WoP/AG, Sergeant Charles Marklew, were taking off on the second leg of a cross-country journey taking six brand-new in Vengeance dive bombers to Madras via Jodhpur and Hyderabad. Flying AN 944, this team were the fourth aircraft to take off from the small airfield at the latter place when a Canadian officer, Air Commodore

---

[1] Confusingly, the Americans called it Pandaveswar when they later moved in.

Thomas Albert Lawrence, RCAF, observing the take-offs aboard the
Lockheed Hudson bomber that was the guide plane of the group, saw
this Vengeance slowly drift onto the grass at the side of the runway in
the strong crosswind. Although Reis's aircraft lifted off the ground it
continued to drift slowly towards an elevated floodlight. Those watching
thought that Reis had cleared the floodlight, but a puff of white powder
emerged as the wing struck the obstruction. The Vengeance flipped
over onto its back and crashed straight into the ground. Reis was killed
instantly; his gunner, Marklew, was pulled out grievously injured and
passed away a few minutes later. Both were interred at Trimulgherry
Military Cemetery the same day.

Two of Reis's close friends were lost in similar accidents, Colin
James 'Poppy' Stower, RAAF, who had been killed in an incident on 21
November 1942, and James Walter 'Sandy' Sandilands DFC. Two other
Canadians, Flying Officer Norman Alexander 'Dutch' Holland RCAF,
and Flight Sergeant Ernest Aubrey Mabee DFC RCAF, flew with 82
Squadron.

The Vengeance I had not been a success due to engine (mainly piston
ring) failures, and was subjected to stringent testing by 82 Squadron
when they got their hands on them. At this point the main party of the
squadron was working from Cholavaram airstrip, near Chennai, Tamil
Nadu, south-east India, which was a converted former race track north-
west of the Red Hills, 13^0 21'N, 80^0 15'E.[2] The advance party was at
another long-forgotten airfield, Madhaiganj, in West Bengal.[3] They had
possession of ten Vengeances at this period, AN 922, 924, 928, 929, 930,
943, 945, 946 and 947 and AP 100. Working with these aircraft occupied
the squadron throughout February 1943 as the following table illustrates
very clearly:

---

[2] Now known as Sholavaram, the airfield is long abandoned but the outline of its runway can
still be made out from the air.

[3] This is another long-abandoned airfield just south of the village of the same name,
north-east of the Konur river, to the north-west of Calcutta, 23^0 38'N, 87^0 21' E. See
Provisional Airfield List: India, Airfield Information. Report No. 7. Assistant Chief, Air
Staff, Intelligence, HQ AAF. Dated 15 September 1944. 18-9-1. National Archives,
Washington DC.

1943	Aircraft	Crew	Task	Time	Details
Feb 7	AN 929	Flt Lt David Metherell RNZAF	Air Test	1100-1130	Cholavaram
Feb 7	AN929	F/O Gordon MacDonald F/O David Berrington	Local Flying	1440-1540	Cholavaram
Feb 8	AN 930	Sgt Ronald Samuel Trigg Sgt H.R. Crichton	Local Flying	1415-1440	Ferrying from St Thomas' Mount to Cholavaram
Feb 8	AP 100	Sgt W. William Melville Tullett RCAF Sgt E. Mason	Local Flying	1415-1440	Ferrying from St Thomas' Mount to Cholavaram
Feb 8	AP 100	Sgt M.J. Croghan	Local Flying	1600-1700	Consumption Test: Ballast. Cholavaram
Feb 8	AN 930	F/O G.G. Thompson	Local Flying	1605-1705	Consumption Test: Ballast. Cholavaram
Feb 8	AN 947	P/O James Sandilands Sgt William F. Webb	Local Flying	1135-1220	Air Test. Cholavaram
Feb 8	AN 947	Flt.Sgt. Alan Parker Sgt D.P. Cartwright-Howell	Local Flying	1555-1655	Cholavaram
Feb 9	AN 947	Sgt George Couttie Flt Sgt R A Gardiner	Local Flying	1410-1440	Cholavaram
Feb 9	AP 100	F/O Gordon MacDonald F/O David Berrington	Local Flying	1400-1530	Consumption Test. Cholavaram
Feb 9	AN 930	Sgt William Melville Tullett Sgt E. Mason	Local Flying	1400-1630	Consumption Test. Cholavaram
Feb 10	AN 928	P/O James Sandilands Sgt W.T. Keefe	Local Flying	1525-1555	Air Test
Feb 11	AN 920	F/O Gordon MacDonald Sqn Ldr Mehar 'Baba' Singh	Local Flying	1155-1245	Cholavaram From 225 Group HQ
Feb 11	AN 928	Sgt D.J. Croghan Sgt G. Davies	Local Flying	1510-1540	
Feb 11	AN 946	F/O James Sandilands Sgt William F. Webb	Local Flying	1540-1610	Air Test
Feb 12	AN 928	Flt Sgt Alan Parker Sgt D.P. Cartwright-Howell	Local Flying	1440-1515	Consumption Test

1943	Aircraft	Crew	Task	Time	Details
Feb 12	AN 946	Sgt George Couttie Flt Sgt R.A. Gardiner	Cross Country	1410–1555	Circle Donakona Landing Ground without landing return Cholavaram
Feb 13	AN 928	Sgt D.J. Croghan Sgt L.R. Jenkins	Cross Country	1130–1340	Circle Donakona Landing Ground without landing return Cholavaram
Feb 16	AN 924	P/O James Sandilands Sgt William F. Webb	Local Flying	1145–1250	Cholavaram
Feb 16	AN 922	Sgt G. Couttie Flt Sgt R.A. Gardiner	Local Flying	1530–1630	Cholavaram
Feb 16	AN 924	Sgt William Tullett Sgt E. Mason	Local Flying	1145–1235	Ferrying from St Thomas' Mount to Cholavaram
Feb 16	AN 928	F/O Gordon MacDonald Cpl Carnera	Local Flying	1710–1730	Ferrying from St Thomas' Mount to Cholavaram
Feb 16	AP 190	Flt Lt David Metherell F/O E.A. Carter	Ferry	0815	Cholavaram to Madhaiganj refuelling at Vizagapatam and Cuttack
Feb 16	AN 930	F/O G G Thompson Sgt. J N O'Brien	Ferry	0815	Cholavaram to Madhaiganj refuelling at Vizagapatam and Cuttack
Feb 16	AN 928	Sgt William Tullett Sgt E. Mason	Ferry	0815	Cholavaram to Madhaiganj refuelling at Vizagapatam and Cuttack
Feb 16	AN 946	Sgt Ronald Trigg Sgt H.R. Crichton	Ferry	0815	Cholavaram to Madhaiganj refuelling at Vizagapatam and Cuttack
Feb 17	AN 924	W/O Alan Parker Sgt D.P. Cartwright- Howell	Local Flying	1355–1500	Test at 6,000ft. Cholavaram.
Feb 17	AN 945	P/O James P. Sandilands Sgt William F. Webb	Local Flying	1420–1520	Air Test. Cholavaram.
Feb 17	AN 922	F/O Gordon MacDonald Flt Lt G.W. Graff	Local Flying	1435–1535	Test at 6,000ft. Cholavaram.

1943	Aircraft	Crew	Task	Time	Details
Feb 18	AN 943	F/O Gordon MacDonald Sgt Sidney Siddle	Local Flying	1030–1130	Air Test. Cholavaram.
Feb 18	AN 945	F/O Robert Dempster Sgt D P Cartwright-Howell	Local Flying	1415–1515	Oil Test. Cholavaram
Feb 18	AN 943	Sgt D.J. Croghan Sgt S.W. Dwight	Local Flying	1440–1540	Local test at 6,000ft
Feb 19	AN 924	Sgt R.G. Holding Flt Sgt Johan Barnard	Cross Country	1500–1720	Cholavaram, circle Tanjore, without landing, Cholavaram
Feb 19	AN 943	Sgt G. Couttie Flt Sgt R. Gardiner	Cross Country	1500–1720	Cholavaram, circle Tanjore, without landing, Cholavaram
Feb 19	AP 100	F/O G.G. Thompson Sgt J.N. O'Brien	Local Flying	1125–1236	Madhaiganj
Feb 19	AP 100	F/O William Boyd Berry LAC L.E. Vaughan	Local Flying	1445–1550	Madhaiganj
Feb 19	AP 100	Sgt William Melville Tullett RCAF Sgt E. Mason	Local Flying	1610–1845	Madhaiganj
Feb 20	AN 928	F/O William Berry Cpl F.G.B. Burt	Local Flying	1130–1215	Air Test Madhaiganj
Feb 20	AN928	Sgt William Melville Tullett RCAF Cpl N. Jakeman	Local Flying	1410–1510	Madhaiganj
Feb 20	AN 928	F/O G.G. Thompson Cpl H. Longley	Local Flying	1515–1625	Madhaiganj
Feb 21	AN 928	Flt Lt David Metherell F/O E.A. Carter	Local Flying	1045–1115	Madhaiganj
Feb 21	AP 100	F/O William Berry Cpl W.J. McGillivray	Low Level Bombing	1200–1245	Madhaiganj
Feb 21	AP 100	F/O G.G. Thompson LAC D.H. Moore	Low Level Bombing	1425–1505	Madhaiganj
Feb 21	AP 100	Sgt William Melville Tullett RCAF Cpl Hiller	Low Level Bombing	1545–1620	Madhaiganj
Feb 22	AN 924	F/O Gordon MacDonald Cpl E. Clark	Local Flying	1110–1125	Air Test – Cholavaram

1943	Aircraft	Crew	Task	Time	Details
Feb 22	AP 100	Sgt Ronald Trigg Cpl H. Longley	Dive Bombing	1115–1200	Madhaiganj – No range party due main body still at Cholavaram – results not recorded.
Feb 22	AP 100	Sgt William Melville Tullett RCAF Sgt E. Mason	Local Flying	1420–1530	Madhaiganj
Feb 22	AP 100	F/O William Berry Cpl W.J. McGillivray	Local Flying	1545–1615	Madhaiganj
Feb 23	AN 928	Flt Lt David Metherell F/O E.A. Carter	Local Flying	1015–1055	Madhaiganj
Feb 23	AN 928	F/O G.G. Thompson Sgt L.R. Jenkins	Practice Bombing	1120–1200	Madhaiganj – No range party due main body still at Cholavaram – results observed by pilot but not recorded.
Feb 23	AN 928	Sgt Ronald Parker Sgt K. Millard	Practice Bombing	1420–1505	Madhaiganj – No range party due main body still at Cholavaram – results observed by pilot but not recorded.
Feb 23	AN 928	Sgt William Melville Tullett RCAF Sgt D.W. Nichols	Practice Bombing	1520–1555	Madhaiganj – No range party due main body still at Cholavaram – results observed by pilot but not recorded.
Feb 23	AN 928	F/O William Berry Sgt G. Davies	Practice Bombing	1630–1650	Madhaiganj – No range party due main body still at Cholavaram – results observed by pilot but not recorded.
Feb 24	AN 928	Sgt William Melville Tullett RCAF Sgt E. Mason	Practice Bombing	1035–1130	Madhaiganj – No range party due main body still at Cholavaram – results observed by pilot but not recorded.
Feb 24	AN 928	F/O G.G. Thompson Sgt J.N. O'Brien	Practice Bombing	1205–1255	Madhaiganj – No range party due main body still at Cholavaram – results observed by pilot but not recorded.

1943	Aircraft	Crew	Task	Time	Details
Feb 24	AN 922	F/O Gordon MacDonald F/O David Berrington	Local Flying	1115-1210	Formation Flying – Cholavaram
Feb 24	AN 943	P/O James Sandilands Sgt William F. Webb	Local Flying	1115-1210	Formation Flying – Cholavaram
Feb 24	AN 924	W/O Alan Parker Sgt D.F. Cartwright-Howell	Local Flying	1115-1210	Formation Flying – Cholavaram
Feb 24	AN 947	F/O Gordon MacDonald LAC J. Hornagold	Local Flying	1510-1610	Air Test – Cholavaram
Feb 25	AN 924	W/O Alan Parker Sgt Cartwright-Howell	Ferry	0840-1440	Cholavaram to Madhaiganj, refuelling at Vizagapatam and Cuttack.
Feb 25	AN 929	F/O James Sandilands	Local Flying	1145-1245	Cholavaram
Feb 25	AN 928	Sgt R.G. Holding F/O Thomas Cox Gilchrist	Cross Country	1425-1635	Cholavaram – circle Tanjore district without landing- Cholavaram.
Feb 25	AN 947	Sgt D.J. Croghan Sgt S.E. Elsmore	Cross Country	1215-1420	Cholavaram – circle Tanjore district without landing- Cholavaram.
Feb 25	AP 100	Sgt Ronald Trigg Sgt H.R. Crichton	Practice Bombing	1110-1150	Cholavaram
Feb 25	AN 928	F/O William Berry Cpl W.J. McGillivray	Practice Bombing	1215-1235	Cholavaram
Feb 25	AP 100	Sgt William Melville Tullett RCAF Sgt E. Mason	Practice Bombing	1430-1505	Cholavaram
Feb 25	AN 928	F/O William Berry LAC L.E. Vaughan	Practice Bombing	1400-1420	Cholavaram
Feb 25	AN 928	F/O G.G. Thompson LAC T.G. Wotton	Practice Bombing	1215-1235	Cholavaram
Feb 26	AN 929	P/O James Sandilands Sgt William F. Webb	Ferry	0745-1930	Cholavaram to Madhaiganj, refuelling at Vizagapatan and Cuttack.
Feb 26	AN 947	F/O Robert Dempster Sgt N.D. Hankinson	Ferry	0747-1500	Cholavaram to Madhaiganj, refuelling at Vizagapatan and Cuttack.
Feb 26	AN 922	Sgt R.G. Holding Flt Sgt Johan Barnard	Ferry	0749-1501	Cholavaram to Madhaiganj, refuelling at Vizagapatan and Cuttack.

1943	Aircraft	Crew	Task	Time	Details
Feb 26	AN 928	Flt Lt David Metherell F/O E.A. Carter	Practice Bombing	1100–1200	Madhaiganj. No range party due main body still at Cholavaram – results observed by pilot but not recorded
Feb 26	AN 928	Sgt William Melville Tullett RCAF Sgt E. Mason	Practice Bombing	1255–1350	Madhaiganj - No range party due main body still at Cholavaram – results observed by pilot but not recorded
Feb 26	AN 928	Sgt Ronald Trigg Sgt H.R. Crichton	Practice Bombing	1425–1505	Madhaiganj -No range party due main body still at Cholavaram – results observed by pilot but not recorded
Feb 26	AN 924	Sgt G.G. Thompson Sgt J.N. O'Brien	Practice Bombing	1500–1550	Madhaiganj -No range party due main body still at Cholavaram – results observed by pilot but not recorded
Feb 26	AN 928	F/O William Berry Cpl W.J. MacGillivray	Practice Bombing	1520–1630	Madhaiganj -No range party due main body still at Cholavaram – results observed by pilot but not recorded

Also in February 1943 168 Wing, under Group Captain Alfred William Hunt, Operational Commander, moved from Asansol to Madhaiganj as part of 221 Group. Squadron Leader Gibbs flew up via Asansol,[4] in a North American Havard with Squadron Leader Anthony Traill of 45 Squadron on 1 March. They found Madhaiganj airfield still under construction, with only a *kutch* airstrip in use and with just *bustie* huts for accommodation; wells were still being dug as there was an acute water shortage. They found 110 Squadron had already arrived. Despite these uninspiring conditions, once the detachments arrived on site from Cholavaram the squadron immediately initiated flying practice to restore morale, with dive-bombing instruction

---

[4]   Asansol was an airfield near Nigah Village, Bihrar Province, West Bengal, which had been established by the RAF in 1941, 23⁰ 39' N, 87⁰ 2' E. It was abandoned in 1945.

on the Salumpur Bombing Range and low-level bombing at Pandar. Flying Officer James 'Sandy' Sandilands flew a Vengeance over to Alipore with a detachment from 110 Squadron for fighter affiliation exercises and cine-gun tests on 4 March while the following day Flight Lieutenant Paulyn Francis Thornelde Smith, RAAF, the squadron adjutant, along with Flight Lieutenant Charles Midwinter-Jones AFM MD, the unit doctor, and Flying Officers Thomas Cox Gilchrist, David Berrington and Pilot Officer Robert Marlborough with the bulk of the personnel left Madras by rail for Asanol, having been temporarily diverted there until the water situation was resolved and, next day, Flying Officer Gordon MacDonald with the equipment train followed on, the two groups arriving on the 8th and 10th respectively. Finally, on the 8th Flying Officer E.A. Carter flew to Bombay to undertake a ship recognition course.

On 10 March 221 Group Air Staff issued Operations Instructions. Flying Standing Orders and 168 Wing Flying Standing Orders were all issued to the assembled aircrew. As circumstances permitted, dive bombing to full serviceability of aircraft and availability of ranges was conducted each day. It was reported that 'line errors are being overcome although under- and over-shooting persists'.[5] Regarding aircraft, on the 18th seven of the eight Vengeances remained grounded awaiting new engines. One Vengeance was therefore attached to 110 Squadron for one of their aircrew to use, but this machine was damaged by a Japanese air attack on the 22nd and destroyed in a second enemy air raid two days later. The squadron's personnel were reinforced by the arrival of Flight Lieutenant Ira Allison 'Sag' Sutherland from Karachi after the Vengeance Development Flight there was disbanded on the 19th, and Flying Officers Henry George Kenneth Pike, Walter Stanley Robinson, William Shipton and Edwin George Westaway, RAAF, all rejoined on the 29th. In April developments included the despatch on the 5th of Flight Lieutenant David William Metherell, RNZAF, Flying Officer David Vincent Starr Berrington, Gordon Webster MacDonald, who had transferred from the RCAF to the RAF, William Berry and Pilot Officer James Sandiland to Karachi to ferry in new Vengeance aircraft; a visit by Air Commodore Henry Hunter on the 6th and instructions from AHQ Bengal for all rear guns on the Vengeance to be converted to .303 Brownings

---

[5]   AIR 27/682/10, March 1943.

and Flight Lieutenant A.F. Wiggins from Engineering/Armament section arrived to supervise this change.

Once again 82 Squadron suffered engine problems with its aircraft and had not been able to fly them for three weeks. This frustrating malaise was reported in the Operational Record Book for 12 April: 'owing to the fact that all the eight-aircraft brought up from Cholavaram have gone u/s through the old trouble of piston rings.' It continued, 'Piston ring trouble started immediately on arrival of aircraft at Madhaiganj, so the ground crews again took the offending cylinder off and renewed piston rings and sometimes the cylinders. In this way it was possible to get a certain amount of practice in, and we concentrated on dive bombing. But things went from bad to worse and it became evident that the aircraft were unsafe to fly.' Flight Lieutenant David William Metherell RNZAF, Flying Officer Gordon Webster W. MacDonald and Pilot Officer James Sandilands did all the air testing, and five aircraft were brought back, sometime after only forty minutes in the air, cutting very badly, and 'engines were found full of shavings from the cylinder rings'.

It was recorded that while 45 and 110 Squadrons were receiving new modified aircraft, 82 which had the old aircraft for the longest period (five months) and experienced the most problems of serviceability was still awaiting improved aircraft. M.J. Croghan ferried the first one up from Karachi via Jodhpur, Delhi and Allahabad on 12 April and others followed at regular intervals. On the 23rd Warrant Officer Norman Holland with Flying Officer William Shipton as aircrew crash-landed Vengeance AN 987 in a river bed about twelve miles from Asanol due to supercharger faults, but they were uninjured. A visit by Air Vice Marshal Douglas Collyer, AOC, HQ Air Forces India, Group Captains Henry James Gemmel and Stanley Albert Checksfield and Squadron Leader James Morgan DSO, RAFVR, took place on the 29th and by the end of the month, with eight new Vengeances on strength, 82 Squadron's morale was reported as 'improved out of all knowledge. The Squadron is now carrying out more flying that either 110 or 45 although it has fewer aircraft, which prove that the ground crews are working extremely hard.' Gibbs added, 'The training at the moment is all dive bombing practice, and as soon as crews reach a satisfactory standard the squadron will be ready for operations.'

Preparations began on 28 May for a detachment of eight of 82 Squadron's Vengeances to move to Chittagong for combat operations. Flight Lieutenant Ira Sutherland and Sergeant D.W. Archer flew over to prepare the airfield for nine air crews and sixty ground crews and these also left by rail and then boat via Calcutta, Gulondo (now Goalundo Ghat) and Chandpur the same day under Flying Officer Arthur Leon Sumner, Intelligence/Operations, and Warrant Officer W.C. Davison, the Squadron Engineering Officer. They arrived at Chittagong on 31 May, the same day as the remaining seven Vengeances, led by Squadron Leader Dennis Gibbs flew in two sections of four and three aircraft, with a refuelling stop at Jessore, without mishap. The makeup of these two flights was as follows:

Aircraft	Pilot	Aircrew	Take Off	Arrival
AN 720	F/O Walter Stanley Robinson	F/O Henry George Kenneth Pike	0746	1155
EZ 859	F/O John Stevenson	Sgt Sidney Siddle	0745	1155
EZ 855	WO Alan Parker	Sgt W.T. Keefe	0748	1155
EZ 845	WO Norman Holland	F/O William Shipton	0745	1155
EZ 810	Sqn Ldr Dennis Gibbs	F/O John Rennie	1000	1518
AN 615	F/O Gordon MacDonald	F/O David Berrington	1000	1518
AN 957	P/O James Sandilands	Sgt William Webb	1000	1518

On arrival the detachment was placed on instant readiness to scramble between dawn and dusk each day as a precaution against Japanese pre-emptive air strikes. The plan was for the defending fighters to get off first to make interceptions with the Vengeances scrambling away immediately upon receiving their 'greens'.

No time was wasted and on 1 June six air crews were briefed for attacks on two factories on a bend of the river on the outskirts of Akyab, each bomber being armed with two 500lb GP NITD .025 bombs, and with 136 Squadron providing fighter escort. However, and not for the first time, the weather had the final say and this mission had to be changed, with an attack on the Buthidaung naval jetty at pinpoints 517436 and 515445 being substituted. Even this had to be abandoned as the weather reports from Ramu were universally bad.

Conditions were better on 3 June and, at 1000, Squadron Leader Gibbs led an attack with six Vengeances on the Buthidaung waterfront. They steered a course of 170 degrees from base to point three miles south of

Teknaf, and then turned 90 degrees to cross the hills screening the target. The weather proved good for once, with 8/10th to 9/10th stratocumulus at 12,000 feet along the whole route, and there was no lower cloud over the coasts, just 5/10th inland at 5,000 feet, with a visibility of fifteen miles. Strangely there was no opposition from ground or in the air and they were able to deliver a textbook attack. Their final approach was recorded in the Operations Record Book as 100 degrees and these dives were made from a left wing-over starting from a height of 10,000 feet down to 1,500 to 1,000 feet.

A total of ten 500lb GP NITD .025 bombs were delivered into the target. Eight bombs burst among buildings along the river bank south of the bend, two burst in the river and two 'hung up'. It was reported that individual pilots could not see their own bombs bursts but could see those dropped by those preceding them. For good measure both front and rear guns were used to ground strafe. A fighter escort had been provided by eight fighters from 136 Squadron and they, having nothing else to occupy them, also ground-strafed after the dive-bombers had finished their attacks.

Because the pre-planned escape route would have taken the Vengeances very low over hills which might have contained machine-gun nests, Gibbs in A went north from the target until he had crossed the British lines, before turning west for the coast, but his team never saw him go and followed the inward route as they exited. All the Vengeances were back safely at Chittagong by 1130.

The following day at 1203 Squadron Leader Gibbs led a six-plane (A, J, X, Y, D and F) attack on important warehouses located in Akyab town itself. They followed the same route and arrived over the target at 1300. The weather was good, with 9/10th cloud at 15,000 feet and a twenty-five-mile visibility with no wind. There was no aerial opposition for their escorts, eight Hurricanes of 67 Squadron, to contend with and they made their left wing over from 10,000 feet down to 1,000 feet, meeting light flak at this height which was described as 'ineffective', the bursts being inaccurate on both sides and astern of the last aircraft down. Gibbs himself, with Flying Officer John Stevenson and Pilot Officer James Sandilands attacked one warehouse, while Flying Officer Walter Stanley Robinson, led Warrant Officer Alan Edward Parker, RNZAF, and Sergeant George Thomas Couttie, RNZAF, down against the other. 500lb GP NITD bombs were dropped and were observed accurate, with timbers flying off one target and a smoke column from the other. Stevenson, flying X, used an F24 camera to photograph the dive.

Shortly after they touched down at Chittagong they were ordered to scramble away at 1430 as an incoming Japanese counter-strike was reported. Sandilands's machine had developed hydraulic problems during the attack and could not get airborne, but the rest got away. Sergeant Couttie aircraft was short of fuel and so, instead of circling at a safe distance for an indefinite period, he flew to Feni, landing at 1545, refuelling and returning to base at 1730. He joined Flying Officer Gordon MacDonald who, at 1500, had ferried in Vengeance AN 929 for the R & SU.

The 5th of June saw the next attack, again by six Vengeances escorted by eight Hurricanes from 136 Fighter Squadron.[6] Their assigned targets were the Buthidaung ferry and nearby warehouses full of enemy army supplies. This time the weather was not so kind, being described as 'thick', with 6/10-7/10th cumulus clouds between 15,000 and 5,000 feet and 4/10th stratocumulus down to 1,500 feet. The six aircraft went in parallel to the Maungdaw to Buthidaung road and made their attack dives through a hole in the clouds at 1615. Again, they deposited twelve 500lb GP NITD .025 bombs onto the enemy positions. Six bombs burst among buildings to the south of the road and within fifty-eighty yards of a large red-roofed building, which remained standing; two more bombs detonated north of the road and two went into the river. The Vengeances strafed the police station with their front guns as they made their exits.

They left at low level, steering north for about twenty-five miles, before turning west out to sea. On their way they sighted what appeared to be a semi-circular 250mm gun emplacement north of Buthidaung, located on the edge of wood on the eastern bank of the river. They also spotted two wrecked fighter aircraft, a partially burnt-out enemy fighter, inevitably identified as a Zero, and a burnt-out Hurricane a mile north of that. There had been no failures and all the dive bombers were back on the ground at Chittagong between 1710 and 1720.

---

[6]   67 Squadron was commanded by Battle of Britain ace Squadron Leader Thomas Campbell 'John' Parker while 163 Squadron was under the command of Squadron Leader A. Noel Constantine.

The planned strike for 6 June was for six Vengeances led by Squadron Leader Ira Sutherland to hit the fuel dumps at Akyab airfield, with the lock at the Royal Lake as an alternative target. They were assigned an escort of ten Hurricanes, but the bulk of these lost contact on the way out and just four stayed with the bombers. An early morning start was made but the weather was poor from the outset and steadily deteriorated throughout the day. They arrived over the target at 0730, found it blanked out, flew forty miles south then returned at 0802. No hole could be found in the clouds over the airfield or the lock, and, although they made a diversion to Buthidaung that was weathered-out also. The same blanket cloud cover ruled out similar plans for attacks on the 7th, 8th and 9th.

To compensate, 82 Squadron made two separate attacks on the 10th. The first took off at 0915, six Vengeances with an escort of eight Hurricanes from 67 Squadron. The mission was to destroy warehouses in the jetty area of Buthidaung, Arakan (now Rakine), Burma, around forty miles north of Sittwe. For this operation they were armed with two 500lb GP NITD .025 bombs apiece. They followed a course which crossed the coast at Teknaf, Cox's Bazar, the southernmost tip in what is now Bangladesh, and then a heading of 130 degrees to the target which was reached between 1025 and 1030. They identified the area by way of a sunken barge (which they machine-gunned) at the junction of the streams. Because of weather conditions, (9/10th cloud from 8,000 feet down to 2,000 feet) it was decided to adopt a shallow dive-bombing method of attack, from 3,000 feet down to 1,000 feet. Fortunately, they were only met by spasmodic small-arms fire, although AN 645 (Sergeant George Couttie) was hit in both wings, the petrol pump and tail, whether by enemy action or by the shrapnel from her next ahead's bomb explosion being unclear, but this damage was not considered serious.

What counted more was that considerable damage was done to the enemy. Two bombs were direct hits on a large 'L-shaped' building on the jetty. Another bomb exploded between this building and the jetty and one went into the water. Four bombs detonated among enemy barrack buildings east of the jetty, four struck a 'U-shaped' building west of the jetty, resulting in both a violent explosion and a cloud of orange-brown smoke which rose to a height of 100 feet. Both the 'L' and 'U' buildings were considered demolished. On their way out, they passed low over several enemy-occupied villages, which were also strafed with the front guns, while

A coastal map of the Arakan region of Burma. (*R.I.N. Official*)

Above: A USAAF A-31 showing the unique Vengeance wing form. (*Smithsonian Institute, Washington DC*)

Below: Original members of 110 (H) Squadron at Quetta, July 1942. (*Adrian Gill*)

A Vengeance with dive brakes in the fully-open position. (*AVCO*)

A *vic* of Vengeances from 152 OTU, Peshawar. (*Flight Lieutenant V B McInnis, RCAF*)

Above: A-31 Vengeances being assembled for the RAF, February 1943. (*Crown Copyright*)

Below: Newly-arrived Vengeances at Drigh Road. (*Crown Copyright*)

A profile shot of Vengeance AF745. (*Adrian Gill*)

Above left: Flight Lieutenant Eugene Ettinger, RCAF. (*R.C.A.F. Official*)

Above right: Flight Lieutenant Sutherland DFC. (*RAAF Official*)

Above: The mixed crews of the Vengeance units is well illustrated in this photograph. (*Cotton, IAF PO2491.350*)

Below: Gill and 84 Squadron meet Lord Louis Mountbatten, Supreme Allied Commander, South-East Asia. (*Arthur Gill Collection*)

Above: Arthur Murland Gill, of 84 Squadron, airborne over Ceylon in 1943. (*Arthur Gill Collection*)

Below: A Vengeance 'warms up'. (*Crown Copyright*)

Above: Like all American-built radial-engine aircraft of its generation, the Vultee Vengeance was a big-nosed beast. (*Crown Copyright*)

Below: Personnel of No. 7 Squadron, Indian Air Force. (*I.A.F. Official*)

Above: Bombs exploding on enemy positions. This image illustrates the difficulty of target selection in Burma. (*Arthur Gill Collection*)

Below: A rare colour photograph of a Vengeance and its crew. (*AVCO*)

Above: Indian Air Force pilots manning their planes. (*Sharma PO2491.349*)

Below: A Vengeance in a typical location with native basha huts as accommodation. (*Adrian Gill*)

That unique wing shape over a typical bridge target. (*AUSTRALIAN WAR MEMORIAL, Canberra A.C.T.*)

Maintenance in the field. Keeping the Vengeance operational in dire conditions always proved a headache. (*Arthur Gill Collection*)

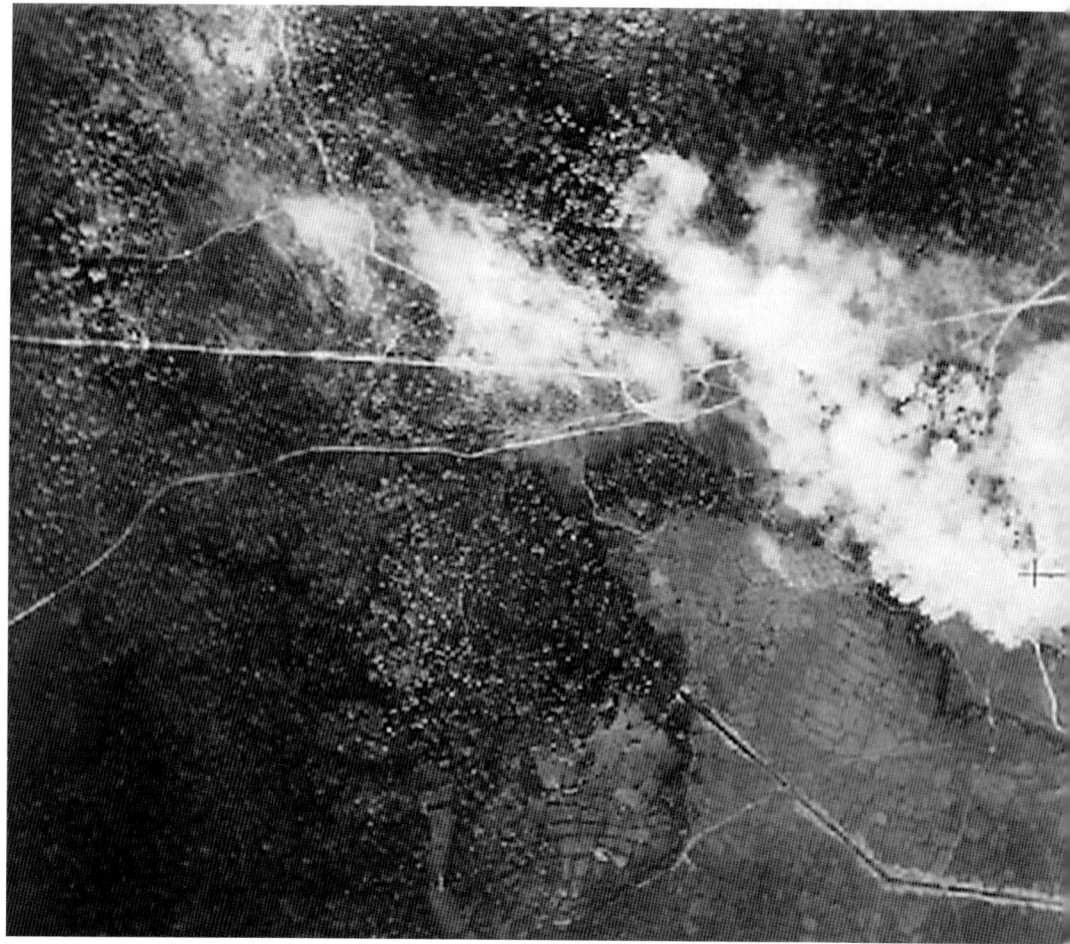

Above: Attack of
18 March 1944.
(*Arthur Gill
Collection*)

Left: Attack of
13 April 1944.
(*Arthur Gill
Collection*)

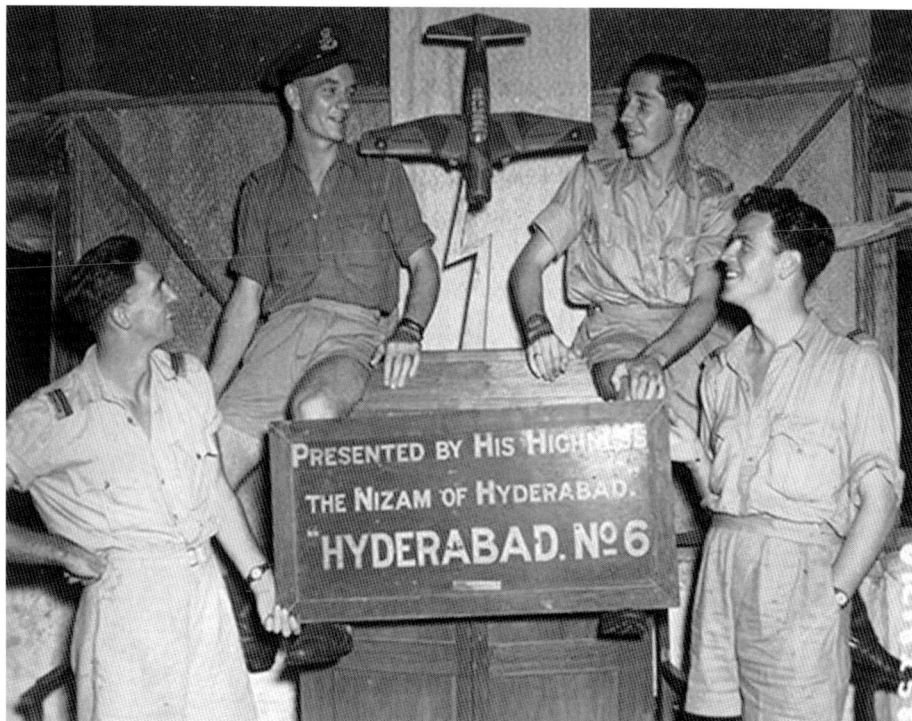

Above: Officers of No. 110 (H) Squadron with a model of a Vengeance presented by His Highness the Nizam of Hyderabad. (*Canadian War Museum*)

Below: Bomb trolley. A fast turn-round between missions was often essential. (*Arthur Gill Collection*)

Above: Take off! A Vengeance roars down the runway. As the monsoon season approached, runways were often 'weathered out'. (*Crown Copyright*)

Below: No. 84 Squadron en route to target. (*Arthur Gill Collection*)

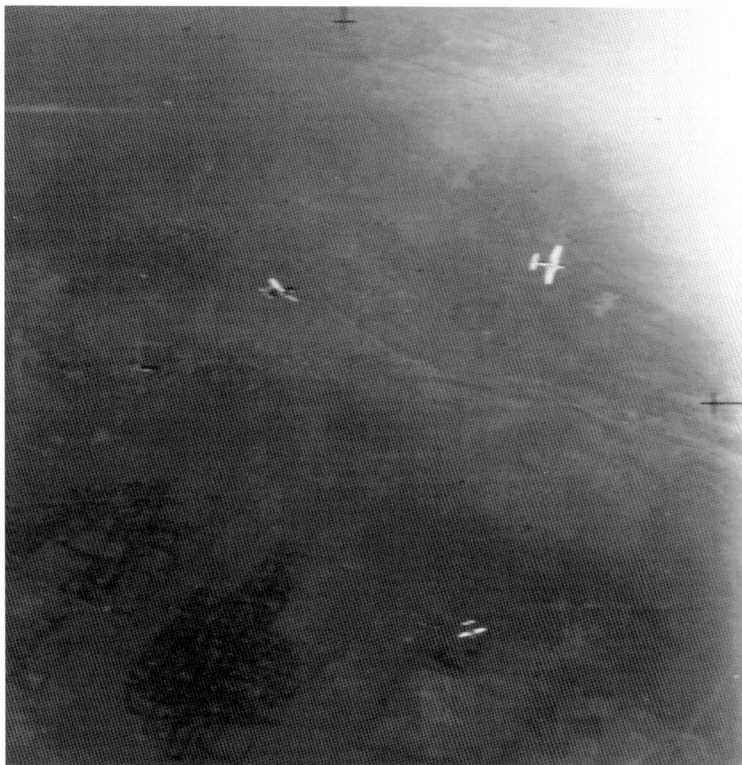

Right: The tip-over into the attack dive. (*Arthur Gill Collection*)

Below: Bombs gone! With nose and tail fuses fluttering, a stick goes down on Japanese positions. (*Arthur Gill Collection*)

An Army-eye view. Tanks prepare to follow up the Vengeance attack. (*Arthur Gill Collection*)

Left: Low-level target check confirms that bombs were on target. (*Arthur Gill Collection*)

Below: De-briefing at the end of a mission. (*Arthur Gill Collection*)

at Indin, Maungdaw, Arakan, in 20⁰ 31'N, 92⁰ 35'E, six 'abnormally high' barges, with flat bows and sterns, possibly landing craft, were also machine-gunned, and at Apuak Myinhlut to the north, a large storage facility covered with camouflage netting was observed and machine-gunned. The six aircraft landed back at Chittagong at 1125.

The second strike of the day took place at 1415. The target selection was once more Buthidaung jetties and town and six Vengeances were allocated, escorted by eight 67 Squadron Hurricanes. Visibility was excellent at forty miles. Their approach was again parallel to the Maungdaw-Buthidaung road. The dives were made at 1505 from 10,000 feet down to 1,000 feet and all twelve bombs fell in the zone, with four hitting a large iron-roofed, U-shaped building, which had two of its sides demolished with four more striking the adjacent buildings and huts to its west. Another large petrol fire followed with black smoke and orange flames; six further bombs fell onto riverside buildings south of the bend. Their exit route was north up the valley at low level and out by Cox's Bazar. En route they observed a variety of enemy movements, including thirty barrack huts (50ft x 18ft) in four lines at Pinpoint PM5640; the landing strip north of Laungdaw which was three-quarters submerged; three Japanese power boats heading south near Mingalagyi and a naval patrol ship, also heading south.

The 11th of June saw another pair of strikes being launched by 82 Squadron. At 0710 six Vengeances lifted off from Chittagong and were joined by ten Hurricanes from 136 Squadron. The bombers formed into two *vics* of three with one being allocated the target of Akyab town jail and the second the courthouse, both of which were suspected of being used as Japanese HQ and admin buildings. Armed with the usual bomb load of two 500lb GP NITD .025 bombs, the Vengeances set a course south twenty miles out to sea then turned due east after circling Fakir Point. The two targets were then approached from the south across Stone Jetty. While no flak was experienced on the approach, heavy AA fire opened as the first Vengeance tipped over into the dive. The bursts were accurate for the initial height but behind the dive bombers, although bursts were seen close to the escorting Hurricanes which were at 17,000 feet.

All bombs fell in the target area and direct hits were made on the jail's outer buildings, sending up clouds of yellowish smoke visible for twenty miles away. Four hits were made on the courtyard of the courthouse, although the roof remained apparently intact. Additional 40mm guns opened up as they made their exit, notably from the vicinity of the airfield and from a site at pinpoint PR.879538, which they machine-gunned with both front wing guns and the rear guns as they flew over. They took an exit route in their respective *vics* which took them at low level out between Fakir Point and the airfield and then across the mangrove swamps. At pinpoint 825544, just south of the *chaung*, approximately one hundred enemy troops, 'Khaki clad', were seen and these too were machine-gunned. It was noted that water on the Royal Lake was very low and that sandbanks were in evidence its centre. All aircraft landed back safely at 0930.

That afternoon a further six-plane raid was launched, escorted by ten 136 Squadron Hurricanes. They took off at 1310 to strike at Padali village on the northern tip of Akyab Island on the main Akyab to Rathedaung highway. There was again no aerial opposition and the attack went in at 1410. Ten bombs were dropped, two falling in the centre of the village among buildings and tents, two more towards the edge among huts and trees while four were aimed at a large two-storey building south of the village, two falling accurately with two overshooting. Vengeance S failed to bomb due to hydraulic pressure failure making the bomb doors inoperational. Both front and rear guns were again usefully employed against tents and buildings

Back at Chittagong, Sergeant Couttie's damaged AN 929 was flown back to Salbani and replaced by Flight Sergeant R.G. Holding with EZ 877.

The steamer station south of Buthidaung, a township in the westernmost part of Burma, and sixteen miles from Maungdaw via a road tunnel, was the object of 82 Squadron's attention on 12 June. Two *vics* of three Vengeances, escorted by twelve Hurricanes from 67 Squadron, left Chittagong at 1100. Cloud cover over the area was heavy but fortunately there was 'a large hole in the clouds' and the dive bombers took advantage of it to attack from 10,800 feet down to 1,200 feet, dropping their twelve bombs with precision. Eight scored direct hits on buildings immediately adjacent to the road intersection, causing flames and a tall column of grey smoke, while four bombs fell into the Mayu river. They met no aerial or ground opposition but engaged targets of opportunity with both front and rear guns, including eight stationary trucks. All were safely back at base by 1235.

There were no operations on 13 June despite the detachment standing to until 1600, due to nil visibility and occasional showers throughout the day.

Combat was resumed on the 14th when six Vengeances, with a ten-Hurricane escort from 67 Squadron, sortied out at 1220 with the aim of silencing Akyab wireless station at Pinpoint 862549 and attacking the jetty at Pinpoint 898548 once more. They found the weather clear over the targets and they were met by the same type of heavy and light flak at 17,000 feet near the airfield and at 1,000 feet from near the W/T station. They made their dives from 10,000 feet down to a bomb release height of 2,000 feet, with a low-level getaway across the island. A very accurate strike was made on the wireless station by Warrant Officer Alan Edward Parker and Flying Officer James Walter Sandilands. They scored four direct hits on the station buildings, starting fires. The following day it was recorded that the wireless station had all its masts down and that all three buildings had been demolished. The second target was also damaged, two bombs striking the northern end on the inner jetty, one hitting the northern end of the 'T' and two more exploded in the buildings adjacent to the jetty to the north-east. They strafed with both front and rear guns during the attack. Passing over the ruins of the jail that they had hit on the 11th they could see several blackened and burnt-out buildings. All the Vengeances landed back at Chittagong safely at 1405 after their most satisfying attack to date.

Spurred on by the excellent results of this strike the next day no fewer than three operations were carried out. The first left Chittagong at 0715, six Vengeances been assigned to attack Japanese motor transport concentrated in trees at Maungdaw. They found the weather clear over the target zone and there was no opposition from the enemy. They made their attack dives from 10,000 feet down to 3,000 feet and strafed with both wing guns going in and rear guns withdrawing. The area was thickly wooded and individual motor transport (MT) vehicles were not seen but the whole area was smothered with ten 500lb GP NITD .025 bombs which all fell dispersed throughout the area, and two red-roofed buildings, thought to be acting as enemy admin blocks, were also demolished.

The second strike left at 1010, six Vengeances which were ordered to make a low-level attack at Letwedet, pinpoint 470452. Their bombs demolished a large *busti* hut in that township, two more were dropped on Palldaung and two others on Kundaing village. Vengeance AN 960 had her bombs 'hang up'. Strafing by both front and rear guns was conducted against five stationary motor transports spotted on the main highway just south of Letwedet and at Buthidaung.

The third strike, again by six Vengeances, and, like the previous two escorted by 136 Squadron Hurricanes, left the base at 1500 to attack the national school (a large grey-roofed building being used as a Japanese HQ). They were met by heavy AA fire which was described as 'plentiful and accurate for height and direction'. The heavy stuff commenced prior to the Vengeances tipping over into their attack dives at 10,000 feet and this was supplemented by light AA from north of the jetty and the jail, and machine-gun fire during their exit. The dive bombers hit the building with eight 500lb GP bombs, with two others being very near misses, the rear pair of aircraft bombing into the demolition dust of their predecessors. Two other bombs overshot and went into the river just to the north of the target.

The next day the detachment was visited by Air Chief Marshal Sir Richard Edmund Charles Peirse KCB DSO AFC, Air Vice Marshal Thomas Melling Williams OBE CD MC, the AOC Bengal Command and Air Commodore Alexander Gray CB MC, AOC 224 (Tactical) Group. The AOC took the trouble to speak to all the aircrew individually and praised the work of 82 Squadron's engineer, Warrant Officer W. Davison, for his work in keeping the detachment in action in difficult circumstances.

Following the visit by the top brass, during that afternoon they were directed to strike at Japanese army troop concentrations at the villages of Athet Nanra and Sinoh and this time the six Vengeances were escorted by 67 Squadron again. They took off at 1305 and although the weather was fine over the target, with 3/10th cumulus to 15,000 feet, the targets were difficult to pick out, being buildings well hidden in trees, and they were unable to observe their results to any degree. The usual bomb load was nonetheless deposited, and strafing conducted against newly-constructed huts at both Sinoh and Buthidaung, to which the enemy made no response.

The weather now deteriorated steadily and made operations increasingly difficult and, eventually, impossible. On 17 June a six-Vengeance strike force, supported by twelve Hurricanes from 136 Squadron, left Chittagong at 0805 with the battle plan of demolishing the British Oxygen Company complex (pinpoint 906566) and the Arakan mills (pinpoint 898565) at Akyab. The weather proved clear until pinpoint PR. 8085 and then it quickly thickened to 10/10th cloud from 13,000 feet down to 300 feet. To get around this mass the Vengeances changed course to 170 degrees to twenty miles out to sea and they tried to reach their targets by crossing the Mayu Peninsula again from the east, then back out to sea and in from the west. The weather remained impossible throughout and they therefore had no choice but to change the plan. It was decided to hit Buthidaung instead, and they altered course northward.

Buthidaung was reached at 0930 and they made shallow dives down to 1,000 feet, distributing twelve 500lb GP bombs along the north–south river road, eight bursting immediately north of the Maungdaw to Buthidaung road and four to the south between the road and the river. There was intense light flak from the ground and two Vengeances were damaged. Sandy Sandilands's AN 615 took a hit in the sternpost from a 20mm shell, while Bill Berry's AN 960 bombed below 1,000 feet and was damaged by the blast, but neither aircraft was seriously impaired, and all the aircraft had returned safely by 1025. Ominously, the bad weather was reported heading north toward Chittagong itself.

The forecast proved only too accurate. By the morning of 18 June torrential rain had started falling and lasted throughout the entire day and on through the next. Only one sortie was possible on the 20th and this was a lone supply drop carried out by Flying Officers Gordon MacDonald and David Berrington in Vengeance AN 960 at Lainkalangpara (Pinpoint PG 4555). Leaving base at 1500 this aircraft had four canisters mounted on the under-wing bomb carriers, but they had to climb to 8,000 feet to get east of Cox's Bazar. The cloud was 8/10th to 9/10ths but they managed to find a gap and followed the course of the Sangu river to the beleaguered British troops. The platoon had laid out a white cross on the riverbank and this was seen at the assigned reference and between 1550 and 1555 all four canisters were dropped 'in positions easy enough for troops to retrieve'. The mission was a very satisfactory one and well executed.

Also, this day two encouraging 'Sitreps'[7] came in following Intelligence received by Headquarters 224 Group. The first, AC 311, read 'V Force[8] reports RAF bombing Buthidaung on 10/6 and 12/6 killed 40 Japs'. The

---

[7] Sitrep = Situation Reports.

[8] V Force was originally a British guerrilla force set up by General Sir Archibald Wavell to operate behind Japanese lines when, as expected, they commenced an invasion of India after the conquest of Burma in 1942. Its first commander was Brigadier Arthur Felix-Williams, 'Felix-Bill', who had commanded the Tochi Scouts on the Afghan border pre-war. It gradually morphed into a mainly reconnaissance and intelligence reporting cadre split into two groups, of which the southern part operated in the Arakan Zone.

second, AC. 338. 'Sitrep 2000. Villagers state bombing Letwedet 15/6 killed 16 Japs in HQ and W/T Station. Bombing Maungdaw 16/6 killed 4 Japs and 100 *Mughs*[9] just arrived from Teknaf.' Later an eyewitness submitted a graphic eyewitness account of the attack. 'After bombing six funeral pyres were seen.' A further Sitrep was received on 24 June: 'AC 375. Most Secret. V Force report 80 Japs killed and wounded RAF raid Buthidaung 3rd June.'

The following three days were also totally rained out and the decision was taken for the detachment to return to Salbani on the 25th to be replaced by a detachment from 45 Squadron which arrived on the 26th. Although only eleven days of the whole month were suitable for flying operations, 82 Squadron had flown ninety sorties, including eighteen in a single day, which, for an eight-plane unit, was pretty good going and reflected well on both air and ground personnel. They were also joined by Flight Lieutenant Gordon Webster DFC, who had transferred from the RCAF to the RAF.

In June 1943, 82 Squadron was transferred to 221 Group, Calcutta, 168 Wing, and was based at Salbati airfield 22°36'N, 87°17'E, alongside the railway in the Bengal Province.[10] During July there was a period of intense training for the understrength force which was not made easier by several periods of appalling weather due to a cyclone in the Bay of Bengal.

Various dignitaries visited them, including Air Commodore Herbert Victor Rowley AOC 221 Group on the 2nd and again on the 7th, and Wing Commander Buchanan, Armaments Officer AHQ Bengal on the 5th. These all made it pretty clear that 82's move forward into combat was imminent. The 25th saw Rowley with them again along with Group Captain Ronald Christopher Wilson, Senior Air Staff Officer (SASAO), 221 Group, Group Captain Percy Ronald Garner 'Paddy', The Earl of Bandon CBE DSO, AOC 224 Group, and a former CO of 82 Squadron, and the commanding officers of 45 and 110 Squadrons, among others. This day also saw the rump of the squadron carrying out low-level formation attacks against a set target on a riverbank which was attacked by three separate '*vics*' of

---

[9]   *Mughs* (*Maughs*) were a mainly Buddhist tribe that had infiltrated this part of the Indian-Burmese border region about a century before and had gradually ousted or cowed the indigenous local tribes. During the Japanese invasion while the Chittagong natives remained mainly loyal to the British cause, the Mughs openly collaborated with the Japanese and their armed bands fought as willing allies of Nippon.

[10]   This is now a long-abandoned airfield at what is still Salbani crossing.

three aircraft simultaneously from three different directions, a dangerous manoeuvre. Bad weather prevented more flying from the following day on, but extensive ground training was initiated with some urgency and at the highest priority. The squadron was divided into four flights under Flight Lieutenants Ira Sutherland, David William Metherell, RNZAF, G.W. Graff and Clifford Smith respectively. When flying did resume next day a box of ten Vengeances practised formation flying and fighter evasion tactics. Two Vengeances, piloted by Warrant Officer Alan Edward Parker, RNZAF, and Sergeant William Melville Tullett, RCAF, with Flying Officer C.A. Carver and Sergeant Eric Mason as their rear-seat men, were detached to RAF Amarda Road on Fighter Affiliation, Gunnery Control, Bombing, Camera Gun operating and Air Firing Courses. The intensive training programme totalled 300 flying hours despite conditions and between ten and fifteen aircraft were serviceable the whole month. Only lack of the same essential spare parts kept four of A Flight's Vengeances grounded earlier on.

During the month two other matters came up; firstly, there was still a need for the harmonization of the front wing machine-guns, Gibbs commenting that 'the results as regards cone of fire were good they still do not seem to realise that when the aircraft is flying straight and level the guns still fire upward. It is realised by all our pilots that this is dangerous when ground strafing.'[11] The second item was recorded on 18 July that 'The markings of all RAF aircraft in this Command are in the process of being altered, and the old familiar roundels of the RAF are no more. The basic colours of the new scheme are blue and white.'[12] On 2 August Squadron Leader Dennis Gibb was hastily recalled from leave due to the impending move forward, and on the 6th resumed command.

The advance party, under Flying Officer A.L. Sumner, left the same day for Feni (Fenni or Fenny) airfield, $23^0 02'$N, $91^0 23'$ E, also in Bengal. Unfortunately for Warrant Officer Parker his journey was not a happy one for the engine of his aircraft, EZ 877, cut out without any warning at 1,500 feet, picked up again after all the pumps had been switched on, and out again half a minute later; it continued picking up for a minute or two then cutting

---

[11]   Flight Lieutenant Ira Sutherland was temporarily commanding 82 Squadron 31 July 1943, AIR 27 682/18.

[12]   *Ibid.*

and would not keep running, indicating carburettor problems. Eventually, Parker belly-landed in five feet of water two hundred yards east of Irda (87⁰8' E, 21⁰39'N. It was still daylight and neither Parker nor his rear-seat man, Flying Officer E.A. Carter, were injured. Two days later Ira Sutherland with four more Vengeances arrived at Feni and assumed command of the detachment; another six aircraft under Flying Officer James Sandilands, RAAF, joined them the next day and Gibbs arrived with Navigation Officer Flight Lieutenant Graff on the 10th. They met with AOC 224 Group on the 16th and discussed targets, current difficulties, range, petrol consumption and other relevant points.

On 18 August 82 conducted its first strike from Feni, Dennis Gibbs leading a six-plane box from Feni at 0945 against concealed enemy *bashas* in the trees along heavily-wooded Thaungdaw Ridge. They found conditions tricky, 10/10th cloud at 6,000 feet with occasional rainstorms en route. Accordingly, they were forced to make their attacks in shallow dives from 6,000 feet down to 1,100 feet, dropping twelve 500lb GP, NITD. All the bombs burst along the ridge itself, but no enemy movement was seen. One of the Vengeances strafed with her rear guns only. There was no return fire and no problems, and they returned to base at 1110.

The 19th saw the second mission of a similar composition, but this time the Vengeances, led by Gibbs again at 0945, hit a Japanese supply dump at Htindaw (Pinpoint PM 4444), just a few miles west of Buthidaung, close alongside the road to Maungdaw which they crossed at an altitude of 9,000 feet, which was smothered in clouds. They dived through the murk over Buthidaung to below the cloud base to 600 feet ASL, but could not distinguish the target, so split and regained height over the surrounding hills before taking their bombs back to Feni where they landed safely at 1120.

They resumed their efforts on the 23rd, returning to Htindaw with Flying Officer G. MacDonald leading. This time they found 3/10th cloud at 6,000 feet and delivered their attack at 1602 in steep dives down to a release height of 2,000 feet on a course of 270 degrees This proved most successful and at least four direct hits were registered in the old village, while a further six 500lb bombs detonated to good effect among the *Busti* spaced along the main highway at Pinpoint PM 441440 which started two fires. On their way out three hastily abandoned military trucks were strafed and they were back at Feni unscathed at 1710.

Flying Officer James Sandilands led the following day's six-plane strike which took off from Feni at 1055. They were briefed to attack a Japanese supply depot at Baguna village (Pinpoint PM 499405) which comprised several *Busti* huts partially hidden in trees along the wood slopes. For once they were blessed with clear weather over the target area up to 15,000 feet. They made steep dives down from 10,300 feet on a course of 260 degrees, bombing from 2,000 feet. Nine bombs fell directly inside the village with three near misses to the north-west, south-west and east respectively.

The 26th witnessed Air Commodore Philip Herbert Mackworth CBE DFC, AOC 224 Group, visiting the detachment and discussing Vengeance tactics, and Dennis Gibbs wryly reported the fact that 'the story was very different from when 82 Squadron was under his Command in 225 Group'. Mackworth was not to be the last senior officer to be forced to curb his original distain for the Vengeance once he had evidence of what they could achieve.

On the 27th a reported Japanese HQ which included an important signals centre, located at Kyauktaw (Pinpoint PN 017393) on the Kaladan river, was allocated as 82 Squadron's next objective. Squadron Leader Dennis Gibbs led a force of five Vengeances which left Feni at 1257. They had been briefed with a stereo pair of photographs which showed the site, which was a quite distinctive pair of rectangular 'and two Geneva-Cross shaped buildings painted red'. These buildings housed these vital targets and were the sole cement-built buildings near the Jetty Steamer Station, to the north of the town market.

On the way to the target the weather was poor with 10/10ths cumulus cloud from 4,000 feet up to 9,000 feet and with occasional towers up to 25,000 feet. A weather reconnaissance aircraft sent out an hour earlier had attempted to transmit a 'PIP' report[13] but her signal was not received and instead a verbal report was received. However, during the hour-long flight, conditions rapidly deteriorated. In addition, Vengeance F, piloted by Flight Sergeant Ronald Trigg, RAAF, which was the camera-equipped aircraft, was forced to turn back with electrical trouble at 1342, leaving just five aircraft to carry out the attack. Nonetheless, on arrival, the buildings were easily identified, and the dive-bombing runs commenced at 1410 from a height of 10,300 feet down to

---

[13] PIP meant Weather Favourable'.

bomb release at 2,000 feet along an attack course of 260 degrees. Ten 500lb GP TD .025 were dropped, of which two were very near misses, with two slight undershoots and four bombs in the river alongside the target.

When the final aircraft left the scene, the building remained comparatively intact, although it was partially obscured by the brown smoke of the bomb blasts. No return fire was encountered, and all aircraft were back on the ground at by 1514.

On the 28th reports from infiltrating friendly forces stated that some 400 Japanese and *Thakins* (the Japanese armed so-termed 'Burma Independence Army') troops were assembled at Tarawaing village (Pinpoint PG 8343). Dennis Gibbs led a force of six Vengeances, both Mk I and Mk IAs, against this concentration, and they carried twelve 500lb NITDR bombs. They lifted off from base at 0855 and, once more, met poor weather, with 9/10ths cumulus from Feni to Chittagong, and then 6–8/10ths up from 4,000 feet to 12,000 feet from Chittagong to the target and with a block of cloud stretching up from 1,000 to 12,000 feet over the village itself.

Tarawaing is on the Kaladan river and surrounded by ranges of forested hills up to 2,600 feet, closing to within two miles to the eastward and six miles from the west. On approach at 0950 they glimpsed the twelve *Busti* huts and one such white building which housed the enemy and were able to refer to the nearby larger hamlets of Kalweta and Daletme for reference points. Because of the conditions, only two aircraft made bombing runs from 6,000 feet to 4,000 feet, and their bombs burst on the edge of the village. Gibbs and the other three headed north, circled back and made another attempted run, but found conditions still unsuitable and took their bombs home. However, Flight Sergeant George Couttie RNZAF, in Vengeance K, was frustrated at not being able to inflict some damage on the enemy, broke from the formation and flew back for yet another attempt. It was in vain as the target was still obscured. While going south over the target ten minutes after the bombs had fallen, Couttie's aircraft flying at 4,000 feet, suffered an explosion which hurled her upward momentarily caused the engine to stop. The machine was flying through layers of thick cloud and no cause for this alarming occurrence could be identified. It was later speculated that a 4–inch (or similar calibre) mortar had been fired off straight into the air with a time fuse. Couttie's aircraft was undamaged but his diversion meant he had to land at Chittagong on his return to base to refuel.

A similar attack was made on the 30th against a strong Japanese redoubt holding around 100 enemy troops which had been constructed under the corner of a building in the old market place at Maungdaw. This bunker was listed as No. 18 on 26th Division's 'Target List'. Dennis Gibbs led a six-plane box from Feni at noon and for once found clear weather over the attack zone. They made steep dives at 1302 from 10,000 down to 1,000 feet which resulted in a highly accurate delivery of their ordnance, which comprised six 500lb GP NITD, two 500lb TD eight hours, three 500lb twelve hours and a single 500lb TD thirty-six hours. There were two direct hits and four near misses within twenty yards of the corner of the building and at least one of the long delay bombs 'also found the target' with others in the vicinity.

It was noted that the vertically-set camera gun used produced photos that were of 'topographical interest, but those taken while the aircraft was in its dive are valueless'. It was suggested that the vertical mounting was unsatisfactory for dive-bombing and that better results might be obtained by substituting a cine-camera for one of the front guns.

The final attack of the month was delivered by six aircraft the next day, and was the first to be led by Flight Lieutenant David Metherell. They left Feni at 0825 and their assigned targets were storage areas and the jetty at Buthidaung It was noted that this township had been extensively bombed already and that there were very few intact buildings remaining and that these were isolated. Therefore, each pilot was briefed to pick his own target. Gibbs wrote, 'It is a peculiarity of Vengeance dive bombing that only rarely is a crew able to see its own bomb bursts; normally each observes what it can of the others.' They attacked through a layer of cloud at 0940 with dives from 11,000 feet down to 2,000 feet utilising a hole in the cloud. Direct hits were claimed on a building near the jetty and there were other very near misses on one of the few larger buildings, caught on camera.

Operations continued apace in this manner from throughout the following period until the weather brought operations to a temporary abatement. No. 168 Wing was advised that, due to the rains, there was a lack of suitable targets for a time. During September, 82 Squadron conducted intensive training flights to Paletwa intersperse with operations where and when the weather allowed. Typical of this unsatisfactory period was an operation to Paletwa on the 2nd. This was a border town in the Arakan situated on the bend of the Kaladan river some eleven-and-a-quarter miles from the Indian border at 21⁰ 18' N, 92⁰E. The practice was for a single Vengeance to make a prior weather reconnaissance flight ahead of the main body to ensure it was worthwhile sending them out and on this occasion this task was done by Flight Lieutenant David Metherell with Flying Officer E.A. Carter as his observer, in Vengeance EZ 819. They left base at 0845 and radioed back that it was worth trying. Accordingly, six aircraft were despatched at 0940, deployed as follows:

Aircraft	Code	Pilot	Aircrew
AN 615	J	F/O Gordon MacDonald	Flt Lt David Berrington
AN 806	C	WO Alan Parker RNZAF	Sgt K.J. Amos
AN 720	K	WO William Tullett RCAF	Sgt Eric Leslie Mason RAAF
EZ 872	P	Flt Lt William Berry	Sgt B.A.E. Winter
EX 869	X	WO Alexander Holland	F/O William Shipton
AN 645	S	Sgt M.J. Croghan	Sgt L.R. Jenkins

This operation was rated as 'successful'[14] and all the aircraft landed back safely at 1135. An identical operation was conducted the following day, this time to Kyauktaw,[15] where the strategically important Kispanadi Bridge crosses the Kaladan, about sixty-five miles north of Sittwe. On this occasion Flight Lieutenant Bill Berry and Sergeant B.A.E. Winter, flying Vengeance AP 116 N, carried out the weather reconnaissance between 0626 and 0810, and the six-plane box left at 0855, with the following teams:

Aircraft	Code	Pilot	Aircrew
AN 615	J	Sqn Ldr Dennis Gibbs	F/O John Rennie
EZ 855	D	Flt Lt David Metherell	F/O E.A. Carter
EZ 902	F	Flt Sgt Ronald Trigg RAAF	Sgt H.R. Crichton
AN 720	K	WO William Tullett RCAF	Sgt E. Mason
EZ 859	X	WO Alan Parker RNZAF	Sgt D.F. Cartwright-Howall
AN 957	Y	Flt Sgt M.J. Croghan	Sgt L.R. Jenkins

After only a short time into the outward leg, Warrant Officer Tullett was forced to return to base with a large fabric patch ballooning on his tail plane and threatening to detach entirely. The squadron had been continually

---

14 Squadron Leader Dennis Gibbs, AIR 27/682/23.
15 Alternately known as Kyauktaw or Kyaukpyu.

complaining about the poor condition of many of the aircraft it had been allocated and this was just another example of how this impinged on their effectiveness. The rest of the force continued and delivered another successful mission, returning to Feni at 1010.

The 4th of September was spent in further practice with calibration, drogue-towing and air-to-air firing, while three aircrews conducted formation bombing on a sea marker in the Sandship[16] Channel in the Meghna estuary but on the 5th they returned to Kyauktaw once more and next day carried out an operation against Hparabyin, Arakan, in $20^0 73'$ N, $92^0 61'$E. The weather reconnaissance was conducted from 0800 by Warrant Officer Alan Parker, RNZAF, with Sergeant Cartwright-Howell as his observer, and the force was despatched at 0910 formed thus:

Aircraft	Code	Pilot	Aircrew
AN 615	J	Sqn Ldr Dennis Gibbs	F/O John Rennie
AN 806	C	Flt Sgt R.G. Holding	Flt Sgt Johan Barnard SAAF
EZ 855	D	Flt Lt David Metherell	F/O E.A. Carter
EZ 902	F	Flt Sgt Ronald Trigg	Sgt H.R. Crichton
EZ 859	X	WO Alexander Holland	F/O William Shipton
AN 987	Y	Flt Sgt George Couttie	Flt Sgt George Davies

The 7th saw weather so bad that even local flying and exercises had to be abandoned. Squadron Leader Dennis Gibbs had flown over to Chittagong on the first day of the month for a conference on a suitable base and 10 September saw a formation of ten aircraft fly from Feni to there and back with various degrees of success, AN 720 K, piloted by Warrant Officer Tullett, suffering electrical troubles but completing the round trip, AN 806 C similarly completing but incurring hydraulic problems which necessitated despatching EZ 836 B again flown by Warrant Officer Tullett, with a fitter, LAC G.L. Longbotham, as his passenger to effect repairs to enable the return leg of the exercise.

The conditions cleared enough for 82 Squadron to mount another operation on the 11th. The preliminary scouting by Flying Officer Robert Dempster and Sergeant N.D. Hankinson found the weather clear over

---

[16] Alternatively known as the Sandwip, Sandvip or Shondip Channel.

Inbauk, Banmauk township in the Kathra district of northern Burma at 24⁰56'N, 95⁰58'E. At 1015, therefore, the following formation left Feni:

Aircraft	Code	Pilot	Aircrew
EZ 855	D	Flt Lt David Metherell	F/O E.A. Carter
EZ 902	F	Flt Sgt R.G. Holding	Flt Sgt Johan Barnard SAAF
AN 720	K	WO William Tullett	Sgt E. Mason
EZ 872	F	Flt Lt William Berry	Sgt B.A.E. Winter
AN 645	S	WO Alan Parker	Sgt D.P. Cartwright-Howell
AN 957	Y	Flt Sgt George Couttie	Flt Sgt R. A. Gardner

This operation also went well, as did another made on the 13th against Maungdaw, but the following day, although weather conditions occasioned an operation to Tazaw,[17] Razabil, which meant crossing the May-Yu (Mayu) mountains, things did not go to plan. The formation was delayed all that morning and on into the afternoon. The first weather sortie was carried out between 1000 and 1150 by Flying Officer Gordon MacDonald and Sergeant N.D. Hankinson in Vengeance AF 116, but they found weather conditions unsuitable. A second reconnaissance was despatched from Feni at 1350, with Flying Officer James Sandilands and Flight Sergeant William F. Webb in Vengeance EZ 859. The squadron stood by ready to go but awaited Sandilands's verbal report before committing. Sandilands returned to base at 1455 and, while his report was marginal, it was decided to commit, and the operation was mounted at 1500 with the following:

Aircraft	Code	Pilot	Aircrew
EZ 810	A	Flt Lt David Metherell	F/O E.A. Carter
EZ 902	F	WO Alexander Holland	F/O William Shipton
AN 720	K	WO William Tullett	Sgt E. Mason
AN 806	D	Flt Sgt R. G. Holding	Flt Sgt Johan Barnard SAAF
EZ 872	P	Flt Lt William Berry	Sgt B.A.E. Winter
AN 957	Y	WO Alan Parker	Flt Sgt S.W. Elgie

However, despite their optimism, the target could not be attacked due to cloud cover and the whole force returned to base at 1725 without having bombed.

---

[17]   Also known as Teza or Tay-Za.

A formation flew another round-trip journey on the 17th, this time to Cox's Bazar and back, again to test the suitability for the Vengeance as a forward operating base and this time there were no untoward incidents. Flying Officer Sandilands, with Aircraftsman Thomas Wootton, also flew out there the next day in Vengeance AN 957, along with Warrant Officer 'Dutch' Holland and Aircraftsman E. Heine, in EZ 859 and Warrant Officer A.E. Parker on his own. The rear seats were then occupied by three senior army officers in order to carry out a reconnaissance before the trio returned to Feni. The overall flying time for this section was four hours, three hours twenty minutes and three hours five minutes respectively. Flying Officer Gordon MacDonald with Aircraftsman Thomas Roy Elliott in EZ 835, Warrant Officer William Tullett with Aircraftsman H. Turrell in AN 720 and Flight Lieutenant Bill Berry on his own, repeated this operation the next day leaving Feni at 0700, each aircraft clocking up three hours twenty minutes. Following on this second sortie a six-plane box, led by Flight Lieutenant David Metherell, was sent to Razabil at 0945 and carried out this mission successfully. Over the next four days the weather was uniformly awful and although a weather reconnaissance sortie was flown by Flight Sergeant R.G. Holding and Flight Sergeant Johan Barnard SAAF, in EZ 859 between 0915 and 1115 on the 23rd they could only report that conditions over the front remained bad. Practice flying only was possible on the 24th but on the 25th an operation was mounted to Dongyaung near Htinsbabyin, a six-plane box being despatched at 0820 with the following composition:

Aircraft	Code	Pilot	Aircrew
AN 806	C	Flt Lt David Metherell	F/O E.A. Carter
EZ 902	F	Flt Sgt Ronald Trigg	Sgt H.R. Crichton
AN 720	K	F/O G.G. Thompson	Flt Sgt S.W. Elgie
AN 957	Y	F/O James Sandilands	Flt Sgt William Webb
AN 645	S	Flt Lt William Berry	Sgt B.A.E. Winter
AN 960	O	Sgt R. McLean	Flt Sgt H. Wyllie

This mission was carried out according to plan save for the fact that Jimmy Sandilands had to return to base early through technical difficulties, landing back at 1045, but the rest of the force proceeded without difficulty and were all safely back at Feni by 1130. This concluded 82 Squadron's operations for September.

October began with a force of six Vengeances under Squadron Leader Dennis Gibbs leaving Feni at 0846 and, after an hour and ten minutes' flying time, finding clear weather over Gwazon (Pinpoint PM 5604) where a Japanese supply dump was their main objective. Here they conducted dives from 10,000 feet down to 1,000 feet scoring near misses on the only buildings visible and plastering the target area with twelve 500lb NITI Rods as well as strafing with both front and rear guns. On the 3rd Gibbs flew to Doharzari to inspect the probable new location of the squadron. He found that this airstrip quickly became unusable after even moderate rainfall and that it was unlikely any future move would take place until around the end of the month. The improvement in weather conditions following the end of the monsoon period could now permit the Vengeances to operate as designed. With targets clearly visible from 10,000 feet the return to steep dive-bombing was welcomed by all concerned.

Therefore, Flight Lieutenant David Metherell, RNZAF, was able to lead a force of six Vengeances from Feni at 0647 to attack Laungchaung, which was described as 'a key point in the defence line Donabik/Buthidaung'. They initially met stratus giving 10/10th cover from 800 feet to 17,000 feet over Cox's Bazar, cloud over the target and the rest of the route much thinner. They attacked at 0755 from 11,000 feet down to 1,500 feet, three of the Vengeances delivering one delayed action and one instantaneous 500lb bombs apiece, with the aim of indicating from the blast of the latter where the former had struck, as these could not be directly ascertained otherwise. They were dropped in short sticks for the same reason. All struck among buildings in the village alongside the Pya *chaung* save for one which 'hung up' on Vengeance D. On leaving the area fresh *Bashas* were machine-gunned at Thayagwin.

Apaukwa village, on the banks of the Kaladan river, was the object of the following day's sorties led by Squadron Leader Dennis Gibbs. The village had been abandoned by the enemy following a previous attack conducted by 82 Squadron on 17 September, but reports had been received that they were filtering back, and it was hoped to catch and kill up to 100 enemy soldiers there. The cloud cover was bad en route but they found a gap and attacked at 1250. Two bombs scored direct hits on the two largest houses in the village, and two other demolished two smaller buildings to the south, with three exploding among huts to the west, while two detonated in the narrow *chaung* that ran through the centre of the target.

An enemy column, estimated to have a strength of around 150 men, advanced along the seventeen-mile track from Tintha towards Keipaw, (north-east of Haka) where they forced the withdrawal of a British outpost and the following day two companies of the enemy (*circa* 400 troops) entered Hata, which lay at the junction of the tracks from Haka to Falam and, simultaneously, the main Japanese column attacked Webula using mortars and an infantry gun and occupied this village. In response 82 Squadron sent twelve Vengeances led by Squadron Leader Dennis Gibbs from Feni at 0714 to attack Natchaung. To do so, they had to cross the 9,000-foot high Chin Hills and go into battle in country completely unknown to anyone in the squadron. Not entirely surprisingly, the wrong target was bombed, the attack being delivered instead on the enemy-occupied village of Kyawya (Pinpoint 5305) on their line of communication between Tintha and Natchaung. The dive-bombing took place at 0830 with the attack delivered from 10,000 feet down to 3,000 feet. Several direct hits were registered and fires with black smoke left. There was no opposition and the force returned at 0930. Gibbs' bombs 'hung up' on him and he took them home. As soon as the aircraft could be refuelled and re-armed, a second strike was launched, this time led by Flight Lieutenant Ira Sutherland who, as he had led the second box in the first attack, was able to locate the correct targets of Tintha village (RU 5822) and Shabo (RU 6824). One red-flamed fire and one white-smoke fire were started in Tintha.

The following day the squadron was on stand-by and, at 0700, was sent to attack Gangaw and Kan-Ywa with six-plane boxes being led by Squadron Leader Dennis Gibbs and Flight Lieutenant David Metherell respectively, but they found the latter village 'weathered out' and all twelve Vengeances hit Gangaw, on the east bank of the Myittka river. The dives were made on a line east to west and several buildings took direct hits and yellow smoke fires were left indicating munition storage. A second attack was launched from Feni at 1140 with Flight Lieutenant Ira Sutherland taking six aircraft against Kalewa which was located at the junction of the Chindwin and Myittka rivers while another six, led by Flight Lieutenant David Metherell, struck at Kaing Village on the eastern bank of the Chindwin, opposite Kalewa. Here they met serious opposition with six heavy anti-aircraft bursts greeting them and being joined during the dives by bursts from Bofors-like light automatic weapons. The attacks went in at 1255 and 1258 respectively and several direct hits were made.

More serious damage was taken on the 11th during attacks on No. 2 Stockade and the supply road to the east, which was delivered by Flight Lieutenant Ira Sutherland with six aircraft at 1335. There was thick weather over most of the outward journey, but a gap, which always seemed to be present, was found and accurate bombing was carried out despite the difficult nature of the target. Although no opposition was noticed, one Vengeance, X, piloted by Warrant Officer Norman Holland, received a direct hit in a junction box as a result of which his aircraft lost a complete inner tank of petrol through leakage on the return flight. Metherell's aircraft was also hit with a machine-gun round through the starboard aileron, probably while circling the area to assess the results of their bombing.

Next day Squadron Leader Dennis Gibbs took one six-plane box against Webula while Flight Lieutenant Ira Sutherland led a second to Sahata. Gibbs himself was forced to turn back with engine trouble after twenty minutes flying time, so the five remaining aircraft were led by Flying Officer Sandilands to complete the mission. In the event bad weather prevented the first target being attacked while the second was missed in the murk. The alternative targets of the adjacent enemy occupied villages of Sihaung Myauk (Pinpoint RU 555675) and Sihaung Ashe were attacked instead at 0943 and 0940 respectively, with direct hits being made on buildings in the centre of each target being attained, and both were ground strafed.

The 13th saw Flight Lieutenant David Metherell as senior officer of a six-plane force which attacked Kan-Ywa, a township on the Chindwin river (Pinpoint PD 3634) at 1000 after a one-hour-twenty-minute flight from Feni. This target was covered by 9/10th cloud with a base at 2,000 feet but the Vengeances dive-bombed through a gap in the clouds from 10,000 feet down to flatten out at 1,000 feet below this murk in almost level flight. All twelve 500lb NITDR bombs fell inside the built-up perimeter and the area was also heavily strafed by both forward fixed and flexible rear machine guns. At the same time Squadron Leader Dennis Gibbs was leading six more aircraft in another strike on Hata (RU 3414) where some 400 enemy troops were reported located. Weather on the way was 8/10th, thinning to 3/10th over the Manipur river with cloud clinging to the mountainsides, but with just one isolated cloud over the villager itself on arrival. The target turned out to be a small group of *Bashas* on the southern side of a hill and required very careful location. The attack was put in at 0950 in steep dives through the cloud, tracking north to south with a wider dispersal of bombs than normal for a maximum spread of ordnance. There was no opposition and all aircraft returned to base at 1050.

At this time, with the occasional cross-mountain, longer-range missions becoming more common, Wing Commander George Byng Grayling MRCS LRCP, the DPMO[18], Bengal Command, advised that the squadron's Vengeances be fitted with oxygen gear and the associated breathing apparatus, but in the event, this proved unnecessary at this time. He also informed them that they would also be equipped with jungle survival kits packed in 'Flat Fifty' tins in case of emergencies. The 14th and 15th had no missions with the squadron stood down due to poor weather but on the 16th a final attack was carried out by 82 Squadron on this IV Corps front, with a six-plane attack mounted by Flight Lieutenant Ira Sutherland which departed Feni at 0855. They were assigned Webula as the main target, with Shaung Myauk as the secondary one, but poor visibility ruled out both villages. However, enemy-occupied Kywaye was identified through a hole in the overcast and selected as a suitable alternative for an attempt, despite difficult conditions. Shallow dives were all that were possible, and these were delivered by four of the Vengeances from 2,500 feet down to 1,500 feet at 190 knots and at least three bombs fell directly into the village with another landing off target in a paddy field, with the four others being unobserved. Two aircraft did not bomb, their pilots deeming that they were too low for safe release. The landed back at base at 1115. This area of operations was then handed over to 45 and 110 (H) Squadrons and they resumed work where they had left off before in the Arakan.

The 17th of October saw a dozen 82 Squadron machines strike the Lower Nawraondaung area of Arakan at 0655. Dive-bombed at 0805. All bombs detonated within just twenty-five yards of target. Unfortunately, Vengeance B crewed by Flight Sergeant R.G. Holding and Flight Sergeant Johan Wilhelm Christiaan Barnard, SAAF, his observer, was hit by AA and crashed 300 yards to south. There were no survivors. Frustratingly also, this Vengeance was carrying experimental VHF equipment to aid fighter protection communication in areas where enemy air opposition was considered possible,

---

[18]   Deputy Principal Medical Officer.

Next up was an attack on Kyauktaw (Pinpoint PN 025388) with six Vengeances under Flying Officer Gordon Macdonald conducted at 1000 on 19 October. Included in the varied ordnance deposited there were three TD bombs with 30-second, three-minute and eight-hour delays. At least one direct was scored and no opposition was encountered. The following day an attack on enemy positions at the Saingdin *Chaung* east of Buthidaung was mounted under Flight Lieutenant Ira Sutherland and this was accompanied by Hawker Hurricanes from 165 Group. They picked these fighters up over Chittagong. The whole force arrived over the target at 1055, with the Vengeances circling and making sure of their target, surrounded as it was by a ring of 1,250-foot hills. They then entered their precision dives at 1100. However, the inexperienced Hurricanes went straight into the attack without any attempt at co-ordination and were lucky to survive without any casualties from the Vengeances' bombs.

There were no operations on the 21st but on the 22nd Squadron Leader Dennis Gibbs led two *vics* of three aircraft, Flying Officer David MacDonald with another and Flying Officer James Sandilands a fourth *vic*, to strike Japanese dugouts atop hill features PM 371399 and PM 371406 and an adjacent road bridge. The latter took at least one direct hit, but examination later confirmed that it remained standing after the strike. Their next objective was an Army request following detailed reports from V Force operatives that the enemy was using a supply dump at Buthidaung Gona Fara, about 1,000 yards to the north-west of Buthidaung itself, as a staging point for supplies and munitions for their forces withdrawing from Synchyn and Awlabyin. In addition, a large HQ building in the town itself was to be targeted. This latter was struck by Warrant Officer Alan Parker while Squadron Leader Dennis Gibbs bombed the town. Two days later another V Force report was received of Japanese soldiers regularly congregating for food handouts between 0600 and 0800 each morning in an area of wooded foothills at Pinpoint PM 5588945 near Indien. An attack was laid on by 82 Squadron at this point on the 25th. Although no enemy were seen the area looked well-used and was comprehensively bombed. Next day Flight lieutenant Ira Sutherland took twelve Vengeances out from Feni as, despite predictions earlier, 82 Squadron was forced by circumstances to return to the IV Corps battle front once more. They split the enemy-held villages of Hata (Pinpoint RU 3414) and Keipaw (Pinpoint RU 348), Chin State, between them as four *vics* under Flight Lieutenant Ira Sutherland, Flying Officer Gordon MacDonald, Flying Officer James Sandilands and Flying Officer 'Dutch' Holland respectively, hit them hard between 1135 and 1140. A second strike that same day left Feni at 1519 on yet further reports of up to 500 Japanese troops digging in along the foothills between Pinpoints of PM 4102609 and PM 420230. These were duly attacked, and the force returned safely to base at 1737.

After another rest day with no target allocations forthcoming, the 28th saw the despatch of Metherell with a six-plane box (map Reference PM 3333) with instructions to destroy a red-roofed building at the northern end of Htindaw village (Pinpoint PM 443443). This was done and enemy positions at Tatmakali were also bombed. Two days on and stick bombing was carried out by six Vengeances under Flight Lieutenant Ira Sutherland at the western end of Kanyidan (Kanyadan) village (Pinpoint 3333) with what was termed 'Excellent results'. Then, on the last day of October, the same officer took six aircraft to strike a hill feature at Zedidaung North (Pinpoint PM 532466) in 20°53' N, 92°43'E, where Japanese trenches and fortifications being prepared on the northerly part of the hill were 'thoroughly plastered'.

In summary, 82 Squadron had flown 191 sorties in October 1943 – the sum total of all missions flown by 224 Group that month. In November 1943 they were to fly 126 sorties, the first of which, led by Dennis Gibbs, on 1 November was against Htindaw again, and subsequently the army signalled later that they killed at least fifty Japanese troops in the attack. Two days later Flight Lieutenant David Metherell took six aircraft to strike an enemy signal station at Sekhaung (Pinpoint PM 700196), Shan State, which was sited atop a small hill at the junction of the *chaungs* there with its control buildings on the western slopes. They dive-bombed and strafed at 0930 and photos showed high accuracy. During the afternoon they were held on standby for army close support missions. Despite very poor conditions they were despatched against Point 1301, an enemy stronghold at Pinpoint 414445, which the army indicated with smoke. On arrival in the murk Gibbs was able to see not only the smoke but the orange bursts of the mortar shells and led his six-plane box through a gap in the clouds at 1430. A subsequent Army Support Control signal read: 'All bombs on target. Good show. Many thanks.'

Fireworks were duly set off on the 5th with Flight Lieutenant Ira Sutherland, RNZAF, leading a dozen Vengeances against remaining buildings in the national schooling area in Akyab town itself, which were occupied by the enemy and factories along Satyoga Creek. The attack was delivered at 1630 from north to south in steep dives from 9,500 feet to 1,500 feet with each pilot selecting his own building. For once they were met with considerable AA fire. The flak bursts were accurate for direction and height, but the enemy failed to open fire until the first box was already on the way down. The second box dived through red bursts unscathed and escaped at low level, encountering machine-gun fire which they strafed with all guns in response. Despite this there were many direct hits confirmed scored and no damage received.

The missions ground on, with Buthidaung struck yet again on the 7th by six aircraft under Ira Sutherland, while the following day a report was received that a senior Japanese commander intended visiting Bathedaung that day. A reception committee was duly assembled with Flight Lieutenant David Metherell taking six Vengeances to greet him. They made their dives at 1632 and no doubt duly impressed their guest. Several direct hits were made on buildings in the southern and central parts of the township. Buildings on the waterfront of Paletwa village on the Kaladae river were bombed on the 10th; an enemy battalion HQ at Chiradan (Pinpoint PM 377322) was bombed at 0736 on the 11th, and a dug-in Japanese artillery piece south of the Ngakyedauk *chaung* was an army requested target on the 12th, and was duly silenced. The 14th saw six Vengeances under Ira Sutherland hit what was believed to be a Japanese headquarters site at Kagyabet (Pinpoint PM 519408). Two direct hits were scored on the assigned building with six more in the village itself and fires with heavy black smoke were left burning throughout.

Two days were spent in fighter-affiliation exercises with various formations being trialled, then it was back to work on the 16th with an ASC mission against two enemy-held hill features at Pinpoints 428484 and 432483 close to the Tatmin *Chaung,* very close to the bomb line. Smoke mortar indicators were fired by the Army, but the Vengeances held off as they indicated areas west of the line which were in friendly hands. The army re-calibrated and then indicated the correct positions and 82 Squadron's aircraft dived from 10,000 feet down to 2,000 and hit these positions so accurately that they extinguished the mortar-shell puffs. Army Signal No. 16 was subsequently received via AHQ Bengal which read that 'a Ground

Source stated that because of this attack two hundred Japs were killed, and three locals wounded'.

The next mission was led by Flying Officer Gordon Webster MacDonald, RCAF, with six aircraft which dive-bombed Apaukwa (Pinpoint PM 9924) at 1532 on 17 November after a V Force report that 500 enemy troops were in the village. The first *vic* hit the east end of the village while the second *vic*, under Warrant Officer Ronald Parker, attacked the west, both diving from 10,000 feet down to 1,500 feet. That same day an advance party from 82 Squadron left for their new base at Dohazari.

The 19th witnessed the last of that series of attacks mounted from Feni during this period when Flight Lieutenant David Metherell led six Vengeances to Kyauktaw (Pinpoint PM 0179). Both the jetty and pagoda area of the township were struck with several direct hits and one 'bright red flash much larger than a normal bomb burst, but without any resulting fire' being obtained. They ground-strafed the area heavily as well.

They also received some news on an earlier exploit, AHQ Bengal signalling: '4 Corps reports 57 Japanese killed, 40 seriously injured during raid on Gangaw on 10th October. Phongyi Kyaung in which Japanese were living badly damaged. After raid Japs started to move out to Pyap.'

On 21 November Dennis Gibbs led fifteen Vengeances from Feni to Dohazari and combat operations commenced from that base on the 23rd. Six Vengeances led by Squadron Leader Dennis Gibbs left Dohazari at 0830 to attack an enemy ammunition dump at a *chaung* junction at Pinpoint PM 420254, near to Rakhan. Latest Intelligence reports indicated that some 200 Japanese troops were billeted near three betel groves nearby. The first twenty miles to the target were clear but then the force met patches of early morning ground mist. The dives were commenced at 0917 stick bombing with both 500lb and 250lb NITD and TD ordnance. They left behind a 1,000-foot high column of dust which remained visible when still twenty miles away, and made at least ten direct hits.

The next day the squadron was at 'Instant Readiness' from 0600 awaiting the Army's call, and this came at 0945. A Japanese redoubt located on the northern slope of Hill PM 442477 was to be taken out. Ira Sutherland led six aircraft and they located the enemy position by means of the map he carried and from cross references with Letwedet and Tatmakhali villages. They attacked on a line from east to west with stick-bombing from 10,000 feet to 1,000 feet and sixteen bombs struck the northern slops of the projection which was immediately cloaked in smoke.

On return to Dohazari they were briefed to carry out Operation GAUNTLET. This was a supply mission in co-operation with the other two services. It was, quite literally, the running of the gauntlet because the Royal Navy was tasked with passing a towed barge with vital supplies for the Allies up the Naf river to Bawli Bazar and this route took them right under the Japanese gun muzzles from their two artillery batteries at Maungdaw. There was a 2-inch gun battery at PM 315394 and a 75mm battery at Ngakhra (Pinpoint PM 321386). For accurate river navigation this attempt could only be made in broad daylight. The attempt was scheduled for 0730 on 25 November. V Force had already accurately located the Japanese gun positions and it was 82 Squadron's task to keep them silent to allow the convoy to get through. A Royal Navy launch would escort the tug and the barge and would lay a protective smoke-screen when required. British artillery had already registered on the enemy gun sites ready to open fire when requested. Twelve Vengeances were to carry out dive-bombing attacks on the enemy guns.

Because of the risk of early ground mist interfering in their work, six of the aircraft led by Flight Lieutenant David Metherell flew down to 'Reindeer' airstrip, Ramu, north of Cox's Bazar,[19] to await Squadron Leader Dennis Gibbs with a further six aircraft which would rendezvous over Reindeer at 3,000 feet at 0708. Should Gibbs's section fail to arrive then Metherell was to carry out the attack on the two batteries with three aircraft against each one. In the same way should Gibbs find Reindeer was not operational he was to proceed with two *vics* against each battery; this would ensure that, should the worst come to the worst, the enemy guns would be fully occupied at the crucial time of 0730 or even later.

In the event, on the day Gibbs's section duly made the rendezvous with Metherell's exactly on time, and both carried out steep dive-bombing attacks on both batteries as scheduled from 9,000 feet down to 1,500 feet, through a thin cloud layer at 3,000 feet Twelve 500lb GP NITD and four 250lb TD .025 were delivered into each battery. No enemy movement was observed during these attacks. On return to base they received a signal from Group HQ which read: 'Operation GAUNTLET satisfactorily completed.' Due to

---

[19]   21⁰43' N, 92⁰, 11' E, Currently Ramu Upazila, Bangladesh.

the surf the barge was lashed to the tug and preceded by the navy launch and the entire group was unmolested. A further signal came in later with a XV Corps Sitrep (W22) which stated, 'Reliable V Force states thirty-seven Japs killed and three wounded in bombing and strafing at Maungdaw.'

Novembers operations continued with Ira Sutherland leading six Vengeances against an enemy supply dump at Kundaung on Akyab Island on the 27th; and this operation was repeated on the 28th, nineteen enemy troops being confirmed killed and three wounded in this raid; while on 30 November a suspected Japanese HQ in a concrete building at Myohaung (Pinpoint PN 260070) was attacked. The target building, heavily camouflaged, was not hit, however, but two adjacent buildings took direct hits Vengeance Y returned to base with machine-gun bullet holes in her starboard wing but that was the extent of the opposition.

The squadron's score board from 31 May estimated from signals received that they had disposed of 1,064 Japanese troops and wounded eighty-three more.in various strikes. The estimates came out thus:

Date	Location	Killed	Wounded	Remarks
3 June	Buthidaung	80	n/a	
10/12 June	Buthidaung	40	n/a	
13 June	Letwedet	46	n/a	
15 June	Maungdaw	104	n/a	Includes 100 *Mughs*
24 August	Baguna	50	n/a	
30 August	Maungdaw	6	n/a	May have included six senior officers
31 August	Buthidaung	170	n/a	
6 September	Hparabyin	100	n/a	
16 September	Buthidaung	60	n/a	
19 September	Razabil	n/a	n/a	Four lorryloads of dead carted away.
10 October	Gangaw	57	40	
23 October	Buthidaung	200	3	
30 October	Kanyindaw	28	2	
31 October	Ladidaung	6	n/a	
1 November	Htindaw	50	n/a	
11 November	Khiradan	3	2	
14 November	Kagyauet	20	20	
24 November	Tatmin *Chaung*	19	3	
25 November	Maungdaw	62	13	
TOTALS		**1,064**	**83**	

Squadron Leader Dennis Gibbs recorded that 'It is possible that some of these reports are exaggerated; but the exaggeration may well be set against the many results which have not been ascertained, and the score is probably more rather than less. 569 have been flown on 91 separate operations against the enemy.'

The squadron remained based at Dohazari for the whole of December. The first day of that month saw an attack on an enemy ration dump at Razabil South (Pinpoint PM 370397) just east of Razabil Village. A six-plane section led by Flight Lieutenant David Metherell took off at 1616 and at 1657 dive-bombed these supplies from 10,000 feet down to 1,000 feet to deliver twelve 500lb GP NITD and eight 250lb GP TD .025 bombs in what were reported to be in 'good concentrations'. There were no incidents and the force returned at 1733. Next day the squadron was on stand-by for Army close support demands, and one was received at 1430. The request was for them to bomb Point 208 (Pinpoint 43612), an enemy strongpoint in the East Mayu area north of Buthidaung. Accordingly, Flight Lieutenant Ira Sutherland led six Vengeances from Dohazari at 1547 and at 1620 they saw the mortar smoke markers and began their dives from 10,000 feet down to 1,500 feet. The marker smoke was obscured by the bomb blasts which indicated they were right on target, with hits on the peak itself and the southern slopes. The force returned unscathed at 1656.

There were no combat operations on the 3rd which was used for training but the next day a difficult target was given them, which was a Japanese pillbox that was holding up the Allied advance. This position was located on a hill feature at Pinpoint 452514 very close to the 'bomb line' near a bitterly-contested area known to the British troops as Jungle Neck. There was no smoke laid on by the ground forces but the leader of the six-plane flight, Squadron Leader Dennis Gibbs, managed to identify the exaction location from photos and a large and distinctive white patch on the ground, which was visible from 10,000 feet. The attack was delivered at 1530, once again the Vengeances commencing at 10,000 feet and releasing at 1,500 feet. All the bombs detonated within a fifty-yard radius of the target and there was no opposition.

The 5th of December saw a strike made against the court house at Buthidaung, reportedly used as a Japanese HQ. Led again by Gibbs, this attack was delivered at 1715 and a direct hit was achieved by Flying Officer

James Sandilands. Gibbs himself dived too low to release and brought his bombs back home. This was followed by another training day. On the 7th Flight Lieutenant David Metherell took six Vengeances against Kanyidan where some three 300 enemy troops had been reported in occupation. The flight attacked at 0800 using stick bombing with each of the two *vics* attacking the northern and eastern areas of the village where the enemy had been reported as located. The weather was good with 'excellent' visibility which led to very accurate deliveries, it being reported that the accuracy on this occasion 'was some of the best they had witnessed'.

Next day Ira Sutherland led six aircraft to strike a reported Japanese divisional headquarters at Kamai (Pinpoint PR 855991). This was a difficult target, the *bashas* housing the enemy again being sited in a narrow *chaung* leading to the foothills. After they landed back at base at 0835 analyses indicated that the attack had targeted the wrong group of huts in similar terrain. Accordingly, a second strike was mounted, and Sutherland led them from Dohazari at 1205. They made their dives at 1250, this time hitting the correct group and were rewarded by 'a large sheet of red flame and black smoke up to 100ft which later became blue', indicating they had hit something vital. The HQ was strongly defended, and they were met with flak, but only one Vengeance, O piloted by Flight Sergeant George Couttie, RNZAF, was hit, receiving three cannon hits on the way in, but suffering only superficial damage and no injuries.

Another training day followed and then, on the 10th, Dennis Gibbs led six Vengeances to Btindaw (Pinpoint PM 442442) to strike an enemy headquarters reported to be located in a building alongside the hill slopes on the Maungdaw to Buthidaung road. Once more they found 'perfect weather conditions' over the target and made their dives at 1000, with the majority of the bombs exploding in the immediate target area. On 11 December 800 enemy troops were reported concentrating at the northern end of a hill feature at Pinpoint PN 035397. Ira Sutherland took six aircraft to bomb this position, but no enemy troops were observed. The flight landed back at base at 1705.

Meanwhile Squadron Leader Dennis Gibbs was attending a war council, planning two days of major attacks in the Fort White area in support of the army. Vengeances from 45, 82 and 110 Squadrons were all to participate. Accordingly, at 0954, Gibbs led twelve Vengeances to Milestone 52, each aircraft carrying just a pair of 500lb GP NITDR bombs apiece due to the distance to the target. This time, however, the weather was less kind and they were unable to locate the main target in the overcast. They were forced to deliver their loads into the secondary target which was Matchaung village (Pinpoint HU 5343). Here they recorded several direct hits. At 1448 a call came to try again at the original target and this time Ira Sutherland led twelve aircraft to Milestone 52 once more. On the way they encountered even more dense cumulus and so had to approach at a much higher altitude to get clear of it, but in vain and, once again, an alternative target was attacked. Direct hits were made on iron buildings and they were enveloped in bright red flames. Dense black smoke, turning to grey, poured from the devastated buildings which was described in the attack report as 'the biggest fire the crews had seen in Burma'.[20] There was more smoke from smaller fires also, but the smoke from the main blaze was still visible at twenty-to-thirty miles distance, rising to between 23,000–30,000 feet.

On the 13th a third attempt was made against Milestone 52 near Fort White on the Tiddim Road, and this time it succeeded. Squadron Leader Dennis Gibbs led a full-strength attack off from Dohazari at 0953. The enemy positions were on a flat-topped ridge and the attack was put in at 1100, all bombs bursting in the centre of the ridge and along its eastern edge. Japanese dug-in positions were seen, mainly craters, and were heavily hit. This flight returned to base at 1155. At 1252 Flight Lieutenant Ira Sutherland was despatched on a lone mission; his task was to act as a target marker for a force of Vickers Wellington bombers. He landed at Feni thirty minutes later and then took off again at 1455 to carry out his pathfinder task. When he was exactly over the target Sutherland made his dive and his pair of 500lb bombs registered direct hits. Sutherland returned to base and landed at 1742, but his work was in vain for the Wellingtons failed to bomb.

A second attack of the day was again mounted against Milestone 52, this time Flight Lieutenant David Metherell leading twelve Vengeances from Dohazari at 1455. They successfully dive-bombed this target at 1600 with their two-dozen bombs bursting in the centre of the ridge and to its northern limits. Squadron Leader Dennis Gibbs noted one important factor in these

---

20   AIR 27/682/28.

long-range sorties. 'The last four operations were undertaken over 'The Hump'[21] and there was an element of cloud which necessitated operating up to 15,000 feet.' None of the Vengeances were equipped with oxygen for this task and Gibbs commented, 'The need for oxygen was felt by all.'

The 14th saw only training but the 15th saw no fewer than three missions undertaken. The first mission resulted in tragedy for the squadron, however, when Flight Lieutenant David William Metherell was killed on operations over Akyab. Six Vengeances had taken off from Dohazari at 0751 that morning and by 0900 were over the target which was the Batyoga creek area of Akyab township. They were greeted by light AA 'of moderate intensity'. An eyewitness, Flying Officer E.A. Carter, reported that 'The leader turned into his dive and was seen going down in flames, and later to crash, explode and burn on the ground.' Neither Metherell, nor his observer was seen to bale out. The precise cause was unknown but was probably the anti-aircraft fire.

Auckland-born Metherell had been an outstanding flight leader with 82 Squadron and had made many low-level attacks. His CO, Dennis Gibbs, wrote that 'Metherell's leadership always showed great skill and determination. He was a great character on the squadron and if any one man was responsible for its success and high morale it was surely this officer who always had a laugh and a joke for everyone.'

The remaining Vengeances continued about their business despite this shock. Four aircraft bombed buildings along the west and to the immediate south of the *chaung*, while the fifth attacked a large twin-engine Japanese bomber which was immobilised on Akyab airfield. These five machines returned safely to base at 0955. Meanwhile a second six-plane section under Squadron Leader Dennis Gibbs was standing by for a ASC call and received a summons to attack some Japanese mortar positions on a hill feature, north of Sin-Shybin (Pinpoint 503484). They duly carried out an attack there, all aircraft safely returning to base at 1229.

---

[21] 'The Hump' was the name given to the eastern arm of the Himalaya Mountains over which continuous air freight from India to China was maintained by the British and Americans after the main 'Burma Road' land route had been severed by the invading Japanese. The Chin and Mizo Hills leading down from this barrier and along the Burma/India border were less high than these but were of sufficient altitude to force the Vengeances to fly at greater heights than they had been equipped to do.

A third mission was mounted at 1457, with Flight Lieutenant Ira Sutherland leading six more Vengeances against enemy-held buildings at Hendya (Pinpoint PM 3379). Several direct hits were recorded on the already badly damaged town. There was no opposition and the force landed back at 1708. The attack went in at 1600.

That afternoon the squadron received a visit from Air Chief Marshal Sir Richard Edmund Charles Peirse DSO AFC, Air C-in-C, along with Air Marshal Sir John Eustace Arthur Baldwin CB DSO DL.

At 0830 on the 16th yet another attack was made on Bathedaung by twelve Vengeances led by Squadron Leader Dennis Gibbs. The dives commenced at 0930 and all save one aircraft, which overshot, delivered their loads into the built-up part of the town, particularly in the area north of the jetty. There was light anti-aircraft fire on this occasion but only one aircraft was hit with negligible damage to her tail unit and no casualties. At 1830 a second full-strength mission with two six-plane boxes was led by Flight Lieutenant Sutherland to strike at a new long-range target for the squadron, this being Ganbale and Mayan (16°16'N, 96°E), villages on either side of the *chaung*. They caused a violent and spectacular explosion in the southern portion of the former which resulted in red flames and blue smoke visible for long after they had let the scene. A large storehouse full of bales and containers was also hit and destroyed. The whole area was also heavily strafed.

That day also 82 Squadron received a visit from Lord Louis Mountbatten, Supreme Allied Commander. He told the assembled aircrew that the end of the war in Europe was imminent and that, although the overall strategy was to defeat Germany first, a heavy Allied build-up was underway to tackle Japan and they would be in the forefront of that effort in this region.

Their own attacks continued with Flight Lieutenant Sutherland leading a mission against Nyoh which they attacked in four *vics* of three-aircraft at 1000. They caused 'an unusually large explosion'. But not all the damage or loss was on the enemy side. On 17 December 1943 further squadron-related losses were incurred at No. 1 Air Gunnery School (AGS) at Bairagah, Bhopal. Two Vengeances, AN 613 and AN 759, from a group of new allotments from 320 MU at Karachi that were en route to 1 AGS, crashed. The most serious casualty was a Mark II machine, which was observed to have dived into the ground at Badnawar, killing Flying Officer Cedric Howie Pierson RAAF, and Flight Sergeant Reginald Royle Burgess RAFVR. A representative of the Vultee Company arrived at Bhopal two days after the crash to inspect the remains.

In December 1943, 167 Wing of 224 Group moved to Dohazari airfield in Bengal and, between 21 and 25 January 1944, new airstrips at Jumchar and Jouri were assigned to 82 and 8 IAF Squadrons respectively; 82 began operations from there on the 22nd. They were to be desperately required. Meanwhile, once Maungdaw port had fallen to 5th Indian Division on 9 January, the Allied ground forces cautiously inched their way toward Razabil village and 'Tortoise Hill'. This was heavily defended with the natural features all lending themselves to the strongest of defensive positions

To assist the army in storming these formidable obstacles held by a fanatical enemy, the Allied air forces mounted a succession of heavy attacks commencing on 26 January. These air strikes were Operation WALLOP and the first in was 82 Squadron who were allocated Japanese bunkers located in the hills overlooking the Maungdaw to Buthidaung road. The composition of this twelve-Vengeance strike, organised in two six-plane boxes, was as follows:

Aircraft	Pilot	Aircrew
AN 747	Flt Lt Ira Sutherland	P/O D.W. Archer
AN 694	Flt Sgt W.A. Garbutt	Flt Sgt E. Widdowson
EZ 867	Flt Sgt B.J. Scowen	Flt Sgt Roderick John Fraser RAAF
AN 665	Flt Sgt M.J. Croghan	Flt Sgt C. Woods
AN 703	WO Alexander Norman Holland	Flt Sgt L.F. Foster
AN 810	WO Kenneth Edward McCrombie	WO Nigel Stark Harrower
EZ 976	Flt Sgt Robert Allan McClean RAAF	Flt Sgt H. Wyllie
AN 782	Sqn Ldr Dennis Gibbs	P/O William F Webb
AN 616	Flt Lt Gordon MacDonald	Flt Sgt K.I. Amos
AN 737	WO Ronald Samuel Trigg RAAF	Flt Sgt H.R. Crichton
AN 812	Flt Sgt D. Kinnell	WO W.I. Rush
AN 806	Flt Sgt M.F. Pettibone	WO George Davies

They carried out precision dives and were then followed by three waves of American North American B-25 Mitchells pattern-bombing in level flight, and then ten Consolidated B-24 Liberator heavy bombers followed; four others bombed the eastern ridge and then 8 IAF Vengeances ended the attack with another dive-bombing attack. On conclusion Allied tanks followed up and found many casualties, but the survivors retreated to the deepest bunkers and still put up fierce resistance. Continued Vengeance assault followed one after another. By the end of January, 82 Squadron had been allocated twenty-eight targets and had carried thirty-seven attacks on them.[22]

During this time the fighting in the Akyab reached a new intensity and the Allied armies found themselves up against a heavily and carefully-prepared and -sited series of Japanese strongpoints and bunkers from which it proved extremely difficult, and costly, to evict them. The enemy fought with ferocious intensity, which was matched by Allied determination and it became a ding-dong struggle for strategic ridges, vantage points among the thickly-wooded hills and steep ravines and gorges. Crucial to the Japanese was the supply road that ran east from Maungdaw to Buthidaung. This route passed under the Mayu mountain range in two tunnels and these were heavily fortified and used as a mustering point-cum-fortress for the Japanese. To the north of these strongest of strong-points was the Ngakyedauk Pass.[23] The enemy had occupied all the surrounding peaks, giving them unrivalled control of both sides of these hills and thus each ridge had to be painstakingly softened up and then, and only then, taken by infantry assault, which, as they mutually supported each other, was a difficult and dangerous task. The Allied and Japanese artillery duelled in counter-battery exchanges but pinpointing the exact locations of these many bunkers called for great accuracy as the two sides were very close together and, indeed in the case of tunnels, one atop the other. It often resembled First World War attritional warfare. The Allies had one distinct advantage, the Vultee Vengeance dive-bomber.

Other types of airpower were brought into play before the powers-that-be were forced to realise what a trump card the Vengeance was. One independent example of how they were finally forced to acknowledge this fact, even if only temporarily, can be cited here. Captain Edward Walter Maslen-Jones RA, served with 656 Air Observation Post Squadron, commanded by Major Denis Coyle, a unit that combined Royal Artillery pilot/observers Royal Air Force ground personnel into an effective and vital spotting, fire-directing and target-laying unit that served Fourteenth Army by co-ordinating the

---

[22] See page 184.
[23] Inevitably nicknamed by the British Tommies as 'Okey Doke' Pass.

work of both these services equally. Based at Deolali in two flights, each with a strength of five Taylorcraft Auster aircraft, for these spotting duties, they performed magnificently in that unique role throughout the campaign. Working from primitive forward airstrips close to the front line, these little aircraft only required ninety-one feet (twenty-eight metres) to take off, and had a top speed of just 113knots (209km/h) with a range of 250 miles, which was more than sufficient. They were unarmed and unprotected, yet operated over enemy lines at heights easy enough for small-arms fire to threaten their existence. Nonetheless, none were lost, although all of them at one time or another were forced to make emergency landings.

Maslen-Jones relates one particular incident that occurred when he was involved in ranging 4th Field Regiment's artillery onto the tunnels area. 'It was especially important to obtain a high degree of accuracy because, apart from using the range for harassing fire, which meant that the Regiment would shoot periodically at the target without the benefit of immediate observation, we also intended to put down smoke shells to mark the target for air strikes. These strikes were to be conducted by Vengeance bombers from the RAF and Mitchell bombers of the United States Air Force.'[24]

Having made an initial aerial reconnaissance of the target at an altitude of fifty feet, Maslen-Jones 'had an excellent view of the tunnel entrance. With ground rising steeply on either side, it was in a cutting'. He concluded from this that

> not only was the accuracy of the "marker" going to be important, but indications of an air strike was likely to be more successful than artillery fire', due to the trajectory of their shooting being largely masked by these confines.
>
> I returned to register the target for the air strike which was due that afternoon. The first attack was by the RAF Vengeances and I was pleased to see the smoke marker was quite accurate, and that their attack, at least from my viewpoint, was well on target.

---

[24]   The North American B-25 Mitchell twin-engined light bomber. The Americans were, in fact, the United States Army Air Forces (USAAF), the USAF was not established until post-war, in September 1947.

All well and good, and then followed the American Mitchells bombing from an altitude of about 10,000 feet. The observer recalled that his expectations of their contribution had been high 'but I did feel disappointed at the result, which was less spectacular and, I thought, rather dangerously scattered, having regard to the proximity of our troops. Reports afterwards verified this and the Vengeance attack went down as effective, whereas the Mitchells largely missed the target'.[25] He also noted that 6th South Wales Borderers were in possession of the 'Ham Bone' feature immediately above the tunnels in readiness to storm and occupy them. However, for the Mitchell attack, they had been ordered to withdraw 100 yards from their positions for their own safety. It was, however, to take much more than one air raid to weaken as tough an enemy as this. Further attacks followed. It was not until 20 March, after three more days of intensive artillery bombardment and dive-bombing attacks that the battalion was able to storm the tunnels and clear them in fierce hand–to–hand fighting.

The Japanese counter-blow, a delayed offensive codenamed HA-GO, was now delivered by the 55th Division, commanded by Lieutenant General Tadashi Hanaya, and fell upon 7th Indian Division, still to the east of Buthidaung, via Taung Bazar. Initial reports of enemy troop movements were not taken too seriously, the estimation being that during the night of 3/4 February, what was believed to be just one company of Japanese troops and sixty mules had infiltrated through Oktaung (pinpoint 5553) but it very soon transpired that they were on the move in greater force than this with no warning but with deadly serious intent. Early on the 4th it became clear that at least one battalion of the enemy had seized Taung Bazar and had split into three columns, heading north towards the Goppe Pass, south toward the Nganyaung Pass and west to cut the Ukhia-Kazabi road near Nganyaung. Not until the 5th was it clear that the whole of 112th Regiment was engaged in carrying out an encircling movement through the hills east of Pyinshe Kala and through Tatmang Yanga. However, this time, instead of immediately retreating as expected when their HQ was directly attacked and enveloped, the British and Indian troops fought it out, being supplied by air drops. The resultant struggle became known as the Battle of the Admin Box and lasted from 5 February until the 23rd.

The really acute crisis period in this area was between 8 and 10 February. Typical of the ARMOP missions mounted by 82 Squadron during this frenetic period were those flown between the 10th and 19th. In January two brigades of 81st (West Africa) Division, commanded by Major General Christopher Geoffrey Woolner CB MC, moved out of Chittagong to Daletme and then on through the Paletwa region at the beginning of February. They moved south along both sides of the Kaladan river and the Pi *chaung* where they were brought to an abrupt halt by strong Japanese resistance at Kaladan village. In an attempt to break the enemy defences an attack was launched on the 10th by 82 Squadron with twelve Vengeances under the command of Flight Lieutenant Ira Sutherland. Escort was provided by twelve Spitfire Vs of 607 Squadron.[26] At 1248 the Vengeances struck at bunker positions just south of the village, diving down from 10,000 to 1,000 feet. Smoke indicators were put down by artillery and all two-dozen bombs struck within the designated area, being described by the crews as 'being one of the most concentrated attacks they had seen'. That same afternoon, at 1615, a strike force of twelve Vengeances under Squadron Leader Dennis Gibbs went in and delivered a follow-up attack against the same enemy positions and, in addition to their bombs, carried out strafing of field guns and motor transport.

Flight Lieutenant Ira Sutherland led a strike of twelve Vengeances in two six-plane boxes from Jumchar at 0850 on the 13th. They were tasked with striking Japanese positions on the Mayu range on the Maungdaw-Buthidaung road. Sutherland's leading box made steep dives against an identified Japanese headquarters in a *nullah*[27] at PM 416420, bearing 350 degrees, where a hairpin bend in the road entered the west tunnel, with a *chaung* flowing through the target area. Every pilot carried photographs for identification. Twelve 500lb NITI and twelve 250lb GP TD were delivered and all fell within the target zone, mainly on the eastern slopes and in the *nullah*, with one stick on west slopes and in the *nullah*. A few *bashas* were seen and attacked at pinpoint 417418. The second box, led by Flying Officer James Sandilands, made similar attacks on troops and stores in the *nullah* from the road bend, placing two sticks at the northern end and two

---

[26]   Commanded by Squadron Leader Patrick Joseph Thomas Stephenson DFC, RAFVR, a Battle of Britain veteran.

[27]   A dry watercourse or ravine, from the Hindi *Nālā* (Rivulet).

in the centre of the *nullah* and another along its eastern side. The force returned to base at 0945.

That night brought new developments. The Japanese attacked Point 1070, a position abutting on to the Ngakyedauk Pass to the north. They inflicted heavy losses on the signals detachment which formed its garrison and occupied it themselves, spending the 14th digging themselves in and beating off counter-attacks. No. 82 Squadron was instructed to strike at these enemy concentrations and early the next day was briefed accordingly, with photographs for each and every pilot. This was vital because the target itself was an isolated hill dominated by pinpoints 1979 and 1778 with another 1,000-foot hill feature overlooking it to the north-east. The target itself falls away in a deep escarpment to the west and north, giving the appearance of an open razor edge, while a *chaung* formed a half-circle around its northern portion. A long, 750-foot-high escarpment runs east and north beyond this *chaung*. Allied artillery fired smoke to aid them, but the Vengeances had already identified the target before the first shells detonated, one halfway down the south-western slope and then more puffs appeared closer to the top and on the razor edge.

The twelve Vengeances were led by Flight Lieutenant Gordon MacDonald RCAF and, at 0925, they made their steep attack dives from 10,000 feet down to 2,000 feet. From photographs taken during the raid, it could be seen that most of the two dozen bombs dropped on the southern tip of the target feature. One attack ran from the top about two-thirds down the western slope, another stick marched from east to west high on the southern slope and one more on the south-western slope. Later a signal was received from the forward troops which stated that this attack was the 'Best Ever'. All aircraft had returned unharmed by 0955.

A second strike was sent out at 1442 that afternoon, again being led by Flight Lieutenant MacDonald. There were no photographs to guide them, but the briefing was that a Japanese cavalry headquarters was located at the end of a cul-de-sac at pinpoint PN 2222152, north of Myohaung, and horses were thought to be concealed in jungle at the foot of a pagoda-topped hill. MacDonald led his force up the 'well-worn road' up from Myohaung and attacked at 1515, again making steep dives from 10,000 feet down to 1,500 feet. The bombs fell 'widely dispersed' on the lower slopes of the hill, while the pagoda was 'very narrowly' missed, but no horses were seen. Myohaung landing ground was crossed and appeared to be in good condition, but inactive.

The next attack was mounted on the 19th, six Vengeances under Flying Officer James Sandilands taking off at 0920 and attacking enemy troops and machine-gun positions on hill features at pinpoint 372398. These were in an elbow of the Maungdaw-Buthidaung road south of the Abkakungbauk *chaung*. They observed a great many tracks, foxholes and trenches with some built-up bamboo on the next hill. They dropped their usual calling cards, a mix of 500lb and 250lb bombs, but one section went around again to strafe these defence works with both front and rear machine guns. A second attack was mounted at 1240 with twelve aircraft under Squadron Leader Dennis Gibbs. They were briefed to attack Japanese positions at PM 449448, which they had hit before. The artillery laid down smoke indicators, which were seen on the approach, but a 15mph wind had dispersed these by the time the Vengeances went down in their dives at 1320. The target was well covered and there were no incidents.

A third sortie was briefed later that afternoon, the aim of which was to bomb Japanese supply dumps in the re-entrant south-west of Punkori village with six aircraft. Gibbs considered that twelve Vengeances would be better employed against this large target and sought, and obtained, permission to have the strike force increased to this number. They left Jumchar at 1655 and were led by Flying Officer James Sandilands. They identified the target from photographs and made their dives at 1721, with the two dozen bombs falling on both sides and the end of the re-entrant, one stick producing a 'long sheet of red flame'. Three Vengeances returned to strafe the area and all machines returned at 1752.

There were no operations on the 23rd but that day saw both Sandilands and MacDonald awarded the DFC, and the CO recorded, 'both really deserve their honours'. The press considered that it was the dive bombing of the tunnels on the Maungdaw to Buthidaung road so successfully that gained 'Mac' his DFC. One local paper back home, *The Edmonton Bulletin*, under the heading 'Daring Attack Made by Alberta Airman' by Harold Guard read:

British and Indian troops of the 14th Army have won full control of the vital Ngakyedauk Pass and the Japanese have been driven from the main crest of the Mayu Mountains, it was announced today in a communiqué on the Burma fighting.

Meanwhile, the Royal Air Force concentrated on the Maungdaw–Buthidaung Road and low level bombing of a tunnel by Flight Lieutenant Gordon Webster MacDonald of Wanham, near Peace River, Alberta, and Squadron Leader Dennis R. Gibbs of London, is described as 'the most daring flying of this campaign'.

Control of the Ngakyedauk Pass was gained when Scottish armoured patrols made contact with the Seventh Indian Division, which had resisted Japanese onslaughts for 17 days. The Scots broke through after assaulting Japanese positions that had dominated the pass.

MacDonald's citation for the award of the DFC read:

During the last six months Flight Lieutenant MacDonald has flown on a large number of bombing attacks against the Japanese in Burma. He has often led the formation in adverse weather and, by his resolution, zeal and courage, has contributed in no small measure to the success achieved by his squadron.[28]

Both Sandilands and MacDonald were back in action the same day as the awards were announced. At 1120 James Sandilands led twelve Vengeances, escorted by five Hurricane IICs from 261 Squadron, to hit pinpoint PM 373390 in the foothills between the Maungdaw-Buthidaung road and the Ngakyedauk *chaung*. Target identification was from photographs made available to the section leaders at the briefing. They found the weather at the target clear, but hazy near the ground. The target was scheduled to be smoke marked but again, although the puffs were duly noted on approach, a 20mph wind had dispersed the smoke before the Vengeances attacked. At 1153 they made steep dives from 10,000 feet down to 1,500 feet and dropped the usual

---

[28]   MacDonald survived the war but was killed flying a mercy flight in a Cessna 180 from Grande Prairie to Edmonton in November 1953 with a doctor (Wilson) and a polio patient (Lloyd Everett Williams) near White Court, Alberta. It was the subject of the most extensive Search and Rescue mission in Canada up to that time.

composite sticks all within a 100-yard radius. Most of the bombs hit the south-western slope on the adjacent ridges in two concentrations. Debris and smoke from the first hits quickly covered the target area and the last aircraft down bombed into this, and may have hit the north-western slope. The planes returned to base at 1220.

A second mission that day left the airfield at 1445, with a further dozen Vengeances escorted by six Hurricanes, and led by Flight Lieutenant MacDonald DFC. They were ordered to hit Point 1301 at pinpoint PM 4144. Friendly forward troops were emplaced at Point 1419 nearby and smoke markers were put down by Allied artillery. The dives commenced at 1515 and three mixed sticks fell atop the hill itself, with a further group along the eastern edge and the rest on the western slopes. It was difficult to estimate damage, but a signal received later from the closest British troops read 'Strikes on 1304 very successful. All bombs on target.'

Two more strikes followed on the 25th, led by Squadron Leader Gibbs and Flight Lieutenant Sutherland respectively, in the same area. The Vengeances were continuously involved at this time but despite their wholesale commitment and an increased Japanese air effort mounted by the 5th *Hikodan*, not a single British or Indian dive-bomber was lost to enemy air attack. On 27 February HQ, AC, SEA issued the following communiqué (No. 15):

No. 82 Squadron in one day flew thirty-six Vengeance sorties against enemy positions on the Maungdaw-Buthidaung Line and claim four direct hits on the entrance to the tunnel on the road connecting the two towns. On many occasions they have placed all bombs within a 150 yards radius of the pinpoint, and the Army have frequently sent signals of congratulations on the results.

An interesting breakdown revealed just how committed 82 Squadron was during the month of February:

82 Squadron Sortie Rate February 1944.

Pilot	Sorties	Aircrew	Sorties
Flt Sgt D. Kinnell	54	WO W.I. Bush	54
Flt Sgt C.S. Macdonald	43	Flt Sgt L.F. Foster	46

82 Squadron Sortie Rate February 1944.			
Pilot	Sorties	Aircrew	Sorties
Flt Sgt B.J. Scowen	41	Flt Sgt C. Woods	45
Flt Sgt N.J. Sinclair	41	Flt Sgt Roderick Fraser	43
Flt Sgt P.B. Herd	33	Sgt J.H. Coombs	38
Flt Sgt H. Rollins	29	Flt Sgt F.R. Casswell	32
Flt Sgt A.P. Bayley	28	Flt Sgt J.E. Allanach	26
Flt Sgt W.A. Garbutt	28	Sgt D.M. Connley	25
Sgt E.P. Hall	20	Flt Sgt J.V.S. Gibson	23
Sgt J.L. Hermelin	18	F/O Maurice Randall	18
Sgt Cyril Armstrong RAAF	16	F/O Alfred Newman	18
Sgt G.H. Ashworth	13	Sgt T.R. Stirton	16
Sgt A.S. Hemingway	7	F/O Mahadeo Ganesh Joshi IAF	3
Sqn Ldr Aizad Awan, IAF	3		

In total 82 Squadron delivered 739 500lb bombs and 745 250lb bombs into enemy positions this month, totalling in excess of 248 tons. Although tiny by comparison to the weight of bombs being dropped over Europe, the Vengeances directed their payloads with high accuracy on enemy combatants, achieving maximum impact with minimal losses.[29] Only three aircraft had to bring their bombs back to base due to technical problems. In an appreciation of their work the squadron was visited by Air Marshal Sir John Sir John Baldwin, Air Commander 3rd Tactical Air Force, on 18 February, while the battle was at its highest intensity. He was accompanied by Air Commodore Alexander Gray, Air Officer Commanding 224 Group. Over lunch he informed the assembled officers that he had 'very good reports from Forward Troops of Vengeance dive-bombing'. He also stated that 'the Army do not wish this squadron to be withdrawn for conversion to another type of aircraft'. Alas for the wishes of the ground troops and the dedication of the aircrew, higher up the chain there was deep prejudice against anything that might hint at any subservience of the RAF to the Army, and, particularly after years of intense propaganda to offset the repeated success of the German Ju87 Stuka, they just could not lose face now, despite all the evidence and all the pleadings from the men on the front line. The Premier,

---

[29]   However, away from the front line, losses were taken by 82 Squadron. On 7 February 1944, Vengeance AN 692 crashed at 1013 at Cuttnick, Orissa, having been caught in a violent thunderstorm and while attempting to make a forced landing in a paddy field. The pilot, Flight Sergeant Robert Thomas Hewetson, was killed on impact.

Winston Churchill, informed the House of Commons just how deep this prejudice ran: 'Most of the Air Marshals, the leading men in the Air Force, think little of dive bombers and they persist in their opinion.'[30]

Another incidence of this attitude was shown in exchanges of correspondence between Air Commodore William Wedgewood Benn, Viscount Stansgate, DSO DFC, Director of Public Relations, Air Ministry and Wing Commander George Basil Houghton, in which the latter stated, 'You will appreciate that we are employing the Vengeance in India with no little success and we shall therefore need to be careful in our reference to the ineffectiveness of the dive bomber and its alleged obsolescence.'[31] AHQ sent another signal which contained the following: 'We have not lost one Vengeance in operations and it has been able to do its job effectively and with impunity.' They added the fact that Burma 'is ideal dive-bomber country where targets are concentrated, camouflaged and surround by woods and hills.'[32] Not wanting propaganda to be influenced by facts, the Air Ministry response was predictable: 'Vengeance dive bomber publicity presents many pitfalls from standpoints both of security and publicity.'[33]

Dive-bombing was practically winning the war at sea in the Pacific, both from US aircraft-carrier task forces and from the island airstrips in New Guinea and beyond. So, it was with interest that Squadron Leader Gibbs was to record that a tactical memorandum describing their methods showed that 'this squadron's tactics are practically the same. An interesting point, considering that there had been no liaison, and that the problem was attacked by this Squadron with no background, tactics being evolved by operational necessity.'[34]

The month of March arrived but the missions continued in unrelenting succession. On the 4th three missions were mounted by 82 Squadron: Flight Lieutenant Gordon MacDonald led twelve Vengeances against a feature codenamed 'Italy' with take-off at 0753, and the attack at 0827. The first six-plane box delivered four mixed sticks precisely on the hill top itself and

[30]   Prime Minister to House of Commons, 2 July 1942, *Hansard*, issue 2.
[31]   Signal contained in 'Army Requirements of the Royal Air Force for Direct Support in Battle', dated 8 April 1943, AIR 20/4249.
[32]   AHQ India to Air Ministry, dated 3 June 1943. WX. 1935. AIR 20/4249 op. cit.
[33]   Air Ministry to AHQ India. Sec. X.49, AIR 20/4249, op. cit.
[34]   Squadron Leader Dennis Gibbs, 82 Squadron Operations Record Book, 29 February 1944. NA, Kew, AIR 27/683/3.

one each on the eastern and western slopes. Pilot Officer Norman Holland led the second box against Point 142 on the southern section of the hill that straddled the Maungdaw-Buthidaung road, and four sticks scored hits on pinpointed enemy machine-gun emplacements with other hits on a hill feature fifty yards to the south. The forward troops signalled this strike was 'excellent'. One Vengeance, H was hit by an explosive bullet which severed the hydraulic ram, but all aircraft returned safely to Jumchar at 0856.

Next up at 1142 was Squadron Leader Dennis Gibbs with two more six-plane boxes and an escort of six Spitfire Vs from 615 Squadron, Squadron Leader D.W. McCormack DFC*. They simultaneously attacked adjacent targets in the same vicinity, but south of the road on the eastern side of the Mayu range. Both boxes attacked at 1215 and both dived steeply from 10,000 feet down to 1,500 feet and each delivered into the enemy twelve 500lb NITD and twelve 250lb GP TD .025. Gibbs's target was the ammunition dump at Dongyaung village (PM 486414) and they caused a large explosion 'which was followed by an orange-red fire with grey-black smoke'. Flying Officer James Sandilands's box went for the valley in the centre of the Inbauk Hill feature (PM 476421), pasting the northern and southern slopes. All planes were back at Jumchar by 1242.

The third attack that day, which left at 1648, followed a similar pattern. This time the attack was put in against the village of Lamadaw, (PN 0339) located on the east bank of the Kafadan river, immediately opposite Kyauktaw. Wing Commander George Frederick Chater DFC, a South African, Battle of Britain veteran, and now the commanding officer of 167 Wing, was also present and observed the attack from a Hurricane. Heavy concentrations of Japanese troops had been reported there and they had already received visits from 8 Squadron's Vengeances earlier, but the Army signalled that there were still many enemy troops remaining. Accordingly, Squadron Leader Dennis Gibbs led a further twelve aircraft to this spot, arriving at 1728 and finding fires still burning on the northern edge of the road at the east end of the village. Each six-plane box attacked in steep dives from 10,000 feet down to 1,500 feet, one to the south and one to the north of the road, with the usual mix of GP and TD bombs. South of the road one direct hit was scored on a building which caused an explosion with red flames up to 150 feet high, followed by dense black smoke, a separate column of grey smoke straight up to a high altitude before mushrooming, and another direct hit on a building on the bank of the river. Two fires were also started north of the road and strafing was conducted by both front and rear guns. In total 82 Squadron mounted thirty-six sorties this day and attacked five different targets.

A Combined Headquarters Daily Intelligence Summary for 5 March (No. 503) gave a concise account of their work.

> 82 Squadron carried out 36 sorties today (4 March) on targets at PM 456438. 6 aircraft, PM 4741 (Pinpoint 124) – 6 aircraft PM 486414 (dumps) – 6 aircraft 476421 – 6 aircraft PM0339 (Lammadaw) – 12 aircraft. In all cases the bombing was accurate. Explosions occurred in the dump and sheets of flame and smoke came from it and from PM 0339. Ground troops report that two bombs on the first raid fall on an M.C. post. In all 54,000lbs of bombs were dropped during the day by this Squadron.

Gibbs recorded that there were 'fires and explosions all over the place'.

Further attacks took place on the 6th, with Flight Lieutenant Ira Sutherland DFC leading one box and Pilot Officer A.E. Parker the second, they dive-bombed positions along the Japanese supply route – and on the 7th, when a Japanese headquarters building on the Kaladan river at PN 019429 was totally demolished by a direct hit by Squadron Leader Gibbs and Norman Holland's section dive-bombed enemy artillery positions 400 yards to the west. The squadron was on stand-by on the 7th and 8th but were not called upon.

Tragedy struck on 9 March, but the enemy was not involved. The squadron was still on standby as on the previous day, but was conducting fighter affiliation exercises with the Supermarine Spitfire Vs of 615 Squadron. A formation led by Flight Lieutenant Gordon MacDonald DFC was some three-and-a-half miles south-south-east of Dohazari and practising diving to escape enemy fighter attack as an alternative to the standard practice of maintaining formation and relying on defensive fire. Flying Officer William Beckensall, RAFVR, the pilot of Vengeance B (FB 976) skidded into the dive and accidentally cut off the tail of MacDonald's aircraft, G (AN 694). Both Vengeances crashed and Beckensall and his rear-seat man, Warrant Officer Ernos George Parkes, were killed. MacDonald and his observer, Flight Sergeant David Berrington, managed to bale out and landed without any harm. Both aircraft were total losses. Gibbs recalled that 'Beckensall, the "Boy" as he was known on the unit, was one of the most popular men on the Squadron. His keenness and hard work in looking after the troops was only excelled in his keenness to bet up Japs.'

Another aircraft was lost on 11 March, during the fourth attack mounted by 82 Squadron which took off from Jumchar at 1158 that day. Ironically it was the first time that Hurricane IIC fighters of 258 Squadron[35] provided six escorts for the six Vengeances led by Flying Officer James Sandilands against enemy positions occupying a hill feature just to the west of Point 124B at pinpoint PM 545473. The weather was clear, but the low sun caused shadows on the north and west sides of the target, which were confusing against the blacked, burnt-out landscape of the battlefield. Sandilands circled and then led his formation into a steep diving attack at 1530. Five aircraft bombed the correct target, dropping four sticks along the top of the feature, and one on the south-western slope. One stick fell on the north-western slope of the last portion of the dog-legged target. The sixth aircraft inadvertently bombed pinpoint 539469. Vengeance A received heavy ground fire with 'an engine full of bullets' and many more bullet holes in the underbody and, crucially, some in the oil tank which proved fatal. Sergeant E.P. Hall and Flight Sergeant J.V.S. Gibson, nursed her as far as a paddy field south of Taung Bazar, on the Chinbyin to Toungup (Taungup) road, inland east from Ramree Island, 21^0 01'N, 92^0 5' E. They were too low to jump for it and both rode the machine down and survived the ditching unharmed. Some Indian troops came out and guided them back to the Bazar itself where they providentially found a little de Havilland Tiger Moth biplane, which took them back to base.

On 15 March the softening-up of the crucial 162 Feature was continued with an attack on enemy positions at Punkori, on the western bank of the Kalapanzin River (pinpoint PM 489476) by twelve Vengeances led by Squadron Leader Dennis Gibbs. The strike took off from Jumchar at 1222 encountering 2/10th cumulus at 4,000 to 6,000 feet. The Vengeances commenced their 'steep dives' from 10,000 feet down to 1,500 feet at 1255. Eleven sticks, totalling twenty-four 500lb GP NITD and twenty-four 250lb GP TD .025, fell directly on target, while one stick landed to the north-east,

---

[35]   258 Squadron was commanded by Squadron Leader Neil Cameron.

including two bombs that went into the Letwedet *chaung* and two more which exploded just north of the *chaung*.

Although nobody observed any enemy fire one Vengeance, W, piloted by Warrant Officer Kenneth Edward William McCrombie, RNZAF, was hit by flak in both the fuel tank and the hydraulics pipe line. Streaming oil, he attempted to force land at the small airstrip at Goppe Bazar. Before he made his final approach, McCrombie told his WO/AG, Pilot Officer Nigel Stark Harrower, to bale out, which he did safely from less than 1,000 feet, surviving with only a strained ankle. McCrombie's luck, unfortunately, ran out because his engine seized up and although he baled out as well he was too low and was killed as the aircraft crashed and totally burned out a mile short of airstrip. This ended 'a very Black Week' for 82 Squadron.

Further accurate bombing was conducted on 18 March, Flight Lieutenant Ira Sutherland leading a force of twelve Vengeances from Jumchar at 1050 in an attack on the northern half of the flat top of Point 1301. They were briefed that British troops were within a radius of 1,300 yards of the target. They found the weather there favourable, it being clear, although it was 10/10th up at 11,000 feet which cast awkward shadow over the actual aiming point. The Vengeances nonetheless made steep dives from 10,000 feet down to 2,500 feet at 1130 and stick-bombed with two dozen 500lb GP NITD and two dozen 250lb GP TD .025, in two boxes of six, with the second box delaying their attack dive until the smoke caused by the first box bomb bursts had died away sufficiently to give them a clear view. All four dozen bombs, save a solitary one which 'hung up' on Vengeance H, hit the northern end of the flat top.

Later in the day a signal was received from the Brigadier CCRA[36] of XV Corps, commanded by Lieutenant General Sir Alexander Frank Philip Christison GBE CB DSO MC*, which read, 'This bombing was more accurate than gunfire. No. 1 hit the foxholes. No. 2 was a little off. Nos.3 & 4 hit foxholes. All the others were very close within 15 to 20 yards. 50 Japs seen to stagger out after the bombing were shot.'

On the afternoon of 20 March, a detachment of sixteen Vengeances left Jumchar for Kumbhirgam, followed by six Dakota transport aircraft conveying ground crews, spare parts and other essentials. They were to be attached to 168 Wing, part of 221 Group commanded by Group Captain

---

[36] Corps Commander Royal Artillery.

James Barclay Black DFC, which 82 Squadron had known at Digri in August 1943. By now they were equipped with the Vengeance III, a great improvement over the earlier versions.

This move was necessitated because, undeterred by the setback they had suffered in the Arakan, the Japanese had launched what was their main onslaught, Plan C or Operation I-GO. This involved twin assaults to take the main British advanced base at Imphal and the huge supply bases at Kohima across the central frontier border in Manipur, India. For this audacious plan, which also caught the Allies totally by surprise, the Japanese Fifteenth Army under Lieutenant General Renya Mutaguchi, whose brainchild this was, threw in two divisions, the 15th and 33rd, which moved up the Manipur river valley against Tiddim and up the Kabaw valley to Tamu. Emboldened by past successes, Mutaguchi largely ignored the tremendous risks involved in supplying and feeding his 65,000 troops over very tenuous terrain with few roads through hostile jungle. Instead he relied on capturing intact the huge stockpiles of Allied food, medicines, munitions and equipment he thought would fall into his hands once his initial two objectives had fallen into his hands, which he confidently expected they would if the Allies adopted their usual policy of retreat. The lure of boundless loot and food would also act as a spur, should that be needed, to his men on the ground. Many of his compatriots thought the policy at least risky, at most foolhardy, and some considered it suicidal, but he stuck to his guns. Once again, although caught on the back foot, Lieutenant General William Slim's reaction was to stand and fight, even when isolated and cut off, and rely on air support, both for sustenance, with Dakota transport planes and gliders and also for direct heavy firepower support in the field.

Now, more than ever before, the accuracy and pounding power of the dive bomber was required and to meet the threat both 82 Squadron with sixteen aircraft, and 7 Squadron IAF, moved their Vengeances across to Kumbhirgram where 168 Wing could now call on four such units with both 84 (which had been hastily diverted from assisting Orde Wingate's latest planned foray) and 110 Squadrons already in place there, to support their hard-pressed colleagues.

On 27 March Flight Lieutenant Ira Sutherland left the detachment to take up his new appointment of commanding officer of 8 Squadron IAF. He left in a North American Harvard and it was noted in the Squadron

Summary that 'Flight Lieutenant Sutherland was very popular in the Squadron which wishes him every success in his Command'.

The squadron was visited on 31 March by Lieutenant Colonel Kenneth Silas Hayes-Palmer, of 2nd East Lancashire Regiment, the officer commanding the troops who captured pinpoint 1301, the key to Razabil. 'He passed on personal messages of thanks to all crews of the Vengeance Squadrons who contributed so devastatingly to the victory over the Jap fortress.' An Air Force officer who had helped provide fighter cover for the squadron in these attacks, Wing Commander George Chater ('Baboon One'), and who later visited the scene of the battle gave a more graphic account, telling how it was 'one mass of bomb craters, and bomb splinters littered the place'. He also added the titbit that 'The stink of dead Japs buried in the bunks was not at all pleasant'.

The work continued, and on 1 April Pilot Officer Alan Parker took twelve Vengeances against Thaungdut (Pinpoint SF 2118) which was situated on a very sharp bend on the in the Cadadwla river with Pilot Officer 'Dutch' Holland, RCAF, leading the second box. They attacked at 0720 and made direct hits on eight buildings, one of which was covered with camouflage netting. Two explosions resulted in red flames and a dirty white column of smoke up to 600 feet, attributed to a direct hit on a petrol dump. The area was strafed despite some return fire from the ground, but no aircraft was damaged. This same village was attacked later in the day by 84 Squadron, who used incendiaries and burnt it out. A later strike with Milestone 109 on the Tiddim Road as its objective was 'weathered out', and 7 IAF Squadron, which ran into the same cloudbank, lost an aircraft in the process.

On 2 April both Nawnpaung (SF 6207) and Paukpyin (SF 6367) were struck by six-plane boxes led by Squadron Leader Gibbs and Flying Officer Sandilands respectively. The increased number of sorties led these Vengeances to sortie with just the two 500lb bombs carried, as 250lb bombs were also being carried by the 'Hurribombers' and this had led to a shortage of these weapons.[37] Later that same afternoon an attack led by Flying Officer

---

[37] According to a later analysis these converted Hurricanes had proved as accurate as the Vengeances in some attacks, but they could not equal them in weight of ordnance per aircraft delivered and had not the same impact on Japanese bunker positions.

Sandilands was delivered into Sittang and its pier on the Caladwin river to disrupt this Japanese supply hub.

The following day two twelve-Vengeance attacks were made, the first under the command of Flight Lieutenant Gordon Webster Macdonald DFC, split with one box bombing Natkyingon on the Myittka river at 0932; while the second box, led by Squadron Leader Dennis Gibbs, hit the enemy on the west bank of the Chindwin river north of the Pauggbyia Bend. All aircraft returned to Kumbrirgram at 1020. The second mission was launched at 1602 against targets in same area and was equally successful. In some kind of belated reprisal 82 Squadron's dispersal area was attacked by a solitary Kawasaki Ki-48 *Sokei* ('Lily') bomber which dropped four 50kg bombs and two phosphorus pellet incendiaries but without causing any damage save earth being thrown over Vengeance F by a near miss. This raider displayed the correct British recognition signals and was unchallenged by the defending AA but was later chased and shot down by a Bristol Beaufighter.

No attacks were made on the 4th but the next day no fewer than four separate missions were flown by 82 Squadron against Toamate (Pinpoint SF 4467) With Flying Officer A.E. Parker and Flying Officer 'Dutch' Holland each leading a six-plane box; the second attack was at Melabum on a knife-edge ridge in the hills east of the Homalin Bend, a very difficult target, but the majority of bombs struck the south-east part of the village, starting large fires. Toamate was hit for the second time by a six-plane box led by Sandilands at 1419 after a difficult approach through bad weather, including a thunderstorm. Finally, Dennis Gibbs put another strike in at Melabum. Planned attacks over the following two days were aborted due to poor conditions.

On 8 April Squadron Leader Gibbs flew the 2,000th Vengeance sortie by 82 Squadron. Both 82 and 110 Squadron attacked targets in the Fort White area, and then 82's twelve aircraft hit Viswena on the second mission of the day, starting many fires, before making a second pass to strafe the area with both front and rear machine-gun fire. Meanwhile, 110 Squadron simultaneously struck at Madsongsang village, a Japanese Army rallying point for their advance along the Imphal to Kohima road. This proved one of their last sorties from Kumbhirgram for, the following day, the 82 detachment was ordered back to Arakan front after carrying out 344 detachment sorties and returned thither on the 10th.

The detachment, with a minimal ground support team of just fifty personnel, had flown 344 sorties on the sixteen days that the weather allowed operations. They flew 700 combat hours while their average take-off time was twelve aircraft in two-and-a-half minutes, their slickest form-up time was five minutes and best landing time around three minutes. At one time the increased work of the Vengeance squadron resulted in a shortage of 250lb bombs and missions had, perforce, to be flown with only 500lb bomb loads. In the words of the Engineering Officer, 'We shook 'em rigid'.

On their return several long-term personnel were posted away, including Flying Officer G.G. Thompson after completing fifty-eight Vengeance sorties and Warrant Officers Ronald Samuel Trigg and H.R. Crichton, who had both flown 101 sorties on the Vengeance. They also lost their Equipment Officer, Warrant Officer M.L. Bignall. The detachment had fulfilled its mission and was returned to Jumchar between 11 and 12 April to resume its support of the offensive from there. Here they found the situation had deteriorated badly. Taking full advantage of the curtailment of Allied air operations and the withdrawal of the ground troops to their monsoon stations once more, the Japanese quickly moved to re-occupy much of the area that had been so painfully and arduously taken from them earlier, including such key locations as 'Italy', 'Ahla', Point 162 and Point 121. The Japanese had the advantage of being able to utilise the Mayu river as his main supply line.

Not content with this the enemy pressed on, hoping to regain control of the Maungdaw to Buthidaung road as well and began an assault on Point 130.

Based back at Jumchar, 82 Squadron flew 400 sorties in the remaining sixteen operational days of April. Squadron Leader Dennis Gibbs noted that 'Back at Arakan operational differences were very noticeable and we once more had good maps and photographs to work with, and were given pinpoint targets. The bombing was therefore much more concentrated and accurate.' It was also recorded how they fought not just the enemy but the sea. 'At the end of the month the tide began to encroach on the strip at high spring tide, but we built a very fine *padi Bund* and with the help of the Climax Pump kept it operational.'

In fact, combat missions soon re-commenced from Jumchar, with no less than four attacks being launched on 12 April. At 1354 two Japanese gun positions were targeted. They had been giving the troops on the ground a hard time as they were firing from cleverly concealed revetments in the vicinity of the re-entrant at the former village of Sinoh (PM 475385). The exact positions of these two guns were determined by registration of their flashes by artillery observation posts and were then given to the squadron as grid references. Both guns were steep dive-bombed from 10,000 feet down to 1,500 feet at 1427 and each one was bombed with twelve 500lb GP TD .025 and twelve 250lbGP TD.012. Squadron Leader Gibbs led the first six-plane box and the target, which could not be made out from 10,000 feet, was straddled but not seen to be destroyed. So, Gibbs went around again to strafe and reported that no gun remained after the bombing. Flying Officer Sandilands led the second box in against the other artillery piece at the re-entrant, but again could not actually see the gun itself. Sticks of bombs were laid across the re-entrant in close concentrations. As they left they could see Allied shells bursting on the adjacent Dongyaung feature. All the aircraft returned safely at 1505.

Sandilands was back in action at 1740 with a six-plane box striking at infiltrating Japanese who had got mortars and artillery. Smoke marking was followed and at 1800 dives were commenced from 10,000 feet to 1,500 feet. Four sticks of bombs fell across the feature, while two other sticks detonated 200 yards away, immediately to the east of the hill. A follow-up attack on this position was carried out at 1807 by another six-Vengeance box led by Flying Officer William Melville Tullett, RCAF, and achieved a concentration on the target. Photographs were taken but proved valueless due to the smoke and dust clouds thrown up.

Pintails were dropped on two occasions that same afternoon. Pintails were, in essence, an elaborate decoy, designed to draw off enemy reserve forces by simulating an aerial landing and could be used in conjunction with dummy parachutists. Pintails were just very small bombs which contained a Very-light cartridge, which was released and activated when the device struck the ground. They were either instantaneous or fitted with time-delay mechanisms, at the end of which mock rifle and machine-gun fire was added to the show. 82 Squadron had already conducted trails with both devices, but this was the first occasion they had deployed them in action. Warrant Officer M.F. Pettibone, RCAF, made a sortie with several of these 'weapons' to the east of the Kaladan river, delivering one instantaneous and one six-hour delay pintail some one-and-a-half miles south-east of Teinnyo Village and two six-and-a-half-hour delay pintails north-east of the same place. Delivery was carried out by Sapper Grimshaw pushing the pintails through the camera aperture of Vengeance H. Both sets were dropped in low scrub near the foothills, but the instantaneous cartridges were not observed to explode.

Next day, 13 April, 82 Squadron made three sorties, but the first, which left Jumchar at 0715, with the intention of attack enemy troops at West Baguan village, was aborted when dense fog was encountered over the Meru valley, which made target identification impossible. They tried again at 1000, Squadron Leader Dennis Gibbs leading twelve aircraft to these positions at 1035 in what was described as a 'very concentrated' strike. There was no opposition and as they left two rear gunners independently noted what appeared to be a red fireball erupt from the hills south of the village, which rose into the sky and was accompanied by a thin column of smoke 200-feet high. It was airborne for about a minute before bouncing on the Dongyaung feature north-east of the village. At 1220 Pilot Officer Norman Holland led six Vengeances against Japanese troops dug in with machine guns to the east of Kanbyin village. Steep diving attacks were made at 1250 and the usual mix of 500lb and 250lb bombs were concentrated on these positions. Reports from forward troops stated that the last Vengeance down, Sergeant E.P. Hall, 'caused an explosion followed by smaller explosions'.

While this attack was in process, Vultee Vengeance AN 810 was detailed to carry out an experimental shallow-dive practice bombing using bombs, in an effort to determine the best angle of dive for use in a planned forthcoming operation. The aircraft, Y, piloted by the very experienced Flight Lieutenant James Walter Sandilands DFC, RAAF, who had 130 combat sorties under his belt, with Leading Aircraftsman Thomas George Wotton, a fitter, in the back seat, took off at 1240 and, after a preparatory circuit, went into a 70-degree degree dive from a height of approximately 3,000 feet with dive-brakes extended and commenced a pull-out at about 600 feet. He was experimenting with dive-bombing techniques and in the last attack planned for the day. However, the Vengeance 'mushed' downwards, probably in a speed stall, and hit the ground at one end of the airfield, bursting into flames on impact and being totally destroyed. Both pilot and passenger died instantly.[38] Gibbs recalled that Sandilands 'was one of the world's best dive bombers, consistently accurate in his own bombing and a leader who by placing his formation in a position immediately over the target, minimised their difficulties of viewing and diving choice. His quiet competence and pleasant forceful character augured great possibilities.' Sandilands's replacement was Flight Lieutenant Donald James Jock Ritchie, RAAF, who arrived in the squadron back at Jumchar on 29 April.

Finally, two six-plane boxes lifted off from Jumchar at 1700 to attack two 70-foot-high telegraph poles, painted red and white, one either bank of the *chaung* opposite Min Kyung Island, east of the Mayu river near Rathedaung, carrying wires to the forward areas from the Japanese Army HQ east of Htizwe. Originally it had been suggested that shallow dives using 11-second time delay bombs might be the best way to tackle this very difficult target, but this idea was not adopted after Sandilands's tragic accident, and so the normal steep dives from 10,000 feet down to 1,500 feet were made at 1740. However, each pilot could attack individually using whichever method, stick or salvo, he preferred. After the fifth Vengeance down, piloted by Flight Sergeant P.B. Herd, had bombed, the telegraph wires were seen to fall into the river, and this was confirmed by their fighter cover who saw the wires dangling down from the tops of the pylons, which, however, were not themselves broken by either of the two attacks. The first was led by Flight Lieutenant Gordon MacDonald DFC, who took twelve Vengeances to dive-bomb enemy troop concentrations at the junction of the track and *chaung* at Pinpoint PM 433435. Two dozen 500lb NITD were concentrated within a 100-yard radius with 80 per cent falling south of the *chaung*. While in his dive MacDonald saw a file of men moving west into the hills. The second strike was led by Flight Lieutenant Donald Ritchie, RAAF, with a further twelve Vengeances which, at 1715 attacked the signal centre at Zediaduang. (Pinpoint PM 829272). All the bombs fell close but once the smoke had cleared a low-level strafing attack revealed that no direct hits had been made on the centre itself.

There were no operations on the 16th and 17th but the 18th saw the squadron standing to for ASC tasks from first light but the monsoon prevented any bombing taking place until mid-afternoon. At 1527 Flight

---

[38] Both men were buried in the Chittagong War Cemetery in what is now Bangladesh.

Lieutenant Donald James 'Jock' Ritchie, RAAF, led a formation of twelve Vengeances against a critical target, a Japanese position to the west of Labawa, Chin Province, (21° 23'N, 92° 43' E) at Pinpoint PG 630312 in direct support of an army assault on a knife-edge ridge. Smoke-laying was not possible on such a difficult geographical feature and it was assumed there would be considerable difficulty in picking out the enemy hill among so many unfamiliar hills when they only had the inaccurate 1-inch map as their sole target indicator. But for one of their final combat missions 82 Squadron rose to the occasion as usual. Don Ritchie was briefed to make an initial dive on his own and, if satisfied, was not to bomb but was to indicate by VHF just exactly where the whole Vengeance formation should bomb. This plan was followed. Ritchie dived but did not release. On rejoining the formation, with the exact location now agreed, they all attacked at 1607, delivering twelve 500lb NITD and twenty-four 250lb TD .025 bombs into the enemy trenches. Five sticks of bombs hit PG 639310 and seven sticks fell into PG 639318. Most of these bombs fell on the knife-edged ridge and its eastern slopes. There were two bombs only that fell higher up on the western slopes. There were no incidents and photographs of this most successful attack were taken. The whole force returned to Jumchar at 1633.

The 19th of May saw 82 Squadron's final attack, with Dennis Gibbs leading a force of no fewer than sixteen Vengeances in excellent attacks on three separate targets. The following day the weather completely closed in and torrential rains rendered further operations impossible. The runway at Jumchar was abandoned as unserviceable due to the combination of this rain and the high tides and the squadron withdrew to Cox's Bazar airstrip on 22 May. This was only a temporary move for, three days later, fifteen Vengeances flew to Asanol and one to Dum Dum. Ten of these then flew on to Allahabad. They fully expected to rest, recoup and then rejoin the fight, but it was not to be.

In summary of this period, the detachment had, in the only eleven days suitable for flying, mounted ninety sorties and one supply drop. The unit maintained 100 per cent serviceability during this period, a squadron record. Many of the squadron's Akyab missions during April and May were in support of 81st (West African) Division. One of these, against a battery of Japanese field guns at Lamadaw, elicited the following signal: 'ASC reports strong possibility probably knocked out field guns as they have not been heard of since.' This was typical of 82 Squadron's achievements.

For his work with the Vengeance Gibbs was awarded the DSO.[39]

Wing Commander Lionel Vivian 'Bill' Hudson, RAAF, who had commanded the Australian Vengeance unit No. 12 Squadron, RAAF, assumed command in July 1944[40] and 82 Squadron became non-operational while it re-equipped with Mosquito VIs. As we have already noted, these were not the initial success that the mandarins in the Air Ministry had hoped for. In Burma, 'despite extended local testing, the extremes of heat and humidity found out weakness in the bonding of the plywood skins and of the laminated wing spars. These led to skin delamination and wing spar failures, which saw Mosquitoes stood down from service in the Far East for a period in late 1944.' [From *de Havilland Mosquito*.] Pilot Officer Victor Abel RAAF, of 82 Squadron, was to be killed on 13 September.[41] Not until 5 October did 82 begin operations with their new mounts, being based at Kolar and Flying Officer Andrew Thynne RAAF, was killed on 19 February 1945.

---

[39] Gibbs later became Administrator of the Caribbean island of Montserrat between 1964 and 1971. See 'Details concerning Dennis Gibbs, Administrator on Montserrat on his departure from his post.' National Archives, FCO 44/591, HWM 25/3. Dated 1971 January to 1971 December. Gibbs died in 1985 after a brain haemorrhage.

[40] Commander Hudson remained CO until Dec 1944.

[41] Abel's Memorial is at Madras cemetery.

Chapter 6

No. 84 Squadron RAF

Scorpiones Pungunt
(Scorpions Sting)

F light Lieutenant Arthur Murland Gill, an RAFVR officer, who had survived the carnage of 84 Squadron in Java in 1942 and had fought tooth-and-nail to get it resurrected from the embers, was placed in command from 30 October 1942 to 19 September 1944 and was subsequently succeeded by Flight Lieutenant Raymond George Ravenscroft on 20 September 1944.

The squadron was based at Karachi between March and April 1942, and then moved to Drigh Road from April to June. The last of the useless Blenheims were withdrawn in June and from then until November that year 84 was based at Quetta, but with no aircraft until the first Vengeance arrived in December 1942.

Some months before, in April 1942, a Japanese naval task force commanded by Admiral Chuichi Nagumo, had carried out a series of raids against British bases in Ceylon[1], hitting both the major British ports of Colombo and Trincomalee, and creating havoc among the dispersed British naval vessels in the area, resulting in the sinking of the aircraft carrier *Hermes*, the heavy cruisers *Cornwall* and *Dorsetshire*, the destroyers *Tenedos* and *Vampire* and numerous naval auxiliaries and merchant ships. A British Fleet under Admiral Sir James Somerville was in the area but totally outclassed and was fortunate to avoid total annihilation, while the RAF on the island suffered heavy losses against the Imperial Japanese Navy's carrier-borne Mitsubishi *Zero-Sen* fighters.[2]

---

[1] Now known as Sri Lanka.

[2] Premier Winston Churchill made highly exaggerated claims in Parliament claiming that the Japanese had 'come up against bone', and similar claims have been repeated since, but the truth was that Japanese losses were minimal and British very heavy, both in the air and at sea, losing more than thirty aircraft against just seven Japanese.

Part of this lesson in the correct use of airpower was that occasioned by the despatch, on 11 April, of an eleven-strong air striking force from No. 11 Squadron, RAF, employing the same obsolete twin-engined Bristol Blenheim Mk IV aircraft that had failed so often before, to deal with the Japanese fleet. Led by Squadron Leader Kenneth Ault, RAF, this strike force left at 0820 with eleven aircraft, their three-man crews being augmented by two Royal Naval observers from No. 806 Squadron FAA, Sub-Lieutenant (Observer) Anthony Pearce and Sub-Lieutenant (Observer) Frank William Bonnell, in order to correctly identify the targets. Two Blenheims developed engine trouble and turned back, landing at 0915 and 0950 respectively. The remaining nine located the enemy fleet, which comprised five aircraft carriers, four battleships, two heavy and one light cruisers, and nine destroyers, and caught them unawares.[3] Despite this advantage, when they made their attacks[4], despite dropping fifteen 500lb SAP and fourteen 250lb SAP (Semi-Armour-Piercing) bombs, they scored only three near misses and caused the enemy no damage or inconvenience. The squadron's ORB states that one Blenheim was shot down by AA fire and then the defending Zero fighters hacked down four more, Charles Henry Adcock SAAF in Z7896, 3911 piloted by Sergeant Hugh Alexander MacLennan, RAAF, 7803 piloted by Warrant Officer Noel Lindsay Stevenson, RAAF and Ault's own aircraft, 5992, which was the last to fall. The remainder staggered back to their base at the Racecourse airfield but were shot full of holes and all were recorded as unserviceable at the end of what the ORB recorded as 'A sad day'.[5]

In truth the RAF were still using the wrong aircraft and the wrong tactics. Many in the media of the day were uneasy, while General Sir Robert Gordon-Finlayson KCB CME DSO, the former GOC Western Command, was scathing at the Air Ministry's attitude towards dive-bombers. 'Perhaps,' he wrote, 'we may learn the reason for our lack of this powerful weapon. We hope that the reason is good; if so we will be delighted that the secret has been kept so well kept.'[6] 'Scrutator', writing in *The Times*, sagely noted: 'There are people

---

[3]   The Japanese ships were not radar-equipped at this period of the war.

[4]   The Blenheims attacked the heavy cruiser *Tone*, the battleship *Kongo* and Nagumo's flagship, the aircraft carrier *Akagi*.

[5]   AIR 27/157/35 & 36.

[6]   Recorded in Memo, ACAS (TR) to VCAS, dated 8 March 1943 (Briny 3167, in AIR 2/5504.

at the Air Ministry who will probably scorn dive-bombers to the end, but I have yet to hear of any soldier or sailor who does so after undergoing attack by them.'[7] Mr T.C.L. Westbrook, a former member of the Ministry for Aircraft Production, also spilled the beans: 'Just lately many confusing and conflicting statements have been made about [British] lack of dive bombers. The true facts are that the Air Ministry decided before the war, against the use of them ….' He added, 'In the early days of the Ministry for Aircraft Production it was impossible to order dive bombers as (1) the British programme was full and production poor, and (2) the RAF did not want them.'[8]

It was deemed opportune therefore that, fearing a repeat carrier-led attack on British possessions in the Indian Ocean at any time (a dread lessened but never abated after the US Navy victory at Midway in June), that the arrival of the first Vengeance dive-bombers in India caused a belated re-think. AHQ Bengal, at the sharp end, signalled to AHQ India back in Delhi, 'I cannot exaggerate the importance I attach to the early arrival of Vengeance dive bombers in the command.' They considered that aircraft like the Blenheim and the Lockheed Hudson were 'quite unsatisfactory for attacks on ships at sea or in harbour'.[9]

A precision instrument was required for use against enemy naval targets, and that was not the only consideration for a re-think; the proposed offensive against the Japanese in the Arakan jungles also merited the positivity of accuracy. 'Had dive bombers been available I consider that our object at Akyab on 9 September could have been achieved at less than half the effort', was the view of AHQ Bengal. They would 'gladly release a Blenheim squadron in exchange' for a Vengeance unit, and wanted 82 Squadron.[10] The success of the US Navy and Marine Corps flyers in the Solomons also resonated, especially regarding jungle warfare. Commander Eric Augustus Feldt, RAN, was to write that 'Indiscriminate bombing of jungle positions is generally harmless, but this precise delivery of high explosives on selected targets was something else again'.[11]

---

[7]   Issue dated 28 June 1942.

[8]   Letter to *The Times*, dated 27 June 1942.

[9]   AHQ Bengal to AHQ Delhi, dated 11 September 1942. AIR 23/4361.

[10]   *Ibid*.

[11]   Feldt, Commander Eric Augustus OBE, RAN, *The Coastwatchers*, Oxford University Press, Oxford, 1946.

Thus, it was that when 45 Squadron went into action with the Vengeance but 84 Squadron's earlier *raison d'etre* was as an anti-naval unit. As the RAF had no dive-bombing doctrine of their own (all their concentration being on German cities in ruins and victory achieved by the heavy bomber alone), the Royal Navy's Fleet Air Arm tactics from the 1930s were examined instead, The Navy was a firm believer in the dive-bomber, but were only allocated minimal funding from which they developed the Blackburn Skua monoplane. Predictably, the RAF, which controlled the Navy's aircraft production pre-war, insisted it also act as a fighter, and no aircraft of that time could possibly do both roles well.[12] The Skua worked as a dive-bomber; the first ever major warship, the German cruiser, the *Konigsberg*, was sunk by them at Bergen, Norway, in 1940, but it was slow and largely impotent as a fighter and soon abandoned. However, all the Royal Navy's earlier dive-bombing training had been done with biplanes and the documents studied by 84 Squadron are strewn with diagrams and sketches showing biplane configurations.

Nonetheless the basic essentials of attacking high-speed, well-armed warships were still relevant and, as No. 11 Squadron's fiasco showed, medium bombing in level flight was *not* the answer, nor was high-level bombing. Indeed, at the Battle of Midway in June 1942, the Boeing Flying Fortresses 'precision' bombed the Japanese Fleet from a great height, went back to base and announced that they had won the battle for the Navy! This was widely accepted by the American Press and became banner headlines across the nation.[13] The truth was that the B-17s did not score one single hit in the whole battle: all four Japanese aircraft carriers, plus a damaged heavy cruiser, were sunk by Douglas SBD Dauntless dive-bombers from the American carriers.

So 84 studied the factors that affected accuracy against jinking warships that were firing back and moving fast, taking into account factors like wind speed and direction and other variables.[14]

---

[12]   See Smith, Peter C., *Skua; the Royal Navy's Dive Bomber*, Pen & Sword Aviation, Barnsley, 2006.

[13]   See *Smith, Peter C., Midway Dauntless Victory: Fresh Perspectives on America's Seminal Naval Victory of World War II*, Pen & Sword Maritime, Barnsley, 2007.

[14]   Among the documents utilised to gain basic knowledge of their expected new role were *Dive Bombing Technique with High-speed aircraft of Clean Aerodynamic Design* (1936); *Notes on Dive Bombing for the Information of Designers of Aeroplanes for the RAF* (1936); *The Theory of Dive Bombing* (1938); and *Dive Bombing* (1940).

Arthur Gill related how, once assimilated, these tactics were practised and honed following a move to Ratmalana, Ceylon, on 19 April 1943. From this airfield they practised with such Royal Navy warships as were available.[15] Static targets for training included Gongala Rock off northern Ceylon, which 84 Squadron dive-bombed 'almost daily'.

After the Japanese Navy had suffered heavy losses in the Pacific at the battles of Coral Sea and Midway, and become further embroiled in the Solomon Islands campaign against the growing might of the US fleet, it became clear that the likelihood of further raids into the Indian Ocean was remote and so the decision was taken for 84 Squadron to join the other Vengeance units on the Burma-India border where they had been achieving great things. Originally this move north-east was scheduled earlier but the monsoon season scuppered that, and it was not until 18 August that they moved up to Ranchi, Bihar, and began training with the Army rather than the Navy. They absorbed these new lessons and prepared to shift to Chittagong in December, sending an advance party off in readiness.

At the very last minute though, fresh instructions were received from 221 Group, informing them of a change of plan; they were instead allocated to provide close air support to Major General Orde Wingate's Chindits, the Long Range Penetration Group (3rd Indian Division), and their move to Maharajpur, Gwazlior.[16]

Arthur Gill's regular navigator had become D'Arcy James Hawke, a highly capable RAAF officer. When 84 Squadron was disbanded he was posted to 221 Group to aid their navigation skills. Flight Sergeant Leonard William Jack Goodfellow was a New Zealand officer while Australians included Philip Mervyn Corney, WOP/AG, who joined 84 in February 1942 and Sergeant John Aldwyn Lovegrove. Other assets were Warrant Officers Edward Gadesden, Allan G. Terry, RAAF, and Arthur Field. Others included

---

[15] There were no carriers on the East Indies Station at this time: they were needed back in the Mediterranean, first to escort convoys to Malta and later for the invasions of North Africa and Sicily, as well as guarding the Arctic convoys and watching the *Tirpitz*, but there were cruisers like the *Sussex* and *Newcastle* and high-speed targets like the destroyer *Scout*.

[16] The name Chindits was given by Captain Aong Thin of the Burma Rifles and referred to the mythical *Chinthe*. When a second group was formed for the 1944 campaign Wingate chose its commander, Lieutenant General Walter David Alexander Lentaigne, and had to accept three brigades (14, 16 and 23) from 70th (formerly 6th) Infantry Division.

Flying Officer Harry Strangeways Pirch Brooke, who was ex-Honourable Artillery Company, and Flight Sergeants Douglas O. Morris, L.R.M. Tibble and Reginald Wilson and Sergeant H. Widdop. Other New Zealanders were Flight Lieutenant Lloyd Sidney Johns (a former 18 Squadron pilot born in Christchurch in 1915) and Flight Lieutenant Colin Ernest Papps DFC.

Lloyd Johns had a very distinguished career. After service in Blenheims in Malaya and Burma, including a period operating with No. 60 Squadron out of Mingaladon at the same time that the AVG (American Volunteer Group, the so-called 'Flying Tigers'), he joined 110 Squadron on 12 November 1942, remaining with them until 27 December when he transferred to 84 Squadron on 30 December. Initially he joined the squadron at Cholavaram, (now Sholavaram) and remained there until 28 April 1943 when the squadron removed via Ratmalana after the rumoured second Japanese carrier strike panic subsided, to Ranchi, where they arrived on 28 August. On 6 December they were on the move again, this time to Maharajpur until 16 December. In total he flew forty-three combat sorties with the Northrop-built Vengeance I and II. He then joined XXXIII Indian Corps at Kumbhirgram, Assam, as a FAC (Forward Air Controller), between 16 February 1944 and 28 April before moving with them via Dinapur on 28 April into Kohima. He moved over to Imphal on 3 May. On 15 May Johns joined Wingate's Chindits at Kawab and on the 29th was attached to 7th Division, remaining with them until 14 October when he returned home.

Flight Lieutenant John Harold Ramsden was the squadron's ever-reliable Engineering Officer and a tower of strength in the many difficult situations they found themselves in. Flight Lieutenant Richard 'Dick' Johns was another New Zealand officer.

Flying Officer Bertram Albert Finnie 'Bert', was involved in two similar incidents. On 6 April 1944, flying Vengeance II AN828, with Flying Officer Ronald Eric Gabrielson, RAAF, he baled out and returned to the squadron on foot on the 10th. On 26 June 1944, Finnie was detailed to attack a fuel depot. Near the target the cockpit filled with smoke. Suspecting it was on fire, he told Flying Officer John Frederick Ellis, RCAF, to prepare to bale out. 'I'm ready when you are' was the reply. Finnie pulled out of formation and turned back to base. Looking round he discovered that Ellis had disconnected the intercom and was about to exit. Finnie was unable to stop him. The gunner's parachute opened, and he apparently landed in trees. Other aircraft spotted the parachute but no sign of Ellis. Meanwhile the cockpit smoke cleared away, although the aircraft hydraulics were unserviceable. The pilot used emergency procedures to open the bomb doors, jettison his bombs and lower his undercarriage to land. The smoke was traced to vaporised hydraulic fluid leaking from the oil cooler. Ellis was presumed to be in Japanese hands, but nothing was heard of him and later his death was officially presumed. His name is on the Singapore Memorial as having no known grave. Warrant Officer Eric Robert Watkins was also killed in action.

There were two Americans flying with 84 Squadron. Flying Officer Owen Andrew 'Curly' Keech, flying Vengeance AN 706, was later killed in action bombing a target one mile west of Yazagyo, on 4 March 1944. His rear-seat man, Warrant Officer Eric Robert Watkins, died with him. Both men are recorded at the Taukkyan War Cemetery. The second American in 84 Squadron was Flying Officer Leonard J. Burnett, who had joined the RCAF. He became the squadron's best photographer during attacks.

Following the already positive results of using Vengeances in both the November 1942 and between March and July 1943 in the Arakan, 168 Wing had analysed all the data and issued their findings in a document designed to form the blueprint for an even larger Vengeance involvement in future offensives, This document was *Tactical Trials on Vengeance Dive Bomber and Dive Bombing in Vengeance*[17] It was supplemented by other detailed reports and, with them, was quite positive and comprehensive.[18]

I have summarised their respective findings elsewhere[19] but, briefly based on these papers plus considerable supplementary trials and training results, the Vengeance squadrons (four RAF and two IAF) earmarked for the next Burma offensive would be called upon for two types of operation – predetermined operations against known targets and direct support operations for the land troops with the Vengeances on call through the Air Support Controller (ASC). The latter called for the dive-bombers to be held in various states of readiness, it being estimated that while the Vengeance

---

[17] Dated 4 October 1943, AIR 19/233.

[18] *Notes on Tactical Qualities of the Dive Bomber*, 9 September 1943, AIR 20/4349; *Vengeance Operations in Arakan*, Tactical Memo No. 35, AHQ India, AIR 23/3288 and *Vengeance Operations in Burma*, 06726, AIR 23/5288/06726.

[19] See Smith, Peter C., *Dive Bomber!* - various publishers in UK and USA) 1982 *et seq.*

could be airborne in fifteen to twenty minutes, local weather conditions and those encountered en route to target would be a limiting factor, as would waiting to collect fighter cover, should any be deemed necessary. This thirty minutes from request to aircraft airborne was taken as a 'norm'. By day, should the weather allow, fully bombed-up and fuelled aircraft could be held 'on call',

It was also estimated that the 'turn around' time between missions, to refuel and re-arm, six Vengeances was forty-five minutes, two hours for twelve aircraft.[20] Three types of bombing were considered: High Dive, Shallow Dive and Low-Level, The first option was overwhelmingly favoured because 'A high degree of accuracy can be obtained in this type of bombing and this is the aircraft's primary role', although under certain conditions Method 2 was not ruled out. The optimum delivery of ordnance was from a high dive in salvo, thus achieving a concentrated cluster. For an average pilot a stick of four bombs (2 internally carried 500lb and wing-mounted 250lb) would cover about 150 yards. This was a concentrated blow. By contrast the much-lauded 'Hurribomber' could only deliver a single bomb which, with Japanese bunkers as deep as twenty-feet or more, had practically no effect whatsoever.

Targets were approached at a cruising speed of around 155-160mph at 12,000 feet. The recommended formation was twelve aircraft split into two boxes of six, the second box disposed in echelon to the leading box and stepped down from it. Earlier operations had not had sufficient aircraft to mount such numbers, other than by two separate squadrons, but twelve-plane strikes were to become the norm during 1944-45 and heavier totals were frequently utilised with several squadrons following each other in sequence. Bomb release was circa 3,000 feet with escape at 1,000 feet.

---

[20] Arthur Gill told me 'that it would take less than an hour to complete a turn-around and be off again. Refuel and the bombs would be already fused. And sometimes you put in your reserve crews'. One of the ground team, Sergeant H. Widdop, involved in this work, informed me that '100-Octane was always used' and that '84 Squadron had three petrol bowsers for the job. Refuelling the VVs was fairly quickly accomplished until a new order was issued to the effect that we had to use a sort of bucket with a spout at the bottom of it to fit the aircrafts' tanks and also three wires were fitted with clips which we had to attach to parts of the aircraft as a sort of earthing device, Furthermore, a chamois leather was supplied to fit on top of the bucket which had to be cleaned regularly.'

The key recommendation was crystal clear: 'The Vengeance should be used against small and precise targets where accuracy is essential ....' It was added to ensure no doubt, 'The Memorandum summed up things this way: With regard to the Memorandum of the Role of the Vengeance, this is an attempt to establish the policy that the use of this aircraft should be confined as far as possible to the role for which it was designed, and in which it is effective, *viz*: dive bombing, and not frittered away on odd jobs for which it is unsuitable.'

While at Ranchi airfield, in Bihar State[21] at the end of 1943, 84 Squadron put in some intensive training in preparation for the proposed move to Chittagong from which base they were preparing to support the forthcoming Arakan offensive early in the new year. This was known as 'battle inoculation' and took place over several days from 11 October after being delayed by low cloud conditions. Live ammunition was used against dummy enemy targets of various types. They worked with the 4th/10th Gurkhas. Squadron Leader Gill broke the dive-bombing record at Amarda Road with an average error of twenty-two yards for four bombs diving from 10,000 feet while, on the 18th, Flying Officer Selwyn Owen RAAF gave a dive-bombing demonstration to a group of American and Chinese army officers. These army co-operation exercises continued into the following month.

The 11th of November saw Flying Officer William Horace Cooper joining the squadron from the staff of 283 Wing as the new Intelligence Officer. On the same date, Pilot Officers Norman Athol Bruce and Aubrey William Pedler led the advance party to Chittagong in readiness for the imminent move. Gearing up for immediate action saw various modifications to equipment in readiness, and this included the air testing of the modified reflector gunsight for the rear guns by Flying Officer John Frederick Ellis, RCAF, on the 16th. These modifications were carried out 'in-house' and were deemed to be a most successful innovation. A new aircrew, Flying Officer Reginald Gordon Miller and Warrant Officer Ronald Herbert Wahlstedt, joined the Squadron from 152 OTU on the 25th to bring numbers up to requirement. All preparations were well in train for the move when, out of the blue, everything changed. Air Commodore Herbert Victor Rowley, AOC 221 (Tactical) Group arrived at Ranchi and announced that 84 Squadron

---

[21] Now Birsa Munda Airport.

had been selected, along with 7 Squadron IAF, to give precision air support to General Orde Wingate's Chindits in their next big operation. This meant that the move to Chittagong was abruptly cancelled and changed to Maharajpur, Gwalior State, airfield five miles north-east of Gwalior City[22] which was used as a Chindit training base. All moves were re-scheduled accordingly and during early December the transition duly took place, with the final party under Flight Lieutenant Richard Johns, RNZAF, in place by the 6th. The following day Major Herbert Gerald Joseph Purcell, Indian Army, of 3rd Gurkha Rifles, arrived at the squadron to assume the position of Air Liaison Officer.

On the 8th Squadron Leader Gill met with Wingate and his entourage who were planning Operation THURSDAY, the flying in of 10,000 troops into the upper Irrawaddy to three secretly-prepared landing strips, from where they were to cut the vital enemy rail and road links at Henu, Hopin and Htindaw[23], being supplied from the air, and now, supported from the air as well, Over the next few days Gill met Wingate and discussed in depth just what was required and what was possible. I asked Arthur Gill how that went, given Wingate's reputation for being cantankerous, plus the inbuilt (through bitter experience) distrust by the Army that the RAF could deliver any meaningful air support, which the German Army had always had but the British only rarely; in Burma soldiers believed the Vengeance to be the best means of delivering effective air support. Gill's response was unhesitatingly honest, as always.

> Wingate was a dedicated genius, a professional down to his fingertips. He would listen, provided he was convinced you knew your job as well as he knew his. We demonstrated this to him by results. As we were all very young men, he first thought of us as a bunch of carefree young kids, but when we started hitting the things he wanted us to hit and doing it consistently, he became convinced and stood firmly behind us, Unfortunately, his early death resulted in dive-bombing again losing its influential support.

---

[22] Now Maharajpur Air Force Station, IAF.

[23] Indaw: The Japanese had two operational airfields there.

As to the man himself?

> He was very quiet. He also had a temper, and could get very cross.
> But he would listen to you. We had many arguments about the
> use of smoke to mark targets, but he would respect expertise. We
> would make our point, and he would argue against you just to
> prove his point. Sometimes he would start an argument just to
> be difficult and make you think. We devised a method of attack
> after many arguments with Wingate himself. He'd ask, 'If I give
> you a map reference of a target I want obliterated fast, can you
> bomb it?' Although both the Army and the RAF used the same
> maps and references, it seemed simple expressed that way. We'd
> reply that the Vengeance could hit anything provided that they
> were sure of what they were aiming at, otherwise we couldn't,
> unless he had it photographed, which of course he couldn't do as
> he would have been deep in hostile jungle and there was a paucity
> of photo-reconnaissance aircraft in Burma anyway. Just giving a
> map reference or latitude and longitude wouldn't have been of
> any use unless the target was identified. We suggested smoke.
> He couldn't see the point of it since smoke drifts and is visible to
> the enemy as well, I then told him that the only way I'd be able
> to find some of these targets would be if he could mark them for
> me, I specified two markers, one on each end, or three to mark a
> triangle, the centre of which I would bomb. These schemes we
> worked out ....[24].

During the 10th and 11th of the month detailed tactical exercises for
Operation THURSDAY were conducted to iron out as far as humanly
possible the closest co-operation between the Army and the Vengeance
flyers. These exercises continued and off with the squadron utilising
Malthone field-firing range as a mock-up of a Japanese base and camp
for target practice, until 19 December, interspaced with conferences

---

[24] Author interview with Arthur Murland Gill, reproduced (in part) as an article, 'Deadly
Diving Accuracy' in *Military History* Magazine, Volume 4, No. 6, pp.18-24. 1988: Leesburg,
VA. Subsequently - Gill Interview op. cit.

and the arrival of the various parties from Ranchi. Meanwhile five more pilots arrived into the squadron from 152 OTU, these being Sergeants Rupert Belval, A.F. Craighill, F.H. Dyer, Frank W. Found and L.T. Hamlyn.

During the rest of December and on into the first week of January 1944, 84 Squadron remained stuck at Maharajpur They continued with their practice bombings, for example on 5th of the month Flight Lieutenant Richard Johns, RNZAF, led six aircraft armed with 11.5lb practice bombs to attack three mock Japanese bunkers at Pinpoint RE864161. The purpose of the exercise was to see if Stinson L5 light aircraft operating from small clearings in the jungle close to the front line could accurately mark targets for the Vengeances to take out. Flying Officer Reginald Gordon Miller, RAAF, was detailed off for this, but the Stinson failed to carry out its mission, so Miller conducted a 'dummy dive' on the approximate target area instead. After this both the Chindits and 84 Squadron decided to rely on mortars for target indication. They were also gearing up for the much larger test of Exercise ENTERPRISE. Live bombing with 500-pounders was carried out for the benefit of the Chindits on both 6 and 7 January and demonstration flights conducted over the Gwalior Exhibition Ground. There were dummy bombing and strafing attacks on Malthone airfield on the 8th. However, ENTERPRISE took place on the 9th without them as an 'extremely heavy and widespread' ground mist grounded all twelve aircrews told off for this duty. It did not clear until midday, by which time the exercise was largely over.

The following day the squadron adjutant, Flight Lieutenant Bryan Lilley, along with Flying Officers Norman Bruce and Aubrey Pedlar, were detached to Bombay while Pilot Officers Gordon Paterson and Raymond Poole and Sergeant Navigator P. Ross joined the Squadron from 152 OTU as did Flight Lieutenant D.J. Lloyd-Davis who joined from 10 CMB.

The 10th saw the squadron visited by the Supreme Allied Commander, Lord Louis Mountbatten, and his entourage, along with Major General Orde Wingate himself. He had obviously been impressed enough with the Vengeance to show them off to his boss on the eve of his next planned foray. In any event, Mountbatten addressed the whole squadron and informed them that they would be moving forward 'in the near future' to co-operate with Wingate's Special Force.[25] On the 19th Arthur Gill confirmed this to his men and further combined training continued and the move was again postulated on the 23rd by Air Command, SEA, as due to take place on the 29th. On the 27th an advance party under Flight Lieutenant Alan Robert McClean Blackburn DFC and Flying Officer Peter Carl Thorns left for Kumbhirgram. Preparations were only slightly marred when, on New Year's Eve, Flight Sergeant Rupert Belval in AN 948 was forced to 'belly land' due to hydraulic problems but little damage was done to either aircraft or crew.

On 4 February Bryan Lilley led the main party to Kumbhirgram via Allahabad and Bishnupur and over the following five days the Vengeances were flown across in batches. Arthur Gill and D'Arcy Hawke flew over for a last-minute meeting with Orde Wingate on the 14th and, two days later, 84 Squadron was back in business about two years after its last combat. As Gill recorded at the time, 'during that time the morale and spirit of all personnel have been very good, but during the last month the morale has risen even higher due to the fact that the Squadron has commenced its eighth campaign of the war.'[26]

The first mission took place on 16 February. The task was set for 'all available aircraft' and in compliance 84 Squadron despatched no fewer than fourteen Vengeances, as follows:

Aircraft	Code	Pilot	Aircrew
AN 725	C	Flt Lt John Goldfinch RAAF	F/O Brian Engall RAFVR
EZ 988	D	WO C.N.M. Thomson	WO Colin Darling RAAF
AN 614	E	F/O Raymond Davies	Flt Sgt Frederick Victor Bird
AN 834	A	Flt Sgt T.A. Davies	F/O Douglas Morris

---

[25] Despite the Army top brass being largely opposed to such special forces, which they regarded as a waste and misuse of resources, and the Air Ministry's opposition to dive-bombing, to quote the AOC 2nd Tactical Air Force, John D'Albiac, 'in any war zone, at any time', the premier, Winston Churchill, had apparently been won over and sanctioned the use of both. D'Albiac's views reflected exactly the view that permeated the majority of the RAF's senior establishment. Focused almost exclusively on area bombing reducing German cities and their populations to rubble and thus, as they viewed it, winning the war 'unaided', they had no time for precision and this was manifest in their total antipathy to dive-bombing in particular, or indeed, anything that might smack of any role that placed the RAF in a 'subservient' position to the other services. Today, of course, it is almost their sole *raison d'etre*.

[26] Gill, Squadron Leader Arthur Murland, ORP 29 February 1944, AIR 27/6971.

Aircraft	Code	Pilot	Aircrew
AN 721	H	Flt Lt George Plumb	F/O Bronte Winchester RAAF
AN 739	F	F/O Aubrey Pedler	F/O Norman Bruce RAAF
AN 964	G	F/O Selwyn Owen RAAF	P/O James Woodhouse
AN 820	B	F/O Stanley Prentice	F/O Allan Thomas RAAF
AN 700	X	F/O Colin Papps RNZAF	Flt Sgt Charles Fou'weather
AN 830	Z	Flt Sgt R.G. Gray	F/O James Farrer RAAF
AN 693	R	F/O Reginald Miller RAAF	WO Ronald Wahlstedt RAAF
AN 713	W	Flt Sgt C.K. Holbrook	F/O Norman Smith
AN 945	S	P/O Kenneth Tonkin RAAF	WO Ronald Gabrielson RAAF
AN 706	V	F/O Raymond Nowland	Sgt John Farr

It is interesting that while some veterans claim that the Vengeances never flew more twelve aircraft on any mission, and others claim only six were ever despatched per squadron, 84's debut involved *fourteen* machines.

Their assigned targets were enemy-occupied huts, ammunition and supply dumps running alongside the eastern side of the main highway that ran north from Tawzi to Mahon. The target zone covered an area of 1,000 yards north of the village to a depth of 100 hundred yards, The Vengeances took departure from Kumbhirgram at 1525 and found the weather over the target area was cloudless, but with some heat haze. At 1634 ten aircraft commenced their dive-bombing runs from 10,500 feet down to a release height of between 3,000 to 2,500 feet along a line running from south to north while the other four completed a semi-circle as this was taking place and then bombed from north to south. In all nineteen 500lb GPNITI and twelve 250lb GPLD of six and twelve hours and two dozen 30lb Incendiaries were deposited. All aircraft returned safely to base but six aircraft suffered some 'hang-ups' 'due to faulty manipulation'. The majority of the bombs burst in the northern sector of the target zone in close concentration, while three or four fell on either side of the strip,

The next strike took place on 20 February, with twelve Vengeances operating in two six-plane boxes, attacking Mektalet village (Pinpoint SF 59440. The formations comprised the under listed:

Aircraft	Code	Pilot	Aircrew
AN 964	G	Sqn Ldr Arthur Gill	Flt Lt D'Arcy Hawke
EZ 988	D	WO C.N.M. Thomson	WO Colin Darling RAAF

Aircraft	Code	Pilot	Aircrew
AN 739	F	Sgt Frank Found	Sgt R.E. Francis
AN 614	E	Flt Lt John Goldfinch	F/O Brian Engall
AN 820	B	P/O Gordon Paterson	Sgt P. Ross
AN 721	H	Flt Lt George Plumb	F/O Bronte Winchester
AN 676	T	Flt Lt Lloyd Johns	F/O Kenneth Dicks
AN 713	W	WO Rupert Belval	WO H.D. Rumohr
AN 945	S	P/O Raymond Poole	F/O Peter Thorns
AN 700	X	F/O Reginald Miller	WO Ronald Wahlstadt RAAF
AN 828	U	Sgt F.R. Dyer	Sgt R.E. Russell
AN 706	V	Flt Sgt D.G. Harrison	Flt Sgt S.H. Gillan

The two boxes attacked at half-hour intervals, the first being airborne at 0946, bombing at 1100 and returning at 1234, the second box taking off at 1016, attacking at 1130 and returning to base at 1116 The dives were made from 9,500 feet down to 2,500-2000 feet. Each Vengeance carried two 500lb GPTI and two 250 GPTI bombs and all loads, save two, were delivered into the assigned target area. There were no 'hang-ups" and all aircraft returned safely. The AOC 221 Group, Air Commodore Stanley Flamank Vincent DFC AFC, visited them on their return and congratulated them on their return to battle.

The squadron repeated the operation again three days later, their objective being Mextalet village (Pinpoint SF 5244) once more and the attacks again being made in two six-plane boxes, the first leaving Kumbhirgram at 0845, attacking at 1000 and returning at 1045. The second box left base at 0913, made their dives at 1030 and landed at 1116. A post-strike reconnaissance by 28 Squadron reported that extensive damage had been inflicted on enemy facilities.

On the 25th a fourth attack was mounted with six Vengeances against Japanese positions at Hmawyonmyaing village, on the Nsam Kwedaing *chaung,* five miles east of Homalin. This was an ARMOP, a requested mission from the Army. Take-off was at 1030 and time over target (TOT) fixed for 1130. Most bombs struck the target, the leader in a stick, the remainder in salvo. Lloyd Johns and Harrison strafed during their runs. They left behind them a column of smoke. Five Vengeances returned safely at 1240, but one aircraft, piloted by Sergeant Frank Found, was forced to put down at Tulihal, near Imphal, to refuel, his machine having suffered excessive fuel consumption during the mission. He finally returned to base at 1358.

Next 84 Squadron attacked enemy troop concentrations and an ammunition dump in thick jungle south of the village of Paukpyin. Twelve Vengeances were sent in two six-plane boxes with a ten-minute gap between them, This strike was a not a successful one at all, with four aircraft from the first box dropping their bombs half a mile to the east of their intended target, while all the second box also made Identification errors and bombed an area in the same vicinity. Gill was to record that 'The similarity of features in the terrain of these jungle targets has caused errors in the past with more experienced crews in this type of target, so the mistake on this occasion is accountable'.[27]

However, the raid did accomplish one thing in that it created a diversion to allow an attempt to rescue a Hurricane pilot who had been shot down and was being held captive in the village. Further Vengeance attacks were made at 1640 by 84 Squadron and at 1650 and 1700 by 110 Squadron.

The final mission of February was mounted on the 29th, with yet a third return to Mextalet village. They hoped to catch the enemy on the hop with an early assault and so the twelve-Vengeance strike left base at 0628. The attack team was:

Aircraft	Code	Pilot	Aircrew
AN 834	A	Sqn Ldr Arthur Gill	Flt Lt D'Arcy Hawke
AN 734	F	F/O Aubrey Pedler	F/O Norman Bruce
AN 820	B	Flt Sgt T.A. Davies	F/O Douglas Morris
AN 721	H	Flt Lt John Goldfinch	F/O Brian Engall
AN 964	G	Sgt A.F. Craighill	Flt Sgt John Paull
AN 614	E	F/O Raymond Davies	P/O Frederick Victor Bird
AN 676	T	Flt Lt Richard Johns	F/O Kenneth Dicks
AN 713	W	Flt Sgt C.K. Holbrook	F/O Norman Smith
AN 706	V	F/O Raymond Nowland	F/O Norman Farr
AN 700	X	F/O Colin Papps	WO Charles Fou'weather
AN 828	U	WO Bertram Finnie RCAF	F/O John Ellis RCAF
AN 693	R	P/O Raymond Poole	F/O Peter Thorns

They arrived over the target and this time carried out a most successful operation. The village was described as receiving 'a good pounding' with a

---

[27]   Ibid.

payload that included incendiaries, with four aircraft adding their machine-gun fire to the mix.

No. 84 Squadron's crews were now beginning to find their stride but, as ever in war, they were discovering that, although it was all very well to have your own plans and offensives, the enemy had his own cards to play. In Burma at this date the great Japanese offensive against the British supply bases at Imphal and Kohima took the British somewhat by surprise. Instead of concentrating solely on assisting the Chindits, 84 Squadron suddenly found itself frequently switched to the defence of those beleaguered garrisons, more and more. Often the two missions coincided, as when the Chindits found that, at the 'Broadway' dropping point, they had landed right in the middle of the enemy supply routes for their invading divisions. I asked Arthur Gill how this dilemma was tackled. His reply was simple: 'We supported both, as the situation demanded. Gradually we spent more time relieving the garrisons under siege at Kohima and Imphal, These were relatively short-range operations, but we interspersed these sorties, sometimes two or three attacks per day, with the occasional long-range sortie in support of Wingate's men as originally planned. The inherent accuracy of dive-bombing suited both mission roles perfectly, because with the Japanese attackers dug in on the very edges of the places under siege, equal accuracy was required in the jungle.'

March saw 84 Squadron try a new tactic. Arthur Gill explained it in detail thus:

> Some of the tasks set on this front are enemy dumps in the jungle with little or no indication of the exact spot which has to be judged from some particular landmark close by, and owing to the similarity of terrain correct identification is at times extremely difficult from attacking height. In order to simplify the correct identification of the target and to minimise the chances of an error in its location, the CO on this occasion put into practice a scheme of a 'pathfinder', in which, on reaching the vicinity of the target, the leader would go ahead and, unhampered by having to keep in formation, could devote more time to identifying the target, Once secure on this point, he would go into the attack with every probability of striking the target, and with his bombs provide a prominent target

marker for the remainder of the formation to pinpoint on the dives, having as they do but a minimum of time to spot the location before going into attack.

On 1 March this idea was tested. The target allocated for a twelve-plane strike this day was Paukpyin village (Pinpoint SF 6267) which was to be hit at 0900. The squadron left base at 0749 and was made up of the following teams:

Aircraft	Code	Pilot	Aircrew
AN 824	A	Sqn Ldr Arthur Gill	Flt Lt D'Arcy Hawke
AN 614	E	F/O Selwyn Owen RAAF	P/O James Woodhouse
AN 820	B	F/O Stanley Prentice	F/O Allan Thomas RAAF
AN 964	G	Flt Lt John Goldfinch	F/O B.W. Engall
AN 721	H	Flt Lt George Plumb	Flt Lt Alan Blackburn
EX 988	D	WO C.N.M. Thomson	WO Colin Darling
AN 676	T	Flt Lt Richard Johns RNZAF	F/O Kenneth Dicks
AN 830	Z	WO R.G. Gray	F/O James Farrer RAAF
AN 713	W	Sgt F.R. Dyer	Flt Sgt R.E. Russell
AN 828	U	F/O Reginald Miller	WO Ronald Wahlstadt
AN 706	V	F/O Kenneth Tonkin	P/O Ronald Gabrielson
AN 693	R	Flt Sgt D.G. Harrison	WO S.H. Gillan

On this occasion the experiment appeared to work as intended. Nearing the target area Gill accelerated and pushed on ahead of the main body and, identifying his objective, he made his attack dive from 9,000 feet at 0856, scoring a direct hit on a row of houses. The remaining five Vengeances then followed in along a line from the north-east to the pull out north-west and west. The second box attacked from 10,000 feet from the north, pulling out of their dives to the south-west at release heights of between 3,000 to 2,500 feet. Eight bomb loads were placed inside the target zone, with resulting clouds of dust, which dispersed fairly quickly. In total, twelve 500lb GPTD .025, twelve 500lb GPNITI and two dozen 250lb GPLD, with settings at six, eight and twelve hours, were delivered into the enemy, while eight aircraft also strafed at various targets of opportunity including rafts on the Uyu river. On their return to base two of the back-seat aircrew reported an enemy landing strip under construction two miles south of the village. Air Commodore Vincent was present at the debriefing session and, on hearing of this, authorised an immediate photo-reconnaissance sortie which subsequently conformed this was a new enemy landing field.

Further attacks followed as 84 Squadron got fully into their stride, with an enemy camp at Pinlieu (Pinpoint SL 9680) hit by a twelve-plane formation on the 3rd, a jungle encampment 500 yards west of Kontha (Pinpoint HP 5803) struck twice by the same number on the 4th, Sakhan village was hit on the 8th and two strikes were made on Le-U village on the 10th with both Gwengu (Pinpoint SL 1883) and Nyaungbintha (Pinpoint SL 15840) villages being targeted by six Vengeances apiece on the 11th.

A Japanese divisional headquarters near to Tonmahe (Pinpoint SF 5588) was assigned to the Vengeances on 13 March. Twelve aircraft left Kumbhirgram at 1130 and found the weather good over the target area, but with a heavy haze which restricted visibility to half a mile. There was 7/10th cloud cover with a base of 10,000 feet. After making a wide circle around the target, the attack went in at 1237 with the first box diving from 9,500 feet and the second from 10,000 feet, all on a heading south-east and east. They deposited twelve 500lb GPTI rods, twelve 500lb GPTD .025, four dozen 30lb incendiaries, seven 250lb GPNITI and five 250lb GPLD, three at six-hour and three at twelve-hour delay, which gave the Japanese commanders much to think about.

The 14th was a busy day for 84 Squadron with two urgent ARMOP missions being flown. The first took off at 0827 with six aircraft disposed as follows:

Aircraft	Code	Pilot	Aircrew
AN 824	A	Sqn Ldr Arthur Gill	Flt Lt D'Arcy Hawke RNZAF
EZ 988	D	WO C.N.M. Thomson	WO Colin Darling RAAF
AN 614	E	WO T.A. Davies	F/O Douglas Morris
AN 734	F	F/O Aubrey Pedler	F/O Norman Bruce
AN 721	H	Sgt A.F. Craighill	Flt Sgt John Paull
AN 820	B	F/O Stanley Prentice	F/O Allan Thomas RAAF

This formation was sent against a reported concentration of enemy troops and artillery along with armoured fighting vehicles (AFVs) stretching from Minthami (Pinpoint BP 7655) to Sunye (Pinpoint RP 7256). The six machines approached the track at 6,000 feet, searching along both sides of it for the reported enemy column, but no signs of it could be seen, even though weather conditions were favourable at six to eight miles visibility and light haze. Therefore, each pilot picked a likely spot with cover where the enemy might be hiding and made his individual attack accordingly. The unit landed back at 1004.

The second strike was despatched from base at 1340, and comprised the same team minus Prentice and Thomas's AN 820 which could not be readied in time due to technical difficulties. This was unfortunate as it was the only camera-equipped aircraft. The Army requested that they hit Japanese trenches and gun positions in thick jungle four miles south of Witok (Pinpoint RF 668634). They reached the area at 1430 and looked for the expected smoke bursts which the Army were to lay on the enemy targets. They circled at 7,700 feet on excellent visibility and two smoke bursts were finally observed six miles off. The attack was duly put in at 1436 with the Vengeances diving from 7,000 feet down to 3,500 feet and placing their mixed bomb loads in between the markers.

Three six-plane strikes were carried out on 15 March, the first against the enemy-occupied village of Zibvugon (Pinpoint RP 7152) at 1340; a second sortie was an ARMOP mission carried out in conjunction with 110 Squadron, each contributing six aircraft, against freshly-prepared enemy positions thee miles east of Tonzang (Pinpoint RP 175154), 84 attacking at 1650; and a third strike was made at 1705 on a Japanese camp and dump just west of Pyingaing village (Pinpoint SQ 308659). One attack was made on the 16th against a reported pontoon bridge across the Chindwin at Sampe but there were no signs of any such structure on their arrival, so the village was attacked instead, while the next day saw a strike on an enemy supply dump at Inbaung (Pinpoint RU 5782). The squadron sent six Vengeances against Japanese troop concentrations at Taungkaugmu (Pinpoint SF 4023) on the 17th.

In response to an ARMOP request the following day 84 Squadron sent nine aircraft to smash an enemy road block on the Imphal-Tiddim road along the top of a ridge south of Milestone 100. The composition of this formation was:

Aircraft	Code	Pilot	Aircrew
AN 649	J	Sqn Ldr Arthur Gill	Flt Lt D'Arcy Hawke RAAF
EZ 988	D	F/O Selwyn Owen RAAF	P/O James Woodhouse
AN 614	E	WO T.A. Davies	F/O Douglas Morris

Aircraft	Code	Pilot	Aircrew
AN 693	T	F/O Colin Papps	P/O Charles Fou'weather
AN 820	B	Sgt A.F. Craighill	Flt Sgt John Paull RAAF
AN 625	S	F/O Raymond Nowland	P/O John Farr
AN 830	Z	F/O Reginald Miller	WO Ronald Wahlstedt
AN 712	R	WO D.G. Harrison	WO S.H. Gillan
AN 828	U	WO Rupert Belval	WO J.J. Foisy

Both Vengeances B and U carried cameras. This force took off from base at 0954 to follow in an attack on the same target by 110 Squadron. They found patchy cloud over the target area from 12,000 feet down to 6,500 feet, with visibility from six to eight miles. The artillery shell bursts were used as markers and the attack went in at 1043. The target itself was 5,000 feet above sea level and the dives were made from 12,000 feet down to 6,500 to 7,000 feet along a course east and south-east, west and north-west. Eight 500lb GPTD .025, eight 500lb GPTI rods and sixteen 250lb GPNITI 50 per cent rods were placed along the ridge and down both sides. Warrant Officer Harrison lost aim due to the poor weather conditions and took his bombs home again. This attack was considered successful and all aircraft had returned to Kumbhirgram safely at 1147.

A Japanese divisional headquarters at Indainggyi village (Pinpoint RU 6175) was struck on 18 March, 84 again following 110 Squadron into the same target. It was reported that 'bombing results proved very successful all strikes being well concentrated' and that they left the target 'one compact mass of smoke and dust'. Next day five Vengeances hit Kuki village (Pinpoint SA 3034) which the Japanese had occupied.

The 21st saw another combined ARMOP with an attack by 110 and 84 on an enemy road-block at Milestone 99 on the Imphal–Tiddim road. Again, the road at this point followed the top of a 5,000-foot ridge and friendly forces were under a quarter of a mile away. The Army marked the target with artillery smoke; they also marked the northern bomb line. The twelve Vengeances left base at 1043 and were composed as follows:

Aircraft	Code	Pilot	Aircrew
AN 693	T	Flt Lt Lloyd Johns RNZAF	F/O Kenneth Dicks RAFVR
AN 712	R	WO D.G. Harrison	WO S.H. Gillan
AN 713	W	WO C.K. Holbrook	F/O Norman Smith

Aircraft	Code	Pilot	Aircrew
AN 826	Q	F/O Colin Papps	P/O Charles Fou'weather
AN 721	V	F/O Raymond Nowland	P/O John Farr
AN 830	Z	WO Rupert Belval	WO J.J. Foisy
AN 649	J	Flt Lt John Goldfinch RAAF	P/O Brian Engall RAFVR
EZ 988	D	WO C.N.M. Thompson	WO Colin Darling RAAF
AN 820	B	PO Gordon Paterson	Sgt P. Ross
AN 799	H	Flt Lt George Plumb RAFVR	Flt Lt Alan Blackburn DFC
AN 824	A	Sgt A.F. Craighill	Flt Sgt John Paull
AN 614	E	F/O Raymond Davies	P/O Frederick Victor Bird

They found 3/10ths cumulus cloud with a base of 12,000 feet with visibility five to eight miles and were easily able to identify the prominent hill they were to hit. They were able to watch as 110 Squadron went about their work and were able to confirm that their bomb bursts were exactly on target before they followed in. Their own attack went in at 1141 making their dives from 12,000 feet down to 7,500 feet with eight aircraft on a heading from west to east and four from east to west. They bombed on the artillery markers and all bombs fell along the ridge from the signal to 300 yards to the south. They subsequently received confirmation from the forward troops that the bombs all fell in the specified area, which photographs from Vengeances E and Z also subsequently confirmed.

Arthur Gill told how actions spoke louder than words in the matter of Army–RAF interaction.

The Army soon began to trust us to hit what we aimed at. I can vividly recall one target where they signalled us that the Japanese commander was in the north-east room of a given house, which was a bit optimistic! We laughed at this, even though it was really a compliment. In any event we took out the whole house to make sure. At Kohima, the Japanese had dug themselves in along the perimeter of the compound itself and were lobbing grenades and mortar fire all the time. We bombed parallel to our own lines so that any overshoots would still land among enemy troops, With Wingate, they would signal the target co-ordinates back to HQ in India. We would be armed and ready to go in order to reach the target very quickly. We then bombed as practised.

The 22nd of March saw a strike by twelve aircraft on Singgel village (Pinpoint RO 9634) on the Imphal-Tiddim road at Milepost 101, north-west of Tonzang, where concentrations of Japanese troops and stores were reported. The force was ordered as below:

Aircraft	Code	Pilot	Aircrew
AN 824	A	Sqn Ldr Arthur Gill RAFVR	Flt Lt D'Arcy Hawke RAAF
AN 693	T	F/O Reginald Miller	WO Ronald Wahlstedt
AN 828	U	P/O Bertram Finnie RCAF	P/O Ronald Gabrielson RAAF
AN 826	Q	F/O Colin Papps RNZAF	F/O Charles Fou'weather
AN 712	R	F/O Leonard Burnett	Sgt S.W. Hinge
AN 625	S	P/O Raymond Poole	F/O Peter Thorns
AN 649	J	Flt Lt James Goldfinch	F/O Brian Engall
AN 739	F	F/O Aubrey Pedlar	F/O Norman Bruce RAAF
AN 779	H	Sgt A.F. Craighill	Flt Sgt John Paull RAAF
AN 820	B	F/O Stanley Prentice	F/O Allan Thomas RAAF
AN 712	W	WO C.K. Holbrook	F/O Norman Smith
AN 614	E	WO T.A. Davies	F/O Douglas Morris

The Vengeances took off from Kumbhirgram at 1028 in two six-plane boxes and headed out. Both aircraft E and S carried cameras. They found 2/10th cloud alto-stratus at 14,500 feet and traces of cumulus at 8,000 feet with a slight haze, but visibility was fair, approximately four miles, so target identification was simple. They commenced their dives at 1135, from an altitude of 11,500 feet down to release heights of between 7,500 and 6,500 feet against the target at 5,000 feet above sea-level. The first box attacked on a line running from east to south-west, the second box from west to east. A few pilots missed the target and attacked an old enemy camp half a mile away to the north in error, but the majority dropped as planned. Nonetheless the results were only claimed as 'fair'. There was no opposition and all aircraft returned safely at 1220.

The raids continued unrelentingly, Singgel village being struck again on the 22nd and Homalin was hit once more the following day, both with maximum efforts. On the 24th it was the turn of Dalati Byung village (Pinpoint RK 745182) to be hit hard while on 25 March four separate attacks were delivered by 84 Squadron. That against the settlement of Maungdaw (Pinpoint SG 0358) on the eastern bank of the Nam-Kadin *chaung* at 1148 produced satisfactory results with 'a particularly heavy explosion observed at the southern end of the hamlet, with a large fire following indicating an ammunition dump had been hit'. At 1150 six more aircraft struck at Sitsawk again, aiming for the bridge and the jungle area immediately to the south-west, with the greater majority of the bombs detonating around the bridgehead area. Also hit was Hpapok village on the Chindwin river which six Vengeances dropped on at 1607 and the final sorties were against their old favourite, Maungdaw, which was dive-bombed by one Vengeance at 1613 and four more at 1617.

An accurate attack was conducted on the 26th by an eleven-Vengeance strike against a precise location gleaned from infiltrated ground troops. This was a position 200 yards north of Homalin township (Pinpoint 423733) comprising a strip of land running 300 yards south to north. The attacking force was made up thus:

Aircraft	Code	Pilot	Aircrew
AN 693	T	Flt Lt Lloyd Johns RNZAF	F/O Kenneth Dicks, DFC
AN 713	W	WO Rupert Belval	WO H.D. Rumohr
AN 712	R	P/O Raymond Poole	F/O Peter Thorns
AN 721	V	F/O Raymond Nowland	P/O John Farr
AN 625	S	F/O Leonard Burnett	Sgt S.W. Hinge
FB 964	N	Flt Lt George Plumb	Flt Lt Alan Blackburn DFC
AN 820	B	WO C.N.M. Thompson	WO Colin Darling
AN 779	H	F/O Selwyn Owen	F/O James Woodhouse
AN 614	E	F/O Raymond Davies	P/O Frederick Victor Bird
AN 739	F	F/O Aubrey Pedler	F/O Norman Bruce
AN 824	A	WO T.A. Davies	F/O Douglas Morris

Take-off was at 1552 and they found the target area with 2/10th cloud f-cumulus with base at 10,000 feet and 5 to 6/10th strato-cumulus with base at 1,500 feet, visibility was three to five miles. They commenced the attack at 1655 from an initial height of 10,000 feet to bomb release heights of between 3,500 and 3,000 feet and dropping eleven 500lb GPTD, 025, eleven 500lb GPNITI, twelve 250lb GPTI, four 250lb with six-hour delay and two with 72-hour delay bombs and sixteen 30lb incendiaries. 'Bombing was accurate.'

The rest of March followed the pattern, with twelve-aircraft strikes on Kaing village on the opposite bank of the Chindwin to Kalewa township, on the 26th, another on an enemy camp and dump at Pinpoint SQ 398659 just west of Pyingaing, plus six-plane attacks on both Naungpin (Pinpoint SA 6316) and Manpa (Pinpoint SA 6322) on the 27th, and a twelve-Vengeance attack on the 28th which hit Hponthet village (Pinpoint SA 1834) and resulted in an exceptionally big explosion causing thick brown smoke to rise up to 500 feet. Four columns of smoke could be seen five minutes after leaving the target until the hills hid them from view. It was thought these were Japanese ammunition dumps that had been struck. Two six-plane strikes were made the same day against Kongyi and Kuntaung respectively, and on the 29th six Vengeances, led by Flight Lieutenant John Goldfinch, dive-bombed Paukpyin once more. The final attack made by 84 Squadron in March was a full strike on another Japanese supply dump situated seven miles north-east of Thaungdut with the following formation:

Aircraft	Code	Pilot	Aircrew
AN 824	A	Sqn Ldr Arthur Gill	Flt Lt D'Arcy Hawke
AN 649	J	Flt Lt John Goldfinch	F/O Brian Engall
AN 614	E	F/O Raymond Davies	P/O Frederick Victor Bird
AN 779	H	Flt Lt George Plumb	Flt Lt Alan Blackburn DFC
AN 820	B	F/O Stanley Prentice	F/O Allan Thomas
AN 739	F	F/O Aubrey Pedler	F/O Norman Bruce
AN 826	Q	F/O Colin Papps	P/O Charles Fou'weather
AN 713	W	F/O Reginald Miller	WO Ronald Wahlstadt
AN 830	Z	WO R.G. Gray	F/O James Farrer
AN 721	V	F/O Raymond Nowland	P/O John Farr
AN 693	T	P/O Raymond Poole	F/O Peter Thorns
AN 712	R	F/O Leonard Burnett	Sgt S.W. Hinge

These aircraft took off from Kumbhirgram at 0644 and reached the target area an hour later. Both F and R were fitted with cameras. They found the weather in the area good with between six to eight miles visibility. Cloud was f-cumulus 3-4/10th at 10,000 feet. The two boxes attacked separately, the first commencing their dives from 8,500 feet, the second from 10,000 feet but all along a path from SSW to NNE. They delivered the usual mix of ordnance into the enemy positions and it was noted that the target 'covered an extensive area of jungle, and all bombs fell in stick well distributed inside'. There was no opposition and all aircraft were back at base by 0855.

The new month began in the same manner. Twelve aircraft were sent against Homalin on the 1st, one being forced to abort, and a second strike, with Hponthet (Pinpoint SA 1834) and secondary of Paukpyin (Pinpoint SF 3401) the same day saw the latter hit at 1249. The next day the objectives were Segyaung village (Pinpoint SF 2801) or Nawngpo (Pinpoint SF 6267). The whole Chindwin Valley was veiled with strato-cumulus with a base of 1,000 feet and top at 2,000 feet, the only clear area being in the Homalin area where there was still 6/10th cover. The twelve Vengeances attacked through gaps in the cloud at 0801, diving from 10,000 feet to 3,500 feet on a course east and north-east to west and south-west. The 3rd saw three attacks launched with the targets being Thitseikkon, Mezali and Monkali respectively, all being accurately hit. On the latter raid Goldfinch had to turn back due to a loose oil cap resulting in his screen being obscured by oil, He took off again in an endeavour to catch the rest of the formation, but they had too great a start and he forced to abort the mission. No doubt some careless 'erk got a tongue lashing because of it.

Also on the 3rd there was an ARMOP mission called in by the Chindits at Hen-U. The exact task was the elimination of troublesome Japanese gun positions on the ridge crest east of the Burma railway, ranging from Pinpoint SG 854337 to SG 855347. The exact target was to be marked by mortar smoke. Twelve Vengeances were sent in to carry out this job, as follows:

Aircraft	Code	Pilot	Aircrew
AN 824	A	Sqn Ldr Arthur Gill	Flt Lt D'Arcy Hawke
AN 816	G	F/O Selwyn Owen	P/O James Woodhouse
AN 820	B	F/O Stanley Prentice	F/O Allan Thomas
AN 779	H	Flt Lt George Plumb	Flt Lt Alan Blackburn DFC
AN 739	F	F/O Aubrey Pedler	F/O Norman Bruce
EZ 988	D	WO T.A. Davies	F/O Douglas Morris
AN 693	T	Flt Lt Richard Johns	F/O Kenneth Dicks
AN 828	U	P/O Bertram Finnie	WO S.H. Gillan
AN 713	W	WO C.K. Holbrook	F/O Norman Smith
AN 721	V	Flt Lt Colin Papps	P/O Charles Fou'weather
AN 712	R	F/O Reginald Miller	WO Colin Darling
AN 830	Z	WO R.G. Gray	F/O James Farrer

The attack was duly delivered at 1346 from an initial height of 9,000 feet down to release heights of between 3,000 and 2,000 feet on a run from east to west. Bomb bursts were observed evenly spaced and, from subsequent reports, were 'most effective'. The importance of this target to the enemy was evidenced by concentrated bursts of AA fire from Bofors-like automatic weapons encountered at heights of between 3,000 and 6,000 feet north and north-east of Mawluu. A subsequent 'Strawberry'[28] signal from the Chindits stated that, after the position was taken, some 265 enemy casualties had been counted, and this was later substantially increased. The capturing of this position was largely due to the fact that the Vengeances had 'rendered useless' these Japanese guns.

Similar excellent results were achieved the following day with full strikes being delivered against enemy positions at Set-Tan (Pinpoint SF 2916) in the morning and Japanese concentrations of motor transport, troops and stores reported immediately to the west of Tamu in the afternoon. On the 5th Kuki settlement (Pinpoint SD 3036) was on the agenda but heavy clouds over the hills to the north and north-west of this target obliged the formation to turn back when some twenty miles along a course bearing 080-degrees from Kumbhirgram as there was little chance of accurate targeting.

From April on the weather increasingly influenced the ability of 84 Squadron to operate at maximum efficiency. A good example of this was an attack launched on the 6th by six Vengeances with Pwelien (Pinpoint SA 4331) as the primary target and Tamanthi (Pinpoint SA 9230) as the secondary. The formation comprised:

Aircraft	Code	Pilot	Aircrew
FB 964	N	Flt Lt Lloyd Johns	F/O Kenneth Dicks
AN 830	Z	WO R.G. Gray	F/O James Farrer
AN 828	U	F/O Bertram Finney RCAF	Flt Lt Ronald Gabrielson
AN 721	V	F/O Raymond Nowland	P/O John Farr
AN 826	Q	Sgt F.R. Dyer	Flt Sgt R.E. Russell
AN 625	S	F/O Leonard Burnett	Flt Sgt S.W. Hinge

The primary target was totally 'weathered out' and so Tamanthi was selected for the strike. However, while flying through thick cloud, Bert Finney lost touch with the formation and turned back for base, only to run straight into a violent thunderstorm. Ron Gabrielson baled out, survived and returned

---

28 'Strawberry' signals of praise and thanks were called such because they were the opposite of the well-known 'Raspberries', which the RAF was much more used to receiving from the ground troops.

to the squadron on foot on the 10th, while Finney managed to land back at Kumbhirgram. Sergeant Dyer also lost contact in the same area of cloud as Finney and eventually crash-landed near Otway (Pinpoint RC 4325). Their mount was a complete write-off and both Dyer and Flight Sergeant Russell were severely injured.

Eventually just four aircraft got through to attack the target and made their dives at 0740, most of their bombs falling on the southern end of the village. On the return flight Warrant Officer Gray was forced to make an emergency landing at Imphal to refuel. Thanan (Pinpoint SF 0639) was also hit at 1148 that day by another six-plane strike. On 7 April a similar attack was delivered at Set-Tan village.

And so, the treadmill continued as the Japanese assault was first halted and then reversed and the Allies started to take the offensive once again. The Japanese had hoped that the deterioration in the weather would be to their advantage in that it would crucially curtail Allied air support operations but, despite many setbacks, 84 continued to punch whenever it was possible, and sometimes when many considered it was considered it was just *not* possible! The 11th of April saw strikes at enemy dumps six miles east of Thungdut by a dozen aircraft while an attack the same day on Htinkinyaung (Pinpoint SL 3499) caused columns of black smoke and the flashes of exploding munitions as they pulled out of their dives.

On 12 April the squadron suffered a 'stop-and-start' day. Two six-plane strikes were planned against Yenan and Kaungkazi respectively, but the first attempts were aborted due to the weather conditions. Second attempts against these targets were underway once conditions improved but were cancelled abruptly on receipt of an incoming enemy air attack warning. Finally, at 1621, and the third the attempt of the day, both attacks went in and were deemed successful. Raids on the next day included Tiddim by twelve Vengeances at 0720 and Thayaung and Tamanthi with six aircraft apiece, later in the day. The 14th saw a different approach with four two-plane raids mounted against Tserhmun, Khuanghi, Taison and Zamual between 0726 and 0742. A larger attack at full strength with two six-plane boxes was mounted later that day with Kalewa (Pinpoint RU 9567) as their objective. Events conspired otherwise for, while en route thither, they met an enormous storm front which stretched right across their path. The second box had straggled since leaving base, dropping behind and losing sight of the leading flight. They nonetheless continued eastward as far as the Chindwin river but could find no way through and eventually took their bombs back to Kumbhirgram at 1800. The leading box had also tried to find a gap in the black mass but equally failed, so they delivered an attack on Japanese-occupied Paukpyin at 1718 instead

Another urgent ARMOP was undertaken on the 16th, when they were ordered to attack area RK 4478, a small area north of the Nungshigum Pimple, The formation comprised:

Aircraft	Code	Pilot	Aircrew
AN 824	A	Sqn Ldr Arthur Gill	Flt Lt D'Arcy Hawke
FB 964	N	F/O Selwyn Owen	F/O James Woodhouse
AN 779	H	Sgt L.T. Hamlyn	Flt Sgt Robert Bovill
AN 739	F	F/O Aubrey Pedler	F/O Norman Bruce
AN 649	J	Sgt Frank Found	Flt Sgt R.E. Francis
AN 820	B	Sgt A.F. Craighill	Flt Sgt John Paull
AN 693	T	Flt Lt Lloyd Johns	F/O Kenneth Dicks
AN 713	W	WO C.K. Holbrook	F/O Norman Smith
AN 721	V	F/O Raymond Nowland	F/O James Farrer
FB 984	F	Flt Lt Colin Papps	P/O Charles Fou'weather
AN 828	U	Flt Sgt Bertram Finnie	Flt Lt Ronald Gabrielson
AN 830	Z	F/O Leonard Burnett RCAF	Flt Sgt S.W. Hinge

They duly struck the enemy positions in dives from 9,400 feet down to 4,000–5,000 feet, with one box tracking east to west and the other north to south. This ensured an even distribution of ordnance and it was subsequently confirmed that the bursts were precisely on target.

On the 15th both Monkali (Pinpoint SF 4566) and Letpantha (Pinpoint SF 3961) were attacked by six-plane boxes each, and the following day saw 84 Squadron make three attacks. The first was an ARMOP request to hit enemy positions at spot height RP 3404 (Pinpoint RK 129134) using ½-inch map No. 83.) The assault was made by six Vengeances, five of them attacking along a north-east to south-west axis, followed by single aircraft which bombed on a south-east to north-west line. All bombs landed close to the spot height. More of the two-plane operations took place this day also, with Tonmate (Pinpoint SF 4467) being hit at 0725, Kettha (SF 4272) at 0726 and Tonleik (Pinpoint SF 3777) at 0728. The main assault was sent against the Manipur Bridge (Pinpoint RP 121215), a key crossing on the Japanese

Army's supply route from Tiddim to Imphal. It proved a tough nut to crack. High and medium-level bombing had failed repeatedly to harm it in any way, so the Vengeances were sent in to have a try, although the perceived wisdom was that heavier bombs than they carried would be required.

This viewpoint was validated for, despite a highly accurate placement of their ordnance on this mission, with most of the bombs concentrated within a 100-yard diameter area, when the smoke had cleared it could be seen that no direct hit had been achieved by any of the twelve aircraft. Flight Lieutenant Raymond Davies and Flying Officer Frederick 'Dicky' Bird had a lucky escape when one of their 500-pounders 'hung up' and when Vengeance E (AN 614) landed back at base it was found to be resting on the bomb doors! Another Vengeance, P, (FB 984) crewed by Warrant Officer R.G. Gray and Flying Officer James Farrer, had a 250lb bomb similarly 'hung up' and this one only finally dropped off during the pre-landing circuit back at Kumbhirgram.

Another Army request was received on 17 April and this was for a strike on spot height 3524, (Pinpoint RK 585773). Twelve Vengeances were despatched and attacked at 0943, bombing on mortar smoke indicators. They dived from 11,000 feet down to 5,000 feet on a track from north to south. This position had just received the best attentions of 110 Squadron and 84 found it 'a mass of dust and bomb smoke'. to which they duly added their quota. No. 23 ASC subsequently sent the squadron the following signal: 'Your bombing this morning T.O.T. 0940 Ground Sources report your bombing a bull's eye. Bloody Good Show.' The only damage sustained was that Vengeance H (AN 779), with Sergeant L.T. Hamlyn and Flight Sergeant Robert Bovill aboard, having to make a forced landing back at base due to the engine cutting out while in the landing circuit. They overran the runway and had to pull up the undercarriage to stop. Bovill, it was reported, 'suffered some head abrasions'.

Both Fort White and Tiddim were assigned to 84 Squadron's attentions the next day, but the former was 'weathered out' and in the case of the latter Tonzang, north of Tiddim, was bombed instead while the 18th saw three separate four-plane missions against Yisi (Pinpoint SA 3274), Akhegwo (Pinpoint SA 3376) and Laruri (Pinpoint SA 3272), all in Phek, District, Nagaland, respectively. The 19th had the Imphal-Tiddim road between Milestones 119 and 120 attacked in a full-strength operation whose principal aim was to induce a landslip to block the road. A further twelve-aircraft attack was mounted later in the day against an enemy dump to the east of No. 2 Stockade at Tamu airstrip (Pinpoint RP 7890).

A planned strike on the bridge on the Burma railway across the Thaw *chaung* (Pinpoint SM 3323) left Kumbhirgram at 1550 on the 21st but, while still on the outward leg, was recalled by the 168 Operations Room at 1620. Visibility had been down to between one and two miles maximum as far as Imphal, from which position the twelve aircraft duly returned to base. The following day, despite similar conditions, (bad visibility, one to two miles only, heavy haze) a full-strength strike was made on Ningthoukhong village (Pinpoint RK 1833) at 0834. Dives were made from the south-west to the north-east, from a tip-over at 9,000 feet down to around 4,000 feet for release. All bombs fell in the target area, one salvo producing 'a particularly big explosion'. The same day 84 Squadron also bombed Kohima Naga village (Pinpoint RE 509678) at 1422 with equally satisfactory results.

The Chindits initiated ARMOP requests on the 23rd, in response to which seven Vengeances were sent against a strongly-fortified Japanese defence point at Thetkegyin (Pinpoint 795070) and another two separate boxes of six aircraft apiece were assigned to take out a petrol dump at the northern end of Indaw West landing ground and three further Vengeances struck specific *bashas* in the north-west part of Yedwigan village near Indaw. A novel feature was the inclusion of twelve Hawker Hurricane fighters fitted with long-range fuel tanks, allocated as nominal fighter protection for both these groups but no enemy aircraft were encountered. Later 168 Wing forwarded a signal from the Advanced HQ of the division which read: 'Secret. Commander Special Force congratulates all ranks 84 Squadron on excellent results obtained bombing targets today.'

After a successful mission against enemy concentrations at Pyingaing (Pinpoint SQ 413654) by twelve aircraft on the 24th, an ARMOP mission the next day, designed to blow up a reported enemy petrol dump to the north-east of Thetkegyin (Pinpoint SG 80076), was aborted while the force was still over the Kabaw valley due to poor visibility once more, which rapidly deteriorated down to just 800–1,000 yards with heavy smoke haze and 10/10th cumulus from 8,000 feet up to 15,000 feet.

Better fortune attended the squadron on the 26th when twelve Vengeances bombed the north-western end of Kohima Naga village. The force left base in this configuration:

Aircraft	Code	Pilot	Aircrew
AN 649	J	Flt Lt John Goldfinch	F/O Brian Engall
FB 945	K	P/O Gordon Paterson	Sgt P. Ross
AN 824	A	WO T.A. Davies	F/O Douglas Morris
AN 614	E	Flt Lt Raymond Davies	P/O Frederick Victor Bird
FB 964	H	Sgt Frank Found	Flt Sgt R.E. Francis
AN 820	B	Sgt L.T. Hamlyn	Flt Sgt Robert Bovill
AN 221	V	Flt Lt George Plumb	Flt Lt Alan Blackburn DFC
AN 713	W	WO C.K. Holbrook	F/O Norman Smith
FB 926	Z	WO R.G. Gray	F/O James Farrer
FB 984	X	F/O Colin Papps	P/O Charles Fou'weather
FB 924	R	F/O Leonard Burnett	Flt Sgt S.W. Hinge
AN 625	S	P/O Raymond Poole	P/O Ronald Gabrielson

Unfortunately, Vengeances A, K, and H each had to return to Kumbhirgram separately with various mechanical problems, and although Vengeance U (AN 828) with Pilot Officers Bertram Finnie and Ronald Gabrielson's crew, was despatched as a replacement, only ten machines made the attack at 1628. Dives were made from altitudes that varied from 8,500 to 6,000 feet, and nine bombloads were released, which resulted in the target being riven by a series of heavy explosions and then fires.

Two further missions were planned for later the same day, with six machines attacking the Indaw petrol dump once more while six others struck at enemy entrenchments at Pinpoint SM 805983. However, on reaching Imphal to rendezvous with their assigned fighter cover, none appeared and instead, at 0910, the Vengeances were instructed to return to base forthwith. It later transpired that this pulling the plug on the operations was due to reports of heavy enemy air activity. When they reached Kumbhirgram they were ordered away again to the 'Scramble Rendezvous' position until the 'All clear' was given.

On 27 April they received another ARMOP task which was to blast Japanese troops who had established themselves in Kohima Fort. Visibility was excellent, from twelve to twenty miles and the dozen Vengeances made their attacks at 0846. The formation was arranged thus:

Aircraft	Code	Pilot	Aircrew
FB 984	X	Flt Lt George Plumb	Flt Lt Alan Blackburn DFC
AN 721	V	F/O Raymond Nowland	P/O John Farr

Aircraft	Code	Pilot	Aircrew
AN 713	W	WO C.K. Holbrook	F/O Norman Smith
FB 926	Z	F/O Reginald Miller	P/O Colin Darling
FB 924	R	F/O Leonard Burnett	Flt Sgt S.W. Hinge
AN 625	S	F/O Raymond Poole	F/O Peter Thorn
AN 649	J	Flt Lt John Goldfinch	F/O Brian Engall
AN 820	B	F/O Aubrey Pedler	F/O Norman Bruce
FB 984	X	F/O Stanley Prentice	F/O Allan Thomas
AN 614	E	Flt Lt Raymond Davies	P/O Frederick Victor Bird
FB 964	H	P/O Gordon Paterson	Sgt P. Ross
AN 816	G	Sgt Frank Found	Flt Sgt R.E. Francis

Another aborted attack took place on the 27th, once again the allocated being the Indaw petrol dump, but before the flight had reached the Imphal area it was ordered to return to base.

Between 30 April and 2 May, 84 Squadron was unable to undertake any combat missions at all due to unfavourable weather. Two new aircrews joined from 22 APC on the 2nd, Sergeant Pilots Ronald Charles Parker, RAAF, and W.L. Salmon, along with Flying Officer Navigators Frederick Holdsworth Coop and Gerald Ralph Pritchett, who were assigned to A and B Flights respectively. The weather remained poor but lifted sufficiently for the squadron to mount an attack on the Treasury area of Kohima (Pinpoint 5167) on 3 May. While Arthur Gill led the first box of six aircraft, Flight Lieutenant Raymond George Ravenscroft headed up the other and they attacked independently. This raid was followed by a second that same day. Many congratulatory messages were received from the various army commanders on their accurate placement of bombs, two from the Chindit commanders and one apiece from 17th Division, 2nd and 3rd V Forces, 23 ASC (IV Corps) and 25 ASC (IV Corps). Gill commented that 'Needless to say, these messages are greatly appreciated by the Squadron, aircrews especially being directly concerned, as they add that extra touch of interest which is brought by direct results being obtained, the majority of targets attacked up to date having been tactical.'

The following day at attack on Pinpoint RE 5167 at Kohima by twelve aircraft had to be abandoned because the time limit set for bombing did not allow sufficient margin for the Vengeances to reach the target and attack before it expired; consequently, they had to carry their bombs back to base.

On 5 May the Chindits requested a mission against Tonbon village (SG 8603). This raid was carried out by eleven of the twelve dive-bombers sent out, one aircraft having to turn back over Imphal with a defective fuel pump in one tank. The squadron had an escort of eight Hurricanes for this mission but, as usual, saw no enemy aircraft. The Hurricanes were, however, able to watch the attack go in and subsequently report that the bombing was 'very accurate'. At midday a second attack began to take-off from Kumbhirgram but, after eleven of the twelve Vengeances had become airborne, the operation was cancelled by Wing Operations Room and the aircraft recalled. The panic aborting of this attack was due to severe enemy penetrations of Allied lines in the Kokaden area, between Pinpoints RK 110380 and 120380, some three miles south-west of Bishenpur, Manipur. Gill led the twelve Vengeances off again against this target, which was attacked successfully.

The 6th saw another request from the LRPG (Chindits) to strike the enemy in the mountainous country north-east of Kohima, but the weather once more made this impossible and the bombs had to be taken back to base. Late in the afternoon of the following day Arthur Gill led an attack by twelve Vengeances against Potsangrem village (Pinpoint RK 175360). Known as 'Pots-and-Pans' to the assailing British forces, this hamlet had been turned into a pivotal strongpoint by the Japanese who were determined to hold it at all cost. The three Vengeance squadrons were called upon to soften it up prior to a planned all-out attack by Brigadier David Alexander Laurence Mackenzie's 7th/8th and 9th/14th Punjab Regiments, supported by tanks. The same day saw the squadron lose three of its veteran aircrew, Flying Officer Selwyn Vernon Owen, RAAF and Pilot Officer James Maurice Woodhouse; Flying Officer Stanley Wood Newland and Pilot Officer John Gabe Farr and Warrant Officer D.G. Harrison and Warrant Officer S.H. Gillan. All were transferred out as their overseas posting time had expired.

No fewer than three Vengeance squadrons, 7 (IAF), 84 and 110, were sent against enemy concentrations at Shwegyin township, Bago region, (Pinpoint RU 77641) on 8 May. As already related, both 7 and 110 met thick and extensive cloud formations and were forced to abort their missions. A similar fate faced 84, which was operating in two six-plane boxes. The two groups became separated while 'dodging around cloud' and the second box eventually also had to give up and returned to base. However, Gill, leading the first box, fortunately found a way through a made an attack, recording 'good results'. Later that day a second twelve-Vengeance strike hit the Japanese troop encampment near Motaik (RU 909662) which was also recorded as successfully bombed.

Two separate targets were struck the next day, Flight Lieutenant George Plumb leading six aircraft against Thanan and Flight Lieutenant John Howard Goldfinch another six against Humine. A full twelve-plane attack was mounted later that day and had taken off and was about to set course when Wing Operations Room abruptly aborted the mission. One-and-a-half hours later Flight Lieutenant Plumb led a further raid on the Kadu *chaung* (RU 975673). The squadron was given three specific aiming points on this attack and all three were hit. Edward Helliwell recalled that 'I flew Vengeances with 110 Squadron and found it stable and easy to fly. The accuracy of bomb placement was amazing, we often had to hit one end of a bridge; at the battle of Kohima the target was two adjacent sides of the tennis court, the other two being occupied by our troops.'

On 10 May both 84 Squadron and 110 Squadrons sent in heavy dive-bomber strikes against Japanese troops across the Imphal road just a mile south of Kohima (at Pinpoint RE 505650). Following the attack by 110 Squadron, Arthur Gill led in twelve Vengeances against the same enemy concentration. The raid was a success, and led to a pat on the back from a relieved army commander. That same day they received a 'Strawberry' from Major General John Malcolm Laurence Grover MC, GOC 2nd Division himself in the shape of a message to Air Vice Marshal Stanley Flamank Vincent DFC, the AOC 221 Group, which read: 'PERSONAL: Grover to Vincent. Please convey to Vengeance Squadrons my warmest thanks and congratulations on their most accurate strikes today 10th May.' They carried out a second strike later that day, this time against an enemy camp near Shwegyin, south-east of Kalewa, Gill reporting that al the bombs were delivered in 'good concentrations'.

And so, it continued day after day. On 17 May twelve Vengeances in two flights were assigned a main target of Moilou village (Pinpoint RK 087276) with a secondary one at Toupoki (Pinpoint RK 171345). On arrival Arthur Gill led the first section of six into the attack after making three entire circuits to clearly identify the target, but the second flight could not make out the enemy positions as indicated in the briefing and so made their dives on Toupoki.

The 19th of May saw a significant attack on Japanese troops firmly and deeply entrenched one mile to the north of Kanglatongbi village, Lamshang, Imphal West, (Pinpoint RK 29984) with the CO leading twelve aircraft. Nos. 7 and 110 Squadrons also contributed their full strength to hitting this enemy stronghold that day, the Vengeances striking on smoke indicators laid down by Army gunners. The heavy and low cloud cover restricted their dives to just 2,000 feet. A subsequent IV Corps *Sitrep*, No. 786, read that these strikes 'were successful and attack was put in by infantry with tank support. Limited objectives capture and consolidated with light casualties to us.'

On 20 May Group Captain James Barclay Black DFC handed over command of Kumbhirgram Station to Group Captain Ernest Alfred Whitely DFC, the former moving on to command RAF Kolar in Southern India.

On 21 May Colonel Henry Templer Alexander again visited the squadron to discuss a target they particularly wished to be destroyed in the Hopin township, Kachin State, on the main Mandalay-Myitkyina rail link, which was arranged to take place the following day. Unfortunately, the weather again intervened but this target was struck on the 23rd. On that day twelve Vengeances were despatched to strike Ywathitale (Pinpoint 123990) a hutted camp east of Indawgyi Lake, Kachin State. Here the enemy, among other activities, was busy constructing a flotilla of small boats in readiness to transport supplies for their front-line forces during the imminent monsoon season. The Vengeances picked up an escort of twelve Spitfires as they crossed over Imphal and attacked as planned.

The following day Flight Lieutenant John Howard Goldfinch led twelve Vengeances to attack enemy ammunition dumps at Humine, and among the ordnance deposited were 40 per cent long-delay bombs. The same group made a second attack that same afternoon, striking an enemy-held hill feature at Tenghnoupal, nine miles south-east of Palael, in direct support of the army. Gill took over again on the 25th after bad weather had cleared sufficiently to mount an operation, and their target was an enemy dump south-east of Kalewa, which was situated at the confluence of the Chindwin and Myittha rivers, Kale District. The weather closed again and made flying impossible throughout the 26th to the 28th. On the 27th one of the squadron's Aussie pilots, Flying Officer Kenneth Victor Tonkin, RAAF, left for special duties in the War Room at 221 Group. A strike was finally mounted against Pantha, Mawlaik, (23⁰ 53' N, 94⁰ 25'E) on the 29th.[29]

The 1st-4th of June was a sterile period due to the weather. A twelve-aircraft attack mounted against a Japanese camp some four miles east-south-east of Kyetpanet in the Kale Valley was sent off at 0559 on the 1st but, while still two miles west of the target, they found themselves flying between layers of 10/10th cloud which joined into a solid wall over the attack zone, making any attack impossible. They were forced to turn back to base where they arrived at 0657 with all their bombs intact. It was the same story the following day, the twelve aircraft, after waiting all day for clear conditions, taking off to hit Ukhrul at 1714 but again running into 10/10th cloud cover and aborting and it was the same again on the 4th, a take-off at 1424, impossible cloud cover over the target and a return to base at 1604.

However, the breakthrough came at last. Typical of the later work of the squadron was a strike mounted on 5 June 1944 against a Japanese HQ at Kangpokpi (now Kanggui), Manipur, and thirty miles north of Imphal on the Kohima road. (Pinpoint RE 377037). The composition of the attack was as follows:

Aircraft	ID	Pilot	Aircrew
FB 964	N	Sgt L.T. Hamlyn	Flt Sgt Robert H. Bovill*
FB 981	A	Sqn Ldr Arthur Gill	Flt Lt D'Arcy Hawke RAAF
FB 941	D	WO T.A. Davies	P/O Ronald Gabrielson
FB 945	B	Sgt W.L. Salmon	F/O Gerald Pritchett
FB 944	C	Flt Lt John Goldfinch	F/O Brian Engall
FB 936	E	Sgt A.F. Craighill	Flt Sgt John Paull RAAF
FB 968	G	Sgt Frank W. Found	Flt Sgt R.E. Francis
FB 943	T	Flt Lt Raymond Davies	F/O Kenneth Dicks
FB 924	H	WO Rupert Belval	F/O John Ellis
FB 991	V	F/O Leonard J. Burnett	Flt Sgt S.W. Hinge
FB 958	W	F/O Raymond Poole	P/O Colin Darling RAAF
AN 649	J	Sgt Ronald Parker	F/O Frederick Coop
FD 105	U	Sgt James Magill	Flt Sgt F.G. Posse

*Weather reconnaissance flight to target area.

---

[29] AIR27/697/7.

Twelve Vengeances lifted off at 0520 but aircraft B, piloted by Sergeant W.L. Salmon with Gerald Pritchett as WO/AG, had to return at 0610 as the pilot was unable to raise the undercarriage after take-off; so only eleven dive-bombers made the attack. The visibility was twelve to fifteen miles, with 10/10ths Stratus cloud in the valleys and on hillsides. They commenced their dives at 0714 from an initial height of 6,900 feet down to between 5,000 to 5,500 feet on a course north to south across the target. The cloud base was 7,000 feet and the target height 4,000 feet, so normal dives could not be conducted; even so their bombing was precise, and they deposited ten 500lb GPTD .025 and the ten 500lb GPTI along with twenty 250lb GPTI ordnance across most of the target. Sergeant Parker in J did not release due to an unsatisfactory dive. Both G and U were 5-inch-lens camera-equipped but photographs were of the bombs falling only.

The same target was attacked again later that same morning by basically the same team. They took off at 1058 and this time all twelve aircraft attacked at 1214 with stick bombing as conditions had not improved at all. In consequence of not being able to dive-bomb 'the majority overshot the specified area'. All aircraft had returned to base at 1259.

The 6th of June saw 84 Squadron launching a strike at 1506 against a defined building at the northern end of Onsansaing village (Pinpoint SG 984783). One aircraft, Z, AN 923, piloted by Flying Officer Raymond Poole with his WO/AG, Pilot Officer Colin Darling, RAAF, was forced to turn back at 1516 with an unserviceable propeller pitch control. The remaining eleven, led by Arthur Gill, pushed on. Visibility was good, cloud cover 3-4/10th and dives were made at 1637 from 9,000 feet down to 2,500 feet. Vengeance U, AN 828, piloted by Sergeant James Magill with Flight Sergeant F.G. Posse, had to dive through cloud and, when he broke clear, found he had drifted off target so did not release his bombs. Two and possibly three of the other six that attacked obtained direct hits on the specified house itself, and the other three obtained close overshoots. Four aircraft, V, FB 991, with Flying Officer Leonard Burnett with Flight Sergeant S.W. Hinge, B, FB 945, crewed by Sergeant W.L. Salmon and Flying Officer Gerald Pritchett, G, FB 962, with Sergeant Frank Found and Flight Sergeant R.E. Francis, and J, AN 649, with Sergeant R.C. Parker and Flying Officer Frederick Holdsworth Coop, dropped their bombs on a similar building in a nearby village in error. Arthur Gill was not pleased: he told me many years later that this was the *only* occasion while with the Vengeances that he had been forced to discipline aircrew for attacking the wrong target. All aircraft were back at base by 1803, a round-trip of almost three hours.

'Followers' Rest Houses at Kadu Railway Station (Pinpoint SG 940645) on the Burma railway were the assigned targets for 7 June. The mission left Kumbhirgram at 1417 with Squadron Leader Gill leading a twelve-plane striking force after Sergeant W.L. Salmon, with Flying Officer Navigator G.R. Pritchett in J, AN 649. flying the preliminary weather reconnaissance flight ahead of them. All thirteen aircraft lifted off at 1417. The line-up for this mission was:

Aircraft	ID	Pilot	Aircrew
AN 649	J	Sgt W.L. Salmon	F/O Gerald Pritchett
FB 981	A	Sqn Ldr Arthur Gill	Flt Lt D'Arcy Hawke
FB 945	B	F/O S.J. Prentice	P/O Ronald Gabrielson
FB 964	H	F/O Gordon Paterson	Sgt P. Ross
FB 964	F	F/O Aubrey Pedler	F/O Norman Bruce
FB 935	E	Sgt Frank Found	Flt Sgt R.E. Francis
FB 962	G	Sgt James William Nattrass	Sgt S.H. Vetters
FB 943	T	Flt Lt Raymond Davies	F/O Kenneth Dicks
FB 984	X	WO Rupert Belval	F/O John Ellis
FB 958	W	WO C K Holbrook	F/O Norman Smith
FB 991	V	F/O Leonard Burnett	Flt Sgt S.W. Hinge
FB 923	Z	Sgt James Magill	Flt Sgt F.G. Posse
FB 928	S	Sgt F.R. Dyer	WO H.D. Rumohr

Over the next three weeks 84 Squadron put in an intensive programme of attacks, hitting targets at Homalin and Tamu village several times (although many sorties were 'weathered out') and Thenung on the 12th, Phubalowa on the 13th. River bridges became regular targets in June also, and the Vengeances hit the Manipur Bridge on the 11th, and those at Ya-Nan and Kokchao, as well as the Williams and Elephant Bridges, all in the Tamu area, on the 18th. They attacked the Yu river bridge at Ya-Nan and the Elephant Bridge over the Lokchao river on the 21st and again on the 28th.

The Yu-Na'n river bridge, a border bridge six-and-a-half-mile (eleven kilometres) south-east of Tamu, Saigang, in position 24^0 11'N, 94^0 23' E, was damaged by near misses but remained useable until 29 June when Squadron Leader Arthur Gill led a three-plane mission using new tactics to take it out with eleven-second-delay fusing from low level as an experiment, twenty-four previous sorties having failed to destroy the bridge. The team was Gill and Flight Lieutenant Robert McClean Blackburn DFC, in aircraft A, FB 981; Flight Lieutenant Raymond Davies and Warrant Officer Kenneth Dicks, in aircraft W, FB 968; and Flying Officer Aubrey Pedler and Flying Officer Norman Bruce in aircraft F, FB 954. They took off at 1506 and found 7/10ths cloud over the target with a base of 2,000 feet rising to 9,000 feet. They made their attack at 1159, with a shallow dive from 2,300 feet down to 1,000 feet along a course south-east to north-west. They dropped six 500lb GPTD 11-seconds and six 250lb GPTD 11-seconds bombs.

Arthur Gill, in an interview with the author, described the method this way:

> On some such specialised strikes we had all bombs fused with 11-second delay. In fact, on the Ya-Na'n bridge which we bombed several times, we would not only drop 11-second delay bombs which would blow the bridge up after we had flown away from it, but we would also drop 12-hour and 24-hour and 36-hour delay bombs. So that as they came back and repaired it and said that was a good job, Boom! But of course, it would worry them once this had happened because they couldn't see where the bombs had dropped into the water and so on and would not know when the next one was due to go off.
>
> With the monsoons the cloud stretched from 30,000 feet down to ground level and so finding the target was a problem. But as the cloud lifted in between the storms one could often get to the target, but at a lower level, say at 5,000 feet instead of our normal 12,000 feet or 13,000 feet. So, we devised this system of nipping in and out of the cloud, but you hadn't got enough height to peel off and dive vertically because you'd kill yourself. So, what we did was introduce this shallow-dive technique of running up alongside the target and doing a gentle turn-off, keeping the target in sight all the way, and diving down at only 45 degrees.
>
> This could never be as accurate as proper dive-bombing which, despite what the 'experts' have since kept on repeating, we *always*

carried out at between 80-90 degrees. So, it would not be as accurate as that, but you had to adjust for conditions and gauge it.[30]

On this occasion each aircraft waited for the bomb of the preceding aircraft to burst before following in to attack. The result was 'very satisfactory' with 25 per cent direct hits being registered. The results were that a quarter of a span was blown away at the eastern end of the bridge, a breach was caused at the western end and they holed the part that remained, 'twisted girders being seen and the deck missing'. Vengeances A and F intentionally dropped only 250lb bombs on the last run to check on results, returning a second time to release their two 500lb bombs. 'It is recognised, though, that a second run is not advisable from any point of view.' However, on this occasion they had got away with it and there were no casualties for an excellent result. The trio landed back at base at 1646.

By the beginning of July 1944, it was becoming very difficult to mount operations due to the steady deterioration of the weather. Typical of the appalling conditions encountered was the mission carried out on the 1st of the month. The target for the dozen Vengeances led by the Arthur Gill was a Japanese army fuel dump and a motor transport park adjacent to the site of the village of Humine (Pinpoint SF 0454). They had to attack at low level and used HE bombs with eleven-second time delay to enable them to clear the explosions. Just as they arrived over the target a fierce rainstorm crossed over the area which instantly reduced visibility to just a quarter mile. This obscuring of the target caused several aircraft to bomb an area wide of the specified aiming point. It also took far longer than planned to deliver the attack itself, which was described as 'excessive' though successful.

This heavy rainfall also hampered their return flight and a heavy local storm developed over the base at the time the force was due to land, and so they were warned to land instead in the Imphal valley, which five of them did, putting down at Imphal itself and Kangla, while the remainder managed to land at Kumbhirgram despite the conditions. A twelve-Vengeance attack was made on the morning of 2 July against Churachandpur, the squadron making the approach in two flights of six aircraft apiece with a quarter-hour

[30] Gill, Arthur Murland to the Author, first published in Smith, Peter C., *Jungle Dive Bombers at War*, John Murray, London, 1987, p.86.

interval between each flight. This was effectively carried out, but a second mission against the same target had to be aborted due to the bad weather. These miserable conditions ruled out any attacks on the 3rd and the 4th so it was not until the 5th that a full strike was again considered possible. Their targets were weapons, munitions and store dumps at Leu which were attacked at midday. Twelve Vengeances went in, but this time in four *vics* of three machines each, with the lead of each *vic* over to port side of the target with Nos. 2 and 3 stepped back on the starboard side at intervals of thirty to fifty yards. The enemy responded strongly with light and accurate flak and two Vultees were hit, but by explosions from the ground, either by the detonation of a landmine set off by their bombs or from one of the bombs of the leading aircraft bursting instantaneously instead of the time-delay working. Sergeant James Nattrass managed to bring his aircraft back to base without difficulty although it was badly holed (Category II), while Flying Officer Gordon Paterson's machine received rather less damage. This attack was repeated exactly during the afternoon, again led by Arthur Gill.

And so, the tempo was, with increasing difficulty, maintained. Three separate raids were made on enemy positions in the Imphal valley at Churachandpur, Thinunggei and Phubalowa respectively, on each occasion being forced to drop from low levels. Next day Flight Lieutenant Raymond H. Davies led nine Vengeance against Leu. Ten aircraft had taken off from base, but engine problems caused her to return to base early. No operations were possible on the 8th as the weather was again atrocious. Two attacks were mounted on 9 July, with strikes at an enemy concentration three-quarters of a mile west of Churachandpur in south-west Manipur, by twelve Vengeances led by Arthur Gill, followed by a second attack.

The next day was notable in that Gill went out in his reconnaissance Spitfire, 'The Looker', and happened on a lone Oscar II, which he duly despatched. This resulted in a pat on the back for his 'kill' and then a stern reprimand for doing so without authorisation (!), which, as ever, is the British way of waging war.

On 11 July 1944, a twelve-plane strike hit Htinkingyaung, Burma (Pinpoint SL 350998), in an accurate attack. The squadron's reward, after six months continuous operations, was notification received at Kumbhirgram that 84 Squadron was to be withdrawn from operations and moved to Samungli Airfield, Quetta, for a rest period. Undaunted, eleven Vengeances, led by George Plumb, successfully bombed Thinunggei, on the road south of Imphal during the fierce fighting of the 12th and the next day made a determined attempt to bomb an ammunition dump to the east of Leu village (SF 435934). Weather conditions made this operation a hazardous business, however, and although twelve machines were despatched, no fewer than seven were forced to turn back. Of the surviving five, three aircraft refrained from bombing due to poor visibility over the target area, which had been reduced to a mere 300 to 400 yards. It was recorded that 'movements of the aircraft in the attack could not be followed nor the target identified with sufficient accuracy'. Pilot Officer Len Burnett had to jettison his bombs and land at Imphal airfield due to engine trouble.[31]

This day also it was confirmed that the squadron would cease operations at 1400 on the 16th. This still left time for three more attacks by the Vengeances. On the 14th the target was, once more, Thinunggei (RE 168307) which was hit by a nine-plane attack led by Flight Lieutenant George Plumb. The following day they struck at an enemy encampment at SF 022523 to the west of Homine; the results were recorded as 'fair'. Next day, 17 July 1944, proved to be the final war operation and they attacked an ammunition and supply dump at Leu (Pinpoint 435234) with a full twelve-Vengeance strike led by Arthur Gill.

This was their swansong, although it was not realised that it was to be so. On the 17th fifteen of 84 Squadron's aircraft left for Allahabad, via a refuelling stop at Bishnupur, on the first leg of their journey north. Although withdrawn to RAF Station Yelahanka, at Bangalore, Kamataka State, in October, 84 Squadron was, for a large part, held *in situ* as the situation regarding the Mosquito operating in tropical conditions looked bleak. The 'Wooden Wonders' were quite literally falling apart in the skies over Bengal and Burma and, while scientists looked around for solutions, aircrew were dying. And they continued to do so. For example, long-serving 84 Squadron member Sergeant James William Nattrass, RAFVR, was killed when his Mosquito disintegrated on 13 May 1945. This continued even into the post-war period, witness the loss of RF 588 from 211 Squadron which broke up in mid-air ten miles south-south-west of Ipoh, Malaya, on 13 December, killing Flying Officer Stephen Falconer Dunnett and his

---

[31]   AIR 27/697/11.

civilian passenger. This accident was thought to be the result of moisture infusion into the aircraft's glued joints. Jefford,[32] and the failing of glued joints. Aircraft parked outside in the Far East for any lengthy time were particularly vulnerable. When the top skinning of the Mosquito swelled up it warped and pulled out the securing screws, which could lead the securing screws to pull through. Those examined in India showed both the wing-spar scarf joints, and the spar-boom joints with the plywood skin and other ply members, were so affected, which meant the upper-surface plywood skin peeled up and off. Panic corrective measures were taken, Modification 638 which involved adding a strip of plywood strip along the front spar in an attempt to seal the upper surface skin joint, and further, from February 1945, applying a coat of protective aluminum dope, but the Mosquito continued to be unreliable in this manner due to local conditions, intense heat and water soakage leading to swelling and shrinkage with the resultant spar defects, which affected the aircraft for a further eight years.]

Meanwhile, it was felt that, in preparation for the forthcoming offensive after the 1944 monsoon season, at least some Vengeance strength should be maintained as the Army were still clamouring for the continuance of their accurate support, even if this plea fell on deaf ears and closed minds back at the Air Ministries in both London and Delhi. A cadre was therefore established with six Vengeances, four Mark IIIs and two Mark IIs (AN 764 and AN 780), along with a North American Harvard trainer, to re-convert Mosquito pilots to the type ready for combat.[33] One of those who served with this unit was Flight Lieutenant Ronald Gilchrist Cameron, RAFVR, who with his navigator, Warrant Officer George Park McMahon, arrived at Yelahanka on 28 October. He had conducted a total of three dives in AN 764 and two in AN 780 up to December. Among others so engaged were Flight Lieutenant Eric Charles Milnes and Flying Officers Alan Richard

---

[32] Wing Commander Clive Graham 'Jeff' Jefford MBE BA, RAF, in his book *The Flying Camels; The History of No. 45 Squadron Royal Air Force*, Annex K, Air Britain Historians Ltd, Tonbridge, Kent, 1995, summarised the structural problems as a combination of poor constructional mating of some structural members, and inferior gluing methods. This was interpreted by some as being a reflection on the two de Havilland construction sites at Coventry and Hatfield.

[33] Neate, Don, *Scorpions Sting: The Story of No. 84 Squadron Royal Air Force*, Air Britain Historians Ltd, Tonbridge, Kent, 1994.

Downer, Gordon Stuart Paterson and Raymond Frederick Poole. When Joseph O'Leary arrived there, it was only to find that, in his words, 'I was out of a job (a better glue had been found and it was "as you were"), but 84 was still there'. Actually, two flights from 84 Squadron, now led by Flight Lieutenant George Plumb,[34] were kept on hand and two flights were scheduled to return to front-line duty on 30 December, but a last-minute further countermand from on high cancelled this move and the Mosquitoes finally arrived to replace them in February 1945.

However, on 28 October, 84 Squadron's command passed to Squadron Leader Ian Lionel Baber Aitkens and then, on 12 November 1944 to Wing Commander Robert Edward Jay. Like 110 Squadron they had been held with two active flights at Yelhanka, pending conversion, and, also like 110, were involved in the furore when the Mosquitoes failed, and panic measures temporarily saw a re-assembly of Vengeance-proficient aircrews in readiness for operations in January, which were just as quickly rescinded. Vengeance aircraft were then buried where they stood and none from either squadron survived.

---

[34] Squadron Leader Arthur Gill, whose last Vengeance flight had been a search for a missing 82 Squadron machine, had finally received a well-deserved DFC for his magnificent work from a very reluctant Air Ministry and gone home. He had been recommended by Vincent for a DSO, but this was refused by the AOC India, Sir Richard Peirse, possibly because his rank was not substantive.

Chapter 7

No. 110 (Hyderabad) Squadron RAF

Nec timeo nec sperno
(I neither fear nor despise)

No. 110 Squadron had three commanding officers in its period of operating the Vultee Vengeance. Squadron Leader John Girdleston Gill was CO from February 1943. He had succeeded a very distinguished officer, Squadron Leader Frederick Frank Lambert DFC, a Canadian serving with the RAF.[35] This was to set a precedent for Canadian participation in the squadron. But, after just a few weeks, in September 1943, Gill was succeeded by Flight Lieutenant Rodney Charles 'Topper' Topley. However, that officer barely had time to warm the seat before he, in turn, gave way in November 1943 to Wing Commander Leonard Frank Penny DFC who arrived at Kumbhirgram on the 10th, and who saw the squadron through their Vengeance combat period and hardest battles.

Although it was early in 1942 that the squadron shed its Blenheims, the first Vengeance (Is, IAs and IIs) did not reach them in a fit state to fly until October and so from 5 June to 11 October 1942. Thus, it was that No. 110 (Hyderabad) Squadron remained based at Quetta (Kuwatah), in north-west

---

[35] Lambert was born in Wilkie, Saskatchewan. After a short service with Royal Canadian Navy Reserve he sailed to England and joined the RAF in 1936. Granted a permanent commission, he qualified as a pilot and served with 27 Squadron on the North-West Frontier. Still serving in India at the outbreak of the Second World War, he continued to serve there and later was posted to 110 Squadron. In 1942 he returned to the UK and, after a conversion course, was posted to 141 on intruder operations flying the de Havilland Mosquito before being posted to 515 Squadron of 100 Special Operations Group. He was awarded the DFC in August 1944 and the DSO in January 1945. During his service he shot down two enemy aircraft. After the war he transferred to the RCAF and held various posts until his retirement in 1962; he died in the UK in 1998. He accumulated a mass of honours including the DSO, DFC, MiD, IGS, 1939-45 Star, Air Crew Europe Star, with Rosette, Africa Star, Burma Star, Defence Medal, Canadian Volunteer Service Medal, War Medal, Canadian Decoration, with Rosette, and the French *Croix de Guerre*.

Balochistan but was non-operational. A small detachment was sent to Karachi between 6 September and 10 December 1942, and another was based, from 11 to 31 October 1942 at Pandaveswar, (Pandabeswar) airfield, West Bengal. The squadron then moved once more and, between 6 December 1942 and 13 June 1943, was based at Madhaiganj, West Bengal, north-west of Calcutta, in 23⁰ 38' N, 87⁰ 21'E. Further detachments were made, with, from 17 to 24 March at Dohazari, near Chittagong in 22⁰ 46'N, 87⁰ 21'E and between 12 to 31 May 1943, at Chittagong itself, while from 13 June to 15 October 1943 the main base became Digri. There were detachments to Ranchi (24 July to 16 August 1943), Amarda Road, West Bengal, a dusty airstrip in the middle of nowhere, many miles south-west of Calcutta, and named after the closest railway station (27 July to 22 September 1943), Kumbhirgram (15 October 1943 to 5 June 1944) and Joari, (Jouri) a dirt 'fair-weather' airstrip east of Cox's Bazar in 21⁰ 27' N, 92⁰ 07'E (11–16 March).

Flying Officer Joseph Dennis O'Leary, with Pilot Officer Robert Robertson as his navigator, (not forgetting Sergeant Das Gupta on the ground as his armourer), flew his own first mission on 17 December, just three days after his arrival at Double Moorings. This, against the jail, thought to be used as Japanese military HQ, and the following two sorties, against the Narigan Bridge (20⁰ 14' North; 92⁰ 51' E) which crosses the Kywede river, due north of Akyab; and Bume (Bhumi), Kisoregonj, radio station, in the village of the same name, closer to the town; were all directed at targets on Akyab Island.

Twelve Vengeances mounted this attack during the afternoon, six from 82 Squadron leading and followed by six others from 110 Squadron. Flight Lieutenant Rodney Charles 'Topper' Topley DFC led 110 Squadron's box of six flying in from the north at 12,000 feet with both formations 'weaving', changing course in a zig-zag pattern every half-minute, to confuse the Japanese predictors. The enemy heavy AA opened up on them and were spot-on for height but about 200–300 feet off laterally. The two squadrons crossed over the island and then made their attack approach from the east, taking advantage of the gloom and haze.[36]

This strategy had an unexpected bonus as it was later learned that the Japanese had assumed that, after the initial crossing, the Vengeances' target

---

[36] The Japanese had great difficulty moving anti-aircraft guns up through the jungle and mountains. The heaviest weapons, as encountered here, were the 75mm M88 dual-purpose

was elsewhere and sounded the 'All Clear'. Lucky or not, the actual attack thus caught them flatfooted. The jail was the largest building on the island, built in a circular plan 200–300 foot in diameter. O'Leary, at the rear of the stern formation of No. 110, later recalled:

> As the last man on the line I could allow myself room to watch the action. 82 were a mile ahead, so I watched them all go down. They were like beads sliding down a string, three spaced out at a time. I could see the bomb flashes dead on target, billowing up in smoke and dust. Then it was our turn. Topper waggles his wings. This is the sign for the rear 'vic' to drop back and move into echelon starboard. A few second later, he waggles again and opens his bomb doors. All open, 3 and 6 (me) swing across into echelon on 2 and 5 respectively. Now we're all in a diagonal line like a skein of geese. (This formation change is made only at the last moment, for although it looks nice on the newsreels, it leaves you practically at the mercy of an attacker – and it advertises your imminent attack to any watcher on the ground).
>
> Mechanically I go through my drill: canopy shut, check bombs open, bomb switches 'live', trims neutral, 2100rpm, mixture rich, gyros caged, cowl gills closed, straps tight. The first three go down. A few seconds later 4 goes over, settles in the dive and pushes his brakes out. 5 puts his out as he rolls over. I put mine out, throttle back to a third and then roll. This gives us an extra bit of spacing for safety. After that, it's simply 'doin' what comes nacherly'. Rolling over, throw my head back and look straight down on the dust cloud over the jail – or what's left of it. Then it's just a matter of sighting down the yellow line and 'flying' it onto the target. Feet braced on my big fat rudder pedals, I sense the dive is as near vertical as dammit – you can feel it with practice. Topper has done us proud, for this is a follow–my–leader operation, and if he's off vertical then the whole thing will be a mess.

---

weapons. Much more common was the 6.5mm Taisho-3 cannon, which the Allies dubbed 'The Woodpecker'. This gun dated back to 1915 but, on a special mounting and on a wheeled-trolley, was both manoeuvrable and efficient, Light AA also featured the 13mm heavy machine-gun.

I can see 4 and 5 ahead for a few moments, then 4 pulls away from my field of vision. Bomb flash. I'm snatching quick glances at my altimeter, which is spinning like a broken clock, one sweep of the 'big hand 'every two or three seconds. 5 pulls away, keep line on target, bomb flash, 5,000 feet, check line, 4,000, check, 3,500, press button (on throttle grip) and pull, pull, pull for dear life ....[37]

Flying Officer Robert Charles 'Bud' Yeates flew full combat sorties with No. 110 Squadron, most of them with Sergeant Noah 'Knocker' Lewis as his back-seat man. During his time in Burma and later, as a crop sprayer, at Takoradi, West Africa, he suffered, like so many, jaundice, malaria and dysentery but survived them all and the Japanese only to lose his life when flying in the Royal Canadian Auxiliary Air Force post-war, being killed when he had to bale out of a Vampire jet fighter on 8 March 1952 when his parachute failed to open.

Several young Canadians were killed flying the Vengeance, including three from 110 Squadron: Billie 'Hoagie' Carmichael from Ottawa, along with his WAG, Sergeant Thomas 'Tommy' Lawton; Anthony John Davies from Lloydminster and Flying Officer P.F. 'Robbie' Robertson from Toronto. Warrant Officer Billie Carmichael was killed on 10 December 1942 in a Vengeance but what is *not* true is the death of another pilot, as related to me in 1980 by one of his contemporaries.

Flight Sergeant Reginald 'Bud' Duncan did *not* die in an aircraft accident, along with his rear-seat man and his pet dog 'Spunky' as related by Vernon Bohdan McInnis. He survived the war and had a long retirement. Nor did Duncan's (and the squadron's) pet dog die in this manner, according to Joseph O'Leary, but sadly had developed an extensive and incurable skin infection and had to be put out his pain by being shot by his owner, despite the best efforts of the squadron doctor, Peter Latcham, which left the squadron desolate.

The true story of this incident is that on 17 December 1943, Flying Officer Anthony John Davies, RCAF and Flying Officer John David Ernest

---

[37] Joseph Dennis O'Leary, http: //www. pprune.org/military-aviation/329990- gaining-raf-pilots-brevet – ww-ii- 133.html with permission of the Author.

Robertson were killed when Vengeance EZ 904, which had been sent to attack Teinkara in Assam, landed back at Kumbhirgram airfield and a bomb which had 'hung up', but of which they were unaware, exploded on touch-down. Davies had joined 110 in November 1941. On 8 April he had written off a Vengeance at Jodhpur while taking off in a strong crosswind. On 21 May 1943 he was taking off for an operational sortie but failed to gain sufficient air speed, stalled and crashed in a *padi* field. On 17 December his remarkable good fortune finally failed him. He was returning to Kumbhirgram from a sortie against Teinkara, Assam. Unknown to him, a 250lb bomb had 'hung-up' under his port wing. As he landed the bomb detonated, completely wrecking his aircraft, EZ 904, and killing both aircrew instantly. Their memorial is at Gauhati War Cemetery.

On 21 April 1943 Warrant Officer Harold Eldon Thorpe and Corporals James Stanley McKay, John William Moseley and Donald Leslie Kay of 110 Squadron were all killed. Another loss was on 23 April 1943 when Pilot Officer George Herbert Lawrenson was killed.

I was fortunate enough to be presented with a copy of Reginald 'Bud' Duncan's Flight Log Book some time after publication of my earlier work and it presents a detailed and unique eyesight into both the training and operational operations of a Vultee Vengeance dive-bomber pilot in India at this time, as seen through this young Canadian pilot's record. It starts with his introduction and initial training on the Vengeance with 110 Squadron's A Flight at Karachi. Many of today's Internet warriors seem to assume that fully-trained pilots just 'turned up' and went into battle. This was far from the case and the additional specialised flying air training involved, interspersed with classroom instruction and examinations, before full combat operations could be undertaken, may be indicated by taking Duncan's example as more or less typical of the period.

On 18 October Duncan had fifteen minutes' back-seat instruction with Flying Officer Vernon James Hedley as his pilot instructor in Vengeance AN847. Two days later a similar brief period followed in the same aircraft, this time with Squadron Leader Freddy Lambert, RCAF, as his front-seat man. He was then deemed proficient enough to fly solo. The same day he had a twenty-minute solo flight and the following day another fifteen-minute solo and then he embarked Sergeant Abbott as his rear-seat man for a one-and-a-half-hour flight to Hyderabad and back. On 28 October

Duncan flew from base to a two-hour-five-minute cross-country route to Nanabshar and on to Hyderabad and back home in Vengeance AN 950 with Sergeant Shaw embarked and three days later piloted AN847 with Pilot Officer Baldwin as his instructor in the rear seat for a twenty-five-minute dive practice run, from a height of 10,000 feet down to 4,000 feet, which was laconically deemed 'OK'. A further twenty-five-minute back-seat instruction flight followed in AN 847 with the officer commanding, Pilot Officer Rodney C. Topley, on 4 November. His further Vengeance training programme was as follows:

Date	Vengeance	Aircrew	Details
11 Nov 42	AN 919	Sgt Robert Harvey	1 hr 25 mins Stalling- Forced & Prec. Landings
24 Nov 42	AN 916	Sgt Stewart-Mobsby	15 mins Local flying
29 Nov 42	AN 920	Sgt Robert Harvey	1 hr 15 mins Low Level Sea Sweep
30 Nov 42	AN 916	P/O Henry Brooke	2 hrs 35 mins flight to Jacobabad
1 Dec 42	AN 916	P/O Henry Brooke	1 hr 25 mins flight Jacobabad to Quetta
5 Dec 42	AN 916	P/O Henry Brooke	1 hr 5 mins flight Quetta to Jacobabad
5 Dec 42	AN 916	P/O Henry Brooke	1 hr 35 mins flight Jacobabad to Karachi
10 Dec 42	AP 121	Sgt Robert Harvey	2 hrs 10 mins flight Karachi to Jodhpur
10 Dec 42	AP 121	Sgt Robert Harvey	1 hr 45 mins flight Jodhpur to New Delhi
11 Dec 42	AP 121	Sgt Robert Harvey, RAAF	2 hrs flight New Delhi to Allahabad
11 Dec 42	AP 121	Sgt Robert Harvey	2 hrs 5 mins flight Allahabad to Madhaiganj
12 Dec 1942	AP 123	Sgt Robert Harvey	50 mins Formation flying
13 Dec 1942	AN 920	Sgt Robert Harvey	1 hr Dive & Low-level bombing
15 Dec 42	AP 118	Sgt Robert Harvey	One hour 5-minute Formation, Dive & Low-level bombing
15 Dec 42	AN 919	Sgt George Davies	20-minute flight Panda and return.
15 Dec 42	AN 895	LAC Belcher	1 hr 30 mins flight Madhaiganj to Maruda Road
16 Dec 42	AN 895	Capt. Appleby	1 hr Army Calibration Test
17 Dec 42	AN 895	Capt. Appleby	1 hr 30 mins Army Calibration Test
17 Dec 42	AN 895	LAC Belcher	1 hr flight Maruda Road to Madhaiganj

Date	Vengeance	Aircrew	Details
18 Dec 42	AN 895	Capt. Smallwood & LAC Belcher	40 mins flight Madhaiganj to Dum Dum, Calcutta.
18 Dec 42	AN 895	Capt. Smallwood & LAC Belcher	45 mins flight Dum Dum to Madhaiganj
19 Dec 42	AN 916	Sgt Robert Harvey	1 hr 10 mins Formation bombing
21 Dec 42	AP 121	Sgt Robert Harvey	1 hr 58 mins Low-Level Cross-Country flight
22 Dec 42	AP 127	Sgt Robert Harvey	1 hr 5 mins Formation bombing
23 Dec 42	AN 826	Sgt Robert Harvey	1 hr 10 mins Dive- Bombing Practice
24 Dec 42	AP 127	Sgt Robert Harvey	1 hr 20 mins Formation Dive-Bombing
26 Dec 42	AP 127	Sgt Robert Harvey	1 hr 20 mins Formation Dive-Bombing
27 Dec 42	AN 908	Sgt Robert Harvey	20 mins Air Test
28 Dec 42	AP 121	LAC Allison	20 mins Air Test
27 Dec 42	AN 998	Sgt Robert Harvey, RAAF	1 hr 15 mins Dive-Bombing
29 Dec 42	AP 121	Sgt Robert Harvey	1 hr 50 mins Dive-Bombing & Air Firing
30 Dec 42	AP 121	Sgt Robert Harvey	25 mins Full War Load Landing
30 Dec 42	AN 998	AC Brotherton	25 mins Air Test
30 Dec 42	AN 919	Sgt Robert Harvey, RAAF	40 mins Low-Level Bombing
31 Dec 42	AP 121	Sgt Keith Stewart-Mobsby	1 hr Formation & Low-Level Bombing
31 Dec 42	AN 920	Sgt Robert Harvey	40-minute Formation & Low-Level Bombing
1 Jan 43	AN 862	Sgt Robert Harvey	40-minute Shallow Dive Bombing
2 Jan 43	AN 998	Sgt Keith Stewart-Mosby	1 hr Formation Dive-Bombing
7 Jan 43	AN 998	Sgt Joseph O'Leary	35 mins Back-Seat Instruction
7 Jan 43	AN 998	Sgt McMath	35 mins Back-Seat Instruction
8 Jan 43	AP 118	Cpl Brown	15 mins Air Test
9 Jan 43	AN 919	Sgt Robert Harvey	55 mins Dive-Bombing
15 Jan 43	AN 919	Sgt Robert Harvey	25 mins Dive-Bombing
18 Jan 43	AN 998	LAC Feather	20 mins Air Test
27 Jan 43	AN 862	W/Cdr McCarthy	2 hrs 5 mins flight Dum Dum and return
29 Jan 43	AN 910	Sgt Robert Harvey	30 mins Air Test & Formation
31 Jan 43	AN 862	Sgt Robert Harvey	45 mins Formation Dive-Bombing DNCO

Date	Vengeance	Aircrew	Details
1 Feb 43	AN 919	Sgt Robert Harvey, RAAF	2 hrs 20 mins Low-Level Cross-Country
2 Feb 43	AN 862	Sgt Robert Harvey	1 hr 10 mins Formation Dive-Bombing
2 Feb 43	AN 850	Cpl Franklin	35 mins Air Test
3 Feb 43	AN 919	Sgt Robert Harvey	45 mins Dive-Bombing
4 Feb 43	AN 862	Sgt Robert Harvey	2 hrs 50 mins Mount Everest to Asansol to Karachi
4 Feb 43	AN 919	Sgt Robert Harvey	1 hr 25 mins Dive-Bombing
5 Feb 43	AN 916	Sgt Robert Harvey	1 hr 20 mins Dive-Bombing
5 Feb 43	AN 862	Sgt Robert Harvey	1 hr 20 mins Dive-Bombing
6 Feb 43	AN 862	Sgt Robert Harvey	1 hr 10 mins Dive-Bombing
8 Feb 43	AN 910	Sgt Robert Harvey	1 hr 5 mins Dive-Bombing
9 Feb 43	AN 920	Sgt Robert Harvey	1 hr 5 mins Formation flight to Ranchi
10 Feb 43	AN 920	Sgt Robert Harvey	1 hr 10 mins Army Co-Operation – 2 x Live 500lb bombs
11 Feb 43	AN 919	Sgt Robert Harvey	1 hr 15 mins Formation flight to Madhaiganj
11 Feb 43	AN 916	Sgt Robert Harvey	40 mins Formation Low-Level Bombing
12 Feb 43	AN 916	Sgt Robert Harvey	1 hr 10 mins Dive-Bombing
12 Feb 43	AN 916	Mr Anderson	1 hr 15 mins Dive-Bombing
13 Feb 43	AN 919	Sgt Keith Stewart-Mobsby	1 hr 15 mins Dive-Bombing
13 Feb 43	AN 919	Sgt Robert Harvey	30 mins Formation Leader
15 Feb 43	AN 920	Sgt Robert Harvey	1 hr 10 mins Dive-Bombing
16 Feb 43	AN 919	Sgt Robert Harvey	1 hr 50 mins to Ranchi and Return
17 Feb 43	AN 919	Sgt Robert Harvey	1 hr 40 mins Instrument and Country
17 Feb 43	AN 919	Sgt Robert Harvey	55 mins Dive-Bombing
18 Feb 43	AN 916	Sgt Robert Harvey	1 hr 30 mins Dive-Bombing
19 Feb 43	AN 916	-	1 hr 5 mins flight to Ranchi
19 Feb 43	AN 916	P/O Kirk & P/O Peter Ganthony	50 mins flight Ranchi to Madhaiganj
20 Feb 43	AN 916	Sgt Robert Harvey	1 hr 55 mins Cross-country R/T Test at 15,000ft.
22 Feb 43	AN 916	P/O Ganthony & Sgt Thomas Harrold Payne, RAAF	1 hr 10 mins to Salbani & Return
22 Feb 43	AN 916	Sgt Robert Harvey	1 hr 20 mins Formation Dive-Bombing

Date	Vengeance	Aircrew	Details
24 Feb 43	AN 919	Sgt Robert Harvey	50 mins R/T Test NCO. Ground Station U/S
24 Feb 43	AN 916	Sgt Robert Harvey	1 hr 15 mins Formation Dive-Bombing
25 Feb 43	AN 919	Sgt Frederick Charles Foakes & Sgt Keith Stewart-Mobsby	1 hr 15 mins Salbani & Return
1 March 43	AN 998	Sgt Frederick Foakes & Sgt Robert Harvey	10 mins to Salabi; NCO. U/S
1 March 43	AN 916	Sgt Frederick Foakes & Sgt Robert Harvey	1 hr 10 mins to Salbani & Return
3 March 43	AN 916	Sgt Thomas Payne RAAF	1 hr Low-Level R/T Test – Salbani
5 March 43	AN 919	Sgt Thomas Payne RAAF	50 mins Formation Leader
7 March 43	AN 916	Sgt Mills	1 hr Formation Low-Level Bombing
10 March 43	AN 920	LAC Newbury	55 mins Air Test
17 March 43	AN 920	Sgt Mills	20 mins Air Test for Ops.
17 March 43	AN 920	Sgt Robert Harvey	50 mins to Jessore.
17 March 43	AN 920	Sgt Robert Harvey	1 hr 35 mins from Jessore to Dohazari for Ops.

On 21 March Duncan and Sergeant Robert Harvey in Vengeance AN 920 took part in their first active combat dive-bombing mission, a one-hour-fifty-five-minute round-trip sortie, when they attacked Japanese troops and supplies at Donbaik, dropping two 500lb bombs. Next day they repeated the medicine, attacking similar targets located at Launchaung, another one-hour-fifty-minute round-trip. On both occasions the Vengeances had an escort of Hawker Hurricanes.

This was just the merest taster of combat, however, for on the 24th the pair flew Vengeance AN 916 from Dohazari the two-hour-fifteen-minutes back to base. They had the satisfaction of live targeting against the enemy but there was still much to do before full commitment. Just what this involved is as below again drawn from Flight Sergeant Duncan's log books.

Date	Vengeance	Aircrew	Details
7 April 43	EZ 857	Sgt Robert Harvey	35-mins Air Test Karachi
8 April 43	EZ 857	Sgt Robert Harvey	2 hrs 45 mins to Jodhpur
10 April 43	AN 619	Sgt Robert Harvey	35 mins Air Test Karachi

Date	Vengeance	Aircrew	Details
11 April 43	AN 617	Sgt Robert Harvey	1 hr 5 mins Air Test Karachi
11 April 43	AN 949	Sgt Robert Harvey	30 mins Air Test Karachi
12 April 43	AN 949	Sgt Robert Harvey	2 hrs 45 mins flight to Jodhpur
12 April 43	AN 949	Sgt Robert Harvey	2 hrs flight Jodhpur to Delhi
13 April 43	AN 949	Sgt Robert Harvey	2 hrs 15 mins flight Delhi to Allahabad
13 April 43	AN 949	Sgt Robert Harvey	2 hrs 15 mins flight Allahabad to Madhaiganj
15 April 43	AN 919	Sgt Robert Harvey	15 mins to Madhaiganj to Allahabad, recalled, aircraft u/s.
15 April 43	AN 128	Sgt Robert Harvey	2 hrs 10 mins flight Madhaiganj to Allahabad
15 April 43	AN 128	Sgt Robert Harvey	2 hrs 10 mins flight Allahabad to Delhi.
16 April 43	AP 128	Sgt Robert Harvey	30 mins flight Delhi to Jodhpur NCO a/c u/s
25 April 43	EZ 853	Sgt Robert Harvey	40 mins Air Test Karachi
26 April 43	EZ 853	Sgt Robert Harvey	2 hrs 20 mins Karachi to Jodhpur
26 April 43	EZ 853	Sgt Robert Harvey	2 hrs Jodhpur to Delhi
27 April 43	EZ 853	Sgt Robert Harvey	2 hrs Delhi to Allahabad
27 April 43	EZ 853	Sgt Robert Harvey	2 hrs Allahabad to Madhaiganj
1 May 43	AN 916	Sgt Robert Harvey	50 mins Dive-Bombing
5 May 43	AN 985	Sgt Robert Harvey	1 hr 15 mins Dive-Bombing
6 May 43	AN 620	Sgt Robert Harvey	1 hr 5 mins Dive-Bombing
6 May 43	AN 620	Sgt Robert Harvey	1 hr 40 mins Fighter Affiliation
6 May 43	AN 620	Sgt Robert Harvey	1 hr 45 mins Fighter Affiliation
7 May 43	AN 638	Sgt Robert Harvey	1 hr 45 mins Fighter Affiliation
9 May 43	EZ 873	Sgt Robert Harvey	2 hrs Fighter Affiliation
8 May 43	AN 620	Sgt Robert Harvey	1 hr Formation to Madhaiganj
11 May 43	EZ 953	LAC Allison	45 mins Air Test
12 May 43	AN 985	Sgt Robert Harvey	1 hr 5 mins Madhaiganj to Jessore
12 May 43	AN 985	Sgt Robert Harvey	2 hrs 10 mins Jessore to Chttagong for Ops.

Combat missions recommenced on 13 May with an attack on enemy supply dumps at Maungdaw. Flying Vengeance AN 985 with the redoubtable Sergeant Robert Harvey aft, Duncan dropped four 250lb bombs on target; the whole sortie took an hour and fifty-five minutes. Two days later the target was Japanese headquarters on Akyab Island where they encountered heavy flak defences. They returned to Akyab Island two days later where the target was the radio station; again, Japanese flak defences were recorded as 'accurate'. Next day enemy supply warehouses were targeted on Akyab, but this time the ground defence were logged as just 'light flak'. On the 19th two 500lb bombs were dropped on enemy supply bases at Kyanktaw. After another two-day interval Akyab was targeted again; they went out and destroyed the Narigan Bridge. Duncan's mount for this operation was Vengeance EZ 853. These were all missions of over two hours duration and, for each of them, 110 Squadron was provided with an escort of Hawker Hurricane fighters.

The last success stung the Japanese into retaliation and on the 21st they attacked the base, Hinge and Harvey in EZ 853 being among those scrambled away to avoid being caught on the ground.[38]

Having survived this counter-strike, 110 Squadron returned to the fray on the 23rd with the dam on the Royal Lake at Akyab being the target. However, thick cloud weathered this out and instead the village where enemy troops had been based was dive-bombed instead. This mission took two-hours-thirty-five minutes in duration and a similar strike was conducted the following day against enemy troops at Alithangyaw, where each Vengeance deposited a pair of 500lb bombs. Again, Hurricane fighters provided a nominal fighter escort but, as ever, no aerial opposition was encountered.

There was another lull in the Akyab operations, and Duncan flew from Chittagong to Madhaiganj on the 26th returning via Jessore the next day, while the 28th saw a twenty-minute air test with LAC Pearse in the back seat. On the 29th the enemy welcomed them back with another bombing raid on the base, and again Duncan and Harvey were scrambled away in Vengeance EZ 853 to avoid the attack. The training routine was again established pending their next deployment on the front line.

Date	Vengeance	Aircrew	Details
26 June 43	EZ 853	Cpl Snowball	20 mins Air Test
27 June 43	EZ 853	Sgt Robert Harvey	40 min Madhaiganj to Digori
28 June 43	EZ 853	Flt Sgt Robert Harvey	2 hrs 10 mins Formation Dive-Bombing
2 July 43	EZ 853	Flt Sgt Robert Harvey	1 hr 50 mins Formation flying.

---

[38] Losses on the ground included Warrant Officer Harold Eldon Thorpe and Corporals James Stalley McKay, plus John William Moseley and Donald Leslie Kay of 110 Squadron, all killed. On 23 April 1943 Pilot Officer George Herbert Lawrenson was killed.

Date	Vengeance	Aircrew	Details
5 July 43	EZ 812	Flt Sgt Robert Harvey	1 hr 50 mins Local flying
6 July 43	EZ 853	Flt Sgt Robert Harvey	1 hr 40 mins Formation flying
17 July 43	EZ 853	Flt Sgt Robert Harvey	1 hr 30 mins Formation & Low-Level Bombing
26 July 43	AN 950	Flt Sgt Robert Harvey	45 mins Digri to Amarda Road
29 July 43	AN 950	Flt Sgt Robert Harvey	1 hr 20 mind Cine Camera Operation and Dive-Bombing. No. 3 Course Air Fighting Training unit Amarda Road.
30 July 43	AN 950	Flt Sgt Robert Harvey	1 hr 30 mins Deflection Shooting (Camera)
31 July 43	AN 950	Flt Sgt Robert Harvey	2 hrs 5 mins Deflection Shooting & Bombing
2 Aug 43	AN 950	Flt Sgt Robert Harvey	2 hrs 10 mins Deflection Shooting & Drogue fire
6 Aug 43	AN 950	Flt Sgt Robert Harvey	2 hrs 15 mins Fighter Evasion & Drogue firing.
7 Aug 43	AN 950	Flt Sgt Robert Harvey	2 hrs 15 mins Fighter Evasion & Drogue firing.
7 Aug 43	AN 950	Flt Sgt Robert Harvey	1 hr Shadow Firing 400 rounds.
8 Aug 43	AN 950	Flt Sgt Robert Harvey	45 mins Air Firing; NCO a/c U.S.
8 Aug 43	AN 950	Flt Sgt Robert Harvey	1 hr Amarda Road to Digri
8 Aug 43	EZ 862	Flt Sgt Robert Harvey	1 hr Amarda Road to Digri
10 Aug 43	EZ 862	Flt Sgt Robert Harvey	1 hr Fighter Evasion
10 Aug 43	EZ 862	Flt Sgt Robert Harvey	45 mins Fighter Evasion & Formation.
11 Aug 43	EZ 862	Flt Sgt Robert Harvey	1 hr 30 mins Fighter Evasion & Drogue Firing
11 Aug 43	EZ 862	Flt Sgt Robert Harvey	1 hr Dive-Bombing
12 Aug 43	EZ 862	Flt Sgt Robert Harvey	1 hr 15 mins Dive-Bombing
12 Aug 43	EZ 862	Flt Sgt Robert Harvey	30 mins Low-Level Bombing
12 Aug 43	FE 474	F/O Michael Charles Folkard	1 hr 20 mins Dual Deflection Shooting
14 Aug 43	EZ 862	F/O Walter James McKerracher, DFM, RAAF*	45 mins Low-Level Bombing
14 Aug 43	FE 360	Flt Lt C.J. Hendrick	1 hr 20 mins Dual Deflection Shooting
16 Aug 43	EZ 862	Flt Sgt Robert Harvey	2 hrs 15 mins Formation Dive-Bombing & Fighter Evasion

Date	Vengeance	Aircrew	Details
17 Aug 43	EZ 862	Flt Sgt Robert Harvey	35 mins Amarda Rod to Digri
17 Aug 43	EZ 812	Flt Sgt Robert Harvey	35 mins Digri to Amarda Road
18 Aug 43	EZ 812	Flt Sgt Robert Harvey	2 hrs Fighter Evasion & Dive Bombing
19 Aug 43	EZ 812	Flt Sgt Robert Harvey	50 mins Fighter Evasion & Bombing. a/c u/s
19 Aug 43	EZ 812	Flt Sgt Robert Harvey	40 mins Shadow Firing. Rear Guns.
20 Aug 43	EZ 812	Flt Sgt Robert Harvey	1 hr 35 mins Fighter Evasion & Dive-Bombing
21 Aug 43	EZ 812	Flt Sgt Robert Harvey	1 hr 45 mins Fighter Evasion & Dive-Bombing
23 Aug 43	EZ 812	Flt Sgt Robert Harvey	1 hr Fighter Evasion
23 Aug 43	EZ 812	Flt Sgt Robert Harvey	1 hr to Kharagpur to refuel
24 Aug 43	EZ 812	P/O Willett	1 hr 25 mins Fighter Evasion & Dive-Bombing
24 Sep 43	EZ 812	F/O Peter Frederick Robinson	55 min Air Test
30 Sep 43	EZ 811	Flt Sgt Robert Harvey	1 hr 30 mins Dive-Bombing
2 Oct 43	EZ 811	Flt Sgt Robert Harvey	2 hrs 35 mins to Baigachi for Fighter Affiliation
4 Oct 43	EZ 811	WO Douglas M McIlroy, RNZAF	To Asansol and return
5 Oct 43	EZ 959	Sgt Maratt	1 hr 10 mins Dive-Bombing
8 Oct 43	EZ 812	WO Douglas M McIlroy, RNZAF	To Asansol
8 Oct 43	EZ 903	–	50 mins Air test to Digri
9 Oct 43	EZ 891	Flt Sgt Robert Harvey	1 hr 15 mins Dive-Bombing
11 Oct 43	AP 119	Cpl Knapp	30 mins Air Test
12 Oct 43	EZ 891	Flt Sgt Robert Harvey	1 hr 15 mins Dive-Bombing
13 Oct 43	EZ 903	Flt Lt Henry Brooke	1 hr 5 mins to Chara Road & return
15 Oct 43	EZ 903	Flt Sgt Robert Harvey	2 hrs Digri to Jessore
15 Oct 43	EZ 903	Flt Sgt Robert Harvey	2 hrs 30 mins Jessore to Kumbhirgram

*McKerracher was killed in a flying accident at the AFTU, RAF Amarda Road, on 13 May 1944.

Flight Sergeant Duncan had emerged from the Air Fighting Training Unit at Amarda Road with a certificate signed by the Officer Commanding that he had completed the course satisfactorily. With the extra flying time also added, they were as ready as they could be, and it was time for 110

Squadron to resume their place in battle. Flight Lieutenant James John McMath, RNZAF, was another Kiwi who joined the squadron.

Operations opened in earnest on the 14th with 110 Squadron moving to the big Kumbhirgram airfield, over fifteen and a half miles north-east of Silchar, under the command of Squadron Leader Leonard Frank Penny DFC. On the first mission, a strike on the supply road leading south out of Imphal towards Tiddim, ten Vengeances under Penny arrived over the target, but Penny was unable to bomb due to a technical fault. The others duly delivered their ordnance as planned. On the second raid in the same area the Vengeances intervened in an artillery duel, tipping the balance in the Allies' favour.

On 19 October there was an attack mounted on the reported Japanese Headquarters at Mowlaik, a two-hour round flight with Duncan and Harvey flying Vengeance EZ 871. The 21st saw the same duo in EZ 871 make an attack on enemy troop concentrations at Kaleymo, an even longer sortie, but three days later Duncan and Harvey had to abort a similar mission half-an-hour into the flight due to aircraft problems with AP 119. Flying Vengeance EZ 905 Duncan dive-bombed enemy troops at Indainogyi in the Chin Hills on 26 October. Whenever the weather allowed, 110 Squadron was striking hard and regularly across their range. The 1st of November saw them dive-bombing Japanese supplies at Sanmyo in the Mittha Valley and they returned to the Chin Hills on the 7th, flying Vengeance EZ 834 to hit enemy supply dumps. Nansaungpu in the Nezinaya Valley was the next target where Japanese troop concentrations were dive-bombed on 11 November with Duncan having Vengeance AN 932 as his mount.

Also on 11 November 1943, in an attack on Khumbirgram by Japanese Mitsubishi *Sally* bombers with anti-personnel bombs, three airmen were killed – Corporal Alfred John Arthur Burrows, RAFVR, Leading Aircraftman John Joseph Crockett, RAFVR and Leading Aircraftman James McKendrick Hall, RAFVR. They are commemorated at the Gauhati War Cemetery, Assam.

Three days later, on 14 November, in EZ 812, Duncan participated in an attack at No. 2 Stockade, in the Chin Hills, where Japanese supplies were again their focus, while their most distant target to date, Kongyi on the Chindwin river, a three-hour round trip, was hit on the 20th, Duncan flying EZ 811. Two days after this another Japanese headquarters, this one at Paluzawa, received the full dive-bomber treatment, Duncan and Harvey flying Vengeance EZ 991; and on the 25th they returned to the Chin Hills once more to hit enemy positions, a two-hour-ten-minute flight. The enemy again retaliated from the air and attacked their base on 29 November. For the third time Duncan scrambled in AN 227 on approach of enemy aircraft. One eyewitness, Flying Officer Kenneth Burton Mosher, RCAF, remembered the incident as taking place when the pilots were driving out to their Vengeances in readiness for another sortie. 'Reg Duncan is sitting on the end of the truck and notices some airplanes overhead, telling the boys, "We have Mohawks for fighter support today".'[39] Then he sees the Rising Sun and shouts, "They're not Mohawks!" The truck comes to a screeching halt and the men dive under it as quickly as the enemy come tearing down in a shoot-up. Bullets ripped the shirt off my back and smashed through my fingers, slicing the guy in front of me. We were banged up, but no one was killed.'[40]

Little harm was done and next day the squadron returned the favour by dive-bombing enemy troops and supplies at Indainogyi again. An attack mounted on 2 December against Japanese positions in the Chin Hills saw Duncan and Harvey having to abort in Vengeance AN 827 due to the failure of the petrol pumps; but they were back in action with AN 234 three days after this with an attack on troop concentrations at Keungkasi near the Chindwin river. On the 10th the target was yet again enemy positions in the Chin Hills, this time close to Fort White, and they returned to blast this target again on the 12th and 13th. Japanese artillery pieces in the Chin Hills that were causing the Army serious problems were obliterated on the14th. They hit enemy infantry concentrations at Tienkava three days later, and were again in action flying EZ891 on the 27th, bombing further Japanese troop concentrations at Yeng in the Chindwin Valley.

A brief interval followed during which opportunity was taken to refresh cross-country navigation and fighter affiliation skills, then it was back to

---

[39] Curtiss P-36 Mohawk IV single-seater fighters, later replaced by Hawker Hurricanes.

[40] Mosher, Sara V., *Remember Me: No. 110 (Hyderabad) Squadron Royal Air Force*, Self-published, Winnipeg, Manitoba, 2011.

work once more. Between June 1944 and January 1945, the squadron was upgraded to operate the superior Vengeance III and IV models.

The 17th of January 1944 saw them striking at Kyaukchaw, close to the Chindwin river, and this was followed the next day by a spectacular dive-bombing of the railway station at Wuntho. Duncan noted in his log book that day that this target was 'Well Pranged!!!' Japanese troops at Pinlebu involving another three-hour round trip, were the target on 22 January, these last four missions seeing the well-tried Duncan and Harvey team flying Vengeance EZ 891. Regrettably, Flying Officer John David Ernest Robertson, along with Flying Officer Anthony John Davies, were both killed on 17 December 1943.

Experimental VHF testing was carried out on the 24th of the month aboard AN 668 while the following day there was an air test of EZ 891 with Aircraftsman King in the rear cockpit. The 2nd of February saw Duncan make a four-hour journey to Bishnapur, in the Bengal jungle, via Sylhet, Comilla, Jessore and Alipore, ready for the next phase. By now the Japanese assault on Imphal was in full flow and the switching of the close-air support units was smoothly carried out to try and blunt the enemy assault. On 18 February A Flight of 110 Squadron, with Duncan and Harvey mounted in Vengeance AN 751, dive-bombed a reported Japanese headquarters east of Homalin but a repeat attack on the 20th was 'weathered out' and AN 835 was forced to land at Imphal itself, returning to base the following day.

The 26th of February saw Duncan and Harvey mounted in Vengeance AN 751 participating in the dive-bombing of a Japanese camp close to Paungbin. Starting on 3 March, the tempo quickened, and the duo were in the thick of 110 Squadron's missions against the rampant enemy. Another Japanese camp, this one at Pinlebu, was dive-bombed this day and on the 4th they hit enemy supplies near Tonzi. The 8th of March saw them hitting yet another enemy headquarters, this one at Sakham, and another at Le-U on the 10th, while the 11th saw them hitting enemy troops at Ta-Anga near Chinwait, while on the 16th, this time aboard Vengeance AN 751, enemy supplies at Nanhanowe were blasted. As the battle reached a crescendo the pace was non-stop and Vengeance operations over this crucial period are best summarised from Duncan's log book as follows–

Date	Vengeance	Target
17 March 44	AN 724	2 hrs 40 mins – Dive-bombed Japanese Divisional Headquarters near Chindwin river
18 March 44	AN 751	2 hrs 25 mins. Dive-bombed Japanese Divisional Headquarters at Indaingoyi
21 March 44	AN 751	1 hr 40 mins. Dive-bombed Japanese troops on Tiddim Road
24 March 44	AN 751	2 hrs 35 mins. Dive-bombed Japanese troops at Konavi
26 March 44	AN 735	2 hrs. Dive-bombed Japanese gun positions in Chin Hills
27 March 44	AN 735	2 hrs 20 minutes. Dive-bombed Japanese supplies east of Homalin
27 March 44	AN 751	2 hrs. Dive-bombed Japanese Headquarters in Chin Hills
29 March 44	AN 751	2 hrs. Dive-bombed Japanese troops near Manipur River
30 March 44	AN 751	2 hrs 30 mins. Dive-bombed Japanese troops at Kaing
31 March 44	AN 751	2 hrs. Dive-bombed Japanese Divisional Headquarters in Chin Hills
2 April 44	AN 751	2 hrs. Dive-bombed Japanese Divisional Headquarters at Menifor River.
3 April 44	AN 751	2 hrs 35 mins. Dive-bombed & Strafed Japanese troops in Naga Hills
4 April 44	An 751	2 hrs. Dive-bombed Japanese positions at Tamu
5 April 44	AN	2 hrs. Dive-bombed Japanese supplies near Chan River
6 April 44	?	2 hrs 40 mins. Dive-bombed Japanese supplies in Naga Hills
9 April 44	?	1 hr 35 mins. Dive-bombed Japanese positions six miles north of Imphal
10 April 44	AN 689	1 hr 15 mins. Dive-bombed Japanese positions north of Imphal
12 April 44	AN 751	2 hrs 15 mins. Dive-bombed Japanese supplies at Keungkesi
13 April 44	AN 751	1 hr 40 mins. Dive-bombed Japanese gun positions north of Imphal.
14 April 44	AN 751	Dive-bombed Japanese supplies near Paungbu
15 April 44	AN 751	Dive-bombed Japanese troops in Naga Hills
3 May 44	AN 716	With Warrant Officer Turner Dive-bombed Japanese gun positions in Kohima
5 May 44	AN 716	Detailed to attack Japanese supplies east of Kalewa – recalled.
5 May 44	AN 716	Dive-bombed Japanese gun positions south-west of Bishenpore
9 May 44	AN 716	Dive-bombed Japanese troops north of Imphal.
10 May 44	AN 716	Dive-bombed Japanese troops south of Kohima.
11 May 44	AN 733	Dive-bombed Japanese positions south of Bishenpore

The Vengeance dive-bomber receives just six scant mentions in the official Air Ministry book on the campaign,[41] and has only rarely been touched upon by later versions like Franks, Norman, *The Air Battle of Imphal*, William Kimber, London, 1985, which barely mentions the Vengeance contribution at all. More recently there is Shores, Christopher, *The Air War in Burma: The Allied Air Forces Fight Back 1942-45*, Grub Street, London, 2005 which is much better but is still perfunctory regarding the Vengeance operations and successes. This shows just how deep-seated prejudice against dive-bombing was; but this record of just one pilot eloquently speaks for itself, despite this strange attitude and modern-day detractors. At the time the Allied troops on the ground were voluble in their praise. Brigadier 'Mad Mike' Calvert said, 'Close Air Support (CAS) was practised extensively during the joint training of the Chindits', adding, 'The pilots flying CAS sorties could drop HE (High Explosives) within 100 to 300 yards of friendly troops.'[42]

One of the last combat missions that 110 Squadron conducted with the Vultee Vengeance took place on 24 May 1944. A force of twelve Vengeances, under Flight Lieutenant Grant Loftus Puttock RCAF, was despatched at 1534 that day, being tasked with the destruction of Japanese motor transport in the harbour area either side of the Tiddim road, just to the north of MS 26 (Pinpoint RK 113088). At 1630 they made their initial dives from an 11,000-foot altitude down to 5,000 feet. As they were on the way down they observed several tracks leading from the Tiddim road into their target area, which was suggestive of much enemy activity. The army laid down artillery indication using white smoke which was clearly seen among the trees. They also saw just three black *bashas* in a line 400 yards due east of the road. The bombs all burst in the target area. All aircraft were safely back at base at 1705.

Shortly after this the monsoon season began in earnest and flying operations were again severely curtailed. When they were ordered to suspend operations with the Vengeance pending her replacement with the de Havilland Mosquito, some other pilots, like 'Bud' Duncan himself, were transferred to 151 OTU where they worked as instructors on the upgraded

---

[41]   Anon, *The Wings of the Phoenix: The Official Story of the Air Force in Burma*, His Majesty's Stationery Office, London, 1949.

[42]   Calvert, Brigadier James Michael DSO, *Fighting Mad: One Man's Guerrilla War*, Jarrolds, London, 1965.

Vengeance aircraft arriving in large numbers. There was evidently considered to be a need for such dive-bombing expertise which appeared to indicate that, until the Mosquito was made fit for service, the Vultee was to be made ready for the resumption of battle after the monsoons, or that, failing to find a solution, the Vengeance would be reintroduced to the war zone as soon as possible and the Air Ministry, despite their inbuilt detestation of the type, were keeping their powder dry.[43] In any event, with regard to Flight Sergeant Duncan, he continued to train a whole series of both Commonwealth and Indian pilots in the technique between June and the end of September. In total he conducted no fewer than thirty-five training flights in the Vengeance during this period. The Vengeances that he flew at Peshawar were AN 101, AN 107, AN 128, AN 673, AN 691, AN 708, AN 715, 746, EZ 806, EZ 807, EZ 857, AN 936 and AN 940, while his trainees included Group Captain Ernest Ralph Bitmead DFC, Major Dales, Flight Lieutenants William Shipton and Kundan Lal Sondhi, Flying Officers Achreta, Hector Beale, Alan Joseph Chaves, Wilmot Horace Derry, Amil Kanta Ganguly, Syed Abbas Hussain, Soli Cursetji Kaikobad, Mohammad Jamiluddin Khan, Maher and Singh, First Sergeant Pinching, and Sergeants Carvalho and Thomas. Among his Indian trainees were some who later went on to achieve senior rankings in the Indian Air Force. He had a total of twenty-eight hours flying time with the 151 OTU, at the end of which his commanding officer rated him 'Average Plus' as an instructor.[44] Duncan's final flight in the Vengeance (AN 107) was a forty-five-minute fighter affiliation trip with Flight Lieutenant William Shipton on 30 September 1944.

This work continued, Flight Lieutenant Norman Edwards, a later Officer-in-Charge of the Air Firing Flight of this unit, noted that the standard of many of the Indian pilots he trained was poor.

> One day I was watching a Vengeance coming in to land. It was holding off far too high. When it lost flying speed, instead of being just inches above the runway for a gentle touch-down, it thumped down

---

[43] The Mosquito was not finally deemed fit for combat in Far Eastern conditions until the end of March 1945 as it happened.

[44] *Summary of Flying and Assessments 151 OTU*, 20 June 1944 to 30 September 1944, dated 9 October 1944.

very heavily and bounced back into the air. The pilot gave it a burst of throttle and then thumped down heavily again – and then again, before remaining on the runway. Fortunately, it was a long runway. I hesitated to think what all this had done to the undercarriage.

The Vengeance taxied past and I saw the beaming face of the pilot, who didn't seem a bit disconcerted. 'What a landing,' I said to a Squadron Leader who was standing next to me. 'It certainly was.' he said. 'That was Flying Officer Sen. It's the best landing I've ever seen him make!'

The Indian Air Force, at that time, was to some degree a political force rather than a top fighting force. The fact that Indians were volunteering to fly and fight with us meant a lot. As a result, pilots who were not up to scratch were not 'washed out' (demoted or grounded) but were sent on another training course round. One of the first pupils I met at Peshawar was none other than Flying Officer Sen![45]

Not all this work was totally wasted. The Indian squadrons who converted to the Supermarine Spitfire found little work for their fighter skills, but spent much of their time acting as dive-bombers, delivering not two 500-lb and two 250-lb bombs into the Japanese, but a single 250-lb bomb. Nonetheless, as the war diary of No. 7 Squadron IAF proudly recorded at the time, 'The spirit of the Vengeance lives on!'

Although 110 (H) Squadron was supposed to convert to the de Havilland Mosquito at No. 1672 Conversion Unit, these aircraft were not yet deemed combat-fit and so alternative employment was found for some of the Vengeances and their crews; between September and November they were used in experimental anti-malarial-spraying operations in the Gold Coast (now known as Ghana). The squadron had Vengeance III and IVs on strength between June 1944 and January 1945.

---

[45] Memoirs of Norman Edwards, courtesy of his son Alastair D.N. Edwards. Edwards cites No. 1 Squadron IAF, but these flew Westland Lysanders and then Hawker Hurricane IICs. However, a Pilot Officer Jitendra Kumar Sen *did* train with1 AGS (Air Gunnery Squadron) of the Indian Air Force at Bairagarh, which trained officers on tactical reconnaissance flights, and which may be the source of this story.

Two detachments of 110 Squadron's Vengeances were sent out to the Gold Coast for mosquito-spraying experiments following the pioneering work of eminent entomologist Lieutenant C. Ronald Ribbands MA FRES, at Accra from 1942 onwards. A signal was received from HQ, AC, SEAC, on 24 June ordering the immediate commitment to 'carry out Special Anti-Malarial Trials in West Africa'. Ten Mk IV Vengeances, along with aircrews and parties of key maintenance personnel, were to carry out the task over a period of approximately two months. These aircraft had to change over their Bendix and VHF radio sets at Allahabad on 1 June, and then be ferried to the squadron at Kalyan, near Nevali, Maharashtra State, by 1 July and they were to depart on the 5th, with a Douglas C-47 Dakota (Skytrain) transport aircraft provided for the maintenance team and equipment. Final briefing was to be at Maripur, four miles north-west of Karachi, and the route was authorised as via North Africa to Cairo then down to Khartoum in Sudan and across to Accra. All the personnel were to receive yellow fever inoculations from the Squadron Medical Officer, Flight Lieutenant John Ley Greaves MB BSc MRCS LRCP and the Vengeances were to be lightly loaded in order to accommodate such spares as could not be embarked aboard the transport plane. Squadron Leader Leonard Penny requested HQ that he proceed with the detachment and supervise their safe transfer before returning to the squadron in India and this was granted. He left on 4 June for a two-hours-fifty-minute flight to Dum Dum and finally got to Kalya but did not reach Kalya until the 12th. The final (planned) composition of the two detached flights was as follows:

First Detachment

Aircraft	Pilot	Aircrew
FD 263	Sqn Ldr Leonard Penny DFC	Flt Lt David Goodall
FD 226	Flt Lt J.D. Hedley	Flt Sgt L.D. Hodges
AN 749	Flt Lt James Corbishley RNZAF	Sgt K.R. Godwin
AN 693	F/O Ronald Francis Norman	P/O Kenneth Burton Mosher
FD 231	F/O Joseph Parrish	WO Robert Coulter Reid
AN 815	WO R. Knight-Clark	Flt Sgt H. Watson
FD 259	Sgt R.C. Merchant	Flt Sgt H. Braden
FD 263	Sgt D.D.J. Carter	WO J. Turner

The Douglas C-47 Dakota, when it finally arrived at Kalyan, was found to be unserviceable and had to be delayed until the necessary spare parts could be obtained from the RAF Maintenance Depot at Santa Cruz, Bombay (Mumbai), but that base did not have the part in stock. The Dakota transport finally left on 14 July with the Squadron Engineering Officer, Flying Officer Claude Winston Steer BEM, one sergeant and three corporals, for Cairo and two days later two Vengeances left to join the six already at Maripur. HQ signalled that ten Vengeances were to move to Karachi on 8 August and proceed to Takoradi the following day. Flight Lieutenant Rodney Topley led eight aircraft off at 1530 that day and two more followed later.

The make-up of the second detachment was originally thus:

Aircraft	ID	Pilot	Aircrew
AN 836	A	Flt Lt Rodney Topley	F/O Norman Laurence Henson
AN 679	D	F/Or John Robertson RCAF	Flt Sgt Ralph Gordon Collingham
AN 623	K	F/O Grant Puttock	Flt Sgt J. Higgs
AN 754	V	WO Robert Yeates	WO L.H. Ward
AN 721	G	WO R.P. Newman	P/O Frederick Foakes
AN 813	Q	Flt Sgt A.R. Fletcher	Flt Sgt Allan James Richardson RAAF
AN 811	B	Flt Sgt M.E.G. Dalton	Flt Sgt David George Cummin
AN 775	R	Flt Sgt John Arthur Douglas Christie RAAF	Flt Sgt A.I. Osborne
AN 749	P	Flt Sgt J.H. Crowther	WO Robert Yates RCAF
AN 804	Z	Sgt D.A. Blair	WO Thomas Harrold Payne RAAF

On the 8th three Vengeances left base but encountered extremely bad weather conditions. Two returned safely, with AN 721 getting down at Santa Cruz, but the third, AN 679, piloted by Flying Officer John David Ernest Robertson, with his navigator, Flight Sergeant Ralph Gordon Collingham, attempted to reach Maripur Air Base, but failed to arrive. Nothing further was heard of this aircraft and it was assumed that it flew off course and ultimately crashed into the sea. Although search flights were flown over the area and Air-Sea Rescue launches scoured the waters off the coast no trace was ever found of the aircraft or her airmen.[46] Eight surviving Vengeances had left for Maripur on the 9th followed by a ninth on 10 July.

After the detachments had departed the base was quiet and the squadron was left in the hands of Flight Lieutenant Harold Keppel Ralph until the

---

[46] Robertson's Memorial is at Gauhati War Cemetery and Collingham's is at Kirklees War Cemetery.

CO could return. It will be convenient here to briefly relate their movements in the interim. Establishment was mainly the docile Airspeed Oxford, for the long-term view was to train aircrew up on two-engined aircraft pending the ultimate arrival of the de Havilland Mosquito VI aircraft. Wing Commander Arthur Ernest Saunders OBE took over from Ralph on 16 September and the latter became OC A Flight, with Flight Lieutenant P.F. Smith as OC B Flight. Between 1 and 6 October the squadron moved base to Kolar and then, between 22 and 26 October, moved on to Yelhanka. It was recorded that the first Mosquitoes arrived on 1 November, with four reaching them on the 3rd, and two more on each subsequent day to a maximum strength of fourteen. But on the 10th a signal from AHQ ordered half of these to be immediately sent to Bengal to reinforce front-line units. Mosquitoes were falling out of the air on a regular basis and, on 1 November, all 110 (H)'s remaining such aircraft were grounded, and later removed.

The adventures, and misfortunes, of both detachment flights make sorry recording, but Penny's group had the worst of it. Two flights of eight and seven Vengeances respectively were to be made available by 8 June but, in the end, only nine aircraft could be readied by the deadline and these did not leave until 3 July, one aircraft being forced to land back at Kalyan with engine problems. On 8 July the first three Vengeances left for Karachi, and three others followed next day but of the third group, two had to return to base and it was not until 16 July that Squadron Leader Leonard Penny and Flying Officer D.D.J. Carter left to join the remaining six at Karachi. From there the detachment left in two flights of three aircraft and one of two, the first led by Squadron Leader Leonard Penny at 0745, the second by Flight Lieutenant James Corbishley, RNZAF, at 0800 and the third by Flight Lieutenant Vernon Hedley at 0815.

Woes soon began. FD 222 was found to be unserviceable (on inspection chunks of rubber were found in the fuel filters); FD 259 was unserviceable due to electrical faults, FD 231 had problems. On 21 July AD 693, flown by Flying Officer Ronald Norman, experienced severe engine trouble and had to turn back, and he, Corbishley and Sergeant R.C. Merchant were soon all stuck at Sharjah on the Persian Gulf. FD 263, flown by Carter, was found to be unserviceable on the 23rd, while FD 231 was found to have used twenty gallons of oil in two hours flying from Lydda airfield in Palestine. No fewer than seven aircraft were thus grounded at Heliopolis, with five of them, FD 222, 225, 226, 228 and 263, found to have major faults, including bent cam rods and shafts badly corroded, and were waiting to have complete engine changes at Aboukir. When this was finally done, 11 August saw a replacement pilot, Flying Officer John J. Sebisty, RCAF, with FD 225, taking off from Aboukir for Cairo West with the other four but, while attempting a normal take-off to get airborne, the engine failed to develop sufficient power to continue and he 'mushed down' back on the runway and belly-landed, fortunately with only slight damage. The remaining four, FD 226 piloted by Flight Lieutenant J.D. Hedley, FD 222 flown by Flight Lieutenant J. Corbshley, FD 263 with Pilot Officer Joseph Parrish and FD 228 flown by Warrant Officer R. Knight-Clark, therefore carried on without him. Two ferry pilots were given crash courses on the Vengeance and one of these, Warrant Officer McLaughlin, was assigned the task of getting Sebistry's machine onward while the other, Warrant Officer Howard, stood by to receive a replacement aircraft, HB 513. Meanwhile an increasingly frantic Middle East Command was sending a stream of signals demanding that 'all available aircraft MUST leave tomorrow', but, in fact, there were only three fit to fly. As Penny recorded there was 'Bags of panic'. It seems remarkable that while 110 (H) Squadron was able to mount full twelve-Vengeance air strikes almost daily in combat operations, such a long-range journey, even in stages, exposed the limitations of their mass-produced American radial engines to an enormous degree.

Also on that date it was found that FD 231 and 254 could not be easily repaired in time and they were replaced by HB 485 and HB 503. Next day Parrish's mount, FD231, developed a high mag drop, running rough on the take off and had to return to base. Three days later HB 513 arrived at Cairo West. The next stage of their journey was routed via Luxor, Wadi Halfa, Khartoum and then on to Takoradi and they commenced this leg on the 18th, but Joe Parrish, flying FD 222, reported his engine running very rough, 'too much 'popping', gave up and turned back. Then HB 513 was found to be unserviceable, with Joe Parrish being forced to stay with her at El Obeid (Al-Ubayyid), Sudan, where he found Flight Sergeant J.H. Crowther and Warrant Officer Robert Yates with AN 749 and Flight Sergeant John Arthur Christie, RAAF, and Flight Sergeant A.I. Osborne with AN 775 in a similar situation.

So, of all the aircraft and aircrew despatched, very few initially arrived safely at Takoradi. The majority of these flights encountered engine failures, extreme weather conditions, breakdowns, lack of spares and other difficulties. Aircrew were lost, others abandoned and even replacement aircraft broke down while an increasingly agitated Air Ministry kept up a steady stream of signals demanding that aircraft which were grounded and totally incapacitated fulfil their original deadlines. It was quite a saga.

It was therefore not until 24 August that Squadron Leader Leonard Penny with Flight Lieutenant David Phillip Goodall in Vengeance FD 263 finally reached RAF Takoradi airfield on the southern coast.[47] In the commanding officer's own words, the rest of the detachments had 'aircraft scattered all over Africa'. The CO was joined the following day by Flight Lieutenant J.D. Headley with his WO/AG Flight Sergeant Bertram Sidney Arthur Smith who arrived in a Lockheed Hudson bomber from Kano airfield in northern Nigeria,[48] having abandoned their mount, HB 485, there as totally unserviceable. They were joined by Warrant Officer R. Knight-Clarke and Flight Sergeant H. Watson from Kano in Vengeance FD 226. Thus, with this tiny nucleus of two aircraft and three aircrew, 110 (H) Squadron was to embark on another, and equally as important, battle, but this time the enemy was not the Empire of Nippon but the deadly *Anopheles Gambiae*.[49]

The detachment now worked with a team from Porton Down, the government research facility near Salisbury, to test the efficiency of aerial spraying of a synthetic pesticide with powerful insecticidal properties known as *Dichlorodiphenyltrichloroethane* (DDT). Highly controversial today, back in 1944 it was hoped DDT would save the lives of tens of thousands of civilians and military alike. Using this chlorinated hydrocarbon as a vector control against the malaria spreading, it was hoped that the disease could be curbed.[50]

The Porton Experimental Unit was commanded by Wing Commander James Black who had a team of service personnel and civilians, including

---

[47] This had been developed from an old Imperial Airways' staging post into a major air ferry terminal for moving aircraft from the UK to the Middle and Far East, thus avoiding occupied Europe. Later American-built aircraft also utilised the base as a short hop across the Atlantic. Today it is known as Takoradi Airport and serves the Sekondi-Takoradi region of western Southern Ghana.

[48] Nowadays known as Mallam-Kano International Airport.

[49] This being the species of mosquito that carries the malaria parasite.

[50] DDT had originated as long ago as 1874, but its important properties were discovered in 1939 by Swiss scientist Paul Herman Müller.

Professor Patrick Alfred Buxton CMG FRS FLS, a distinguished entomologist, Mr S.H. Fryer and Flight Lieutenant M.R. Siddorn, along with Lieutenant Colonel Eric Frances Edson MB, RAMC and Lieutenant Borrice, and Squadron Leaders Buckingham and Phillips and Flight Lieutenant Hoster, with whom 110 (H) was to work. For this experimental work selected areas of jungle had been selected, each approximately one square mile in area. Each of these areas were to be sprayed from the air in turn with the insecticide, the purpose of the spray being to affect lethally the mosquitoes and mosquito larvae in the area. Data was to be collected and assessed on the concentrations of spray deemed necessary for effect mosquito control, and the best method of spraying was to be investigated. All the flying involved was to be undertaken by the Vengeance detachments.

Until sufficient Vengeances finally reached West Africa, opportunity was taken to conduct practice flights with the spray containers. Each Vengeance was fitted with two containers, one under each wing on bomb carriers. The first practice flights took place on 28 August, with empty containers mounted on Vengeance FD 226. Three runs were made, one of twenty minutes and one of ten minutes duration by Squadron Leader Leonard Penny and Flight Sergeant Bertram Smith, and one of fifteen minutes by Warrant Officer R. Knight-Clark and Sergeant H. Watson. As anticipated, it was found that the carrying of these spray containers had 'little or no effect on the flying characteristics of the Vengeance aircraft'. Late the same day tests were carried out on a trial area adjacent to the airfield, utilising low-level spraying with an oil spray. Again, Vengeance FD 226 was the aircraft employed and three runs were made by the teams Penny/Watson, Hedley/Smith and Knight-Clark/Watson respectively. The spray was released from a height of approximately 180 feet and the tests were considered to be satisfactory.[51]

Following a day of analysis, 30 August saw Squadron Leader Leonard Penny take Porton engineer Mr Fryer on a thirty-minute test run in Vengeance FD 263, and the next day a further twenty-minute test run was made in FD 226 by the team of Warrant Officer R. Knight-Clark and Flight

---

[51]   See AIR 27/860/11. Also, Roberts, Jonathan, 'Korle and the Mosquito: Histories and Memories of the Anti-Malaria Campaign in Accra, 1942-5', *Cambridge Core*, Vol 51, Issue.3, pp.343-65, November 2010, and Annand, Percy Nicol, *Tests Conducted by the Bureau of Entomology & Plant Quarantine to Appraise the Usefulness of DDT as an Insecticide*. (1944).

Sergeant H. Watson, while Squadron Leader Leonard Penny flew FD 226 with Squadron Leader Phillips from the Porton team on a thirty-minute reconnaissance flight over the first spray area near Ajumako (04^0 54'N, 02^0 01' W). Later a second reconnaissance flight of one-hour duration was made by Hedley with Flying Officer Ballantyne of Air Sea Rescue as passenger to familiarise the latter with the area in case of accidents.

No. 110 (H) Squadron's detachments, working from Takoradi, continued the first series of aerial spray tests trials on 2 September 1944, Squadron Leader Penny DFC, with Pilot Officer Bertram Smith as his rear-seat man, making a fifteen-minute run in Vengeance FD 263 on that date. The next day Flight Lieutenant Hedley, with LAC White as a passenger, went out on a trial run in Vengeance FD 226 over the first designated spray area at Ajumako, in the central region of the country.

But the first official use of the spray was conducted on 4 September when Squadron Leader Penny and Flight Lieutenant David Phillip Goodall in Vengeance FD 263 and Flight Lieutenant Hedley and Warrant Officer Knight-Clark with FD 226 conducted a fifty-five-minute run in line abreast. It was concluded from this trail that this formation was unsuitable for future operations with a larger number of aircraft and that, instead, they would adopt an echelon-starboard formation, which would provide all the pilots with a better line of sight for safety while flying at low level. There matters stood awaiting the arrival of the second detachment, although on the 5th both aircraft conducted a low-level 'beat up' of the fleet in Takoradi harbour to give anti-aircraft practice to the naval gunners.

The second detachment finally arrived from Imeja, Nigeria,[52] On 8 September six aircraft had made it and these were as follows:

Aircraft	Pilot	Aircrew
AN 826	Flt Lt Rodney Topley	F/O Norman Henson
AN 693	F/O Grant Puttock RCAF	Flt Sgt J. Higgs
AN 754	WO Robert Yeates RCAF	Flt Lt D. Cummin
AN 813	Flt Sgt D.A. Blair	Flt Sgt Allan James Richardson RAAF
AN 811	Flt Sgt Crowther	WO Robert Yates
AN 721	WO H.P. Norman	P/O Frederick Foakes

---

[52] Now known as Murtala International Airport.

With their safe arrival Squadron Leader Penny, Flight Lieutenants David George Cummin and Rodney Topley and Pilot Officer Frederick Foakes all returned to 110 (H) Squadron in India in a Lockheed Hudson on the 12th to resume their duties and prepare for the forthcoming deployment back at the front in Burma. Meanwhile, the newly arrived aircrews took part in practice spraying next to the airfield to acclimatise themselves, FD 263 taking part with Sergeant D.D.J. Carter and Warrant Officer J. Turner, and a reconnaissance was done of the second spray area at Ataraso, slightly to the west of Takoradi, by Flight Lieutenant Hedley and Flight Lieutenant David Goodall in FD 226. The following day a fifty-minute practice formation spray was carried out by seven Vengeances adopting the echelon-starboard layout. Further practices followed over the next few days and, on 16 September three more Vengeances arrived from Kano, AN 749 with Flight Lieutenant James Corbishley, RNZAF, and Flight Lieutenant Kenneth Mosher DFC FD 254 with Pilot Officer Joseph Parrish and Warrant Officer Robert Coulter Reid and AN 775 with Flight Sergeant John Christie, RAAF, and Flight Sergeant A.I. Osborne. One further Vengeance was left unserviceable at El Oeneina, a fuelling airfield in Dafur, Western Sudan,[53] with her crew, Sergeant Hooper and Warrant Officer Gatling, arriving at Takoradi aboard a Lockheed Hudson the same day. The initial rehearsal spray runs conducted on the 18th by ten Vengeances in two five-plane formations covered a section of the area in turn using the now standard formation, while ground personnel used smoke flares to indicate the confines of the spray area. It was confirmed that wind conditions, naturally, affected the accuracy of the lays and made accurate placement very difficult. It was agreed that for future runs an increased number of smoke indicators would be used to give the pilots good forward and lateral lines aiming lines.

On 20 September, therefore, a full scale spray of the Ataraso area was carried out, and the conclusion of this led to the abandonment of the echelon formation and the adoption of the vic formation approach as being more satisfactory 'from the point of view of the pilot's vision of the correct spraying run and his simultaneous view of the other aircraft in the formation'.

---

[53] Known then, and still unflatteringly today, as 'The Airport at the end of the World'.

A third area, Busua (4^0 48 N, 1^0 56W) on the Gulf of Guinea, was selected and the usual practice runs were made between the 21st and 23rd and, on 25 September, the rehearsal took place with two *vics* of five commanded respectively by Flight Lieutenant Hedley and Flight Lieutenant James Corbishley, RNZAF. Each covered the area twice, a different section being taken on each pass for a total of forty-five minutes duration. The composition of the teams was thus:

Aircraft	Pilot	Aircrew
FD 263	Flt Lt Vernon Hedley, RAAF	Flt Lt David Goodall
AN 693	Flt Sgt John Arthur Christie RAAF	Sgt D.A. Blair
AN 811	Flt Sgt J.H. Crowther	Flt Sgt A.I. Osborne
AN 813	WO K. Clarke	Flt Sgt A. Watson
FD 254	P/O Joseph Parrish	Gp. Capt. Lipscomb (MO)*
FD 263	Flt Sgt J. Hadley	Flt Lt David Goodall
AN 693	Sgt Hooper	Sgt Allan James Richardson RAAF
AN 813	WO Alfred Newman	P/O Bertram Smith
AN 754	Sgt D.D.J. Carter	WO J. Turner
AN 775	Flt Lt James Corbishley RNZAF	Flt Lt Kenneth Mosher RCAF

*Group Captain Lipscomb was a medical officer visiting from the Porton unit from England and accompanied the formation as a passenger in this Vengeance.

Full-scale spraying took place on the 27th, with two teams of five apiece making runs that varied from thirty-five to fifty minutes. On this occasion the smoke delineating the spray area was clearly seen by everyone 'and gave good and clear-cut boundary lines'. The fact that the area was on the coast meant that they could make clear approaches from out at sea, which gave a very good line of vision. Further trials were accomplished by four crews on 3 October, and were designed to ascertain the degree of penetration which normally took place through varying types of foliage and jungle undergrowth. Yet a fourth spray area, Natien (4^0 53' N, 2^0 12' W), was duly subject to photographic reconnaissance as before on the 4th, and after rehearsals, was subjected to full-scale spraying on 11 October with four *vics* of five aircraft apiece, which worked in successive waves. One week later, Ataraso was re-visited and a full-scale spray was made with four *vics* of five Vengeances each. The Fairburn area near Accra was the sixth area selected and this was duly tackled, as before, from 20 October onward, while a seventh zone, Awusiejo (4^0 88'N, 1^0 89 W), was given the full treatment on the 26th but attempts to spray the eighth, Asani, on the coast east of Accra (4^0 88'N, $1°$ 89'W) failed due to bad weather conditions. One a single *vic* of three aircraft out of the five *vics* despatched managed to reach the spray zone, but turned back after thirty minutes without releasing the spray.

The ninth area selected was Ntangupo, eight miles north of Takoradi (4^0 93' N, 1^0 73' W), and, on 3 November 1944, this area was given a full-scale spray with four *vics* of five aircraft that covered the area in successive waves. The composition of the force was as follows:

Aircraft	Pilot	Aircrew
FD 226	Flt Lt Vernon Headley	Flt Lt David Goodall
AN 775	Flt Sgt John Arthur Christie RAAF	Flt Sgt J. Higgs
AN 811	Flt Sgt J.H. Crowther	Flt Sgt A.I. Osborne
AN 721	WO R.P. Newman	P/O Bertram Smith
AN 749	Sgt Hooper	WO Robert Yates RCAF
AN 749	Flt Lt James Corbishley	Flt Lt Kenneth Mosher
FD 263	WO K. Clarke	Flt Sgt H. Watson
AN 693	P/O Joseph Parrish	WO Robert Reid
AN 836	Sgt D.D.J. Carter	WO J. Turner
AN 754	Flt Sgt Blair	WO Gatling
FD 226	Flt Lt Hedley	Flt Lt David Goodall
AN 775	Flt Sgt John Arthur Christie RAAF	Flt Sgt Higgs
AN 811	Flt Sgt Crowther	Flt Sgt A.I. Osborne
AN 721	WO Newman	P/O Bertram Smith
AN 749	Sgt Hooper	WO Robert Yates
AN 749	Flt Lt Corbishley	Flt Lt Kenneth Mosher
FD 263	WO Knight-Clark	Flt Sgt Watson
AN 693	F/O Joseph Parrish	WO Robert Reid
AN 836	Sgt Carter	WO J. Turner
AN 754	Flt Sgt Blair	WO Gatling

This proved a significant operation, not only because this was the final spray carried, as the work of the Porton Down unit was considered to be completed, but, for 110 (H) Squadron's connection with the Vultee Vengeance, this proved to be the last mission flown in earnest.

It was fully expected that the detachments would ultimately return to the Burma Front and from 4 November onward the containers were abandoned, and the unit began to prepare themselves for their main mission, dive-bombing. Flight Lieutenant James Corbishley, Flying Officer Grant Puttock, Warrant Officer Ross Harrold, RAAF, Robert Yeates, and Flight Sergeants John Arthur Christie, RAAF, and J.H. Crowther commenced refresher training that day. Similar dive-bombing training took place on 13, 14 and 15 November.

Meanwhile, back at Yelhanka, the rest of the squadron, far from continuing to convert to the Mosquito aircraft at this time, suddenly, on 21 November, had all these aircraft taken away from them.[54] The Commanding Officer, Wing Commander Arthur Ernest Saunders OBE, received Signal AT/49 from 225 Group at Bangalore, 'ordering the re-conversion of 110 (H) Squadron to Vengeance aircraft'. It was recorded, 'This will alter many of the Squadron's recent plans, and also effect many of the aircrews. The establishment for Squadron Leader CO and Flight Lieutenants Flights OCs will mean replacements of our present commanders, all of whom are one rank higher. The signal suggests that experienced Vengeance pilots and crews still be posted to the squadron and some of the existing Nav/WOs will be trained. 110(H) and 84 Squadron are required to operate from forward areas as soon as possible.' Signal Q 452 was that same day received from 226 Group notifying them of 'an allotment of eight Vengeance III aircraft from 319 MU in operational condition'.

On 27 November the AOC 225 Group, Air Vice Marshal Noel Lloyd Desoer[55] addressed 110 (H) Squadron, 84 Squadron and conversion units in the station cinema at 1000. He first explained why all Mosquito aircraft had been grounded in India. 'It is estimated that prefect replacement Mosquito aircraft from UK will not be available until March. 110 (H) Squadron and 84 Squadron will reconvert back to Vengeance aircraft and are required to operate as soon as possible. The Air Vice Marshal then gave an account of the grand work of all Vengeance squadrons, operating from Assam and the Arakan in Army close support during 1943/44.'[56]

---

[54] The ORB merely recorded on that date, 'Flying has ceased, due to Mosquito VI aircraft being taken from the Squadron.' AIR 27/860/11.

[55] Air Commodore Desoer, as he later became, was one of the joint authors of *War Against Japan: Vol. III. The Decisive Battles. History of the Second World War: UK Military Series*, HMSO, London, 1961.

[56] The withdrawal of the Mosquito at this time was embarrassing for another reason. The Prince of Berar (General His Highness Azam Jah Walashan Sahebzada Nawab Mir Sir Himayat 'Ali

Things began to hot up at RAF Yelhanka, Bangalore, Kamataka, where the rest of 110 (H) was now based. On 6 December two Mk III Vengeances arrived from Bishnupur and Wing Commander Dennis Gibbs DSO, from 225 Group Training, held a conference in the CO's office with A and B Flight commanders, the adjutant (Flight Lieutenant Thomas Kerr Campbell) and the Engineering and Intelligence Officers. The squadron's move to the front in January was discussed and aircrews were place into three categories, 1 – Vengeance trained, 2 – Vengeance to be trained and 3 – Mosquito to be trained for wastage. The following day another pair of Vengeance IIIs arrived from Bishnupur and later Flight Lieutenant Patrick Bernard Finlay flew in a fifth from the same base. Next, on the 8th, two crews left the base in an Airspeed Oxford to collect a couple more Vengeances from Allahabad. They returned empty-handed on the 9th as nobody had apparently warned Allahabad they were coming, and the aircraft would not be ready for another ten days.

Also on the 9th Squadron Leader Ira 'Sag' Sutherland DFC, arrived in the squadron. It was noted that, 'This officer will command Vengeance operations when the squadron goes to the forward area in the near future.' Two days later Sutherland, given the official title Officer Commanding Vengeance Operations, spoke to all the crews making up that section and introduced himself. His reputation preceded him, however, and all were aware he knew his stuff. He told all the flying personnel to arrange themselves in crews and that formation flying would commence as soon as possible. 'Time is short!'

Two more pilots, Flight Lieutenants William Brandon Lucas and Raymond Rootes, rejoined the squadron. In the period from Tuesday 12 to 16 December, Vengeance flying training clocked up thirty-two flights totalling thirty-five hours thirty minutes. That day also Flight Lieutenant Spence Harold Swaffer, DI and CA SAC, SEA, left for Madras with Vengeance Pilot Flight Lieutenant J.L. Hermelin, and they made a propaganda recording entitled 'Hitting the Japs with a Vengeance' in readiness for their next combat missions. This was broadcast from

Khan Siddiqi Bahadur GBE) was to receive the gift of a model Vengeance on behalf of his father, the Nizam of Hyderabad, at a ceremony on 1 December. Rehearsals for a full-dress parade were being even then being organised!

Madras at 1130. The 18th of December saw Flight Lieutenant Patrick Finlay appointed as OC Vengeance A Flight and Flying Officer William Melville Tullet, RCAF, as OC Vengeance B Flight. Vengeance training flights increased to sixty-one flights totalling eighty hours thirty-five minutes.

None of this frenetic activity, not one iota, has ever been recorded in any of the many books on the air war in Burma.

The end came abruptly, with yet another *volte face* on the part of the Air Ministry. A phone call from Air Vice Marshal Desoer on 19 December, just a couple of weeks away from the deadline, signalled it was all over for the Vengeance. He informed the CO that 110 (H) Squadron would *not* re-convert to the Vengeance after all! 'Apparently Mosquito aircraft will be available sooner than at first expected. It is anticipated that Mosquitoes would arrive in the squadron from the first or second week of January, when training will continue as speedily as possible. It is not yet certain what will happen to the Vengeance crews posted to the squadron or to the twin-engined crews who were posted away.' At this time the squadron personnel comprised thirty-one officers, (twenty-eight British, two Australian and one Canadian) and seventy-four senior NCOs (seventy-two British and two Canadian, as well as the New Zealand Cs). In view of the many changes of mind that they had been subjected to, it is not surprising that the ORB contained the comment that 'we hope this information is accurate this time'. But it was not! In fact, it was not to be until the end of March that sufficient modified Mosquitoes appeared, so the Allied armies were denied three whole months of effective and accurate close air support: a very strange decision indeed.

As Joseph O'Leary, who finally arrived at Yelanhanka as an instructor on 25 October, later recorded, 'When the Mosquitoes first started to fall apart, the official reaction was "this isn't really happening, it's just a bad dream, if we close our eyes tight it'll go away". The decision to re-convert Mosquito aircrews back to the Vengeance was not taken until mid-October (*sic*), whereas the Mossies had been claiming lives since May. If the Air Staff had seen the red light then, there would still have been time to "hold" the six Vengeance squadrons at readiness west and south of Calcutta (just in case).' He also stated that 'The RAF ignored our many successes; they'd no more enduring interest in dive bombers now than they had in '39. They scrapped the lot – nobody thought of keeping any Museum specimens.'[57] He also ruminated that, even had the Mosquitoes been operational, there was room, and use enough for *both* aircraft to be utilised at the front, as the Vengeance aircrews were of proven quality, but this was ignored also.

> We could have continued operating from the end of the '44 monsoon (October) till the onset of the '45 (May) – seven or eight months, in conditions for which the Vengeance might have been designed. The Army had broken out of Imphal and got the upper hand in Arakan; the Jap was in fighting withdrawal mode on both fronts, building bunkers to hamper our advance. And the Vengeance was a 'bunker-buster' extraordinaire! Our brand-new Mk IIIs were coming out to replace the old Is and IIs which had flown all the 'ops' the year before.
>
> The argument that the squadrons were withdrawn to 're-equip with the Mosquito' was specious. The 'old' Blenheim crews had come out in mid-'42; the new influx in the December of that year – and we were all only [single-engine] trained. Where would be the sense in converting us to operational standard on the Mosquito when (at the end) we would (at the most) only twelve months to serve in our tours?
>
> In fact, as we know, the Mossies came out with their own trained crews to start a full Tour (at that time the war out there looked as if it could go on for years yet). All they wanted from us was the Squadron Names and Numbers. I think they should have been formed as new squadrons, and we keep ours for the rest of our Tours.
>
> It is hard to resist the conclusion that the Air Staff never warmed to the Vengeance, decried its achievements and simply wanted rid of it. Even if the Mossies had not started to fall apart, it would have made little difference.[58]

---

[57] The Australians did; they preserved one and are working on salving others. One might even fly again.

[58] Joseph O'Leary to the Author, 14 March 2017.

Over at Takoradi training had been abruptly halted earlier than this, a signal being received that all the Vengeances at that base would be made redundant with immediate effect and their aircrews returned home to the UK or Canada. As for Joseph O'Leary, he recalled for me, 'I kicked my heels for a bit, then flew with a Calibration Flighty, then spent my last year with my own Special Duty Flight (using three Vengeance IIIs which had never fired a shot in anger) And then the end.'

Chapter 8

Other Vengeance Operators

The Royal Australian Air Force was the second largest user of the Vultee Vengeance in combat. Orders were received both from RAF allocations and direct from the American plants. In the matter of designations, the RAF and the RAAF both used Mark I, IA and IIs, but whereas the RAF listed the subsequent deliveries of the Mark III, the RAAF termed them as Mark IVs. Thus, British Mark IIIs (serials FB918-999 and FD918-999) were built as Vengeance A-31Cs, the RAAF Vengeance Recognition Guide lists them as the A-35A-VU. The RAF's Mark IV, the best of the bunch, were known as the Mark IVA in Australia. Under the Australian listings the RAAF took delivery of ninety-nine Mark IAs, 122 Mark IIs and 121 Mark IVAs for a total Vengeance complement of 342 aircraft. The RAAF Vengeance Recognition Guide, dated March 1944, lists the various computations thus:

RAAF Mk	I	IA	II	IV		IVA	
RAAF Nbr A27-	1-15	16-199	200-399	400-499	500-559	560-599	600-
RAF Mk	I	IA	II	–	IV	IV	IV
RAF Serials	AN838 – AN999	EZ800- EZ999	AF715-AF944 AN538-AN837 FP686 (?)	FB918- FB999 FD100- FD117	–	–	–
US Model Nbr	V-72	V-72	V-72 (A-31)	A-35A-VU	A-35B-5-VN	A-35B-10-VN	A35B-15 VN
US Serial Nbr	–	–	–	41—31148 – 41-31246	41-31264 41-31299 – 41-31310 41-31411 t- 41-31447	42-94149- 42-9438	42-94349- 42-49548 42-101235 – 42-101765
Manufacturers Nbr	401-562	101-300	4101-4299 4301-4600 4600A	–	–	–	–
Manufacturer	Northrop	Northrop	Vultee	Consolidated-Vultee			

N.B. By the above date the Mark I and IVA machines had been relegated to the role of target tug and had all their defensive armaments removed. The Mark IA and II had four .303-inch wing-mounted machine guns and two .303-inch machine guns on a flexible mounting in the rear cockpit. The Mark IV had three .50-inch machine guns in each wing and a single .50-inch machine gun on a flexible mounting in the rear cockpit.

No. 4 Operational Training Unit was established to prepare pilots and aircrew of the highest standard, and had skilled instructors like Flight Lieutenants Douglas Macdonald Johnstone, Cyril John McPherson, Bernard William Newman and John Ewan Gerber, but the pressure for results meant that the green dive-bomber crews were pitched into combat scenarios somewhat prematurely. They formed No. 77 Wing, commanded by Wing Commander Edwin Glen Fyfe RAAF.

Five RAAF Squadrons were allocated the Vultee and four of them employed them in the combat mission. They were successful, but were subsequently treated with distain by their American allies in particular by Major General Ennis Clement Whitehead of the US Fifth Air Force, and by *force majeure*, were abruptly ordered to abandon their mission after a series of highly questionable allegations about their efficiency. I have written about their work, and shabby treatment, elsewhere[1] so only a brief outline follows here.

No. 12 Squadron RAAF

On 12 September 1942 Commonwealth Wirraways were replaced by the Vultee Vengeance. The first attacks were made against the enemy forces on Tanimbar and Selaru Islands, north of Darwin, in June 1943. In July 1943 the squadron moved to Merauke airfield, Dutch New Guinea, and undertook army co-operation and coastal patrols. One year later it was back to Australia and it became non-operational, but later reformed with Consolidated B-24 Liberators.

The squadron's first commanding officer, Flight Lieutenant Neville Gerald Hemsworth RAAF, was wounded when a Lockheed Hudson in which he was a passenger was attacked by Mitsubishi Zeros and shot into the sea off Hanko on 26 December 1942. Squadron Leader John Neirne Hooper became the new commanding officer, while Douglas McDonald Johnstone AFC was the last CO with the Vengeance. Many experienced 12 Squadron personnel joined the RAF's 45 Squadron in Burma.

No. 21 (City of Melbourne) Squadron RAAF

Formerly a Brewster Buffalo fighter outfit the squadron took heavy losses over Malaya and returned to Australia in March 1942 to re-build. However, it was not until the summer of 1943 that the squadron received its first Vengeance

[1]   See Smith, Peter C., *Jungle Dive Bombers at War*, pp.54-71, John Murray, London, 1987.

dive-bombers. After training and familiarisation, No. 21 Squadron, under Wing Commander Thomas Russell Philp, moved up to New Guinea for two weeks, attacking Japanese airfields, barges and infantry positions. It was then withdrawn to NSW where it converted to the Consolidated Liberator.

No. 23 (City of Brisbane) Squadron RAAF

At Amberley, Queensland, with Bell P-39 Airacobras and Commonwealth Wirraways, No. 23 Squadron was first equipped with the Vengeance in Queensland and underwent training in dive-bombing. In February 1944 the squadron, under the command of David Fotheringham Miller AFC, moved up to the battle front at Nadzab and began operations near Saidor, Madang and Alexishafen, and also along the Markham Valley but again, after only a few weeks operations, and despite the unit striking the Japanese with great accuracy, No. 23 Squadron, along with other RAAF Vengeance squadrons, was withdrawn to Australia and reduced to cadre. It also later converted to the Liberator.

No. 24 (City of Adelaide) Squadron RAAF

The composite Commonwealth Wirraway and Lockheed Hudson component of No. 24 Squadron had been almost annihilated in the fighting around Rabaul in spring 1942 and the shattered remnants had been withdrawn to Townsville and then Banksville to recover and rebuild with Brewster Buffalo and Bell P-39 Airacobra aircraft in the interim.

The first RAAF unit to convert to the Vultee, No. 24 Squadron first received the Vengeance in May 1942 and employed it in conjunction with other types. By August 1943 the squadron had standardised on the Vengeance and, under the command of Squadron Leader Barton Honey, RAAF, moved up to Nadzab, New Guinea, with eighteen aircraft. From here it operated with great success against Japanese positions on Shaggy Ridge under Wing Commander T.R. Philp DFC, and supported the Allied landings at Cape Gloucester. Despite their success they were withdrawn in March 1944 and returned to Australia. Honey was awarded the DFC on 13 April 1944. They subsequently re-equipped with the Consolidated Liberator heavy bomber.

No. 25 (City of Perth) Squadron

This unit was the last to be equipped with the Vengeance, and being last meant that they received the superior Mark IV model at Fremantle, Western

Australia. They employed them for coastal patrol work from the middle of 1943 onward, but, apart from the Japanese 'invasion' panic of 7 March, when it was thought a Japanese naval task force was approaching to 'do a Colombo' on the Australian ports, saw no action. Like the RAF the RAAF subsequently only used the Vengeance as a target tug while older dive-bombers, like the Douglas SBD Dauntless, were used by the US Marine Corps to support General Douglas MacArthur's land forces in the Philippines.

Royal Australian Navy
The RAN took delivery of several Vengeance aircraft which it used mainly for target towing. Among those transferred were: A27-502 on 7 October 1945; EZ 997 (A27-97), EZ 998 (A27-98), EZ 999 (A27-99), A27-400, 16 May 1946; A27-404 on 27 April 1948, A27-402, 2 March 1949 and A27-403, 2 March 1949.

RAF Second-Line Duties
Like their RAAF counterparts the RAF subsequently employed the newer Vengeance aircraft that were now arriving in numbers, for target towing and similar miscellaneous duties. A large number of such squadrons found themselves with the Vengeance on their books, and such aircraft continued in service well into the post-war era. The following RAF units are known to have flown Vengeance aircraft.

No. 288 Squadron RAF
This unit was formed from No. 12 Group Anti-Aircraft Co-operation Flight in 1941. It employed. Vengeance II aircraft at Church Fenton, North Yorkshire, from November 1944 to August 1945 and from August 1945 to May 1946, at Hutton Cranswick, East Yorkshire. Final use was between May and June 1946 at East Moor, north of York. The commanding officer from October 1944 was Wing Commander A.M.G. Lywood DFC.

No. 289 Squadron RAF
Originally formed from No. 13 Group Anti-Aircraft Co-operation Flight in 1941 it operated in the Southern Scotland and Northern England area. The squadron employed the Vengeance II. Bases included, from May 1942 to May 1945 Turnhouse, Edinburgh, in May 1945 Acklington, Northumberland,

between May and June 1945 Eshott, Northumberland, and then finally Andover, Hampshire, in June 1945 before being disbanded on 26 June 1945.

No. 291 Squadron RAF

First formed on 1 December 1943 from Nos. 1613, 1629 and 1634 Flights at Hutton Cranswick, Yorkshire, it utilised the Vengeance II between November 1944 and June 1945. Commanding officers in this period included: May 1944, Squadron Leader R.E.A. Mason; December 1944, Squadron Leader R.H. Fletcher and, from June 1945, Squadron Leader J.R. Graham. The squadron was disbanded on 26 June 1945.

No. 577 Squadron RAF

Formed on 1 December 1943 at Castle Bromwich, Warwickshire, from detachments of Nos. 6, 7 and 8 Anti-Aircraft Co-operation Units. Though mainly flying Supermarine Spitfires and Airspeed Oxfords, between July 1945 and June 1946, it also flew the Vengeance IV.

On 13 July 1944 Wing Commander H.N. Garbett was appointed as commanding officer and he was succeeded in August 1945 by Wing Commander Matson. The squadron's work was mainly anti-aircraft co-operation with the Army and Navy with the planned coming invasion of mainland Japan in mind. The unit had detachments in Wales and the Midlands.

No. 587 Squadron RAF

This squadron had been originally formed at Weston Zoyland, Somerset, on 1 December 1943, from Nos. 1600, 1601 and 1625 Flights. The role was to assist the calibration of AA guns and radar, towing targets and providing aircraft to fly known courses and speeds. On 13 July 1944 Wing Commander H.N. Garbett had responsibility for the unit and in August 1945, as noted above, Wing Commander Matson took over until August, when Squadron Leader P. Green OBE AFC, assumed command. The Vengeance IV arrived in October 1944 and served until the squadron's disbandment on 15 June 1946.

No. 631 Squadron RAF

This was a target-towing and gun-laying training squadron based in Wales from its formation on 1 December 1943 by the merger of 1605 and 1628 Flights until the end of war. It used the Hawker Henley (another abandoned dive-bomber) and Miles Martinets until September 1944 and then the Vengeance IV from May 1945 to May 1947 as well as Spitfire XVIs. Until May 1945 It was based at Towyn, Conway, then moved to Llanbedr, Caernarfonshire, until 11 February 1949, when it became No. 20 Squadron with de Havilland Vampire F.1s. Commanding officers were: from December 1944 Wing Commander A.H. Drummond and then, in July 1946, Squadron Leader T.N. Hayes DFC.

No. 667 Squadron RAF

This squadron carried out target-towing and gun-laying duties from Gosport. (Lee-on-Solent), Hampshire. Formed first on 1 December 1943 from Nos.1631 and 1662 Flights using Boulton-Paul Defiants until January 1944, then Fairey Barracudas in May 1944 and Vengeance IVs from October 1944 to December 1945. Until 20 December 1945 Wing Commander A.H. Drummond was in command. The unit was finally disbanded in June 1946.

No. 679 Squadron RAF

Formed on 1 December 1943 from the merger of Nos. 1616 and 1627 Flights and based near Ipswich, Suffolk, it operated in East Anglia on anti-aircraft co-operation duties. In March Fairey Barracuda naval dive-bombers were used, and they were replaced between April and June 1944 by the Vengeance IV. From December 1944 the commanding officer was Wing Commander A.H. Drummond. The squadron was disbanded on 26 June 1945.

No. 691 Squadron RAF

This was an anti-aircraft co-operation squadron and served South-West England. Formed in December 1943 from No. 1623 Flight at Roborough, Devonshire, the squadron utilised Bolton-Paul Defiants, Hawker Hurricanes and Airspeed Oxfords. The first two were replaced by Fairey Barracudas in January 1944 and the Vengeance IVs arrived in April 1944, serving until May1947.

This squadron moved to Harrowbeer, Devonshire, in February 1945, then to Exeter in August 1945, next to Fairwood Common, Swansea, in January 1946 and finally worked from Chivenor, North Devon, under the command of Squadron Leader T.N. Hayes DFC, followed by Squadron Leader D.E. Proudlove before being disbanded on 11 February 1949.

No. 695 Squadron RAF

Originally formed in 1943 from Nos. 1611 and Nos. 1612 Flights and served in East Anglia based initially at Bircham Newton, Norfolk, and then, from August 1945, at Horsham St Faith, Norwich. The Vengeance IV served between March 1945 and May 1947, replacing Hurricane IICs and Spitfire VBs.

The commanding officer was Squadron Leader D.E. Proudlove from July 1948. In February 1949 the squadron was disbanded and redesignated No. 34 Squadron.

Fleet Air Arm

The Royal Navy's Fleet Air Arm made no attempt to adapt the Vengeance for carrier-borne operations, preferring to utilise the Fairey Barracuda in that role against the German battleship *Tirpitz* at her Norwegian anchorage, but they were allocated 113 of the Vultees from RAF allocations for land-based use. Of this total some eighty-eight were received up to the end of August 1945. The first batch arrived in the UK aboard the SS *George the Knight* on 28 August 1944 and were transferred to the Lockheed Overseas Corporation facility at RAF Langford Lodge, Lough Neagh, west of Belfast and then on to Speke airfield, Liverpool. The first Vengeance received was FD 171 on 8 March 1944, but an accident on the 17th wrote this machine off almost immediately. Three squadrons were assigned the Vengeance, but their main employment was as a target tug. When the Allies were still planning to make landings on the Japanese mainland, the Royal Navy was allocated twenty-five Vultee target tugs to work up the task force's gunners to face the threat of the Kamikaze. However, after the dropping of the two Atomic bombs and the abrupt surrender of Japan, these numbers were superfluous and only nine of these Vengeances actually arrived on station aboard the British escort carrier *Smiter* in December 1945. Some of these were modified as DDT crop-sprayers. The final Royal Navy Vengeance, FD 404, was retired from service at RAF Changai, Singapore, in April 1947.

No. 721 Squadron

This outfit, another Fleet Requirement Unit, was based at RNAS Ponam (HMS *Nabaron*) on the islet of Ponam, just north of Manus Island in the

Admiralty Group, itself north-west of Rabaul, with MONAB IV[2]. The squadron initially had six Vengeance aircraft which it had received in March 1945. J. Dickson, who was serving aboard the light fleet carrier *Vengeance*, spent some time there in August. He wrote how 'I remember there were some Vultee Vengeance dive-bombers of 721 Squadron there. They had only ever been used for towing targets and now they were engaged in spraying DDT on the mosquitoes!' On 15 October, with the Pacific war over, the Royal Navy light fleet carrier *Unicorn* picked them up and they were transferred to RAAF Archerfield, near Brisbane, to re-equip. Among the aircraft on the squadron's strength were to be twelve Vengeance target tugs which were transferred to Kai Tek airfield, Hong Kong, HMS *Nabcatcher*, at MONAB VIII.

No. 733 Squadron

This was another Fleet Requirements Unit and the first Vengeance to arrive in the Squadron reached it in July 1945. The Squadron was operating from HMS *Garuda* (Coimbatore, Cochin, southern India), RNAS Puttalam (HMS *Rajaliya*), Ceylon and at China Bay. The first Vengeance was a TT Mark IV, FD 404 (ex-42-94288) which went into service at Trincomalee (HMS *Bambara*) having shipped out aboard the escort carrier *Khedive*.

No. 791 Squadron

Although re-formed from a unit that had served at HMS *Condor* (RNAS Arbroath) and disbanded in December 1944. It was not until 27 September 1946, that this squadron, by this date based at Sembawang, Singapore (HMS *Simbang*), took delivery of its six Vengeance aircraft. As an air target towing outfit, 791 operated until 1947 before again disbanding.

RNEAD

One aircraft, FD 368, was allocated to the Royal Navy Experimental Air Department which had been established at Thame, Haddenham, Buckinghamshire, in 1943. Here they tested this Vengeance in its role as a target tug, along with Miles Martinets and Fairey Swordfish. Later this aircraft went to Oakley on CS (A) duties for International Model Aircraft Ltd in June 1945, on target towing duties.

---

[2]   MONAB – Mobile Naval Operating Base.

The RAF transferred several Vengeances to the Fleet Air Arm post-war, including 41-31360 (FD 171), 41-31370 (FD 181) and 41-31410 (FD 221). Several ex-RAF, ex-RAAF Vengeance were handed over to the Royal Navy, and these included 41-31316 (A27-512), 41-31317 (A27-513), 41-31319 (A27-514), 41-1326 (A27-515) and 41-31329 (A27-516) on 16 May 1946.

Brazilian Air Force
The Brazilian Air Force received twenty-eight A-31 and five A-35 Vengeances. They formed two dive- bombing squadrons.

1st Dive-Bombing Squadron
In February the first batch of Vengeances was delivered to Brazil. These were V-72s. They arrived in two deliveries, the first with Serials AN581 to AN592 and they received Brazilian serials 6000 to 6011; the second set were R–V-72s with serials AN593 to AN608 which received Brazilian serials 6012 to 6025. One of these aircraft, AN608, was lost on the journey south.

2nd Dive-Bombing Squadron.
A second delivery of A35B-15-VN Vengeances was made in September 1944, and these five aircraft carried USAAF serials 41-101412, 41-101421, 41-101422, 41-101426 and 41-101435, which received the Brazilian serials 6056, 6057, 6058, 6059, and 6060 respectively.

The 1st Group of the 1st Aviation Regiment, based at Santa Cruz Air Base, Rio De Janeiro, was allocated the Vengeances under Presidential Decree 6796 dated 17 August 1944. They flew anti-submarine missions along Brazil's long Atlantic coast line protecting Allied convoys. Between 1942 and 1946 they operated from Caravelas, southern Bahia, and Santos, Sao Paulo, but principally over the waters off Rio itself. They were based at the old Zeppelin hangar at the base.

In addition, the former 41-31252 was also transferred and used as a ground instruction hulk at the Technical School.

French Army Air Force
Two deliveries of the Vultee dive-bomber were made to the Free French, one in July 1943 and a second in December 1943. Vengeance aircraft received

by the Free French Air Force in North Africa included 41-31224, 41-31225, 41-31226,41-31227 and 41-31228, 41-31262, 41-31263, 41-31264, 41-31265, 41-31266, 41-31267, 41-31268, 41-31269, 41-31270, 41-31271, 41-31272, 41-31273, 41-31274, 41-31275, 41-31276, 41-31277, 41-31278, 41-31279, 41-31280, 41-31281, 41-31282, 41-31283, 41-31284, 41-31285, 41-31286, 41-31287, 41-31288, 41-31289, 41-31290. One aircraft, 41-31200, was lost while being flown by an American ferry pilot before delivery had been completed. The rest equipped the GBI/17 *Picardie* and the GBII/15 *Anjou Escadrilles.*

GBI/32 *Bourgne*

One Vengeance, 41-31193, was lost in a crash at Gazes airfield, Casablanca, Morocco on 22 January 1944. Other serials which served with this unit were 41-31198, 41-31292, 41-31293, 41-31294, 41-31295, 41-31296, 41-31297 and 41-31298. Of these 41-311294 was written off on 2 January in a crash at Agadir.

The French were in an inordinate hurry to get these aircraft into active service as soon as possible, but the adage of 'more haste, less speed' prevailed here. Thus, instead of incorporating many of the British and Australian modifications found necessary after many hard lessons in the field, the French attempted to use them straight from the factories with all the engine and hydraulic faults still unresolved. The only exceptions were 41-31202, 41-31203 and 41-31204, all three being re-fitted with the A5B5 engine in an effort to solve these problems. As a result, the high oil consumption and other woes resulted in frustration and none of the French Vultees saw active service. Instead they were used as training aircraft for dive-bomber pilots and, later, inevitably, as target tugs and the like. The Vengeance was therefore withdrawn from service in September 1944, and French dive-bombers went into action in Europe in 1944-45 with the much older semi-obsolete Douglas Dauntless, which could only carry a single 500-lb bomb externally.[3]

United States Army Air Forces

The USAAF distributed some Vengeance aircraft to their Combat Crew Replacement Centres (CCRCs) with bases throughout the United Kingdom.

---

[3]   See Pelletier, Alaine J., 'Consumptive Vengeance, Vultee A-35s in French Service.' *Air Enthusiast*, No. 128. March/April 2007, Key Publishing, Stamford, Lincs.

There were seven at RAF Cluntoe, Ardboe, County Tyrone, Northern Ireland; seven more at RAF Greencastle, Kilkeel, County Down, Northern Ireland; ten at RAF Sutton Bridge, Lincolnshire; and six more at RAF East Wretham, Thetford, Norfolk. After these CCRCs were closed down, these Vultees were distributed around various UK-based bomber squadrons as target tugs and hacks.

In the US itself the dive-bomber programme was mainly instigated by General George Catlett Marshall, the US Army Chief of Staff, who, impressed by the German *Blitzkrieg* methods, had initiated the equipping of no fewer than sixteen dive-bomber groups in a crash programme in 1940. Various types were ordered straight off the drawing boards, among them the Brewster SB2A Buccaneer and the A-25A Shrike, the Army equivalent of the Navy's Curtiss SB2C Helldiver. But the most instantly available such aircraft was the Army equivalent of the Navy's Douglas SBD Dauntless, the Douglas A-24 Banshee.[4] General Marshall found little support among his United States Army Air Corps colleagues, many of whom did all they could to oppose, delay and halt those such types then being introduced. Under the auspices of Senator Harry S. Truman of Ohio, the Truman Committee was established in 1941 and immediately reversed this policy. General Orvil Arson Anderson, Head of the Air War Plans Division, deleted Marshall's entire programme. Marshall overrode him and the initial batch of seventy-eight A-24s was reinstated and the first unit planned to be so equipped was the 27th Bombardment Group (Light) in the Philippines. Fifty-Two A-24s were to be despatched in November 1941, but none reached that area before it fell to the Japanese. Instead they were diverted to Australia. The 91st Bombardment Group (Light) also received the A-24, but, with both groups, it was only utilised in penny packets and without the enthusiasm the Navy flyers showed for dive-bombing and with a total lack of commitment and flair. Losses were disproportionately high and achievements almost nil.

Subsequently the squadrons allocated the Vengeance (V-72, A-31a and A-35) were classified in September 1942, as the 55th, 56th, 57th and 88th Bombardment Squadrons (Dive) respectively. They were based at Key

---

[4]   Like the Brewster Buccaneer and Curtiss Shrike, Banshee was the USAAC name applied to the Douglas dive-bomber, but it was never widely used in the USAAC at the time, and, indeed, has been disputed by some.

Field, Meridian, Mississippi, where most USAAC dive-bomber training was done. A year later, in August 1943, these were re-classified as the 492nd, 493rd, 494th and 495th Fighter Squadrons. The Vengeances were used operationally. Other units which had the Vengeance briefly on strength were the 309th, 311st, 312nd, 623rd, 628th, 629th, 630th and 631st Bombardment Squadrons (Dive). The 311th Bombardment Group (Dive) comprised the 382nd, 383rd and 384th Bombardment Squadrons but, before moving to India, its Vengeances were replaced by the North American A-36 Apache dive-bomber and the P-51 Mustang, used as a fighter-bomber, both being single-seaters. The 312th Bombardment Group was supplied with some V-72s and was reputed to have used some for anti-submarine work in the winter of 1942-43, but the main workhorse was the A-24.

Some 25 A-35As built for the RAF were requisitioned by the USAAC, some serving at the Gunnery Training Centre at Patterson Field, often still carrying RAF camouflage; these included AF 769, AF 829, AN 838 and FD 186,

According to Wally Blackwell, one Vengeance, 41-31396, was transferred from the 91st Bomb Group to the 398th Bomb Group on 26 September 1944 and became the last-ever aircraft assigned to that unit. They used her as a 'monitor ship' for commanders and senior pilots to assess the group's formation assemblies. She carried a large white letter F on her tail. The 398th Group, in turn, later passed her on from Nuthampstead, Hertfordshire, to the 438th Air Service Group on 1 June 1945.[5]

Even the US Navy almost got in on the act. There was a proposal to adapt the Vengeance as a carrier-based dive-bomber with tail-hook and other modifications. This would have been the TBV-1 Georgia, a 'navalised' version of the A-35B. The idea was dropped before any converted aircraft were evaluated.

The well-advertised initial problems with the Vengeance continued unresolved in the States right through to the end of the war.[6]

---

[5]   398th Bomb Group Memorial Association, October 2004.
[6]   See Smith, Peter C., 'Trouble with the Vultee, Parts 1 & 2.' *Army & Defence Quarterly* 1993, Tavistock, Devon.

Bibliography

Andrade, John M., *US Military Aircraft Designations and Serials 1909 to 1976*. Midland Counties Publications, Earl Shilton, Leicester, 1997.

Air Ministry, *The Wings of the Phoenix: The Official Story of the Air Force in Burma*. His Majesty's Stationery Office. London: 1949.

Anon, Japanese Studies in World War II – Monograph No. 59(1) – *Burma Operations Record, Phase III, 1944-45*. Military History Section, HQ Army Forces Far East. Chief of Military History, US Department of the Navy. Washington D.C. 1962.

Bishop, Edward, *The Wooden Wonder: The Story of the de Havilland Mosquito*. Max Parris Publishing, London: 1971.

Calvert, Brigadier James Michael DSO, *Fighting Mad: One Man's Guerrilla War*. Jarrolds. London: 1965.

DSIR 23/12244, (Design of elevators, ailerons and brake flaps on Vultee Vengeance Aircraft: Tunnel Tests – Department of Scientific and Industrial Research: Aeronautical Research Council: Reports and Photographs. Farnborough :1942.)

Brown, Captain Eric, *Wings of the Weird and Wonderful. Vol. 2*. Airlife Publishing. Shrewsbury: 1985.

Carlan, Alan, *Eagles in the Sky: The Royal Air Force at 75*. Mainstream Publishing. Edinburgh: 1993.

Douhet, General Giulio, *The Command of the Air*. Air Force History and Museums Program, Washington D.C.: 1998.

Franks, Norman, *The Air Battle of Imphal*. William Kimber. London: 1985.

Gooderson, Dr Ian, *Air Power at the Battlefront: Allied Close Air Support in Europe 1943-45*. Routledge. Abingdon: 2013.

Grant, Brian Lyall, *Burma: The Turning Point*. Pen & Sword. Barnsley: 2014.

Jefford, Wing Commander Clive Graham MBE BA, RAF, *The Flying Camels; The History of No. 45 Squadron*. Royal Air Force. Jefford/Air Britain. High Wycombe: 1995.

Mead, Richard, *Churchill's Lions: A biographical guide to the key British Generals of World War II.* Spellmount. Stroud: 2007.

Mosher, Sara V., *Remember Me: No. 110 (Hyderabad) Squadron Royal Air Force.* Self-published. Winnipeg, Manitoba: 2011.

Lal, Air Chief Marshal Pratap Chandra, *My Years with the IAF.* Lancer Publications LL.c. Atlanta, Ga.:1986.

Maslen-Jones, E.W., *Fire by Order: Recollections of Service with 656 Air Observation Post Squadron in Burma.* Pen & Sword Aviation. Barnsley: 2012.

Neate, Don, *Scorpions Sting: The Story of No. 84 Squadron Royal Air Force.* Air Britain Historians Ltd. Tonbridge, Kent: 1994.

Royal Air Force Historical Society, *The RAF and the Far East War 1941-1945. Bracknell Paper No. 6: A Symposium on the Far East War.* Royal Air Force Historical Society and Royal Air Force Staff College. Bracknell: 24 March 1995.

Seekins, Donald M., *Historical Dictionary of Burma (Myanmar).* Rowan & Littlefield. Lanham, MD: 2017.

Shores, Christopher. *The Air War in Burma: The Allied Air Forces Fight Back – 1942-45.* Grub Street. London: 2005.

Singh, Pushpindar, *Aircraft of the Indian Air Forces 1933-1973.* B. Chowdn. New Delhi: 1974.

Singh, Pushpindar. *The Battle Axes No 7 Squadron Indian Air Force 1942-1992.* Society for Aerospace Research Studies. New Delhi: 1993.

Singh, Pushpindar. *Himalayan Eagles: History of the Indian Air Force, Volume 1 (of 3).* Society for Aerospace Research Studies. New Delhi: 2007.

Slim, Filed Marshal 1st Viscount William. *Defeat Into Victory.* Cassel. London. 1956.

Smith, Peter C. *Close Air Support: An Illustrated History, 1914 to the Present.* Orion Books. New York: 1990.

Smith, Peter C. *Deadly Dive Bombing Accuracy* – Interview with Arthur Murland Gill - *Military History*, Vol. 4, No. 6. June 1988, pps18-24. London: 1988.

Smith, Peter C. *Dive Bomber – An Illustrated History.* Moorland Publishing/ United States Naval Institute Press. Ashborne/ Annapolis :1982.

Smith, Peter C. *Impact! The Dive Bomber Pilots Speak.* William Kimber/ Nautical & Aviation Publishing. London/ Annapolis: 1981.

Smith, Peter C. *Jungle Dive Bombers at War.* John Murray. London: 1987.

Smith, Peter C. *The Junkers Ju.87 Stuka,* pp 182. – 20. Crecy. Manchester: 2011.

Smith, Peter C. 'Trouble with the Vultee' – Pts. 1 & 2. *Army & Defence Quarterly Journal,* Vol 123, No. 3 July & Vol 123, No. 4 October. Tavistock: 1993.

Smith, Peter C. *Vengeance! The Vultee Vengeance Dive Bomber.* Airlife/Smithsonian Institute Press. Shrewsbury/Washington D.C.:1986.

Thetford, Owen. *Aircraft of the RAF since 1918.* Putnam. London: 1962.

Thomas, Squadron Leader Thelkethil Joseph, *Memories of 8 Squadron, IAF.* Veteran Project Interview, Profiles and Memoirs. Wing Commander Joseph Thomas. Delhi: 2015.

Tiwary, Air Marshal Arun Kumar, *Indian Air Force in Wars.* Lancer LL.c. Delhi: 2012.

Yeats-Brown, Major Francis Charles, *Martial India.* Eyre & Spottiswood. London: 1945.

Index